SENATOR
ROBERT F.
WAGNER

and the Rise of
Urban Liberalism

Senator Robert F. Wagner studies his bill to renew the OPA on June 13, 1946

SENATOR
ROBERT F.
WAGNER

and the Rise of
Urban Liberalism

J. JOSEPH HUTHMACHER

New York

ATHENEUM

1971

COPYRIGHT © 1968 BY J. JOSEPH HUTHMACHER
ALL RIGHTS RESERVED
LIBRARY OF CONGRESS CATALOG CARD NUMBER 68-16869
MANUFACTURED IN THE UNITED STATES OF AMERICA BY
THE MURRAY PRINTING COMPANY,
FORGE VILLAGE, MASSACHUSETTS
PUBLISHED IN CANADA BY MCCLELLAND AND STEWART LTD.
FIRST ATHENEUM PAPERBACK EDITION

For my wife

MARILYN

with love

Preface

"THE PROPER PROBLEM of the biographer is to assess the role of men in history. His subject is not the complete man, or the complete society, but the points at which the two interact. At these points the situation can throw light on the character of the individual, and the individual's reaction can illuminate the situation."

In these words Oscar Handlin has provided a definition of the biographer's task that is somewhat less demanding than that which prevailed when ponderous "life *and times*" elaborations were in vogue; and more modest, too, than the current approach favored by some who set standards of biographical "psychoanalysis" almost as rigid as those that govern practicing psychiatrists dealing with living, breathing human beings. I quote Handlin's dictum approvingly, in part because it has made my work somewhat less arduous, but mainly because it has seemed to me the best way to approach the challenge of writing a biography of Robert F. Wagner.

I think it would be impossible, and probably uninteresting in any event, to attempt to portray Bob Wagner, "the complete man." ("He is 'Bob' to his friends," a journalist wrote when the Senator was well over fifty, "and those who know and admire him refer to him in this manner." I have adopted that usage.) For Wagner was not a meditative person, and he left behind little in the way of personal reflection that would help tell a historical psychoanalyst what made him tick, or why his philosophy and public record developed the way they did. The biographer of an individual "can only call attention to his most important characteristics, infer their probable source from available evidence, and relate them to the culture in which they flourish," Arthur Mann, the biographer of Fiorello La Guardia, has written in his most recent volume. I quote that approvingly too, for it summarizes the approach I have been content to use in this book.

Moreover, Wagner was not a colorful politician—not an Al Smith or a Little Flower—and thus any attempt to probe "the complete man" might soon turn into a dull affair. "Why write about such a drab figure," a colleague who served with Wagner in the United States Senate once asked me, "when you could spend your time on men like Huey Long or J. Ham Lewis, who always put on a good show?"

But the answer to the question asked by Wagner's colleague is probably known already to the readers who will pick up this volume. For most of us living in the welfare state that is now America are at least vaguely familiar with some of the ways in which the interaction between Bob Wagner, the man, and the society that he served during the first half of this century have affected our own situations. "Whether you like his laws or deplore them," a reporter once wrote, "he has placed on the books legislation more important and far-reaching than any American in history, since the days of the Founding Fathers." In compiling that record, Bob Wagner not only "illuminated the situation" of modern American society, he also did about as much as one individual can do to profoundly alter and remodel it.

Not that this book undertakes to portray "the complete society" in which Bob Wagner operated. To do so would require writing virtually a textbook covering fifty years of American history—the span of Wagner's public service was almost that long. Moreover, to chronicle and assess the ramifications of each of the ideas that Wagner the lawmaker institutionalized during his career would require a preliminary series of monographs detailing the history of many of the instrumentalities of government that vitally shape our lives today. My objective is less ambitious.

Yet Bob Wagner and his career can be understood and evaluated only against the background of the societal forces that shaped him and that he grappled with. Wagner was an immigrant, a city dweller who "became uneasy whenever the el train near his apartment ceased to rumble," and the product of an industrial–working-class environment. And who today is not familiar with the deep impress that the immigration-urbanization-industrialization syndrome has made on the nature and quality of American civilization?

Wagner started his career under the aegis of Tammany Hall, the

most notorious of the big-city machines that first embodied and served
—in however unsatisfactory and tainted a way—the aspirations and
needs of the urban industrial masses. During the course of his work,
first in Albany and later in Washington, the kind of Americans whom
Tammany represented grew in numerical importance and political
power, and so did the intensity of their demands that society as a
whole acknowledge and satisfy their ambitions for a greater share of
"recognition," social security, and economic opportunity. In part
through the labors of Bob Wagner, one of their earliest and most
devoted spokesmen, they gradually succeeded in bending the instruments of American politics and government to their liking—at considerable expense to the public treasury, and at considerable expense,
too, to the cluster of values that the nation had inherited from its
more homogeneous, rural, and agrarian past.

The result, in the eyes of some, has amounted to the conquest
of America by alien ideas and ideals, the nationwide Tammanyizing
of the country's governmental and social processes, and the establishment of a debasing political philosophy built on the precept "Spend,
spend, spend; elect, elect, elect." But to others it has signified part
of the nation's Age of Reform, the Big Change—in the sense of a
change for the better; the fruition of a half century of peaceful
revolution that has laid the groundwork for exploring the New Frontiers of the Great Society.

To Bob Wagner, who regarded Tammany and its schooling as
"the cradle of modern liberalism," the path that he and his society
traveled during his lifetime represented nothing more or less than
"the next step in the logical unfolding of man's eternal quest for freedom"—the translation of "the virtues, aspirations, and ideals of a
rural people so as to serve in the development and progress of an urban
people."

I began work on this book with a built-in liberal bias in Senator
Wagner's favor. In the ten years of research, reading, interviewing,
talking, thinking, and writing that have intervened since then nothing
has happened to change my evaluation of him. It is just as well to
say so at the outset, for the fact of my favoritism will assuredly become evident in the pages that follow.

Nevertheless it should be stated also that the present work is in
no sense an "authorized" biography in the pejorative meaning of that
term. True enough, those who jointly control the disposition of the
Robert F. Wagner Papers—Robert F. Wagner, Jr., Miss Minna L.
Ruppert, the Reverend Joseph T. Durkin, S.J., and the Rector of

Georgetown University—have authorized me to make use of the papers in preparing a full-scale biography of the Senator. (The papers have been, and are, open to use by other scholars working on tangential subjects.) But none of these individuals directed or censored in any way the construction of my study.

The Wagner Papers, deposited at Georgetown Universtity in Washington, D.C., constitute the core source I have relied on in writing this volume. Footnotes will indicate the kinds of material the collection contains. They will indicate also the books, unpublished manuscripts, periodicals, newspapers, and other printed sources that I have found useful.

The personal papers of other figures with whom Wagner was associated in public life proved generally disappointing in their yield of pertinent material. The Franklin D. Roosevelt Papers at Hyde Park were moderately helpful. On the other hand, the Wagner correspondence in the Harry S Truman Papers, at Independence, Missouri, which Dr. Philip C. Brooks and the staff of the Truman Library were kind enough to search out and send to me, told me more about the President than about the New York Senator. Fred Greenbaum supplied me with microfilm copies of material from the Senator Edward P. Costigan Papers (University of Colorado Library at Boulder), which shed light on several legislative matters that jointly interested Wagner and Costigan in the early 1930s. Otherwise, the mutually negative reports that I exchanged with biographers of Wagner contemporaries—Arthur Mann, Richard Lowitt, and Richard Kirkendall, for example, who are writing on Fiorello La Guardia, George L. Norris, and Harry S Truman, respectively—were disappointing to all of us. They served to reinforce what is our common conviction, I think, that in the age of the telephone and rapid transportation, politicians simply do not communicate very much with each other on paper— to history's loss.

One source that was invaluable to me was Columbia University's Oral History Research Office, in which are deposited transcripts of interviews by the office staff with several state and national figures who knew Bob Wagner well. Even more rewarding were the interviews I conducted personally in the quest for information and insight about the Senator. They began with Robert F. Wagner, Jr., Jeremiah T. Mahoney, Minna L. Ruppert, Marguerite Cummins Hayes, and Claire Dittrich Denzer, all of whom were relatives or close friends of the Senator. Exceedingly helpful also were my discussions with Simon H. Rifkind, Leon H. Keyserling (who kindly opened to me portions of his private papers), Philip Levy, David Delman, and Joseph P. Mc-

Murray, who successively served Wagner as secretary or administrative assistant during his years in Washington. Others who gave generously of their time and knowledge were Irene Osgood Andrews, Henry Ashurst, John A. Bell, Jr., Hugo Black, Mrs. Frederick W. Brooks, Jr., Howard Cullman, Paul H. Douglas, Mary E. Dreier, Morris Ernst, Clarence Galston, Theodore Granik, Edythe Griffinger, James Hagerty, Milton Handler, Carl Hayden, Dorothy Kenyon, John L. Lewis, Isador Lubin, John Morrissey, Warren Moscow, Frances Perkins, Frank J. Quillinan, Victor F. Ridder, Eleanor Roosevelt, Anna Rosenberg, Rose Schneiderman, Boris Shishkin, Kenneth Steinreich, Nathan Straus, Mrs. Myron Sulzberger, Harry S Truman, and Burton K. Wheeler. To all these men and women I extend my heartfelt thanks for their patience and cooperation.

It is also a pleasure to record my indebtedness to three institutions—the American Council of Learned Societies, the Eagleton Foundation for Research in Practical Politics, and the Georgetown University Faculty Research Fund—without whose financial support this book would have taken even longer to complete. Equally valuable were the moral support and encouragement afforded me over the years by colleagues and friends like Hisham B. Sharabi, W. Richard Walsh, Donald R. Penn, and Father Durkin of Georgetown University; Frank Freidel of Harvard University; and William E. Leuchtenburg of Columbia University, who have an uncanny knack for making themselves of service, in the midst of their own busy researches, to co-workers in the field; and especially helpful was Oscar Handlin of Harvard, whose teaching and writing have done most to prepare me to recognize and develop what I think are the relevant and important points at which Wagner, the man, interacted with his society to produce results that were meaningful for history.

As already indicated, work on this biography was begun in 1957, shortly after Marilyn Catana Huthmacher became my wife. Thus she has "lived with" Senator Wagner about as long as we have been married, and the satisfaction she derives from the work's completion is exceeded only by my own. To credit her with much of a direct role in the actual compilation and composition of the book would be ritualistic; raising our son and pursuing her own career have kept her more than busy enough. But her interest in and devotion to the book, and to the man whom it concerns, have become deep and absorbing, even to the point of prompting her to spontaneously "interview" New York City cab drivers old enough to remember Senator Wagner. For that and much more I am grateful, and I am happy to acknowledge my debt to her on the dedication page.

J.J.H.

CONTENTS

CONTENTS

ILLUSTRATIONS

PART I

New York & the Progressive Era

CHAPTER 1

The Fire

THE FIRE began in the late afternoon of Saturday, March 25, 1911. A passer-by in New York City's Washington Place was puzzled, momentarily, as he looked up and saw the girl, hysterically screaming and waving her arms, standing high on a ledge of the loft building across the street. Just as he shouted to her not to jump, she did; and a few wisps of smoke drifted out the window behind her. Stunned now, he watched her fall past floor after floor, until her head struck the pavement. Turning to run to a nearby alarm box, he saw more bodies tumbling toward the street. "They jumped with their clothing ablaze," wrote a reporter who came on the sickening scene. "The hair of some of the girls streamed up in flames as they leaped. Thud after thud sounded on the pavements. On both . . . sides of the building there grew mounds of the dead and the dying."

Forty-seven employees of the Triangle Shirtwaist Company plunged to death from its windows that day. Inside, firemen found another hundred dead of suffocation or burning—"there were skeletons bending over the sewing machines." A dozen or so of the bodies were beyond recognition. Some of the victims who smothered to death were identified by the pay envelopes still clutched in their hands: Rosie Crebo, $10.00; Mrs. Rosen, $12.00—and tied in a handkerchief tucked in her bosom were Mrs. Rosen's life savings, $847 in bills. Saturday, the end of the six-day week, was payday. In half an hour, at five o'clock, the Triangle workers would have been free to enjoy their "weekend," had not the tragedy struck.

The Triangle Company occupied the top three floors of the ten-story building. The fire started on the eighth floor, in a pile of scrap probably ignited by a cigarette. Some occupants of the tenth floor made their way to the roof and then to an adjoining building. Two elevators, one outside fire escape, and an enclosed stairway were the only means of exit available to the others.

Elevator boys made heroic ascents to the inferno, until smoke forced them to abandon their rescue efforts. The "fire escape" amounted to a single ladder hanging directly from one of the narrow windowsills; it led down into an enclosed courtyard, which filled with smoke as the fire raged. Those who managed to scramble down the ladder panicked when they found that the iron doors leading from the yard into the cellar of the building were locked, and they would have smothered there had not firemen finally battered the doors open from the inside. Some contended that the door leading to the enclosed stairway had been locked, too, in order to prevent employees from loitering there, and that the delay in getting it open accounted for the mound of suffocated corpses the firemen found piled up behind it. The charge was never proved to the satisfaction of a court, though only a short while before, a Labor Department inspector had warned employers in the building to stop the "locking-in" practice.

The proprietors of the Triangle Company were not held criminally responsible for the disaster; nor were the owners of the building, for they had complied with all the existing fire regulations governing loft structures. The Asch Building was classified as "fireproof," and, amazing as it seemed, the inadequate means of escape that it afforded were all that the law required.[1]

The Triangle Fire was the greatest industrial tragedy in New York's history and, as might be expected, especially in the midst of a nationwide Progressive Era, it touched off a chorus of protest and demands for varying degrees of "reform." Socialists, particularly strong in New York City, pointed to the disaster as still another evidence of capitalism's inhumanity. The Women's Trade Union League, defeated shortly before in its efforts to unionize the Triangle Company's employees, organized a public funeral demonstration in which a hundred thousand workers marched through the East Side in tribute to the fire's victims. A few nights later the league joined other labor, business, civic, and religious groups in a mammoth protest meeting at the Metropolitan Opera House, where a Committee of Fifty was established to formulate a program of action. Shortly there-

[1] New York *World*, March 26, 27, 1911; Albany *Evening Journal*, March 27, 28, 1911; Leon Stein, *The Triangle Fire* (Philadelphia, 1962), *passim.*

after representatives of the committee delivered to the state capitol at Albany a petition demanding a legislative investigation of working conditions in the state. In the majority leaders of the Senate and the Assembly—Tammany Democrats Robert F. Wagner and Alfred E. Smith, respectively—they found a receptive audience. In May the legislature approved the Wagner-Smith resolution creating the New York State Factory Investigating Commission. That summer the most intensive study of industrialism yet undertaken, not only in the Empire State but in the nation, got under way.[2]

The Triangle Commission, as it became known, consisted of Senators Wagner and Charles M. Hamilton; Assemblymen Smith, Edward Jackson, and Cyrus Phillips; and four public members appointed by the governor: Simon Brentano, the publisher, realtor Robert E. Dowling, Samuel Gompers, president of the American Federation of Labor, and Mary E. Dreier, president of the Women's Trade Union League. From year to year its tenure was renewed and the scope of its investigations broadened until with the return of the Republicans to power in 1915, it expired. In 1911 alone the commission held twenty-two public hearings, examined 222 witnesses, published 1,986 pages of testimony, and met in fifteen executive sessions to formulate recommendations. The four annual reports that it submitted to the legislature, totaling thirteen volumes, were masterly analyses of America's new industrial order. The commission's proposals for humanizing that order were embodied in more than sixty bills that Wagner and Smith introduced in the legislature during these years. Under the guidance of the two Tammany politicians, fifty-six of those reform measures became law.[3]

The commission engaged a number of experts and technicians who supervised studies in their special fields of competence: for example, George Price in industrial sanitation, H. F. P. Porter and James

[2] New York *World*, April 3, 1911; Albany *Evening Journal*, June 8, 21, 1911; Henry Morgenthau, *All in a Life Time* (Garden City, N.Y., 1922), pp. 107–108; interview with Rose Schneiderman, who was an official of the Women's Trade Union League at the time of the Triangle fire.

[3] New York (State) Factory Investigating Commission, *Reports*, 13 vols. (Albany, N.Y., 1912–15), *passim*. See also Alfred E. Smith, *Up to Now* (New York, 1929); pp. 90–98; Frances Perkins, *The Roosevelt I Knew* (New York, 1946), pp. 17–26; Josephine Goldmark, *Impatient Crusader: Florence Kelly's Life Story* (Urbana, Ill., 1953), *passim*; J. William Gillette, "Welfare State Trail Blazer: New York State Factory Investigating Commission, 1911–1915" (unpubl. master's essay, Columbia Univ., 1956), *passim*; and Laurence A. Tanzer, "Reminiscences" (Oral History Research Office, Columbia Univ., 1949), pp. 48–50. The author is indebted for interviews and correspondence concerning the Factory Investigating Commission to Rose Schneiderman, Frances Perkins, Mary E. Dreier, and Irene Osgood Andrews, who was an official of the American Association for Labor Legislation at the time of the commission's work.

Whiskeman in fire protection, and a young Consumers' League social worker named Frances Perkins in wages and working conditions. But the commissioners were not mere figureheads, nor did they base their recommendations on second-hand knowledge and academic theory. They personally visited most of the important manufacturing cities in the state, and a good many of the mill towns, frequently surprising flustered factory managers and seeing for themselves—or remembering once again—how "the other half" worked and lived. They saw unguarded machinery that could, and often did, "scalp a girl or cut off a man's arm." "Robert Wagner," one of the commission's investigators has written, "personally crawled through the tiny hole in the wall that gave egress to a steep iron ladder covered with ice and ending twelve feet from the ground, which was labeled 'Fire Escape' in many factories." [4]

The commissioners saw the "doctored" company records of hours and wages that were sometimes used to dupe Labor Department inspectors. They went to the rope works at Auburn and interviewed some of the 150 women as they came off the ten-hour night shift, 7:00 P.M. to 5:00 A.M., to return to their husbands and children. At times they met enlightened employers who had succeeded, on their own, in improving working conditions, and came away more convinced than ever that laws to compel the recalcitrants to follow suit would benefit workers, industry, and the public alike.

In New York City and elsewhere Wagner and his fellow students climbed the dimly lit steps of rat-infested tenement houses where "home work" flourished. In some flats they found mothers, victims of tuberculosis or scarlet fever, supervising the work of youngsters gathered about the bed and making paper flowers, infants' clothing, macaroni, or cigars. The commissioners toured upstate vegetable farms at harvest time, where women worked as many as nineteen hours a day in the fields or in the canning sheds, their children at their sides. "What do your children do while you're working?" Wagner asked one mother. "They fall asleep, wake up, and begin to work again when they are awake," the woman replied. "I have nowhere else to keep them." At some canneries children five, six, or seven years old were employed full time as a matter of course. Arriving at one establishment at 7:00 A.M., two hours after it had opened, Wagner noticed a six-year-old leaving. "Where are you going?" he asked. "They say they don't need me today," the boy answered. "I'll have to come back at five o'clock tomorrow morning." [5]

[4] Perkins, *The Roosevelt I Knew*, p. 22.
[5] Mary E. Dreier to the author, May 21, 1962.

Thus the Triangle Commission, between 1911 and 1914, reached far beyond the fire-hazard problem that had called it into existence. Bob Wagner and Al Smith, as its chairman and vice-chairman respectively, had a comprehensive look at modern labor conditions, "and from that look," Frances Perkins has written, "they never recovered. They became firm and unshakable sponsors of political and legislative measures designed to overcome conditions unfavorable to human life." [6] The first series of Wagner-Smith labor bills passed in 1912. Some of the more controversial among them encountered strong opposition in the Republican-controlled Assembly of that year and had to be postponed. But 1913 was a banner year, and the legislature, Democratic again in both houses, enacted virtually the entire agenda of reform.

As embodied in the Wagner-Smith acts, the Factory Commission's program touched many facets of industrial life. Parts of it naturally concerned fire protection. Construction codes were upgraded so as to require a greater number of enclosed stairways, fire escapes, and automatic sprinkler systems in factory buildings. Limitations were placed on the number of workers who might be employed on a given floor space, and fire drills became mandatory. But industrial safety and sanitation regulations of a much broader sort also received attention. Some bills prescribed the safeguards that must be maintained in the operation of dangerous machinery. Others regulated in minute detail the lighting and ventilation of factory workrooms and the provision of washrooms and first-aid facilities for employees. One of the major enactments of 1913 reorganized the State Department of Labor along up-to-date lines. It authorized a five-member Industrial Board to enforce safety regulations recommended by newly established bureaus of medical and sanitary experts. Conservatives complained that the format "reads more like a prospectus for a scientific school than a plan for a State bureau." [7] But the measure extended to the labor field the kind of flexible and discretionary administrative authority that progressives favored, and it became a model for other states that overhauled their labor regulatory machinery in the progressive years.

Determined to end the kind of gross exploitation of women and children that they had observed, the Factory Commission and its legislative spokesmen also pressed to enactment a series of laws that drastically tightened regulations regarding hours of labor. In 1913 the legislature outlawed the employment of women in any factory or cannery between the hours of 10:00 P.M. and 6:00 A.M. The employment of

6 Perkins, *The Roosevelt I Knew*, p. 17.
7 Albany *Evening Journal*, Jan. 21, 1913.

children under fourteen years of age was forbidden, and the legal number of working hours permitted for persons under twenty-one was further reduced. Moreover, provision was made for physical inspection of minors before they might be hired, and the procedures governing the issuance of "working papers" were surrounded with additional safeguards.

In 1914 the commission broadened the scope of its mandate still further by launching an intensive study of wage levels. Investigation of several industries revealed an appallingly low pay scale, especially for women—an average of $6.00 a week in confectionery manufacturing, for example, and $6.50 a week in the paper-box industry. In submitting the commission's preliminary report to the Senate, Wagner commented that "something must be done to remedy this situation." [8] By the end of the year he and Smith had prepared a bill for the coming session that would establish minimum wages for women and children.

Progressives were particularly pleased with the Factory Commission's achievements in the control of tenement home work. In 1885 the state's highest court had nullified a statute forbidding tenement manufacture of cigars on the ground that it was an unconstitutional interference with the "liberty" of employers and slum dwellers. Since that time the home production of forty-one articles had been subject to license, but the commissioners found at least sixty-two others that went completely unregulated. A bill passed in 1913 subjected all such industries to control by the State Department of Labor. And, despite the adverse precedent set by the Court of Appeals, Wagner and Smith succeeded in enacting a measure that outlawed completely the most pernicious aspects of tenement industry—the manufacture of infants' wear, dolls, and food products, for example. During the Senate debate Wagner asserted, hopefully, that "the point of view of the courts in such matters is changing." [9]

Constitutional objections, serious as they were, posed only one obstacle that the sponsors of the reform measures had to overcome. Conservative businessmen and realtors strenuously opposed the bills, and sometimes it was necessary to compromise with them. For example, as originally introduced, the bill requiring enclosed staircases applied to factory buildings of four or more stories. In deference to upstate manufacturers, who claimed that their plants should not be subject to the same requirements as the "skyscraper" factories of New

[8] *Ibid.*, Feb. 17, 1914.
[9] *New York Times*, March 11, 1913; Goldmark, *Impatient Crusader*, pp. 122ff.

York City, the measure was amended so as to apply only to structures of five stories or more, even though Wagner declared that "the time will come when the wisdom of the original provision will be appreciated." That time wasn't long in coming, for shortly thereafter fire swept a Binghamton clothing factory and claimed thirty lives; consequently the original proviso of Wagner's bill was restored.[10]

As the regulatory statutes piled up—"this foolish legislation," a prominent realtor called it—the laments of aggrieved interests grew louder. "You can no longer distinguish the real estate owner by the smile of prosperity," complained the counsel of the Real Estate Board of New York, "because his property is now a burden and a liability instead of a comfort and source of income. To own a factory building in New York is now a calamity." Spokesmen for the Associated Industries of New York asserted that the Wagner-Smith acts would mean "the wiping out of industry in this state." And years later there still hung in the press room of the State House a yellowing cartoon, clipped from a conservative newspaper, and bearing the caption: "Young Bob Wagner won't be satisfied until he closes down all factories altogether." [11]

Nor did passage of a measure mean that it was permanently secure. Manufactures, canners, and real-estate operators maintained powerful lobbies at Albany and could always find lawmakers who were willing to sponsor bills that would repeal, or amend into insignificance, the Factory Commission laws. On the last day of the 1914 session, for example, newspapers reported that during the hectic closing hours conservative legislators had managed to slip through a bill that practically exempted certain types of factory buildings from regulation. The story was a false alarm, however, and Frances Perkins issued a reassuring statement from Consumers' League headquarters: "Those who think the real estate interests gained these concessions no doubt read copies of their bill *before* it was passed, and not *after* we had amended it. . . . The result is that the status remains unchanged." [12] Miss Perkins, along with Bob Wagner and Al Smith, learned in those years that vigilance is the price of reform, and they never forgot it.

Wagner's confidence in the ability of the Triangle laws to withstand attack in the courts proved well founded. Not one of the Wagner-Smith statutes was ruled unconstitutional—a remarkable record

[10] Albany *Evening Journal*, July 23, 29, 1913.

[11] *New York Times*, May 3, June 21, July 17, 1914; undated memorandum in the Robert F. Wagner Papers (Georgetown Univ., Washington, D.C.), hereafter referred to as RFW Papers.

[12] *New York Times*, March 31, 1914.

in an era when the phrases "due process of law" and "liberty of contract" still spelled the doom of progressive measures in many jurisdictions. The sponsors of the Factory Commission bills had learned to
relate their objectives clearly to the preservation of the health, safety,
and welfare of the citizenry and thus to bring the enactments within
the purview of the state's "police power." When tests did come in the
courts—and they came frequently—organizations like the Consumers'
League helped the state's lawyers prepare "sociological briefs" of the
sort made famous by Louis D. Brandeis in his defense of reform legislation. Those briefs touched not only on the legal aspects of the cases
and on the precedents, which were often unfavorable, but even more
on the economic and sociological justification for novel exercises of
the police power amid the changing conditions of American life.

In New York such arguments proved singularly effective, as
when, in 1915, the Court of Appeals completely reversed a decision
only seven years old and thereby sustained the Wagner-Smith act outlawing night work for women. "There is no reason," the justices
declared in their opinion, "why we should be reluctant to give effect
to new and additional knowledge on such a subject as this." The new
and additional knowledge consisted of data that the Factory Investigating Commission had gathered at Auburn and elsewhere.[13]

The commission's accomplishments were, in the opinion of the
progressive journalist Oswald Garrison Villard, "epoch-making in
their improvement of labor conditions in the Empire State." Former
President Theodore Roosevelt agreed and personally endorsed the
Wagner-Smith bills. "Any measure which betters the child's surroundings . . . has my hearty support," he told a legislative committee
considering the tenement bills, even though the pugnacious Republican could not resist adding a thrust at their Tammany sponsorship
—"no matter who proposes it." "We doubt if any State in the Union," resolved the New York Federation of Labor at its 1913 convention, "can now compare with our Empire State in its present code
of labor laws." [14]

The Triangle Commission experience was no less significant in
the molding of Robert F. Wagner. He never forgot it, and three
decades later he would win a bet by recalling the exact date and hour
that the fire began. Service on the commission was the most important event in his public life up to that time, for it focused and made

---

[13] Goldmark, *Impatient Crusader*, pp. 165–167; *New York Times*, April 28,
May 1, 1914.
[14] Oswald Garrison Villard, *Prophets True and False* (New York, 1928), pp.
11–12; *New York Times*, Feb. 20, 1913.

impregnable the reformist leanings he had exhibited earlier. It also made him, and the political organization he represented, essential links in the chain of reform that spanned the Progressive Era and marked the emergence of modern, urban liberalism on the American scene.

CHAPTER 2

Good Intentions

THE TRIANGLE COMMISSION investigation was not simply an objective, intellectual experience for Bob Wagner; it was an emotional one as well. For it evoked memories of the poverty and deprivation that had marked his own youth in the immigrant, working-class neighborhood of New York's upper East Side. "My boyhood was a pretty rough passage," he would recall later.

Wagner remembered, too, the series of fortuitous happenings that had enabled him to overcome the handicaps imposed by his environment and to fulfill his ambitions for a better life. "I came through it, yes. But that was luck, luck, luck! Think of the others!" [1] His work on the Triangle Commission, and in much of his later career, was designed to ease the rough passages and to reduce the hazards of chance for those others. And because Wagner remembered these things and succeeded in doing something about them, he would leave his own deep mark on the history of his adopted country.

In the Rhineland village of Nastätten, near Wiesbaden in Germany, Reinhard Wagner had operated the local dyeing and printing establishment to which farmers and townspeople brought their homespun woolens for finishing touches. His wife, Magdalene, occasionally

---

[1] Oliver Pilat, "A New Dealer—Sunday, Monday and Always," New York *Post Weekly Picture Magazine*, Dec. 31, 1943, p. 2; Henry F. Pringle, "Profiles: The Janitor's Boy," *The New Yorker*, March 5, 1927, p. 24; Beverly Smith, "Thanks to Brother Gus," *American Magazine* (Dec. 1939), p. 84.

taught school, and as things were measured in Nastätten, theirs were not particularly poor circumstances. At the urging of their older sons, nevertheless, the Wagners uprooted their family in 1886 and moved to America. They brought six of their seven children with them; the youngest of them, Robert Ferdinand, was nine.[2]

But there was little use for Reinhard Wagner's handicraft trade in the rapidly mechanizing industry of late-nineteenth-century America. His age was another factor that counted against him when he sought employment. And so, in the "land of plenty," the father of the Wagner immigrants found himself working as janitor in a succession of tenement houses in Yorkville, the "little Germany" of polyglot New York City. His income hovered around $5.00 a week, plus use of the basement apartment as home for his family.

To make ends meet, every member of the family had to contribute. Magdalene took in washing, and the older sons and daughters found jobs of various sorts. Only Bobby, the "baby" of the brood, was fortunate enough to go through the public schools. In after-school hours and on weekends he, too, helped stretch the family's meager resources: selling newspapers, delivering groceries, or peddling candy in nearby Central Park. It seemed certain—for his father expected it—that on graduation from high school the youngest boy would join the others as a full-time wage earner.

But Bob's oldest brother, August, was determined that at least one member of the family should enjoy the opportunities extended by their new country, such as the tuition-free education afforded by the City College of New York to those who could qualify. After all, Bob was a bright boy and an avid student. A sister remembered that on Christmas morning, 1886, the day after their arrival in America, he pestered the family with an insistent "Nun kann ich nach schule

2 For information on Wagner's background and youth the author is indebted for interviews to Robert F. Wagner, Jr., the Senator's son; Jeremiah T. Mahoney, his first law partner; Kenneth Steinreich, his nephew-in-law; and John Morrissey, who during the 1940s and 1950s was Tammany leader of the Yorkville assembly district where Wagner cut his first political teeth. The Senator's sister, Clara Wagner Jenkins, and two of his nieces, Claire Dittrich Denzer and Helen Dittrich McCartan, were not only informative in interviews but also ransacked their attics for pictures and clippings. Among the more useful articles on Wagner written after he became famous are the following: Pilat, "A New Dealer," pp. 2ff; Pringle, "Profiles: The Janitor's Boy," pp. 24–26; Smith, "Thanks to Brother Gus," pp. 42ff; Owen P. White, "When the Public Needs a Friend," *Collier's*, June 2, 1934, pp. 18ff; Jack H. Pollack, "Bob Wagner: Liberal Lawmaker," *Coronet* (April 1946), pp. 36–39; and John C. O'Brien, "Robert F. Wagner: Pilot of the New Deal," in J. T. Salter, ed., *The American Politician* (New York, 1938), pp. 109–123. See also Jeremiah T. Mahoney, "Reminiscences" (Oral History Research Office, Columbia Univ., 1949), *passim*.

gehen?" At the high-school commencement exercises in 1893 he was valedictorian of his class. Gus promised to contribute to Bob's support, and also to help him get a job at the New York Athletic Club, where Gus worked as a cook. At length he persuaded his father to allow Bob the luxury of a try at a college education. The youngest Wagner easily passed the qualifying exams, and in the autumn he was enrolled at the City College of New York.

City College, "the People's University," was not one of the country's chief centers of learning· near the turn of the century, but it offered a portal of escape to professional careers for boys whose talents might otherwise have lain dormant, buried under the burden of urban poverty. Through that portal passed such luminaries as Felix Frankfurter and Bernard Baruch, as well as Robert Wagner. Because he worked part time, it took Wagner five years to win his degree, but during that time he savored enthusiastically just about every facet of college life that was available at City. He commuted, but was elected to a social fraternity, Phi Sigma Kappa. He worked as a bellhop at the N.Y.A.C. (Gus made good his promise), yet managed to find time to join City's debating team and athletic squads. Bob was a "fair miler" on the track team and played shortstop on the baseball nine. Football was his favorite sport, however, and as quarterback he led his mates to a celebrated 12–6 victory over archrival New York University in 1895. The college yearbook reported that Wagner's playing "left nothing to be desired," while his passing "was superb," and the following year he captained the team. Most important of all, young Wagner mastered the academic curriculum which a contemporary described as "tough but not original"—well enough to graduate near the top of his class.[3]

In 1896, while Wagner was still in college, his parents returned to Germany to live out their remaining years among the more familiar surroundings of Nastätten; America did not materialize as the "promised land" for all the immigrants who landed on its shores in those years. Bob then moved in with brother Gus and his wife, an Irish woman named Margaret Hogan who learned to cook a good *sauerbraten* and the other "foreign" dishes of Yorkville. At the same time Bob converted from the conservative German Lutheranism of his parents to Methodism, whose secular functions had become more important to him than matters of theology. He taught Sunday school for a time and joined the Epworth League, whose social activities were

[3] Lawrence D. Weiner (C.C.N.Y. Public Relations Office) to the author, May 16, 1962; Jeremiah T. Mahoney, interview. See also the centennial issue of *Microcosm* (1947), the C.C.N.Y. yearbook, for a memoir by Wagner regarding his college days.

much to his liking. After his immersion in politics Wagner became only an occasional churchgoer, but he remained formally a Methodist until his conversion to Catholicism many years later, in 1946.

When he graduated from City College in 1898, bearing the title of "Class Orator," it appeared that Wagner's formal education was over. He'd decided to become a public-school teacher and had already acquired the necessary certificate. But during the summer Wagner's boyhood chum Jeremiah T. ("Jere") Mahoney, who had just completed the law course at New York University, painted an alluring picture of a career together in legal practice. Gus agreed to the further strain on his wallet (it's said, too, that a loan was arranged with the wealthy father of a student Bob had tutored), and in the fall Wagner enrolled at New York Law School, downtown near City Hall, on William Street.

He negotiated the prescribed two-year course—Elementary Law, Contracts, Real Property, Wills and Equity, Partnership, Corporations, and Evidence—with little difficulty. His highest grade was 96, his lowest, 93; and in 1900 he graduated again with honors.[4] In view of what was to come, the training was mediocre. Labor law, administrative law, and constitutional law, which were to be so important in Wagner's career, were nonexistent or neglected subjects at the turn of the century. These things Wagner would have to learn on his own— and help to create.

In October 1900, following Bob's admission to the bar, he and Jere Mahoney formed the law partnership that was to last nearly twenty years until one member, followed by the other, assumed a seat on the bench of New York's Supreme Court. Their original office at 229 Broadway, as Mahoney described it, was shared with another couple of fledgling lawyers. The quarters were so small that when one "firm" had business to transact the other withdrew to the corridor to make room for the client until the deal was concluded.

Like so many young lawyers, however, Wagner and Mahoney relied on participation in local politics to augment their practice. Since Tammany Hall firmly controlled the 29th and 30th Assembly districts in which the two men were domiciled, it seemed natural and sensible that they should cast their lot with the Democratic machine. Indeed, the first reward for his election-day services in the 29th A.D. had already come to Mahoney in 1899, when he was appointed an assistant counsel to the city controller in the administration of Democratic Mayor Robert A. Van Wyck. It was the heyday of Boss Richard

---

[4] Constance J. Lawson (Secretary-Registrar of the New York Law School) to the author, April 30, 1962; Jeremiah T. Mahoney, interview.

Croker's regime at Tammany Hall, and Van Wyck was his pawn.
From his position on the inside, Mahoney was able to observe city
administration, or maladministration, at its worst. "I'm afraid prosti-
tution was more or less their business," he wrote later, along with
gambling syndicates, shakedowns, the selling of jobs, contracts, and
franchises, and every other form of graft and corruption imaginable.
A legislative investigation blew the lid off the mess, and in 1901 the
voters elected Seth Low mayor on a reform Fusion ticket, ending
Croker's leadership of Tammany and turning the rascals out, at least
temporarily.

But Mahoney came through it all unscathed and kept his position in the controller's office during the Fusion regime. Under George
B. McClellan, the reform Tammany mayor who succeeded Low in
1903, he rose to be counsel to the controller. Jere became a respected
figure in political circles, and, needless to say, all this benefited his law
firm.[5]

On Wagner's part, introduction to active politicking had come
even while he was a student. In the fall of 1898 he visited Tammany's
30th A.D. headquarters on East 87th Street—the Algonquin Club,
presided over by "Whispering Larry" Delmore, who signed his name
with an X—and offered to make a speech for Augustus Van Wyck,
the Democratic candidate running for governor against the triumphant Rough Rider, Theodore Roosevelt. The men in charge were
willing to let anyone speak for their ticket, apparently, and assigned
the new recruit to one of the wagons scheduled to tour the neighborhood a few nights later. Wagner wrote out his speech, memorized it,
and, to brother Gus's disgust, practiced it for two hours before the
bedroom mirror. But it made a hit, although, as Wagner recalled
later, "If anybody had interrupted I would have been in a hell of a
fix!"[6]

In the years that followed, Wagner became an habitué of the
Algonquin Club, and of Mike Cosgrove's tavern down at the corner,
which served as a sort of club annex. He also joined the Elks, the
Eagles, the Buffaloes, the Mozart Verein, and numerous other local
organizations. Weddings, wakes, picnics, balls, and other social functions absorbed much of his time. All this was good for his law practice
and for paving the way to what was called at the time "political pre-
ferment."

The chance came in the fall of 1904, when the incumbent assem-

[5] Jeremiah T. Mahoney, "Reminiscences," pp. 13ff.
[6] Robert G. Spivack, "Valiant Crusader for Social Betterment," New York
Post Daily Magazine, Oct. 9, 1944, p. 1.

blyman from the 30th A.D. announced his retirement to private business after serving the customary two or three years at Albany. Mike
Cosgrove, a powerful figure in the neighborhood, had become Wagner's chief political mentor, and his influence in helping Bob secure
nomination to the vacancy counted a lot. In addition, the younger
element of Algonquins backed Wagner's claim, arguing that since he
was the only aspirant—and one of the few members of the tribe—
with a college degree, he ought to be in the legislature. The district
convention nominated him, Wagner had a new photograph made,
handbills and posters were printed, and the campaign was on. At its
end the Tammany candidate won, as was usual in Yorkville. Wagner
secured 6,365 votes; his Republican opponent got 3,428.[7]

Some of the old-timers were skeptical about their new assemblyman's ability to meet the generally accepted specifications for a successful Tammany politician. Only shortly before, these had been
spelled out authoritatively by State Senator George Washington
Plunkitt, Tammany sachem and warhorse, in an interview reported by
newspaperman William Riordon. "A young man who has gone
through the college course is handicapped at the outset," Plunkitt
explained. "He may succeed in politics, but the chances are 100 to 1
against him." Admitting that there were a few "bookworms" in Tammany Hall, the elder statesman professed to see little real function or
future for them in the organization: "We keep them for ornaments
on parade days." Equally misguided were those who "think that the
best way to prepare for the political game is to practice speakin' and
becomin' orators," for this type, too, were "chiefly ornamental." "The
men who rule have practiced keepin' their tongues still, not exercisin'
them."

Another awful temptation, which Plunkitt admitted that he
himself found hard to resist, was "the hankerin' to show off your
learnin'." "Don't try to show how the situation is by quotin' Shakespeare," who was all right in his way, "but didn't know anything
about Fifteenth District politics." The promising young aspirant
would be careful in such matters as dress, too, so as to make even the
poorest man in the district "feel that he is your equal. . . . Puttin'
on style don't pay in politics." Most important of all, he must for-
swear the use of intoxicants. "I honestly believe that liquor is the
greatest curse of the day," Plunkitt pronounced, "except, of course,
civil service." "You won't make a lastin' success of it if you're a
drinkin' man." For the fellow who followed the sachem's advice to
the letter the rewards would be great; in life he would "get his share

[7] *New York Times*, Nov. 9, 1904.

of the good things that are goin'," and at death he might merit on his gravestone the kind of epitaph that Plunkitt envisioned for his own: "George W. Plunkitt. He Seen His Opportunities, and He Took 'Em." [8]

Young Bob Wagner plainly violated many of the precepts. Not only was he a college graduate, but thus far just about his only claim to political fame was his speech-making. In an interview he even admitted that reading history and Shakespeare was his only hobby, and "preferably Shakespeare." [9] His taste for good clothes—which developed from the time when, at thirteen, his newsboy profits enabled him to buy his first "store suit"—lasted throughout his life; photographs at the time of his first nomination show a handsome young dandy who might have just stepped out of a men's fashion magazine. And Wagner was known to enjoy a drink now and then—quite a few, on special occasions—especially the imported German beers and Rhine wines so plentiful in Yorkville.

The picture seemed clear to the wise ones: the twenty-seven-year-old assemblyman would be good for one or two terms in Albany. But surely that was all, unless Tammany Hall had ceased being the Tammany of old, and of George Washington Plunkitt.

During his first year in the legislature Wagner played his role according to traditional Tammany rules. He kept quiet, took orders from those who knew "the good things that are goin'," and voted as he was told. The net result was that he was defeated in his bid for reelection in November.

The year 1905 marked the beginning of the Progressive Era in New York State; and neither Wagner nor Tammany Hall knew it yet. A legislative investigation of alleged monopolistic practices among the gas and electric companies of New York City heralded the dawn of the new day. Under the brilliant direction of its counsel, Charles Evans Hughes, the committee relentlessly unearthed corporate chicanery, while Joseph Pulitzer's New York *World* and the Hearst newspapers whipped up grass-roots support for the regulatory measures that the committee proposed. Most of the bills passed, but toward the end of the session a coalition of conservative Republicans and Tammany Democrats in the State Senate managed to defeat a bill that would have set the price of gas at eighty cents per thousand cubic feet in place of the dollar being charged by the monopoly.

[8] William L. Riordon, ed., *Plunkitt of Tammany Hall* (New York, 1905), pp. 10, 12–13, 69, 84–85, 93, 98–99, 143, 145.
[9] Albany *Knickerbocker Press*, Jan. 12, 1913.

"Cheap Gas Is Killed!" "Tammany Did It!" the *World* blared.[10] William Randolph Hearst announced that a new party, the Municipal Ownership League, would appear on the ballot in the fall elections. It ran Hearst himself for mayor and entered a full slate for the Assembly. In some districts the League's candidates also won Republican endorsement as the result of a bargain struck between Hearst and G.O.P. state leaders.

Reducing the cost of gas and electricity was the kind of reform issue that New York City's masses could readily understand and, through their votes, endorse. That became apparent in the November election returns when Hearst nearly beat the incumbent Tammany mayor, McClellan. (Indeed, Hearst may well have been "counted out" by Tammany election officials, as the publisher himself contended.) Republican–Municipal Ownership fusion candidates for the Assembly unseated a number of incumbents in hitherto Democratic strongholds, and four straight League assemblymen were elected. One of them was Maurice Smith, who in the 30th District received 4,197 votes to Robert F. Wagner's 3,934 (the Republican candidate had 1,186). The reform wave had engulfed Yorkville, and Wagner—his vote cut 40 percent below 1904—was one of its victims.[11]

Repudiation was a great disappointment to Bob Wagner; he had enjoyed his year at Albany and the prestige that went with it, and he wanted to return. For another thing, he had already formed close attachments to some of his legislative colleagues. This was especially true of a young Tammany assemblyman named Alfred E. Smith, who came from the lower East Side and with whom, purely by accident, Wagner had shared a dingy hotel room at the outset of the session. The two men took an immediate liking to each other and were to remain linked together thereafter, tied by close bonds of personal affection that not even the deepest of political disagreements, years later, could sever.

During 1906 Wagner had a chance to ponder the lessons of his defeat, and perhaps he sought ways to ensure that his first would be his last; so it turned out to be. But just as Bob had had little to do with the high-level political deal between Hearst and the Republicans that had cost him his seat the year before, so now he had little hand in the arrangement that regained it for him. As it became apparent that the Republicans were prepared to nominate Charles Evans Hughes for the governorship, Tammany Boss Charles F. Murphy cast

10 New York *World*, May 5, 6, 1905.
11 W. A. Swanberg, *Citizen Hearst* (New York, 1961), pp. 230–238; *New York Times*, Nov. 8, 1905.

about for a reform candidate of his own. He lit upon none other than
William Randolph Hearst. The mercurial publisher, whose cartoon-
ists had customarily depicted Murphy garbed in a jailbird's striped
uniform, accepted the Boss's support and the Democratic nomination
that went with it. Now Hearst's Independence League (the successor
to his Municipal Ownership League) fused with the Democrats in
many local elections, in contrast to the year before. Assemblyman
Maurice Smith, unceremoniously bereft of the Hearst organization's
blessing, ran for reelection as a Republican. But he was powerless
against the doubly endorsed Democratic–Independence League candidate, and Bob Wagner reentered the winner's circle by an overwhelming 6-to-1 vote.[12]

That Wagner had learned well the lessons of recent political history soon became apparent. For he returned to Albany a reformer, a
breed no longer so rare with Hughes ensconced in the governor's
mansion and leading the state through the first phase of its Progressive Era. The measure that earned Wagner his own degree of fame as
a liberal crusader against the "interests" in these years was the Five
Cent Fare bill, which would compel the Interborough Rapid Transit
System and the Brooklyn Rapid Transit System to issue transfers and
thus limit to a nickel the cost of a ride from the crowded tenements
of Manhattan to the cooling breezes of Coney Island. The New York
World had mounted a campaign for such a law for some time past to
no avail, for the interests behind the IRT and the BRT wielded powerful influence in both political parties. Nonetheless a *World* reporter,
a fellow Yorkvillite whom Wagner knew well and frequently dined
with in the German restaurants that lined 86th Street, interested him
in the reform measure following his election in 1906. When the legislative session of 1907 opened, Wagner dropped his Five Cent Fare
bill in the hopper. He'd made his first move in the direction of independence, and partly because of it, he never had to worry about
reelection again.[13]

Like eighty-cent gas, the five-cent fare represented the kind of
reform that readily commanded the support of the urban masses. As
spring brought on the first heat waves, the *World* stepped up its front-
page campaign for the measure that would guarantee "Five Cents for
a Ride from the City to the Sea." Other dailies joined in, and the
New York City correspondent for an Albany newspaper found it the

[12] Swanberg, *Citizen Hearst*, chap. v; *New York Times*, Sept. 25–28, Nov.
7–9, 1906.
[13] The legislative history of the Five Cent Fare bill can be followed in the
Journals of the Assembly and State Senate, but see especially the New York
World, 1907–1908. Jeremiah T. Mahoney, interview.

most discussed topic in the metropolis, more important than foreign relations, national issues, or even the upcoming baseball season! [14] Naturally, the bill's sponsor reaped a great deal of publicity.

The Assembly passed Wagner's measure in 1907, but with the connivance of several Tammany senators, conservatives bottled it up in committee in the upper house. In November voters expressed their displeasure with the offenders; in 1908, consequently, the bill passed both houses by large majorities. The first "Wagner Act" of any significance seemed about to become law, but in the end Governor Hughes vetoed it. By now the governor had established a State Public Utilities Commission, and he preferred to leave rate-setting problems to the discretion of the commission's experts.

Strictly from Wagner's career point of view, however, it made little difference whether his pet measure became law or not. He had made a name for himself not only in his district but in the city at large—and in the inner sanctum of Tammany Hall. Older hands had warned Wagner at the outset about the risks involved in bucking the likes of August Belmont, Thomas Fortune Ryan, and Nicholas Brady, millionaires who were equally influential in the affairs of both the city's transit corporations and Tammany Hall. And there is little doubt about the names those gentlemen applied to the upstart legislator in their conversations with Boss Murphy. But Murphy himself had not interfered or retaliated. Indeed, in 1908 his word made Wagner's Five Cent Fare bill an official "Tammany issue," and helped ensure its passage. The Boss read the papers and the election returns, and he knew "a good thing that's goin'," votewise, even when it involved something other than what George Washington Plunkitt had in mind.

Murphy also possessed a sharp eye for promising young votegetters, and in the fall of 1908 he decided to use Bob Wagner as the agent for quashing a suspected cabal against his leadership in Yorkville. The 16th Senatorial District, in which Wagner lived, embraced two assembly districts: Wagner's own 30th and the adjacent 31st, ruled by "Silent Maurice" Featherstone. By long-standing tradition the senatorial nomination was Featherstone's to bestow. But lately Murphy had become suspicious of "Silent Maurice's" loyalty, and he threw down the challenge by letting it be known that he wanted young Wagner to replace Featherstone's incumbent minion in the upper chamber. The atmosphere was tense on the night the nominating convention assembled, and the meeting lasted until four in the morning. But at the end of the marathon session Wagner emerged

[14] Albany *Evening Journal*, June 11, 1907.

from the steaming hall the victor—by a margin of one vote. Feather-stone's power was broken, and a short time later he retired from politics. Moreover, Bob Wagner, on the basis of Tammany's vote-pulling strength and his own, was assured of a seat in the State Senate the next time the legislature met.[15]

Promotion to the upper house meant even more than a political triumph to Wagner. It gave him a feeling of confidence that he had advanced to a secure and promising position in life, with perhaps still other triumphs lying over the horizon. On the basis of that assurance Wagner, always conservative in personal matters, took the step he had been contemplating for some time—the proposal of marriage to the girl he had courted for almost three years. Margaret Marie McTague was her name. A Jersey City girl, she worked in a Wall Street brokerage office, and the couple had met at a house party during the summer of 1906. "She was the typical Irish beauty," Bob wrote of her, "a twinkle in her eyes, a ready smile, and an equally ready tear." With Jere Mahoney as best man, the wedding ceremony took place in the rectory of a Catholic church in Brooklyn. Following a honeymoon in Atlantic City, the newlyweds took an apartment in a building at 87th Street and Lexington Avenue owned by Mike Cosgrove, Bob's old political mentor. Sparkling, witty, and socially graced, it's said that Margaret was the perfect wife for the aspiring young politician to whom she was married. "She enjoyed life to the fullest, and was so terrifically human," Wagner later recalled.

Two years after their marriage, in the spring of 1910, the Wagners became the parents of a boy, who was promptly named after his father. To celebrate the event Wagner bought a shore home at Woodmere, Long Island, so that in the heat of summer his family could escape "from the city to the sea." The affluence of a second residence was easily manageable now, for the firm of Wagner and Mahoney was well established and prospering—even expanding to take in several junior partners. The progress of his private and professional life warranted a great deal of satisfaction on Wagner's part.[16]

On the political front, moreover, developments in 1910 also proved gratifying to Bob Wagner and those close to him. For in the election of that year, as part of a nationwide trend, New York's Democrats won control of the governorship and of both houses of the legislature for the first time in a generation. Since he was a member of what had now become the majority party, Wagner's role in the legis-

15 Interviews with Jeremiah T. Mahoney and John Morrissey. See also Murphy's obituary in *The New York Times*, April 26, 1924.
16 Robert F. Wagner, "Growing into Catholicism," in John A. O'Brien, ed., *The Road to Damascus* (Garden City, N.Y., 1951), *passim;* interviews with Robert F. Wagner, Jr., Jeremiah T. Mahoney, and Claire Dittrich Denzer.

lature seemed bound to be even more interesting and important than in the past.

Of course some well-meaning admirers of the expiring Hughes Administration winced at the prospect of Democratic control of the state's lawmaking body. For if seniority and service to the party meant anything—and they usually did—Thomas F. Grady, Tammany's "Silver-Tongued Orator," would become majority leader of the Democrats in the State Senate, while "Paradise Park Jimmy" Oliver would assume the counterpart role in the Assembly. With these two seasoned Tammany spoilsmen in control, liberals and progressives feared a resurgence of the forces of reaction and corruption, "allied, as of old, under the legislative leadership of . . . the mercenary Old Guard of both parties." [17]

Except that this time seniority counted for nothing with Charles F. Murphy. Moving to head off a revolt against his party leadership being readied by State Senator Franklin D. Roosevelt and other upstate reform Democrats, the Boss passed over Grady's and Oliver's claims. Instead, he reached down into his "kindergarten class" and named two of his "fair-haired boys," Bob Wagner and Al Smith, as Tammany's choices to head the Senate and Assembly. When the party caucuses met in January 1911, the upstate reformers acquiesced, and Murphy's selections were ratified.

At thirty-three, after only two years in the State Senate and a total of five years' experience in the legislature, Bob Wagner became the youngest president pro tem in the Empire State's history. The immigrant boy unable to speak a word of English at Castle Garden had come a long way—and had remained remarkably unsullied—in the rough and tumble of urban politics, Tammany style. Wagner was proud of his achievement. "It typifies the opportunity that America affords to the young man with the 'right stuff' in him," the newspapers were saying. The pleasantly surprised *New York Times*, which had hitherto harbored the mistaken notion that "Senator Wagner . . . [has] shown more independence than is relished in Tammany Hall," greeted his promotion to the majority leadership with enthusiasm, for here was a man "capable, and of unquestioned integrity."

At the same time Franklin D. Roosevelt noted in his diary that Wagner would be "fairly good. He has good intentions; the only obstacle is the pressure of his own machine." [18]

[17] *New York Times*, Nov. 9, 1910.

[18] *Ibid.*, Nov. 10, 1910; New York *World*, Jan. 4, 5, 1911; Albany *Knickerbocker Press*, Jan. 12, 1913; Franklin D. Roosevelt *Diary*, Jan. 3, 1911, Franklin D. Roosevelt Papers (Roosevelt Library, Hyde Park, N.Y.), hereafter referred to as FDR Papers; Jeremiah T. Mahoney, interview.

CHAPTER 3

The Front Ranks of
the Progressive Movement

THE REPORTERS SMILED when, in reply to a question about Charles F. Murphy's power at Albany, Senator Bob Wagner told them, tongue in cheek, that "Adhering closely to his long-established policy, Mr. Murphy has not attempted to influence the legislature in any way." They laughed outright when Assemblyman Al Smith chimed in and added that "Mr. Murphy is not any more concerned in the deliberations of the legislature than any other good Democrat." For the newsmen knew that although the two legislative leaders conferred frequently with the governor, they made no move without the approval, or at least acquiescence, of the chief of the Tammany wigwam in 14th Street.[1]

Mister Murphy, as even his most intimate political associates called him, was the essence of dignity and propriety. A short, stocky man, "his face was not unpleasant, rather intelligent," a reporter once wrote, but his mouth was a closed straight line, and his expressions were inscrutable. His private life was unblemished, and a long-time acquaintance confessed that "I would have just as soon thought of telling an off-color story to a lady as I would to Mr. Murphy." He neither smoked nor drank, but he chewed gum incessantly, and, when agitated, "his jaws worked like a trip-hammer." If there was one game he loved more than politics, it was golf. He bought an estate, Good Ground, on Long Island, and fitted it out with a nine-hole course. Some old-timers thought he was going high-hat, as Croker had done

[1] Henry F. Pringle, *Alfred E. Smith: A Critical Study* (New York, 1927), pp. 130–131.

by cavorting at Lakewood in a full-dress suit. But the Boss was the Boss, and some of the skeptics eventually got used to the idea and took up the game. It was at Good Ground that Wagner and Smith learned, among many other things, to drive and putt in mediocre fashion.[2]

By 1911 Murphy had been the leader of Tammany Hall for nearly nine years. He had weathered many storms, but his position was still insecure, and more challenges were to come. To Murphy the Democrats' control of the state government meant a chance to stabilize his power, and his "boys in the legislature," as he called them, were the agents for carrying out his designs. Wagner and Smith loyally accepted this aspect of their roles, conferring regularly about "practical politics" with the Boss at Good Ground or at his sumptuous private dining room above Delmonico's restaurant in New York City. Consequently they shared the blame and opprobrium for the "sins" committed at Albany in Tammany's name between 1911 and 1914.

There were transgressions, to be sure. But whether they were venial, or as mortal as the political purists claimed, depends upon one's attitude toward the realities of politics as practiced at the time. "The Democratic Party," the Citizens Union complained at the end of the 1911 legislative session, "devoted much attention to the pursuit of patronage and to bills legislating out of existence Republican office-holders and providing for the appointment of their successors by the Democrats." And it's true that a good many "ripper" bills were put through. A typical one amended the charter of Mount Vernon to allow the Democratic mayor to appoint all city officials without confirmation by the Republican-controlled Common Council; another abolished the Republican-staffed Bronx Sewer Commission and empowered the Democratic governor to appoint a new one. When the Republican minority leader of the State Senate protested, Tammany-ite Jim Frawley bluntly replied: "Go ahead, squeal. We're taking this because we want it. You took it away from us, and now we're recovering our property." But even that reform Democrat Senator Roosevelt supported some of these measures as being "justified by the partisan acts of the Republicans while in power." In any event, the Republicans would reciprocate and recover "their" property again when they resumed control in 1915.[3]

2 Lawson Purdy, "Reminiscences" (Oral History Research Office, Columbia Univ., 1948), p. 22; James W. Gerard, "Reminiscences" (Oral History Research Office, 1950), p. 22; obituary of Charles F. Murphy in *The New York Times*, April 26, 1924.

3 Pringle, *Alfred E. Smith*, pp. 160–161; Albany *Evening Journal*, April 18, May 3, June 20, 28, July 21, 1911; New York *World*, July 21, 1911.

Unseemly political wrangling also blackened the Democrats' record in the eyes of "good government" elements. In 1911, for example, the state's legislative work was tied up for the first three months of the session as Wagner and Smith, marshaling Tammany's forces at Albany, staved off a revolt among upstate Democrats, led by Roosevelt, over the questions of choosing a United States senator. The insurgents managed to block Boss Murphy's first choice for the post, "Blue-Eyed Billy" Sheehan. But they failed to elect one of their own number, and in the end, according to some observers, the compromise choice, Judge James O'Gorman, turned out to have even closer connections with Murphy and Tammany than Sheehan had. Nonetheless the hassle won considerable favorable publicity for the meteoric young Roosevelt and a great deal of notoriety for Tammany. In the annual Assembly election in November 1911 (state senators were elected for two years) the voters returned control of the lower house to the Republicans.[4]

Then followed, in 1913—after the Democrats had regained full control of the state government again the previous fall—the spectacle of the Democratic legislature impeaching its own governor. William Sulzer, elected to the governorship with Murphy's backing in 1912, harbored strong presidential ambitions. ("A good many people say . . . he suffers from hallucinations," a prominent Republican commented.[5]) Taking his cue from the career of President Woodrow Wilson, "Plain Bill" Sulzer set out soon after inauguration not only to build an image as a dedicated progressive ("A man," said Mr. Dooley in Finley Peter Dunne's humorous political column, "who has to blow his nose ivry time he thinks iv the troubles iv others") but also to usurp control of the party machinery by launching a crusade against "boss rule" in the Empire State.[6] The latter course constituted a direct challenge to Charles F. Murphy's leadership, but, unfortunately for Sulzer, Murphy was prepared for such a contingency. During the summer of 1913 a Senate investigating committee, appointed by Bob Wagner, probed into the governor's financial affairs and produced evidence that he had filed a false report of campaign expenditures. (Indeed, it appeared that the governor had diverted a

---

[4] An excellent account of the Sheehan fight is given in Frank Freidel, *Franklin D. Roosevelt: The Apprenticeship* (Boston, 1952), chap. vi. New York newspapers of Jan., Feb., and March 1911 cover the contest in minute detail. See also Alfred B. Rollins, Jr., "The Political Education of Franklin Roosevelt" (unpubl. doctoral dissertation, Harvard Univ., 1953), chaps. v–vi.

[5] Albany *Evening Journal*, April 29, 1913.

[6] Dunne is quoted in Jacob A. Friedman, *The Impeachment of Governor William Sulzer* (New York, 1939), p. 22. Friedman's book gives an exhaustive and balanced account of the whole Sulzer affair.

considerable amount of campaign contributions to private speculation on the stock market.) In August Al Smith's Assembly returned articles of impeachment against Sulzer. A month later the High Court of Impeachment, consisting of the State Senate and the ten justices of the state's Court of Appeals—Sulzer called it "Murphy's High Court of Infamy"—voted to remove the governor from office.

"It is a just verdict," the New York *World* concluded. The *Times* agreed, but added its hope that "Since we are now rid of one party to this sordid political quarrel, in Heaven's name let us be rid of both! The impeachment of Sulzer should be the sure portent of the defeat of Tammany in the . . . election." [7] And so it turned out to be. In November 1913 the Republicans regained control of the Assembly, and in 1914 the voters returned the State Senate and the governorship to the G.O.P.—a party that conducted its squabbles with more decorum!

That ended the period of Democratic ascendancy in New York, at least temporarily. For a while (it turned out to be four years) Tammany was consigned to licking its wounds and atoning for its sins. Not even under promising new leaders like Bob Wagner, some concluded (indeed, Wagner was among "the devil's minions," one clerical champion of Sulzer's innocence proclaimed from his pulpit), could the Tiger be expected to change its stripes.[8]

Yet it would be unfair and misleading to judge the Democrats' record at Albany between 1911 and 1914—the highpoint of the Progressive Era—solely in terms of Tammany's abuses of patronage and political power. For amid the flying fur of the Democracy's internal disputes her legislators managed to enact a volume of reform measures that far exceeded the achievement of any earlier period. "By 1914," a historian of the Empire State has written, "New York had not reached the millennium, but it had adopted a body of forward looking legislation that placed the state in the front ranks of the progressive movement." In that process Bob Wagner and Al Smith, who were jointly responsible for channeling progressive sentiments into concrete statutes, "compiled a record that has never been surpassed in the history of the New York legislature." And since we're told by an experienced politician that "nothing could be done at Albany unless Charles F. Murphy permitted or encouraged it," it seems only proper to assign the Tammany Boss some responsibility for the Hall's "good works" as well as for its faults.[9]

[7] New York *World*, Oct. 17, 1913; *New York Times*, Oct. 18, 1913.
[8] New York *World*, Aug. 12, 1913.
[9] David M. Ellis, James A. Frost, Harold C. Syrett, and Harry J. Carman, A

For the truth was, as a perceptive official of the Citizens Union observed in his memoirs years later, that during the Progressive Era "Tammany was in a flux, so that . . . the reformers were no longer in exclusive possession of reform, if you know what I mean. That was a very subtle change," he added, "which I have never seen referred to very much." [10] But in terms of the nation's future development, it was a change of vital importance. The signs of it had begun to appear early in the Hughes Administration—in the individual case of Bob Wagner and the five-cent fare, for example. Its wider progress could be charted in the legislative debates and roll calls that took place as the Republican governor's reform program unfolded between 1907 and 1910. For while unreconstructed Tammanyites like Tom Grady continued to condemn Hughes's proposals as "communistic" proposi-tions, a younger and broader-visioned band of Hall spokesmen lent unexpected support to a good many of the governor's recommenda-tions throughout his term. After a caucus of Assembly Democrats, led by Wagner and Smith, decided to vote in favor of Hughes's bill to create an effective Public Utilities Commission in 1907—without Murphy's interfering—even the New York *World* had a good word for the Tammany delegation: "The Democrats have heard from the people. Their decision merits the highest praise. Only by breaking away from the Gradys . . . only by heeding the people's will, can the Democracy regain its ancient standing in New York." [11]

So while it appeared between 1911 and 1914 that in matters of patronage and political bickering Tammany remained much the same, it became evident also that in many and more important ways Tammany was changing. Her spokesmen continued to heed "the peo-ple's will," and her legislative leaders in the State Senate and Assem-bly were among the most attentive and effective listeners.

Not that Wagner and Smith or the lawmakers whose votes they controlled showed much enthusiasm for some of the purely political reforms touted by the "good government" forces. Those appealed mainly to the middle- and upper-income voters who paid the city and state tax bills, not to the working-class tenement dwellers who made

---

Short History of New York State (Ithaca, N.Y., 1957), pp. 376, 389; Edward J. Flynn, "Reminiscences" (Oral History Research Office, 1950), p. 8.

[10] Robert S. Binkerd, "Reminiscences" (Oral History Research Office, 1949), p. 59.

[11] Albany *Evening Journal*, April 4, May 9, 14, 15, 22, 1907; New York *World*, May 15, 16, 17, 23, 1907. The author's generalizations in this paragraph and those that follow are based on intensive study and analysis of legislative de-bates and roll calls during the years 1907–1914, as reported in newspapers and in the *Journals* of the State Senate and Assembly.

up most of Tammany's constituency. Even so, however, the Democrats did become identified as the champions of certain progressive political reforms in New York State. In 1913 Bob Wagner placated the women suffragists—and won their enduring support—by introducing a bill authorizing a statewide referendum on the subject. (The Republican minority leader of the Senate, on the other hand, compared woman suffrage to the "mistake" that had been made in giving the vote to Negroes!) [12] That same year Wagner sponsored the resolution whereby New York became the third state to ratify the Seventeenth Amendment, requiring popular election of United States senators. (Republicans, favored by the state's antiquated system of legislative apportionment, preferred to keep the selection in the hands of the legislature and denounced the pending amendment as "an insidious advance against the foundations of the Republic.") [13] Greater "home rule" for cities, freeing them from interference by rural-dominated state legislatures—a proposition generally favored by Progressive Era municipal reformers—was another cause espoused by Tammany, especially for New York City, where the Hall usually was in control. Tammany even became the defender of the primary system of nomination in New York State against Republicans who were ideologically opposed to "direct democracy"—at least *after* the machine's leaders learned that the primary method would not hamper, and might even enhance, their influence in naming party candidates.

Of much greater interest to New York City's masses, however, were the kinds of "bread-and-butter" economic reforms that more directly touched their daily lives. Tammany, mindful of the adverse election returns of 1905 and other occasions when her representatives had sided with the "malefactors of great wealth," now joined in the movement that during the Progressive Era severely curtailed the reign of "free enterprise" in the American business system. The Public Utilities Commission, created during the Hughes Administration, had its powers expanded and strengthened during the Democratic regime at Albany. Strengthened also were the laws regulating insurance, banking, "loan sharks," and tenement housing, while additional businesses, such as the cold-storage food industry, were brought under regulation for the first time. Farmers benefited from laws that encouraged the formation of agricultural cooperatives and established a system of public markets; even rural upstate Republicans were willing to vote for "welfare state" measures that benefited *their* constituents. In the realm of electrical power generation and distribution the Demo-

[12] Albany *Evening Journal*, Jan. 23, 1913.
[13] *Ibid.*, Jan. 14, 15, 1913; *New York Times*, Jan. 16, 1913.

crats between 1911 and 1914 went far beyond the position of Governor Hughes—who had ended the pernicious system of outright giveaways of invaluable water sites to private utility interests—and committed their party to the policy of *public* ownership and operation of power facilities. And it was the Democrats who, in 1911, added New York to the list of states approving the federal income tax authorized by the Sixteenth Amendment, a reform that even Hughes had shied away from.

But most important of all was the Democrats' role in enacting the kinds of welfare and labor legislation that were designed particularly to preserve, in an urban, industrial society, the American promise of equal opportunity for all that had flourished previously in an agrarian, rural setting. In teeming cities like New York across the nation the greatest challenge of all to that American dream was emerging during the Progressive Era, and, to its credit, Tammany under its new brand of leadership lent support to those social-justice crusaders who were determined to prove that the dream could be sustained. To rehabilitate those who cracked under the strains of modern life, for example, the Democrats sought expansion of the state's institutional and welfare agencies. Even more important was the augmentation of the public-school system that took place. Throughout his career Bob Wagner was especially proud of the 1913 measure that established scholarship grants to enable poor but talented young people to attend the state's colleges and universities (after all, not everyone had a Brother Gus!).

In 1914 the legislature created a system of public employment offices to free jobseekers from reliance on extortionate private agencies. (A prominent Republican member denounced the act as "an illustration of open-hearted, generous-minded Democratic legislation" of the sort that would soon bankrupt the state.) [14] Old-age pension systems for public employees became more common. ("You are simply making a mollycoddle lot instead of encouraging independence," a Republican state senator proclaimed.)[15] Employers throughout the state were compelled to give their workers at least "one day's rest in seven" by a law enacted in 1913; seven-day weeks and twelve-hour days had not been uncommon before. That same year the legislature approved a compulsory workmen's compensation act, sponsored by Wagner and Smith, which President Samuel Gompers of the American Federation of Labor described as "the best law of the kind ever

[14] Albany *Evening Journal*, Feb. 27, March 6, 25, 27, April 8, 1914; *New York Times*, Feb. 28, March 1, 27, 1914.
[15] Albany *Evening Journal*, May 3, 1910.

passed in any state, or in any country." During the debate on the measure Wagner declared that "The cost of repairing human machinery should enter into the cost of a product, just as much as the expense of repairs to machines made of iron and steel." Years later, in Washington, he regarded workmen's compensation as the beginning of America's social security system.[16]

The capstone of the Democrats', and of Robert Wagner's, contribution to social reform during New York's Progressive Era was, of course, the work of the Triangle Commission. The many enactments that resulted from its labors did most of all to place New York "in the front ranks of the progressive movement," and to compile for Wagner "a record that has never been surpassed." And the prominence of Tammanyites and Tammany votes in creating the Triangle laws testifies, indeed, to the fact that the Hall "was in a flux." The urban political machine, undergoing "a very subtle change," was beginning to play a new and crucial role not only in the Empire State but in the development of American industrial society as a whole.

For, as Frances Perkins wrote in a reflective mood years later, after a lifetime of service to reform causes: "The extent to which this legislation in New York marked a change in American political attitudes and policies toward social responsibility can scarcely be overrated. It was, I am convinced, a turning point." [17]

The era of that turning point, the Progressive Era, in the Empire State and elsewhere, was the first phase in the evolution of modern American liberalism, and in many ways it set the pattern and precedents for later milestones that would be labeled New Deal, Fair Deal, New Frontier, and the Great Society. Obviously it was the product of many forces and many hands. Individual reformers—muckraking journalists, religious leaders devoted to the social gospel, educators, social workers—gave impetus to causes close to their hearts. But it was also the age of the "organizational revolution," and usually reformers banded together in order to pool their strength more effectively. Labor organizations, farm groups, and a host of "professional" reform organizations, such as the Citizens Union, Consumers' League, Child Labor Committee, and the American Association for Labor Legislation, represented a response to the issues raised by the growth of organized business and to that other form of organized living that goes under the name of urbanization. The motives of all these groups

[16] *Ibid.*, March 31, April 3, December 11, 13, 1913; *New York Times*, December 9–14, 1913.

[17] Frances Perkins, *The Roosevelt I Knew* (New York, 1946), p. 23.

were selfish, in one respect, for they were out to protect their own
interests against real or imagined enemies. But they shared a degree of
altruism, too, which resulted from a mounting realization that under
modern conditions of interdependence all Americans are "in the same
boat." Indeed, that realization constituted the essence of "the awakening of the public conscience," as the New York *World* once
expressed it, and in briefest compass it accounted for the coming of
the Progressive Era.[18]

Sometimes reformers and their organizations worked at cross-
purposes, for their programs were not identical in all respects. (Some
progressives felt that "moral" reforms like Prohibition were desirable,
for example, while others believed that economic and social "environmental" reforms would suffice.) Moreover, mutual suspicion and distrust existed to an extent (as between organized labor and some
middle-class reformers). But on those points where their programs
overlapped, and especially on measures of broader application where
altruism met altruism, the combined strength of the reform elements
was capable of producing lasting results. Sometimes those results involved nothing more than voluntary, nongovernmental action—the
attainment of collective bargaining rights for workers with their employers, for example, or the establishment of settlement houses in slum
areas, or the compliance of some manufacturers with the Consumers'
League sanitary code in return for the right to exhibit the league label
on their products.

Most often, however, the reformers turned sooner or later to the
government to achieve their reforms more quickly and effectively
through statutory enactment. Legislative success required research
and bill-drafting services, propaganda campaigns to educate the public,
lobbying, and funds; these things the reform organizations provided.

---

[18] New York *World*, May 4, 1906. On the Progressive Era in general see
Robert H. Wiebe, *The Search for Order, 1877–1920* (New York, 1967); Samuel
Hays, *The Response to Industrialism, 1885–1914* (Chicago, 1957); Richard Hof-
stadter, *The Age of Reform* (New York, 1955); Frederick Lewis Allen, *The Big
Change: America Transforms Itself, 1900–1950* (New York, 1952); George
Mowry, *The Era of Theodore Roosevelt, 1900–1912* (New York, 1958); Arthur S.
Link, *Woodrow Wilson and the Progressive Era, 1912–1917* (New York, 1954);
Eric Goldman, *Rendezvous with Destiny* (New York, 1952); and J. Joseph Huth-
macher, "Urban Liberalism and the Age of Reform," *Mississippi Valley Historical
Review* (Sept. 1962), pp. 231–241. On New York in particular see Irwin Yel-
lowitz, *Labor and the Progressive Movement in New York State, 1897–1916*
(Ithaca, N.Y., 1965); Robert F. Wesser, "Charles Evans Hughes and the Urban
Sources of Political Progressivism," *New-York Historical Society Quarterly* (Oct.
1966), pp. 365–400; and J. Joseph Huthmacher, "Charles Evans Hughes and
Charles F. Murphy: The Metamorphosis of Progressivism," *New York History*
(Jan. 1965), pp. 25–40.

But ultimately it also required that there be legislators and political leaders who were amenable to the reformers' ideas. Without them the campaign for a measure would come to nothing, and by no means did all politicians respond to the reformers' entreaties. Some did respond, however, and New York's progressives were fortunate indeed to have Governor Hughes heading the Republican party for the four years 1907–1910. But after 1910, when the G.O.P. again turned conservative, New York's liberals found themselves relying on the Democrats, especially on the "new Tammany" element headed by Wagner and Smith, and perhaps without fully realizing it, on Boss Charles F. Murphy himself. That reliance was not misplaced.

Just why Bob Wagner proved so responsive to the reformers, rather than to conservative or even corrupt interests that earlier had made prisoners of so many Tammany men, is difficult to fathom, for he was not an introspective man. Undoubtedly political expediency counted a good deal for his liberalism. He happened to enter politics just as reform was coming into its own. Anyone who read the *World* or Hearst's New York *American*—as Wagner and most of his East Side neighbors did—could sense that. Certainly his defeat for reelection in 1905 at the hands of a Hearst progressive jolted him into an awareness of the trend of the times if nothing else had. Young and willing to take a chance, Wagner quickly became a reformer of sorts himself, a spokesman for the *World* in its crusade for the five-cent fare and for other measures that Pulitzer's muckraking journal promoted. The subsequent popularity that he gained with his constituents—and the favorable newspaper publicity—was gratifying, and thereafter the election returns ran consistently in his favor. Wagner had found a "good thing that was goin'," different from the sort of thing that attracted George Washington Plunkitt, but a sure-fire method of keeping himself in office nonetheless.

It would be possible to let the explanation rest there, and to view all of Wagner's later reform efforts similarly, as political catering to the influence of reform-minded (or self-seeking) pressure groups. But what of Wagner's contemporaries who were surrounded by the same progressive tendencies of the day, yet failed to respond? "You can talk social reform to a hundred men," a devotee of progressive causes has reminded us; "only those will react whose hearts and minds are attuned to the gospel preached." [19] Somehow, it would appear, Wagner's background and experience had attuned him to the preachments of the reformers. Not that his parents were directly responsible for

[19] Oswald Garrison Villard, *Prophets True and False* (New York, 1928), p. 14.

that result, or that his teachers and ministers were; Wagner hardly ever mentioned them in his later life, and there is little evidence that he imbibed liberal principles from them. Nevertheless the school of poverty in which Wagner grew up left a lasting impression of the meaning of deprivation. "Things were hard for us," he once reminisced, "and I realized then that heavenly rewards are not enough —a man must have some happiness and some security on earth." [20]

Wagner's personal ambition and striving—"I have tried hard to be successful. I love work," he frankly admitted to reporters on more than one occasion—helped him overcome his own handicaps. But as he became able to enjoy the good things of life he didn't forget his "luck" or "the others" who lacked it. Many of the ideas that progressives confronted him with seemed to be proper means for insuring that, as Wagner frequently told newsmen who interviewed him, "The boy of this country has the opportunity to build himself up no matter how low his beginning or how little money he possesses." He adopted the reformers' proposals and, as legislative leader of his party, formulated them into law. "He learned at $1.50 a week how to succeed as a youth," a journalist once wrote of New York's Senate majority leader, "and that lesson taught him how to perform not only the work essential to his personal success, but to act and succeed for others—*pro tempore*." [21]

If the political currents of the times and Wagner's own early environment generated his progressive tendencies, his service on the Factory Investigating Commission nourished them toward maturity. Between 1911 and 1914 Wagner saw conditions that made even the East Side squalor of his youth seem idyllic. He was thrown into intimate contact also with labor's spokesmen and with individuals and organizations that had sparked "the awakening of the public conscience." He learned that not all unionists were racketeers or anarchists and that not all reformers were the kind Al Smith once complained of: people who only wanted "to fix it so that no Tammany man could ever run for office." [22] Some of them were sincerely interested in bettering conditions for the kind of people that Wagner and Smith and Tammany Hall represented, and they were willing to collaborate with Tammany in doing so.

Moreover, the breadth and scope of the factory investigation began the process of directing Wagner's liberalism, heretofore rather

[20] Unidentified Washington, D.C., newspaper clipping dated June 6, 1937, RFW Papers.
[21] Albany *Knickerbocker Press*, Jan. 12, 1913.
[22] *New York Times*, Nov. 11, 1913.

disjointed and sporadic, into a more consistent philosophy regarding the role that welfare legislation and labor organization might play in fulfilling America's promise for all its citizens. The tenacity with which he thereafter fought for measures in line with that philosophy suggests, certainly, that Wagner's heart and mind, as well as concern for his political well-being, lay behind the strenuous leadership—and much more than a vote—that he contributed to the liberal movement for the rest of his life.

Wagner remained an "organization man" nonetheless, but fortunately for his strong sense of party regularity, his commitment to economic and social reform in the progressive years did not necessitate a break with Tammany Hall and its boss. For in that same era the Tammany organization as a whole, under the influence of men like Wagner and then on Boss Murphy's orders, gradually emerged as a potent force for implementing the new liberalism of twentieth-century America. In contrast to the earlier liberalism of *laissez faire*, the new approach emphasized an active and positive role for government in fostering society's well-being. The propaganda of assorted reformers and agitators educated Tammany's constituents to an understanding that their political strength could, if properly directed, compel the enactment of measures, such as utilities regulation and social insurance, that would directly benefit them. They began to expect such programs from their political spokesmen—as those who watched election returns could see—and Tammany responded. The Hall discovered that "there is something more important than ward picnics and balls," and it learned to bank on its record of support for welfare measures as its most effective appeal for votes at election time. Such developments, historian Frank Freidel has written, "were the first intimations of a shift of basic significance in American politics." Its significance was stressed years later by Bob Wagner himself when, in the midst of the New Deal, he referred to Murphy's Tammany Hall as "the cradle of modern liberalism in America." [23]

Not that Charles F. Murphy planned it that way. The earliest years of his regime seemed to mark little change from the era of Boss Croker. Murphy did indulge in one deviation from his predecessor's course, however, and that was his penchant for opening up avenues of advancement in the organization to youngsters, even when their youthful enthusiasms led them toward an uncommon degree of independence from the older establishment. Wagner, Smith, Jere Ma-

[23] Freidel, *Franklin D. Roosevelt: The Apprenticeship*, p. 120; Wagner speech file, July 5, 1937, RFW Papers. See also Perkins, *The Roosevelt I Knew*, pp. 23-26.

honey, and James Foley were the standouts among Murphy's first
crop of "young men," and there would be others. Perhaps he used
them as "window dressing" at the outset; they might help give the
organization and the Boss a good name. But as the Progressive Era
wore on, with a reformer like Hughes leading the Republicans to victory, with third parties and reform Democrats challenging the Boss's
power in the state, and with several varieties of Socialists distributing
their handbills on the sidewalks of New York, Murphy became more
attentive to his youngsters' insistence that "a political party . . .
couldn't remain static." [24] Increasingly he let them have their way at
Albany, and he was pleased to see how the "good side" of Tammany's
record, which they contributed, produced favorable results at the
polls. When the "bad side" of its record—culminating in Sulzer's impeachment—brought a stinging rebuke to Tammany in the 1913 election, the Boss's conversion to the young men's viewpoint was made
complete. "Give the people everything they want," the newspapers
quoted him as saying; and those orders stood during the remainder of
his regime.[25]

The conversion of a powerful political organization like Tammany Hall to the support of legislative liberalism was a major feat,
and Murphy's reward for being wise enough to permit it came in the
fact that thereafter, until his death in 1924, his supremacy in the city
and state Democracy was unshaken. Political purists who continued
their efforts to unseat him found little to work with; indeed, many
liberals were quite satisfied with the character of Tammany's major
nominations after 1914 and regarded the Boss in a tolerant, if not
entirely kindly, manner. Murphy was left to watch with pride as his
"young men" rose ever higher in public esteem; one of them, Al
Smith, even became a serious contender for the presidency while the
old man still lived.

When Murphy died, some who wore blinders remembered only
the sins that marked parts of his rule. But wiser men offered more
accurate evaluations of his significance. "He was a great leader, because he kept his hand on the pulse of the people" observed Republican Representative Fiorello La Guardia. "He was a genius who . . .
recognized that the world moved on," added a mellower Franklin
Roosevelt. "It is well to remember that he has helped to accomplish
much in the way of progressive legislation and social welfare in our

[24] Jeremiah T. Mahoney, "Reminiscences" (Oral History Research Office,
1949), pp. 13–14, 46, 50, 106–107.
[25] Albany *Evening Journal*, Dec. 8, 10, 1913; *New York Times*, Nov. 13,
Dec. 7, 10, 1913. See also the analyses of Murphy's political career that appeared
after his death in *The New York Times*, April 26, May 4, 1924, and Jan. 25, 1925.

state." "The Murphy kind of boss," wrote political analyst Silas Bent in *The New York Times*, "is a guarantee of the future." Needless to say, Bob Wagner and the other graduates of Murphy's "kindergarten class" echoed these sentiments.[26]

As it turned out, none of Murphy's successors in the leadership matched his political acumen. "The brains went out of Tammany Hall when he died," Arthur Krock once remarked.[27] But in committing the organization to liberal legislation Murphy and his supporters did a thorough job, and Tammany's constituents saw to it that, in Albany and in Washington, the Hall's legislators thereafter cast their votes almost invariably on the liberal side. New York's Democracy became a major force in promoting the trend toward welfare statism not only locally but on the national party level, and in national legislation as well. So effective did this role prove in winning votes at elections that eventually New York's Republicans also cast off their conservative role, and thus the Empire State was one of the first in which twentieth-century liberalism became a bipartisan ideal. Near midcentury a Dewey could contest for the governorship against a Lehman, or a Rockefeller against a Harriman, with little difference in their mutual support of principles and programs that only the Democrats had endorsed in the time of Wagner, Smith, and Murphy. Certainly the Progressive Era reformers, who taught New York's people and Tammany Hall what to expect of modern government, worked even better than they imagined.

[26] *New York Times*, April 26, May 4, 1924. See also Rollins, "The Political Education of Franklin Roosevelt," pp. 458ff.

[27] Arthur Krock, "Reminiscences" (Oral History Research Office, 1950), p. 5.

CHAPTER 4

The Decade of "Normalcy"

WHEN THE REPUBLICANS resumed control of New York's government in 1915 their conversion to bipartisan liberalism was still a generation and more away. The G.O.P.'s victory, one of its spokesmen asserted, meant the return to power of "the party that gave the people not what they wanted, but what the party thought they ought to have." Thereafter progressives were on the defensive, and the creative period of Bob Wagner's career at Albany had come to an end. When the 1915 legislature met, Wagner promised that he would make no patronage deal with the Republicans, in order that he would be free to "pound." "That's all I'll be able to do," he conceded, "but I hope we may block some of the reactionary legislation that will be attempted." [1]

During the next four years the Senator from Yorkville served as the chief legislative spokesman for the liberal forces at the state capital, and "pound" he did. So vigorous was his opposition to the conservative counterattack that the Republican Senate majority leader publicly marveled at Wagner's "gymnastic" style of debate and at times expressed concern that his Democratic counterpart might suffer a heart attack if he didn't let up. Wagner's efforts to prevent "a return to barbarism," as he once put it, did not impair his health. But they did net him a great deal of favorable publicity, and enduring support, in liberal circles. [2]

[1] Alfred E. Smith, *Up to Now* (New York, 1929), p. 133; *New York Times,* Nov. 8, 1914.

[2] Albany *Evening Journal,* Feb. 26, March 23, April 2, 8, 9, 1915; *New York Times,* April 2, 1915.

During these years Wagner's ties with reform groups such as the Consumers' League and the American Association for Labor Legislation became closer than ever. He sponsored or supported the projects for an expanded program of social justice that they initiated—bills for minimum-wage laws, widowed mothers' pensions, state health insurance, and municipal ownership of public utilities, for example. On their part the social reformers, as Frances Perkins has observed, learned to head "straight for Wagner's door" when they had business to transact at Albany.[3]

At the same time Wagner's association with organized labor solidified into a virtual alliance. During election campaigns Samuel Gompers personally visited the Sixteenth Senatorial District to speak on behalf of the candidate whom the state's labor organizations periodically feted as "our Bob." Wagner reciprocated by stepping up his legislative contribution to labor's cause. In 1918, for example, he introduced a series of bills that would exempt unions from the state antitrust law, limit the issuance of injunctions in labor disputes, and in other ways protect the worker's right to organize, strike, and picket.[4]

Virtually none of the social welfare and labor reform bills introduced at the state capitol between 1915 and 1918 became law, of course. "This is such a dreadful legislature," Florence Kelley of the Consumers' League complained at one point, "that it is no use asking anything of them but that they stop sinning a little." [5] But the frustrated efforts of Wagner and the reform alliance did serve to keep alive the spark of progressivism in a period of retrenchment, a spark that, in New York at least, would flourish again in a relatively short while.

In the meantime, however, the liberals' prospects seemed further blighted by war-inspired circumstances that reinforced the conservatives' drive and raised new issues of repression for liberals to cope with. During 1916, as American sympathies moved closer to the side of the Allies, conservatives lost no time calling into question the allegedly "Germanic" origins of progressive social legislation. When America entered the war in 1917 the Republican leader of the New York Senate declared that "Every law which stands in the way of efficiency during this crisis ought to be gotten out of the way"—heralding a renewed attack on the state's code of labor regulations in the

[3] Frances Perkins, interview. The legislative history of the years 1915–1918 may be followed in the *Journals* of the State Senate and Assembly and in the newspapers of the period.

[4] *New York Times*, May 7, 1915, Jan. 11, 1917; Jeremiah T. Mahoney, interview.

[5] Albany *Evening Journal*, April 6, 1915.

name of patriotism. And after the Bolshevik revolution shook Russia
later in the year, conservatives added a new epithet, "Communist," to
their antiprogressive lexicon.[6]

The war and the Red Scare, by generating a wave of "antihy-
phenism" and demands for conformity, also intensified ethnic cleavages that sapped the unity of progressive forces and at the same time
raised basic questions regarding the future *cultural* direction of American liberalism. The issues involved had already been encountered in
New York, as at the state constitutional convention that met in 1915.
There conservative nativists, generally upstate Republicans, sought to
add to the constitution amendments that would virtually outlaw social welfare ("class") legislation and at the same time impose a literacy test as a qualification to vote. The connection between the recent
wave of progressive legislation in the state, on the one hand, and Tammany and its working-class "newer American" constituents, on the
other, certainly was not lost on the conservatives. One of their spokesmen, Judge Alphonso T. Clearwater, lashed out against "the proletar-
ians . . . crowding the seaboard cities. They elect legislatures
. . . ," the Judge complained, "and are strong enough in number to
enforce their demands for 'equality,' according to their ideas, which
are not American ideas." [7]

In 1915 the progressive forces at the constitutional convention,
marshaled by Wagner, Al Smith, and moderate Republicans from
New York City, managed to turn back the antiliberal, anti-immigrant
proposals. In the wartime atmosphere of superpatriotism a short time
later, however, the nativists gained some points. In 1917 the federal
Congress adopted a literacy proviso for the immigration laws. In
New York book-censorship and alien-registration laws were passed
during 1917 and 1918, and the legislature added the literacy test to
the suffrage regulations. Bills were even introduced to limit officehold-
ing to native-born citizens. Had they become law, the minority leader
of the State Senate would have been deprived of his seat.

In addition to restrictions on immigration and political participation, the cult of "100 percent Americanism" also fostered among native elements a determination to "uplift," or at least circumscribe, the
allegedly unhealthy cultural influence wielded by the "foreigners"
who dominated the nation's large cities. Drives for "moral" reforms,
such as Prohibition, blue laws, and the outlawing of parochial schools,
took on a new intensity as they became identified as the means to
preserve the supremacy of the white, Anglo-Saxon, Protestant way of

[6] *New York Times*, March 8, May 5, 24, June 4, 10, 1917, and March 27,
1918.
    [7] *Ibid.*, Aug. 13, 17, 18, 25, 26, 27, 1915.

life. To some extent such crusades commanded the support of native progressives, distracting their attention from the kinds of economic and social environmental reforms that had absorbed their energies earlier. Like other side effects of American involvement in the World War, therefore, "100 per cent Americanism" proved inimical to the kind of intergroup cooperation that had been essential to the prewar triumphs of the liberal coalition.[8]

In view of Bob Wagner's own ethnic origin, it's not difficult to understand why he took his stand with the cultural liberals in the years when narrow nationalism began to run rampant. Indeed, in 1917 he personally felt the sting of the rash prejudices being spawned in a war-spirited nation. Early in the year Wagner had joined others in the legislature in blocking a plan proposed by Fusion Mayor John Purroy Mitchel involving an exchange of public and private lands in New York harbor, on the ground of allegations that private real-estate interests stood to benefit exorbitantly thereby. Since the matter involved the War Department's wish to improve the harbor's fortifications, the legislature quickly approved an alternative method of bringing about the desired rearrangements. Infuriated nonetheless, Mitchel told newsmen that "It would appear that certain members of the Legislature are working in the interest of the German Government. Of course you know . . . I mean Bob Wagner." Hailed before the bar of the Senate on the day after President Wilson asked Congress to declare war, the mayor denied that he had meant to accuse Wagner of "conscious and intentional disloyalty," and by unanimous vote the upper house commended the "diligence, loyalty, and patriotism" of its minority leader. But given the temper of the times, Mitchel had successfully eliminated Wagner as a possible opponent in the fall mayoralty election, which up to then Wagner had confidently expected to win.[9]

Even without such incidents, however, it's likely that Wagner's background in the polyglot politics of Tammany Hall would have made him the cultural liberal that he proved himself to be throughout his career. Tammany represented a host of minority groups, and, despite the differences and hostilities that existed among them, they resented in common the growing tendency of the native "majority" to label them all as "inferior" or "un-American." Responding to its con-

[8] Oscar Handlin, *The American People in the Twentieth Century* (Cambridge, Mass., 1954), pp. 113–162; J. Joseph Huthmacher, *Massachusetts People and Politics, 1919–1933* (Cambridge, Mass., 1959), pp. 26ff. See also John Higham, *Strangers in the Land* (New Brunswick, N.J., 1955), *passim.*

[9] *New York Times,* Feb. 13, 14, 21, 22, March 23, 24, 27, 29, April 4, 5, 6, 1917; Jeremiah T. Mahoney, interview; Robert S. Binkerd, "Reminiscences" (Oral History Research Office, Columbia Univ., 1949), pp. 55–56.

stituents' needs and aspirations ("Give the people everything they want"), the Hall opposed the newer-American phobia of the war and postwar years that helped produce discriminatory immigration quotas, voting restrictions, Prohibition, anti-Semitism, anti-Catholicism, and the Ku Klux Klan. Bob Wagner joined those who viewed America as an open, pluralistic society, rather than a cultural monolith enforcing conformity to white, Anglo-Saxon, Protestant standards. To its support of economic and social liberalism, therefore, Tammany now added defense of cultural liberalism. At a later date that concept, too, would gain wide acceptance as an essential ingredient in the making of America's twentieth-century liberal society.

For the time being, however, as the World War came to an end, cultural liberals—indeed, liberals of every sort—seemed to be overwhelmed. The war that had been fought to make the world safe for democracy abroad had not served democracy well at home, for the Progressive Era was among its casualties. In place of trust and cooperation between old-stock and new-American progressives, and between reformers drawn from the ranks of the working class and of the middle class, there now existed suspicion. Fears of radicalism and "class legislation" combined with fears of "un-American" influences emanating from minority groups and the big cities to produce a postwar decade that was inhospitable both to liberalism in the economic sense and liberalism in the cultural sense. Instead, the nation as a whole experienced the decade of "normalcy."

It did not work out that way, however, in New York State. For in the election of 1918, while voters across the nation handed keys to executive mansions to men like Calvin Coolidge, the Empire State chose Alfred E. Smith as its governor. Liberals, some of whom may have voted Republican in 1914 as a rebuke to Tammany's arrogance in the Sulzer affair, now welcomed this favorite son of the Tiger with open arms. There was no doubt where Smith stood on the issues of either economic or cultural liberalism, and three times during the 1920s his stand was rewarded with reelection. The damage that had been done to the structure of progressivism during the interlude of Republican rule between 1915 and 1918 was quickly repaired, and during the postwar decade, as one historian has written, New York constituted "an island of progress and reform" in a nationwide era of complacency and conformity.[10] That fact was to mean a great deal to the state, to the nation, and to the career of Robert F. Wagner.

[10] David M. Ellis, James A. Frost, Harold C. Syrett, and Harry J. Carman, *A Short History of New York State* (Ithaca, N.Y., 1957), p. 393.

The election that promoted Al Smith to the governorship also elevated Bob Wagner to a seat on New York's State Supreme Court. The circumstances that accompanied his reward for thirteen years of service to Tammany and to the legislature were gratifying indeed. Not only was his candidacy endorsed by the Bar Association, the Citizens Union, and overwhelmingly by the press of New York City, but he rolled up the largest vote among the eight contested aspirants for the three vacancies that existed on the court. As Wagner prepared to assume his new role, the editor of an Albany newspaper, a seasoned reporter who had seen politicians come and go at the state capital over the years, penned a tribute that might have turned any man's head:

> In ability and character, in honesty of purpose and manliness of action, Senator Wagner has been an inspiration to younger legislators and a beacon light to men older than him in years. He was the friend of the laboring man and the defender of women and children who have to earn their bread by the sweat of their brow—and yet he never was a demagogue. All the gold in the world could not buy him; all the beckonings of ambition could not induce him to abandon the cause that was righteous and the issue that was true. There is not a black spot upon him. He has served the people well.[11]

In thus serving the people well over those many years Wagner had been forced to forego many of the amenities that other family men enjoyed. During the legislative season he lived away from home for extended periods, and during all seasons his political responsibilities curtailed the leisure that he might spend with his wife and son. The demands on his time and devotion became especially trying when, in 1915, Margaret Wagner contracted a disease from which there was no recovery. The doctors called it locomotor ataxia, a form of creeping paralysis. Within two years she had become a total invalid, deprived of the use of her legs.

It may well be that his wife's condition prompted the longing that Wagner frequently expressed after 1915 to exchange his legislative position for one on the Supreme Court, in order that he might spend more time in New York City with her. But if such was the case, fate soon cut short the Wagners' elation. Early in the summer of 1919, during Bob's first year as a judge, Margaret's chauffeur-driven automobile was struck by a trolley while she was returning from a ride in the country. The accident produced a state of shock from which she

---

[11] *New York Times*, Aug. 1, Oct. 9, 27, Nov. 6, 1918; clipping from an unidentified Albany newspaper, 1918, RFW Papers.

never recovered, and at the house at Woodmere, on July 28, she died.

Bob was only forty-two at the time, and his position as a judge and then a United States senator subsequently gained him friends and acquaintances among a widening circle of interesting and gifted people. Since Wagner was fairly well off financially, distinguished, and affable and charming in social situations, there is little doubt that he was considered "eligible" by some of the women he met—and certainly he enjoyed their company. From time to time rumors appeared in the gossip columns that he was about to remarry. But Wagner remained a widower the rest of his life. And some believed that his conversion to Catholicism in 1946, when he thought his own death was near, resulted in part from his wish to be buried next to the wife he had lost nearly three decades before.

Following Margaret's death, Wagner became exceptionally close to his son. They spent their vacations together at mountain or seaside resorts, and annually during the 1920s there were trips to Europe. The excursions abroad invariably included a visit to Nastätten, where, with much feasting and toasting, relatives and friends of the family greeted the "local boy who had made good." In 1927 the townspeople made Wagner their honorary mayor, but seven years later the Nazis had his "election" revoked in retaliation for his "unfair attitude toward the Fuehrer."

In the mid-1920s Bobby, Junior, went off to prep school, and later he entered college. The apartment that Wagner continued to occupy in Yorkville was quieter than ever after that. To compensate for his loneliness, the man who had already told reporters at Albany, "I love work," immersed himself even more deeply in his official responsibilities. The public benefited thereby, and perhaps Bob Wagner did too. For public service helped fill the void that personal tragedy had left in his private life.[12]

The First District Supreme Court bench, on which Wagner sat between 1919 and 1926, embraced Manhattan and the Bronx, and it has been described as the busiest jurisdiction to be found anywhere in the legal world. The thirty-six justices who served it in Wagner's time did their best to keep abreast of the sixteen thousand new cases instituted annually, but in an average year they succeeded in disposing of only nine thousand. The result was that in 1923, when Wagner was

[12] *New York Times*, July 31, 1919; interviews with Robert F. Wagner, Jr., Jeremiah T. Mahoney, Claire Dittrich Denzer, Simon H. Rifkind, and Leon H. Keyserling. Rifkind and Keyserling were Wagner's administrative assistants during long periods of his career as a United States senator.

appointed head of a commission to reform procedure and reduce congestion, a backlog of twenty-two thousand cases awaited trial. Even the indefatigable judge from Yorkville, who must have found in such circumstances an outlet for his passion for work, had to report that the burden tested both the "mental and physical endurance" of the justices.[13]

The Supreme Court was a court of original jurisdiction in both civil and criminal actions, and most of the cases tried there involved "a large measure of . . . dull routine," one of Wagner's colleagues has written.[14] Occasionally, however, issues did arise that cut though to the basic principles of legal interpretation and philosophy that were undergoing significant transformation in the first third of the twentieth century. As a result of the Progressive Era, the conservative doctrines of constitutional absolutism and judicial "objectivity" inherited from the late nineteenth century had come under increasing attack by a liberal school of judicial realists who insisted that changing times and circumstances must be given due weight in the decisions of judges. That Wagner adhered to the liberal approach had already become clear during his career in the legislature. It was made even more explicit in the ceremonies that marked his induction as a judge on January 6, 1919, for there wasn't a judicial conservative among the many who made speeches on that occasion. Instead, Bob's well-wishers reminded him to render his decisions so as "not only to conform to precedent where conditions permit, but to promote justice, to prevent oppression, to protect the weak and to curb the strong." During the next eight years Wagner expounded judicial pragmatism in his own speeches: "In our . . . study and practice of the law we worship too much the importance of precedent and antiquity," he told a Fordham Law School audience in 1925. "Why speak and act upon the past in all things?" In addition he entertained his share of socially significant cases in which practical effect could be given to the principles of judicial modernism.[15]

For example, Wagner exhibited little patience with arguments based on fine legal technicalities, which in some jurisdictions served to nullify the popular will and strike down progressive measures. In 1925 conservative real-estate interests that viewed home rule as "home ruin" for taxpayers brought suit to invalidate the home-rule amend-

[13] *New York Times*, March 14, 1923; Joseph M. Proskauer, *A Segment of My Times* (New York, 1950), p. 93.

[14] Proskauer, *A Segment of My Times*, p. 85.

[15] *Addresses Delivered on the Occasion of Honorable Robert F. Wagner Assuming His Seat as Supreme Court Justice* (n.p., n.d.), RFW Papers; *New York Times*, April 30, 1925.

ment to the state constitution that the voters had approved by referendum two years earlier. Their action was based on the contention that the legislature, in voting approval of the amendment for the required second time in 1923, had merely entered the number and title of the resolution on its journals rather than the complete text; thus the constitutional requirement of "entry on the journals" had not been fulfilled and the amendment was void.

The case was of considerable importance to New York City and other municipalities that had in the meantime enacted numerous ordinances on the basis of the amendment's authority. Lawyers of national stature, such as Louis Marshall and Bainbridge Colby, argued the case in Wagner's courtroom, and it commanded front-page headlines. Wagner kept the complicated matter under consideration for three months, but in the end his opinion sustained the validity of the amendment. "Words must be interpreted and understood in their most natural and obvious meaning," he wrote. "A record describing and identifying the proposed amendment is an entry as popularly understood and intended." He prefaced his decision with a long history of the struggle for home rule in New York State, which clearly indicated the intention of the legislature and the people to bring it about by their votes in 1923, and he concluded with an incisive observation that summed up the whole philosophy of the movement for judicial realism. "We as courts," Wagner declared, "are not bound to close our eyes to what as men we know." [16]

Wagner's inclination to uphold the state's right to protect the public welfare, even at the expense of traditional "property rights" narrowly conceived, was expressed in an even more important decision that he rendered in 1921 sustaining the constitutionality of the rent-control laws enacted by the legislature during the postwar housing crisis. At the time of their passage the Bar Association of New York City characterized the acts as "a wanton interference with one of the important attributes of private property" and "unquestionably unconstitutional." But in the first case that tested the issue Wagner sided with the lawmakers. "I cannot subscribe to any doctrine that hinders or restrains our legislative power from enacting a clear and reasonable design to relieve the actual distress of thousands of tenants who would otherwise be made homeless. The protection of their health and morals," he asserted, "commands a vastly more important position to my mind, and is of far greater moment to the welfare of the state, than any strict adherence to the private rights of property."

The Appellate Division of the Supreme Court reversed Wagner's

[16] *New York Times*, Feb. 7, May 12, 1925.

decision on the ground that the rent-control statutes violated "due process of law" and impaired the obligation of contracts. But the judicial realists who dominated the state's highest tribunal, the Court of Appeals, sustained the lower-court judge with the observation, "It is with a condition, and not with economic theory, that the State has to deal in the existing emergency." Later in the year a 5-to-4 majority of the United States Supreme Court upheld the New York laws in an opinion written by Justice Oliver Wendell Holmes, whose language was more eloquent than Wagner's, but whose reasoning was the same. "Had the decision gone the other way," commented a New York City housing official, "the streets . . . would be so littered with furniture that there wouldn't be traffic room for a sparrow." [17]

In the increasingly important field of contacts between labor and the law Wagner's attitude as a judge represented an extension of the position he had begun to develop in the legislature; it added up to an insistence that workers, like employers, must enjoy the fullest freedom consistent with order in organizing and acting collectively to further their legitimate ends. He was extremely cautious, for example, in granting antilabor injunctions—court orders inhibiting unions and strikers from picketing or performing other actions, on the ground that such actions represented real or potential interference with the property rights of the employers. His position contrasted sharply with that of judges who issued such orders almost automatically in the 1920s; it contrasted also with the conservative majority of the United States Supreme Court, who, during the postwar decade, tended to stultify labor action by prescribing, among other things, the number of pickets legally allowable during a strike.[18]

In justifying his reluctance to intervene judicially in labor-management disputes, Wagner echoed the views of the more liberal judges throughout the country and of Justice Holmes and other minority members of the Supreme Court. But he became a pioneer in another direction when, in 1922, he issued the first injunction in American industrial history designed to compel *employers* to honor an agreement signed with their workers' union representatives.

The case arose out of a complaint by the International Ladies Garment Workers' Union against the Cloak, Suit & Skirt Manufacturers' Protective Association, on the ground that the association had violated its labor contract by lengthening hours and introducing the

[17] *Ibid.*, March 8, 1919, Nov. 27, 1920, and March 9, 10, April 19, 1921. A copy of Wagner's decision is in the RFW Papers.
[18] See, for example, Wagner's opinion in the Neutral Embroidery Works case, reported in *The New York Times*, Jan. 20, 1922.

piecework system without first resorting to the arbitration machinery that the contract established. The employers contended that their unilateral action, which touched off a major strike involving 55,000 clothing workers in the city, was justified in that the union had abrogated the contract first. Many disinterested observers sympathized with the workers, however; *The New York Times*, not often found on labor's side in the 1920s, called the action of the managers "lawless in purpose and insolent in manner." The *Times* credited the ILGWU with belonging to "a small but increasing number of unions that are trying steadily, and on the whole intelligently, to build up a permanent system of regulating . . . conditions of employment by means of discussion, conciliation, and arbitration. It is, or is at least capable of becoming, a movement toward local self-government thoroughly in keeping with our instincts as a people."

The Garment Workers' experiments in stabilizing labor relations through industrial democracy appealed to Wagner, too, and so did the pleas of the union's counsel that the Manufacturers' Association be enjoined from violating the agreement, "in order that collective bargaining may be safeguarded." Wagner's opinion "deplored" the employers' action, specifically restrained them from lengthening the workday or introducing piecework, and enjoined them to abide by all the provisions of their union contract. Citing the many instances in which employers had secured orders prohibiting employees from violating agreements, Wagner observed: "The only distinguishing feature in the instant case is that the applicants are workers. They are entitled to have exercised in their behalf the restraining power of the court, when their legal rights are obstructed, to the same extent as it had been exercised to protect the contractual rights of employers." [19]

As it turned out, a "battle of injunctions" between employers and employees, which Wagner's 1922 decision might have presaged, did not become the accepted means of conducting labor-management relations thereafter. In New York State some unions, and particularly those operating in the more stabilized garment industry, occasionally sought and obtained orders compelling employers to adhere to working agreements, and Wagner's opinion served as a precedent in such instances. But on the whole the injunction's reputation as an unfair and one-sided weapon grew even worse in progressive circles as the 1920s ran their course. Conservative judges issued an increasing volume of antilabor orders, not only in compliance with *ex parte* allega-

[19] *New York Times*, Dec. 13, 1921, and Jan. 12, 1922. A copy of Wagner's decision is in the RFW Papers. See Felix Frankfurter and Nathan Greene, *The Labor Injunction* (New York, 1930), pp. 109–110.

tions of impending violence lodged by employers but against peaceful picketing, persuasion, and publicity. By the time Bob Wagner entered the United States Senate in 1927 he, too, had come to regard the injunction as a device that generally "gags one of the debaters" in labor disputes, and he was prepared to support legislation designed to limit, if not abolish, resort to court orders in such disputes. The injunction, he had concluded, was one of the chief obstacles to the achievement of that "partnership between corporate industry and organized labor" that, "in place of the old relation of master and servant, the new day demands." Since the prolabor injunction had proved incapable of bringing that relationship about, Wagner was prepared to consider other means.[20]

Thus the nature of his more important decisions as a judge during the 1920s compelled Bob Wagner to further develop his position on the kinds of social questions he had first come to grips with in the legislature. In that process he revealed the experimental cast of mind —tempered always with special consideration for the underdog—that stamped him as one of the judicial modernists of his time. In acknowledging the lack of precedents for granting an injunction to a labor union, for example, Wagner remarked: "Precedent is not our only guide . . . for many are worn out by time and made useless by a more enlightened and humane conception of social justice. That progressive sentiment of advanced civilization, which has compelled legislative action to correct and improve conditions which a proper regard for humanity would no longer tolerate, cannot be ignored by the courts. Our decision should be in harmony with that modern conception, and not in defiance of it." And overriding all was his conviction, as expressed in the rent-control case: "Our constitutional government is not an impotent one. Not so readily can its arms of protection for those whose benefit it is imposed be bound and made helpless; its scope and vision is wide; its power flexibly adaptable; its aim the protection of human rights."

Progressives, who were sometimes inclined to regard the courts as "one of the greatest obstacles to human progress in this land," found sympathetic allies in pragmatic judges like Wagner.[21] In time their liberal viewpoint would permeate the state and federal judiciaries throughout most of the land, but not before many more battles during which Wagner, in a capacity other than that of a judge, would

[20] Jacob Seidenberg, *The Labor Injunction in New York City, 1935–1950* (Ithaca, N.Y., 1953), pp. 38–39; Frankfurter and Greene, *The Labor Injunction, passim*; Wagner speech file, Aug. 28, 1928, RFW Papers.

[21] Peter Brady, an official of the A. F. of L., quoted in *The New York Times*, Jan. 17, 1923.

help challenge still further the conservative legal doctrines inherited
from another age.

Wagner's ability to influence the practical course of events in a
liberal direction remained limited while he served as a member of the
New York judiciary, even after he was promoted to the Appellate
Division of the Supreme Court in 1925. And there is evidence that
after a while his political instincts began to chafe under the restraints
imposed by membership in that cloistered fraternity. "The work is
accompanied by no public acclaim," he lamented on one occasion.
"There is no admiring audience to welcome each opinion with its well-
deserved applause." [22]

But even if Wagner had viewed election to a fourteen-year term
on the bench in 1919 as the end of his political career, his attractive-
ness as a candidate in the eyes of Democratic politicians was bound to
test his determination. In 1922, for example, the newspapers reported
that if Al Smith persisted (which he did not) in his intention not to
run for the governorship again, the party would turn to Smith's old
partner of the Albany days "as an almost ideal alternative." In 1924
Wagner's name was again in the political news, this time as a possible
successor to Tammany leader Charles F. Murphy. Probably Wagner
did not want *that* ticklish job, but one reporter felt that only his religion saved him from it: "Tammany hesitates at having other than a
Catholic as its Boss." [23]

Two years later came the severest test of all. Smith was up for
reelection again in 1926, and he wanted to win in a way that would
assure his nomination for the presidency in 1928. But rumors that an
"old-time Tammany deal" was in the offing, designed to ensure the
victory of both Smith and the incumbent Republican United States
Senator James W. Wadsworth, worried Smith and his managers. One
solution seemed obvious, and that would be for the Democrats to
name for the senatorship "a man of the highest calibre," one whom
neither Smith nor the party could be suspected of deliberately sacrific-
ing. There was Franklin D. Roosevelt, for example, who had nominated Smith for the presidency two years earlier; but Roosevelt, still
recovering from polio, insisted that his health would not yet permit
him to run for public office. And of course there was Smith's bosom
pal, Bob Wagner.

The decision was a hard one for Wagner to make. Wadsworth

[22] Wagner speech file, Oct. 3, 1927, RFW Papers.
[23] *New York Times*, June 26, Sept. 5, 11, 1922, and May 4, 1924; Henry F.
Pringle, "Profiles: The Janitor's Boy," *The New Yorker*, March 5, 1927, p. 26.

would not be easy to beat; he'd already been senator for twelve years, and in 1920 he even carried every one of New York City's five boroughs. Moreover, the "safe harbor" of the bench, as Wagner once called it, did have its attractions. In the end, however, Bob gave in to the urgings of the politicians, of friends like Jere Mahoney, of his sixteen-year-old son, Bob, Junior, and of prominent liberals like Eleanor Roosevelt. On August 5 he announced his availability. All talk of a bipartisan "deal" ended, and a month later the state convention ratified the Wagner-Smith ticket by acclamation.[24]

"This is the most glorious moment of my life," Wagner told the cheering delegates, and he meant it; the senatorship was the highest elective office that he, an immigrant citizen, could hold. He also asked the party's indulgence if it took him a little time to "put on my fighting clothes," for Wagner realized that his political talents had grown rusty during "the calm period" of his life on the bench. As a judge he had come to rely heavily on the brain power of others, such as Joseph Force Crater, a brilliant young lawyer who served as his legal secretary throughout the 1920s. Wagner knew he would need similar help in the months ahead, and at the outset he demonstrated that uncanny ability for finding it that was to become a distinguishing mark of his senatorial career.

In preparation for his first campaign address Wagner invited a group of "bright young men" to his apartment. Among them was Claude Bowers, the scholar-journalist who had recently come east from Indiana to edit the *New York Evening World*. After an elegant dinner the discussion turned to the kind of speech that the new candidate might make. "I fell in love with Bob Wagner the moment I saw him," Bowers later recalled. "When we got through, he astonished me by saying, 'Now that I know what we've decided upon, I'm going to ask Mr. Bowers to write the speech.'" The surprised recruit complied and thus became the first in that succession of idea men who were to contribute much to Wagner's imposing stature in the upper house of Congress.[25]

However, not even the pen of a gifted writer like Bowers could dramatize issues very effectively at the height of "Coolidge prosperity." In making charges Wagner's speeches during the 1926 campaign ran the gamut of accusations that Democrats customarily harped on in the 1920s: the Harding scandals and Republican corruption, the

[24] *New York Times*, June 4, 5, 13, 28, July 4, 28, Aug. 4, 5, 16, 19, Sept. 3, 27, 29, 1926; interviews with Robert F. Wagner, Jr., and Jeremiah T. Mahoney.
[25] Claude Bowers, "Reminiscences" (Oral History Research Office, 1954), pp. 57ff.

Administration's tax policies that favored the rich, and the high tariff that oppressed the poor. Frequent denunciations of Prohibition and of the "unjust and bigoted" Immigration Quota Law of 1924 identified Wagner as a northern Democrat appealing to a big-city, immigrant-derived constituency. (At one point Bowers was asked to delete from a speech the phrase "Beware of Greeks bearing gifts." "Then I knew I was in New York," the Hoosier editor later reminisced, "and not in Indiana.") But aside from some premonitory efforts to probe beneath the tinseled surface of "Republican prosperity," and their generally progressive tone, Wagner's pronouncements bore no special distinction.[26]

Nor did Bob's delivery add luster to the campaign. Eight years on the bench had suppressed his oratorical abilities to such an extent "that he quite forgot the art," wrote reporter Henry Pringle, who found the Democratic candidate's performance "a sad disappointment." Wagner's platform manner did improve considerably later on, after he again became surrounded by "men who talk for a living." But he never resumed the "gymnastic" style of debate. Service as a judge had produced a marked effect on Wagner's lungs as well as his mind.[27]

Nevertheless, Wagner did have two things going for him in 1926 that turned out to be decisive in the end. One was the smooth efficiency of Tammany's well-oiled election machinery, which was thrown into high gear on behalf of the Hall's favorite-son ticket of Wagner and Smith. In alliance with organized labor and independent liberal forces, Tammany had forged over the years a voting coalition that seemed certain to carry the popular and seasoned Al Smith, at least, to another victory.

But second, and even more important in determining the outcome of the senatorial race, were the internal frictions that disrupted Republican unity and reacted particularly in Wagner's favor. By 1926 Jim Wadsworth had become an outspoken opponent of Prohibition. In the estimation of the drys, who swung considerable weight in New York's Republican party, he was therefore a traitor to the greatest "reform" of all time. Unable to prevent Wadsworth's renomination at the G.O.P.'s state convention, the more fanatic of the Prohibitionists organized the Independent Republican party—for the senatorial contest only—and nominated Franklin W. Cristman as their can-

[26] *Ibid.*, pp. 59–60. A complete file of Wagner's 1926 campaign speeches, together with the publicity and financial records of the campaign, are in the RFW Papers. His major addresses were reported in *The New York Times* and other newspapers, Sept.–Nov. 1926.

[27] Pringle, "Profiles: The Janitor's Boy," p. 25.

didate. Financed by the Anti-Saloon League and the Women's Christian Temperance Union (it's said that Tammany Hall also helped keep the divisive Independent Republican organization supplied with money), Cristman and his associates waged a vituperative campaign against the incumbent senator. The beneficiary of their efforts was neither Cristman nor the cause of Prohibition, but Bob Wagner.[28]

On election day Cristman polled nearly 232,000 votes in rural upstate counties that were traditionally dry—and traditionally Republican. And although Wagner ran behind Al Smith and everybody else on the Democratic statewide ticket, he managed to beat Wadsworth by about 116,000 votes, or one half of the Independent Republican's tally. The drys believed, mistakenly as events proved, that they had taught the G.O.P. a lesson. But much more important in the long run was the role they played in helping launch a new and memorable senatorial career.

On March 4, 1927, Bob Wagner strode down the aisle of the United States Senate and took the oath as a member of the Seventieth Congress. As he returned to his seat in the rear of the chamber a few wags among his new colleagues hummed the strains of "Tammany"; up above, in the visitors' gallery, a band of Tammany braves beamed with pride.

Wagner established living quarters at the Mayflower Hotel, while in Suite 125 of the Senate Office Building a hastily assembled staff put his office in order. In charge was a young lawyer named Simon H. Rifkind, whom Wagner hired as his secretary (the position now called Administrative Assistant) on the recommendation of the dean of the Columbia University Law School. Another secretary handled office routine, and there was one typist. That was all the help a United States senator, even one from the country's most populous state, was thought to require in the easygoing Washington of the Coolidge era.[29]

Henry Pringle, who sized up the freshman lawmaker in a *New Yorker* "Profile" shortly after his arrival in the nation's capital, observed correctly that "the elevation of Robert F. Wagner was a politi-

[28] *New York Times*, Sept.–Nov. 1926; James W. Wadsworth, "Reminiscences" (Oral History Research Office, 1952), pp. 344ff; Alden Hatch, *The Wadsworths of the Genesee* (New York, 1959), *passim*; interview with Howard Cullman, who served as Wagner's campaign treasurer in 1926.

[29] New York *Daily News*, March 5, 1927; interviews with Simon H. Rifkind and Minna L. Ruppert. Miss Ruppert served as Wagner's secretary in Washington from 1930 until his retirement from the Senate in 1949.

cal accident." But unlike some others, this was "a happy accident," Pringle continued, for Wagner would "bring to the upper house of Congress a high measure of intelligence, a sympathy for the masses that does not sour to demagoguery, and a talent for hard work." The journalist assessed the novice well, for the qualities he cited were the very ones that had built Wagner's reputation in the past and would sustain him in the future.

Pringle also pointed out that the Empire State's new Senator had "merely a layman's knowledge of national affairs," a fact that Wagner readily admitted to Claude Bowers and others at the outset of the campaign. But, added the reporter, "few of his colleagues have more, and he has the ability and the persistency to settle down and find out what it is all about." [30]

With the help of Si Rifkind and others, Wagner did just that. When he left Washington twenty-two years later, the country was much different for his efforts.

[30] Pringle, "Profiles: The Janitor's Boy," pp. 24, 26.

PART II

*Washington & the
New Deal*

CHAPTER 5

Not the Whole Journey

BOB WAGNER had gone to Albany only two years before the inauguration of Charles Evans Hughes as governor signaled the beginning of the Progressive Era in the Empire State. Coincidentally, he took his seat in the United States Senate just two years before the Wall Street crash marked the start of still another historical era for the nation as a whole. In both cases he began his service in an atmosphere of complacency and indifference, but in neither case could fate have timed more favorably the debut of a lawmaker with Wagner's background and interests. For in the winter of 1927—even with "a Coolidge in every garage"—the forces that were soon to make a mirage of the "prosperity" of the 1920s were already building. Few understood that yet, nor did Wagner understand it fully. But his first speech on the floor of the upper house in March 1928 carried the unlikely title, "Unemployment," and his major legislative efforts during the months that followed were devoted to pushing for passage of a series of measures that would probe the extent, nature, and possible remedies for joblessness. When the Great Depression materialized the freshman Democrat from New York stood out as something of a prophet, and in later years he would be described as "a New Dealer long before there was a New Deal."

The timeliness of Wagner's career was "amazing," the editors of *Fortune* once wrote, and partly because of it, "he may well turn out to be the most famous Senator of his generation." But "luck like Mr. Wagner's," the editors acknowledged, "cannot be put down merely to

the three old ladies with the scissors. There is obviously a man's will
behind it." Another writer enumerated the essential ingredients of
that will. "By sheer hard work, by an extraordinary singlemindedness,
by a sure sense of the difference between the trivial and the important," read a New York *World* editorial of 1930, "Wagner has in a
very short space of time become a national figure." In 1932 talk of
"Wagner for President" arose among people who were unaware of his
constitutional ineligibility. At any rate, by then there wasn't any
doubt that this national figure would be reelected to represent the
Empire State for a second term in the upper house of Congress.[1]

Wagner's quick rise to prominence in Washington was due
partly to his close association with Al Smith. During 1927 and 1928
the New York governor loomed as the likeliest Democratic candidate
for the White House, and many observers believed that Wagner's
views on national issues provided a key to the positions that Smith
might be expected to take in the forthcoming presidential campaign.
Thus when Wagner denounced the Republican Administration's
intervention in the affairs of Latin American countries, endorsed armaments reduction, the World Court, and the Kellogg-Briand Pact, or
spoke in favor of creating a Tennessee Valley Authority and other
public power projects, his pronouncements received more press coverage than was usually accorded a freshman senator.[2]

Preparation for the 1928 campaign also provided the backdrop
for Wagner's initial probing of unemployment, the subject that was
to be the vehicle for promoting his reputation over the next several
years. During the 1920s some Americans—the hard core of Progressive Era social reformers—did continue to concern themselves with
social problems like joblessness and with possible means for ameliorat-
ing them. Wagner and Al Smith were on intimate terms with many
of these people as a result of previous associations; Smith's Industrial
Commissioner, Frances Perkins, was prominent among them. In January 1928 the governor ordered a study of unemployment in New York
State, contending that it was assuming considerable proportions. On
February 13, in what was probably a concerted move, Wagner introduced a Senate resolution calling on the Secretary of Labor to report
on the extent of unemployment and part-time employment in the
United States; the method used in his calculations and means

[1] New York *Post*, Dec. 31, 1943; *Fortune* (March 1935), p. 116; New York
World, July 23, 1930.
[2] Brooklyn *Eagle*, Nov. 20, 1927; Wagner speech file, 1927–28, RFW
Papers.

whereby the collection of relevant statistics might be made more inclusive and reliable were also to be covered in the report.

The newspapers, especially those of Republican persuasion, characterized Wagner's resolution as "a major political move in the interest of Al Smith's campaign," and in that they were partly correct.[3] But Wagner's maiden speech on the floor of the Senate, on March 5, indicated that his concern with unemployment and its attendant evils went far deeper than that. Recounting his efforts to obtain pertinent information from Administration sources, Wagner declared, "There were figures on the production of our factories, on the traffic of our railroads, on bank loans, on the status of our wheat, prune, cherry, and apricot crops; there were statistics on the cold storage holdings of cheese and pickled pork. "But" he complained, "when I made inquiry of the Department of Labor as to how many people were unemployed, I was told that they did not know. The only available official information which in any way answered the questions that were troubling me, were the monthly reports showing the number of persons on the payrolls of a relatively small number of manufacturing industries and Class I railroads." [4]

Pointing to the conflicting "guesses" emanating from government agencies about the seriousness of the unemployment situation, and to increasing reports of bread lines forming in various cities, Wagner repudiated the traditional assumption that unemployment would take care of itself. "The cityward drift of population, the increasing size of the industrial unit, and the corporate enterprise are making an ever-increasing proportion of our population depend upon wages as the sole means of gaining a livelihood," he declared. Those trends had carried the nation to "the threshold of a new industrial age," in which the old *laissez-faire* attitudes were worse than obsolete. For "with bread lines and idleness," Wagner warned, "comes diminution of purchasing power, a gradual slackening of business and industry, and greater unemployment. Behind this economic curtain stalks misery, want, hunger, and discontent in our cities." To the New York member the conclusion seemed obvious. "If we are going to provide any basis of security for American life, we must at once begin to chart the phenomena of employment and unemployment and, insofar as it is possible, to subject them to our control." The collection of adequate statistics bearing on the nation's economic health was the nec-

[3] *New York Times*, March 6, 1928.
[4] Simon H. Rifkind, interview; Wagner speech file, March 5, 1928, and Oct. 9, 1932, RFW Papers. Copies of all bills and resolutions that Wagner introduced during his senatorial career are contained in the RFW Papers.

essary first step. "Where that will lead, no one can foretell. But that it is only a step, and not the whole journey, is plain."

When Wagner finished, the Senate—perhaps out of courtesy to one of its newest members—agreed to take that first step and, without a roll call, approved the pending resolution. Surely none of those present realized then how many more steps the New York lawmaker would lead them to take during the years ahead.[5]

Secretary of Labor James J. Davis' report, in compliance with Wagner's resolution, reached Congress on March 26 in two parts: the complicated calculations made by his Commissioner of Labor Statistics, Ethelbert Stewart, and Davis' own covering letter purporting to summarize the commissioner's figures. "Commissioner Stewart finds that the actual number now out of work is 1,874,050," Davis stated categorically; and while he admitted that the situation was serious enough, the slump was "not so extensive or grave" as some contended. For a day or two thereafter Senator Reed Smoot of Utah and other Administration stalwarts took turns exulting over the report and berating those Democratic "alarmists" who had tried to play fast and loose with the reality of "Coolidge prosperity." (Besides, intoned Smoot, "remedies for unemployment cannot be supplied by laws.")

But the Old Guard's exuberance soon subsided when Bob Wagner and others, politicians and statisticians alike, having had time to digest the elaborations contained in Commissioner Stewart's calculations, pointed out that his 1,874,050 figure pertained *not* to the total number unemployed but merely to the *shrinkage* in employment that had taken place since the base year, 1925. It took no account of the number of jobless already existing in 1925 or of population increase and the effects of the city-ward trend since then. Some Democrats and insurgent Republicans, like Henrik Shipstead of Minnesota, charged Davis with deliberately misrepresenting Stewart's figures and upped their estimates of the number unemployed, based on projections of the commissioner's methods, to eight million. Wagner was charitable enough to concede that Davis' misreading might have been "inadvertent," and he stuck to the four million estimate he had presented in his maiden speech.[6]

It was further confirmed that more than political expediency and "Al Smith's campaign" lay behind Wagner's concern with the unemployed when, in April, he introduced a series of measures designed to

[5] Wagner speech file, March 5, 1928, RFW Papers; 69 *Congressional Record*, 4081.

[6] 69 *Congressional Record*, 5337ff, 5434ff, 5724, 6839–42; file on "Senate Resolution 147, 1928," RFW Papers.

augment the federal government's role in efforts to stabilize business conditions. One bill would improve the government's statistics-gathering facilities, "so as to permit business to be guided intelligently by reference to the facts." The second sought to perfect channels between job-seekers and employment opportunities by creating an effective system of public employment agencies. The third called for utilizing "the tremendous spending power of government as a great balance wheel to stabilize the vibration of the entire industrial machinery." [7]

The principles involved in the Three Bills, as they soon became known in Suite 125 of the Senate Office Building, were by no means original with Wagner, or with Simon Rifkind, who supervised the actual drafting of the legislation for "The Boss." [8] President Harding's 1921 conference on unemployment, presided over by Commerce Secretary Herbert Hoover, devoted ten consecutive pages of its report to the need for collecting more adequate statistics concerning the extent and character of joblessness. During the 1920s the American Statistical Association and other interested groups tried to implement the recommendations of the conference to no avail. Early in 1928, however, Wagner turned to these groups for help in drawing up appropriate legislation, and a subcommittee of the Statistical Association, headed by Mary Van Kleeck of the Russell Sage Foundation, advised Rifkind what to put in Wagner's S. 4158. The bill boosted the appropriation authorized for the Bureau of Labor Statistics by $100,000 so that it might extend its reports to include statistics on *part-time* as well as total unemployment, based on data obtained not only from a larger number of manufacturing industries and railroads but also from the mining, construction, agricultural, transportation, and retail and wholesale trade industries.

Interest in the idea of employment exchanges was also anything but new in 1928; it will be recalled that, as a legislator at Albany, Wagner had been instrumental in getting New York's system started. Other states followed suit, and during the First World War the federally created United States Employment Service collaborated effectively with the state agencies in helping man the nation's industrial

[7] Robert F. Wagner, "Senator Wagner Tells How To Keep Tab on Unemployment," *Printers' Ink*, March 8, 1928, pp. 85–86; "Sound Policy To Break the Bread Lines," *Independent*, April 14, 1928, pp. 353–354; "Senator Wagner Tells How To Help the Idle," *New York Times*, May 20, 1928.

[8] Simon H. Rifkind, interview. For material relevant to the origins of the Three Bills see RFW–Van Kleeck correspondence, RFW–Andrews correspondence, Wagner speech file, March 5, April 20, 1928, and files on "The Three Bills, 1928–1933," all in the RFW Papers. See also *Congressional Digest* (Jan. 1931), *passim*.

war machine. But during the economy drive that came with peace the
U.S.E.S. languished; by 1928 it was a skeleton bureau in the Department of Labor, engaged in little more than the collection of reports
from the operating state placement systems. Since 1917 every Congress had seen the introduction of a bill, formulated by the American
Association for Labor Legislation, providing for a federal-state system
of employment services to be financed by federal grants-in-aid with
matching state appropriations; but it had never been enacted. A version of that bill, brought up to date in consultation with Dr. John B.
Andrews, the executive secretary of the A.A.L.L., constituted the second of the measures Bob Wagner introduced in April 1928.

Nor was the idea of using governmental expenditures to stabilize
the economy—so often regarded as an innovation of the New Deal or
of Lord Keynes—of such recent origin. President Harding's conference endorsed public works as a countercyclical measure, and in ensuing years such organizations as the Association for Labor Legislation,
the International Labor Office, and the National Unemployment
League sought to institutionalize the procedure through statute. Republican Senator Wesley M. Jones of Washington seemed to be a
convert to their cause, and his "prosperity reserve bill," which would
divert part of the government's annual surplus income of the 1920s to
a special fund held ready to finance public works in periods of recession, was actually reported favorably by a Senate committee in 1928.
But Jones failed to push his measure beyond that point, and thereafter
Wagner's bill, which was a composite of the earlier suggestions, held
the center of the stage. It called for long-range planning of public
works by the federal agencies concerned with such programs, and
prior Congressional authorization, so that the projects might be ready
for launching when hard times struck. A Federal Employment Stabilization Board would be established, composed of certain Cabinet
officers charged with the duty of keeping the President advised on
the state of the economy as gauged by employment, construction, and
other indices. By presidential directive, the government's public
works enterprises would be accelerated when, on the advice of the
board, recession was deemed to loom ahead for the nation as a whole
or any part of it. "When everybody is buying let the Government
stand by," Wagner explained in the speech that accompanied introduction of the measure in the Senate. "When everyone else stops
buying then the Government can step up to the counter. That in
general is the stabilizing principle of the long-range plan."

Wagner's first package of antidepression proposals, then, was
based on concepts that had been familiar to economists and reform-

ers for some time past. But never had these measures been introduced in the national legislature in conjunction with one another as part of a concerted, rounded attack on the problems of cyclical and technological unemployment. "Those who suffer from cyclical changes will be helped by the long-range plan which will tend to stabilize the cycle," Wagner told the Senate. "For those who are released . . . because their jobs have been supplanted by machinery we have a major task of adjustment to accomplish; to find them new places, possibly in new industry. For those men we need the machinery of the employment exchange to bring about that adjustment. And all the time facts and figures of employment and unemployment must be carefully watched and studied."

Moreover, never had even one of the bills been sponsored by a senator who told his colleagues, with the kind of "Teutonic tenacity" for which Wagner had become known: "We may as well determine right here and now that we are going to wage relentless war until we abolish involuntary idleness as surely as we abolished involuntary servitude." [9]

The Three Bills were referred to the Committee on Education and Labor. Their sponsor was enough of a political realist to know that that Administration-dominated body was unlikely to take action in an election year on measures that implied that Republican rule had *not* put "a chicken in every pot and two cars in every garage." But interest had been aroused, and before the Senate adjourned late in May it adopted a resolution sponsored by Robert M. La Follette, Jr., of Wisconsin, directing the committee to undertake a wide-ranging investigation of unemployment and possible measures for its relief. As expected, however, the committee put off its study until after the election.

While Wagner thus quickly resumed in Washington the familiar role as spokesman for advanced social thinkers and reformers that he had filled at Albany, he also took up the cudgels for organized labor, as might be expected in view of his record as a judge and legislator. Early in 1928, as a member of a subcommittee of the Senate's Interstate Commerce Committee, Wagner took part in an on-the-spot investigation of conditions in the coal fields of Pennsylvania, West Virginia, and Ohio. The group's three Republican members, all millionaires, together with Wagner and fellow Democrat Burton K. Wheeler of Montana, spent several weeks touring the region accompanied by a young New York *Daily News* reporter-photographer

[9] Wagner speech file, March 5, April 20, 1928, RFW Papers.

named Lowell Limpus. The committee was charged with studying the
depressed state of the bituminous coal industry—one of the obviously
"sick" industries of the 1920s—but, instead, its attention centered on
the frightful conditions of life and labor that the mine workers were
forced to endure. The pictures that Limpus brought back with him
graphically told the story of the poverty the investigators had encountered. Wagner's personal handouts to the women and children he
met left him broke before the tour had ended, and he was obliged to
borrow money from Philip Murray, a United Mine Workers official
who served as guide to the senators, for the trip back to Washington.

Striking for union recognition, the mine workers had been fired,
turned out of their company houses, and replaced by Negro strike-
breakers imported from the South. In one town an injunction issued
by a company judge, and enforced by company police, forbade the
strikers to picket, to accept food or other assistance from the
U.M.W., or even to make use of the company church. "Had I not
seen it myself," Wagner told an audience later, "I would not have
believed that in the United States there were large areas where civil
government was supplanted by a system that can only be compared
with ancient feudalism." Even the conservatives among the investigators were affected—like Wagner and Wheeler, they had been threatened with arrest by company police in some localities—and the subcommittee's report, which severely condemned the mine operators'
labor policies, bore the signatures of all five members. It made no
specific recommendations for legislative relief, but did shed additional
light on abuses, such as those connected with the labor injunction,
which Congress would attempt to cope with in succeeding years.[10]

Not that it took the coal-mining investigation to make Wagner
aware of the feudalistic use to which injunctions lent themselves in
labor disputes. During the early part of 1928 Wagner's law firm (he
had opened an office for private practice soon after his election to the
Senate) won two decisions that served as landmarks in the
unshackling of labor from its injunctive chains. The cases, *Interborough Rapid Transit Co. v. Lavin* and *Interborough Rapid Transit Co.
v. Green*, involved attempts by the IRT to secure orders forbidding
the Amalgamated Association of Street and Electric Railway Employees and its parent body, the American Federation of Labor, to
proselytize its employees, on the ground that the workers had signed
agreements—"yellow-dog" contracts, unionists called them—promis-

[10] Interviews with John L. Lewis and Burton K. Wheeler; Wagner speech
file, March 15, 1928, and file on "Conditions in the Coal Fields of Pennsylvania,
West Virginia, and Ohio, 1928," RFW Papers.

ing not to join an outside union while in the company's employ. Wagner, assisted by Joseph Force Crater, who was now his law associate, Simon Rifkind, and Professor Herman Oliphant of Columbia Law School, drew up briefs contending that since the "contract" was terminable at the employer's will and guaranteed the worker nothing, it was inequitable and unenforceable. Contrary to precedents established in other jurisdictions, where such agreements were enforced as a matter of course, the New York Court of Appeals sustained the reasoning of the unions' lawyers. The litigation, which Professor Oliphant hailed as "the most significant since the Dred Scott case," virtually ended the use of "yellow-dog" contracts in New York State, and requests for copies of "the Wagner brief" flowed in from lawyers, judges, and scholars across the country. It found a place in casebooks, and for years it served as a model in labor-law classrooms.[11]

Wagner's prominence in the anti-injunction fight in New York lent an air of authority to his voice, when, in 1930, he helped lead the opposition to Senate confirmation of John J. Parker as a justice of the United States Supreme Court. In a floor speech that minutely examined Parker's record as a circuit court judge, Wagner charged him with slavishly following outdated precedents in decisions involving labor injunctions, and he contrasted Parker's rigidity with the forward-looking flexibility of New York's Court of Appeals. Parker failed to appreciate that constitutions and laws "are not a lifeless set of wooden precepts moved about according to the rules of a mechanical logic," Wagner contended, and therefore he lacked the judicial statesmanship requisite for occupancy of the highest bench. A few days later the Senate rejected the President's nominee—one of the few such instances in history—and liberals throughout the country hailed the contribution that Wagner's speech had made to the outcome. "It was on a very high level," wrote Harvard's Felix Frankfurter in a congratulatory note, "and provided a powerful analysis of . . . the deeper issues regarding the criteria that ought to govern selection for the Supreme Court." [12]

During his first term Wagner became a firm ally of those congressmen who made it their special business to perfect federal anti-injunction legislation that would be workable and constitutional. Senator George Norris and Congressman Fiorello H. La Guardia, and the

11 *New York Times*, Nov. 29, 1927, and Jan. 20, 24, Feb. 16, 1928; file on "I.R.T. Injunction, 1927–1928," RFW Papers; Simon H. Rifkind, interview; Felix Frankfurter and Nathan Greene, *The Labor Injunction* (New York, 1930), pp. 40–42, 63, 87, 95, 111, 270.
12 RFW Papers: Wagner speech file, April 30, 1930; file on "Judge John J. Parker, 1930"; Frankfurter to RFW, May 7, 1930.

labor leaders and lawyers with whom they hammered out successive drafts of the bill, frequently turned to the New York Senator for advice, particularly on legal technicalities with which his service on the bench had made him familiar. When the Norris–La Guardia bill finally reached the point of floor debate in February 1932, Wagner delivered one of the culminating speeches that built the case for its proponents.

Depicting how industrialization and the concentration of capital had made a myth of the legal conception of equality between the corporate employer and the individual employee, Wagner pleaded that the government cease to allow use of its courts as "strike-breaking agencies." The government's role in the field of contacts between labor and management, he contended, should be a neutral one, at least, if not one affirmatively favorable to unionization. "Simple justice commands that we unfetter the worker in his effort to achieve his goal," Wagner told his Senate colleagues. "Statesmanship dictates that we encourage him to take this road of organized action to responsibility, to self-mastery, to human liberty, and to national greatness. We can convert the relation of master and servant into an equal and cooperative partnership, shouldering alike the responsibilities of management and sharing alike in the rewards of increasing production. We can raise a race of men who are economically as well as politically free." [13]

The bill passed, and President Hoover signed it. It made "yellow-dog" contracts unenforceable in federal courts, and marked one of the relatively few important advances made by progressives during the years when the "Great Engineer" occupied the White House.

Hoover came to the presidency by defeating Al Smith in the fall of 1928. "Today Tammany is as proud as a bride in June," Bob Wagner had exulted when, that summer, the Democratic convention at Houston named his best friend as its candidate for the highest office in the nation. But by the end of the campaign Wagner was crestfallen. Not only did unemployment and other economic and social issues prove unavailing against the Republicans and "prosperity," but many aspects of the campaign against Smith, based on his religion and background, had dealt heavy blows to the cause of cultural liberalism. "The virtue of a man, we are pleased to believe, rests only within him, and is not predetermined by race, nationality, or religious affiliation," Wagner had told a group of newly naturalized citizens in his

[13] Wagner speech file, Feb. 29, 1932, RFW Papers; Simon H. Rifkind, interview.

courtroom only a few years before. But the whispering campaign of 1928 must have caused him—and Al Smith too—to wonder again just how many "native" Americans really subscribed to that ideal.[14]

Despite his disappointment with the outcome of the election, however, Wagner could reasonably feel that the presidential campaign improved the prospects for enactment of the unemployment legislation he had introduced earlier in the year. Smith discussed the problem of unemployment when he invaded the textile centers of New England and other depressed areas. Even the Republican candidate had been forced to take up the subject; in a speech at Newark Hoover called for collection of more complete statistics on unemployment and suggested that, as far as possible, the government's public works program "should be carried on in such a way as to take up the slack of occasional unemployment." Late in November, moreover, in a message to the annual governors' conference, at New Orleans, the President-elect even endorsed creation of a "construction reserve fund to do for labor and industry what the Federal Reserve has done for finance." Hoover's spokesman at the conference, Governor Ralph O. Brewster of Maine, credited "the economic foundation of this policy and the specific ways of putting it into operation" to economists William Trufant Foster and Waddill Catchings, who had written extensively about the need for countercyclical planning throughout the 1920s. Since those two gentlemen had become ardent exponents of the Wagner public works planning bill, it appeared that the legislative vehicle for implementation of Hoover's policy was ready at hand. Or so Foster and Catchings presumed, and they said so in their nationally syndicated newspaper column.[15]

By then other publicists, such as radio commentator William Hard and the editorial writers for *The New York Times*, had gotten behind Wagner's measures, and endorsements of them flowed in from many sources. During the summer of 1928 Rifkind sent copies of the bills to over two hundred nationally recognized leaders in education, the labor movement, and business, soliciting their reactions. When the lame-duck session of Congress met in December Wagner inserted their replies in the *Record*. The overwhelming majority of the comments were favorable; among them were laudatory letters from Professors John R. Commons and E. R. A. Seligman of Wisconsin and Columbia, respectively, Dean Roscoe Pound of Harvard Law School, Henry S. Dennison and Sam A. Lewisohn, two of the nation's

[14] Wagner speech file, April 18, 1927, and July 4, 1928, RFW Papers.
[15] *New York Times*, Nov. 22, 1928; RFW–Foster correspondence, RFW Papers.

most progressive industrialists, and scores of other prominent figures.[16]

Equally gratifying was the enthusiasm shown for the Three Bills by the expert witnesses who appeared before the Senate's Education and Labor Committee when, in November, the committee began hearings, in compliance with the La Follette resolution of the previous spring. The committee's chairman, Republican Senator James Couzens of Michigan, was a millionaire businessman, forward-looking and apparently quite sympathetic toward the Wagner bills. The preponderant Old Guard sentiment of his colleagues prevented endorsement of any specific legislation, however, and the committee's report, presented in February 1929, was phrased in generalities. Yet it did subscribe to each of the ideas contained in Wagner's program—more and better statistics, a better system of employment exchanges, and advance planning of public works—and, in addition, suggested further development of private and state unemployment insurance and old-age pension schemes. The hearings, which Wagner sat in on occasionally and Rifkind attended faithfully, provided suggestions for the improvement of Wagner's original program and also served to introduce the two New Yorkers to a young economist named Isador Lubin, who was "on loan" from the Brookings Institution to Couzens' committee. Rifkind and "Lube" soon became close friends, and Wagner's brain trust gained an important recruit.[17]

But if the unveiling of the "Hoover prosperity plan" at the governors' conference encouraged Wagner's hope for quick action on his Three Bills, he was soon disillusioned. The special session of Congress that Hoover summoned in April 1929 was asked to complete action on a few routine matters, such as the bill authorizing the decennial census in 1930, and thereafter to confine its deliberations to the redemption of "two pledges given in the last election—farm relief and limited changes in the tariff." The President's message made no reference to industrial unemployment or to proposals for its mitigation. Even the suggestion that the 1930 census include a count of the unemployed—a recommendation made by the Commissioner of Labor Statistics in testimony before the Couzens Committee, and subsequently indorsed in the committee's report—found no place in the new President's program. With the assistance of the American Statistical Association, and despite the opposition of the Director of the Census, Bob Wagner fashioned and managed to secure Congressional adoption of

[16] *New York Times*, Dec. 9, 1928; Hard to RFW, Nov. 26, 1928, RFW Papers; 70 *Congressional Record*, 218, 438, 976.

[17] U. S. Senate, 70th Cong., 2nd Sess., Committee on Education and Labor, *Causes of Unemployment*, Senate Report 2072 (Washington, D.C., Govt. Printing Office, 1929), *passim*; interviews with Simon H. Rifkind and Isador Lubin.

an amendment to the census bill implementing the committee's proposal. A narrow victory resulted for the proponents of economic fact-finding: in the House the Administration stalwarts lined up solidly against Wagner, and the amendment was retained by the scant margin of one vote! [18]

Through the summer of 1929, then, Wagner joined in the wrangling over farm relief and the tariff. In fact, at the expense of "considerable trouble and study" Wagner even introduced a substitute farm-relief measure, drawn up in consultation with Professor Seligman of Columbia University, but it got nowhere.[19] Nor was he any more effective in attempting to keep tariff schedules, particularly those affecting consumer goods, within reasonable bounds; as summer gave way to fall, and as the special session rolled on, Congress was well on the way to writing the most overly protective tariff legislation in the nation's history. Meanwhile Wagner's Three Bills continued to languish in a committee pigeonhole, while the "Hoover prosperity plan" languished somewhere in the back of a complacent President's mind.

But October 1929 brought more than a change of temperature that soothed the perspiring brows of harried lawmakers in Washington; it also brought a "wind that blew through Wall Street," and soon the entire nation's climate would change. Wagner happened to be in New York on "Black Thursday." A few days later his Washington secretary, Minna Ruppert, penned a postscript to a routine letter going off to Marguerite Cummins, Wagner's New York secretary: "The Senator returned this A.M., looking quite upset. I hope you remained outside the disaster." Few Americans did so in the months and years ahead.[20]

[18] *New York Times*, April 17, 1929; file on "Census Act Amendment, 1929," and RFW–Van Kleeck correspondence, RFW Papers.

[19] Wagner speech file, May 2, 1929, and file on "Farm Relief Act Amendment, 1929," RFW Papers.

[20] Boston *Transcript*, Oct. 31, 1929; Ruppert to Cummins, Nov. 14, 1929, RFW Papers.

CHAPTER 6

Prosperity by Proclamation

A T FIRST Wall Street hoped that the crash might result in nothing more than a passing financial panic. The "irresponsible" elements would be shaken loose from the stock market, but the underlying structure of the economy would remain as sound as always. President Hoover shared this view. In his State of the Union report to Congress in December 1929 the President made no direct mention of the economic disturbance until the seventh page of his printed message. His analysis was highly optimistic and, in retrospect, naïve. In Hoover's estimation the trouble lay solely in the "wave of uncontrolled speculation in securities" which produced the "inevitable" crash. The "unwarranted pessimism and fear" among businessmen that had resulted, throwing a number of people "temporarily" out of work, could be remedied by "voluntary measures of cooperation with the business institutions and with State and municipal authorities to make certain that fundamental businesses of the country shall continue as usual," and by a "prudent expansion" of the federal government's public works program. The objective should be the restoration of "normal conditions"—presumably those of the Coolidge era.[1]

[1] U. S. House of Representatives, 71st Cong., 2nd Sess., *Message of the President of the United States*, House Document 176 (Washington, D.C., Govt. Printing Office, 1929), *passim*. For the history of the Hoover Administration see Herbert Hoover, *The Memoirs of Herbert Hoover: The Great Depression, 1929–1941* (New York, 1952); H. G. Warren, *Herbert Hoover and the Great Depression* (New York, 1959); Albert U. Romasco, *The Poverty of Abundance: Hoover, the Nation, the Depression* (New York, 1965); and Arthur M. Schlesinger, Jr., *The Age of Roosevelt: The Crisis of the Old Order* (New York, 1957).

Bob Wagner's appraisal of what was happening differed from the outset. True enough, he sympathized with Hoover's initial efforts to restore confidence through a series of conferences with business and financial leaders. In December, when the President proposed a reduction in income tax rates as a stimulus to consumption and investment, Wagner defended the measure against a group of insurgent Republicans who asserted that it was too favorable to big business.

But in a radio speech of January 18, 1930, Wagner questioned whether "we can . . . indefinitely continue to have 'prosperity by proclamation.'" In defining the causes of the recession he did not mention the Wall Street crash, as such, at all. Instead he concentrated on the figures of the Bureau of Labor Statistics that indicated a long-range downward trend in employment in every major industry. "I see before me the continuous performance of a tragedy," Wagner observed. "The scene may shift from the textile mills of Massachusetts to the coal fields of West Virginia, from radio manufacturing to automobile construction . . . but the plot is throughout essentially the same: always the atmosphere of anxiety and apprehension and fear; always the daily round of futile search for work and the morale-breaking refusals; always the exhaustion of savings, the depletion of credit, and finally the outstretched hand for relief; for work or no work, men must eat and children must be fed."

It seemed axiomatic to Wagner that the solution for bad business conditions lay in waging the all-out war against unemployment that he had urged for nearly two years: "When I plead for measures calculated to prevent unemployment I plead for the welfare of every business man in the country. There is a great, wide, open space in American political life which can be filled with economic idealism. To remove the pall of want and poverty from the great masses of our people is an economic ideal, and none the less an ideal though it is economic. To lift up those who are now low, to provide a fuller life, a more leisurely life for those who now lack it, to create opportunities for the development of men and women capable of spiritual growth, these are economic ideals to strive for in this day and age. *They are today within the province of political action.*" [2] That the great mass of depression-weary Americans came to accept his approach, and to reject Hoover's, accounts for Wagner's prominence—and his party's accession to power—in 1933.

The first breakthrough in Wagner's war against unemployment came in April 1930, when the Republican-dominated Senate passed his Three Bills. The stock market crash of the previous fall had

[2] Wagner speech file, Jan. 18, 1930, RFW Papers.

created an atmosphere more favorable to their consideration. Months of lobbying carried on by such individuals as William Trufant Foster and organizations such as the American Association for Labor Legislation familiarized lawmakers with the merits of the measures. Wagner himself, for example, personally distributed copies of Foster's influential book, *The Road to Plenty*, to every member of the Senate in the summer of 1929.

However, it took a bit of the political maneuvering that Wagner had learned so well at Albany. By the time he reintroduced his bills in January 1930 Bob had arranged that instead of being consigned again to the Senate's Committee on Education and Labor, they be referred to insurgent Senator Hiram Johnson's Commerce Committee. Johnson, who, according to newsmen, harbored "no love for either the Old Guard or the Administration," honored his promise to take early action, and hearings before a subcommittee were held in the middle of March.[3]

Early in April the Commerce Committee reported favorably to the Senate, and by the middle of the month Wagner had secured the Republican Steering Committee's approval for consideration of the two bills concerned with statistics and long-range planning. In the meantime, however, the National Association of Manufacturers filed a brief that, while approving these two bills in principle, assailed the unemployment exchange scheme as a centralizing, bureaucratic assault on states' rights. Apparently because of the N.A.M.'s objections, the Steering Committee refused to give right of way to S. 3060; on April 28, when the Senate approved the first two of Wagner's bills without a roll call, the Republican leaders assumed they were finished with the troublesome New Yorker.

But at that point the majority leader, James E. Watson of Indiana, was caught napping, and his failure to immediately move the taking up of an "approved" piece of legislation provided Wagner with an opportunity that was ready-made for a Tammany-trained parliamentarian. In an instant Wagner was on his feet, proposing that S. 3060 be made the next order of business. Despite the belated protests of Watson, Hiram Bingham, Simeon Fess, and others of the G.O.P. general staff, a coalition of Democrats and insurgent Republicans sustained Wagner's motion by a vote of 37 to 32. A few days later, after a debate in which Bingham served as chief spokesman for the N.A.M. position—the bill, the Connecticut lawmaker warned, was another one of those propositions "which strike at the very roots of our form of goverment"—the unemployment exchange measure passed 34–27. Congratulatory messages flowed in on the Three Bills' sponsor, but he

[3] St. Louis *Post-Dispatch*, April 4, 1930.

knew that the fight was only partly won. "I am afraid," Wagner responded to his well-wishers, "that we must prepare for a stiff battle to secure passage of this program in the House." [4] And when the House hearings finally came, Wagner and his staff again coordinated the activities of the individuals and groups who were supporting his campaign.

By now the latter had grown into an impressive phalanx, which included individuals such as Democratic Representative Emmanuel Celler and Republican Representative Fiorello La Guardia, who were Wagner's chief liaison men during the proceedings in the lower house; Paul Kellogg, the editor of *Survey* magazine, who collected 415 signatures petitioning for passage of the Three Bills at the National Conference of Social Work meeting in June; Professor Samuel Joseph of City College in New York, who circulated a round robin to economists throughout the country and eventually collected over a thousand names; Walter White, who, in response to an appeal from Florence Kelley of the Consumers' League, passed the word on to congressmen who had received N.A.A.C.P. backing in the past; and Professor Paul H. Douglas of the University of Chicago, who reported that "a group of us here are working on a number of Illinois congressmen."

Organizations such as the A.A.L.L., the National League of Women Voters, and the National Board of the Young Women's Christian Association also worked on congressmen across the country with literally tons of mail, pamphlets, and propaganda. On June 11, the day hearings began in the House, a delegation headed by William Trufant Foster and comprising educators, representatives of the three major religious faiths, labor leaders, and social workers called on the President to petition that he implement the "Hoover prosperity plan" by lending his support to the Wagner bills. Wagner's secretary arranged the White House appointment.[5]

Still, the onslaught had only a limited impact on the Old Guard stalwarts who controlled the House of Representatives. The statistics bill, referred to the Labor Committee, was reported unscathed by that sympathetic body. But the other two measures encountered strong opposition in the predominantly conservative Judiciary Committee, and they emerged from under its knife in emasculated form. Next the all-powerful Rules Committee buried the unemployment exchange, bill altogether by relegating it to the bottom of the calendar. As in the

---

[4] 72 *Congressional Record*, 7796ff, 8741ff; RFW to Samuel Joseph, May 14, 1930, RFW Papers.

[5] RFW Papers: Kellogg to RFW, June 11, 1930; Joseph to RFW, May 14, June 10, 1930; White to RFW, Dec. 16, 1930; Douglas to RFW, Nov. 5, 1930; files on "The Three Bills, 1930."

Senate, only the statistics bill and the now disemboweled long-range planning bill (which no longer provided for long-range planning) received the imprimatur of the Republican strategists. Those two passed the House on July 1, but the Senate, on Wagner's motion, refused to accept the House version of the public works measure. "The bill as amended is largely an empty shell, depending for its content on the whim of the Executive," Wagner complained, adding, "The President could not have more completely destroyed the bill if he had vetoed it." A Senate-House conference committee was appointed, but by the time Congress adjourned later in the month only the statistics part of Wagner's program had become law. Hoover signed S. 3061 on July 7, 1930.[6]

Up to this point the Administration's attitude toward the Three Bills had indeed ranged, as Wagner told newsmen, "from indifference to active opposition," and there was a good deal of confusion in its approach. In February Acting Secretary of Labor Carl Robe White informed Senator Johnson and the Commerce Committee that the statistics bill was unnecessary and "not in accord with the financial program of the President." But the action of Republican Congressional leaders in both the Senate and House, and President Hoover's signing the bill when it passed, indicate that a change of heart took place later. On the matter of long-range planning of public works the confusion was even more compounded. In February, for example, Secretary of Labor Davis told a radio audience that the government couldn't predict unemployment, and that when it came, appropriations for public works would "mean but little." A short time later, on the other hand, Assistant Secretary of Commerce Julius Klein told another radio audience that "the effect of brisk and widespread construction activity in reducing unemployment is apparently so generally recognized today, that I need not dwell long on it." By the time the Three Bills reached the hearing stage in the Senate Commerce Committee Davis had changed his mind; and in a letter to Senator Johnson he urged passage of the long-range planning bill. But two months later the secretaries of the Treasury and of Agriculture told the House Judiciary Committee that long-range planning of government works was impracticable! And while Davis also endorsed the employment exchange bill, he was the only Administration official to do so publicly.[7]

[6] 72 *Congressional Record*, 12238ff, 12267; Wagner speech file, June 19, 1930, RFW Papers.

[7] *New York Times*, Aug. 3, 1930; Senate Committee on Commerce, *Hearings on Unemployment in the United States*, pp. 110–111; texts of speeches by Davis, Feb. 13, 1930, and Klein, April 6, 1930, in files on "The Three Bills, 1930," RFW Papers; 72 *Congressional Record*, 12238–39.

Meanwhile Hoover himself continued to espouse, in a general way, the concepts involved in Wagner's measures, but apparently he felt that existing laws and the existing agencies for implementing them were sufficient. The Bureau of Labor Statistics *was* collecting better information now, he claimed; the United States Employment Service *was* expanding its operations; and the construction agencies of the government were already stepping up the tempo of public works. In a speech to the United States Chamber of Commerce on May 1, 1930, the President agreed that study should be made of ways by which the government might help promote greater stability within the business cycle, but he felt that it was too early to move yet. Instead he promised to organize a study group representing businessmen, economists, labor, and agriculture "when the situation clears a little." [8]

Perhaps the President's hesitancy to endorse new anti-unemployment legislation like Wagner's was due to a sincere conviction that the focusing of public attention on the malady would only disrupt business confidence further and make the situation even worse, a conviction that—as one Administration official put it—"Calamity howling only creates calamity." The frequency with which Republicans on Congressional committees asked witnesses favorable to the Three Bills for their opinions on that proposition indicates that it exerted a strong influence in Republican circles. But others, like Robert J. Caldwell, believed that "the chief trouble with these bills is that they were not proposed by a Republican," and a growing number of observers shared Bob Wagner's own feeling that "For petty political reasons the Administration refuses to permit the bills to pass." [9]

The Administration's renunciation of "calamity howling" failed to alleviate the depression, and by the fall of 1930 conditions had only gotten worse. Political repercussions came in November when returns in the mid-term elections indicated that the Republicans would not control the House in the Seventy-second Congress and would have but a bare majority in the Senate. When the Seventy-first Congress returned for its lame-duck session in December, President Hoover's message reflected the growing seriousness of the situation. While still affirming that the "fundamental strength of the Nation's economic life is unimpaired," the President conceded that there had been "some" increase in unemployment since the spring. And though he

[8] *New York Times,* May 2, 1930.
[9] RFW Papers: text of radio address by Secretary of Labor James J. Davis on May 8, 1928; Caldwell to RFW, July 8, 1930; Wagner speech file, June 19, 1930.

still maintained that "The best contribution of government lies in encouragement of . . . voluntary cooperation in the community," Hoover saw room for further acceleration of job-making federal public works in the amount of $150,000,000—the maximum amount that government departments could make use of in view of the "engineering, architectural, and legal preparations" that must precede actual construction.

At the same time Hoover viewed the government's problem in terms of increasing employment "for the next six months" only; he regarded as unwarranted any proposals that would extend commitments beyond that period. He had no use for the flood of bills introduced on the first day of the session calling for large federal relief expenditures in one form or another; a short time later he denounced their sponsors as men who were "playing politics at the expense of human misery." Nor did the President's message make any reference to the two remaining of Wagner's Three Bills—the measures for long-range planning and employment exchanges. While conceding again that "we shall need to consider . . . what action may be taken by the Government to remove possible governmental influences which make for instability, and to better organize mitigation of the effect of depression," Hoover still could believe that "it is as yet too soon to constructively formulate such measures." He preferred to wait until "after the passing of this depression, when we can examine it in retro spect." [10]

Wagner was prepared to support the Chief Executive's request for an additional $150,000,000 worth of public works, although, as he told reporters, he felt the amount should be larger, and could be, if his long-range planning bill had been put into effect in time. But what irked the New York lawmaker most was the President's continued procrastination regarding the creation of permanent machinery to stabilize the economy. And on December 11, before packed galleries, the Democratic "expert" on unemployment had his say.

Ninety-two of his ninety-five colleagues were on hand as Wagner —"the regular spokesman at the Capitol for scientific and progressive economists," one newsmen called him—delivered his rebuttal to the President's message. Castigating Hoover's plea for delay as "an apology for previous inaction," Wagner pointed out that despite increased appropriations, the federal government's actual expenditures on public works during 1930 would exceed those of 1929 by a mere four

[10] U. S. House of Representatives, 71st Cong., 3rd Sess., *Message of the President of the United States*, House Document 519 (Washington, D.C , Govt. Printing Office, 1930), *passim*; *New York Times*, Dec. 10, 1930.

million dollars, and all because the government's construction agencies found themselves "uninformed, unorganized, and unprepared." Such were the effects of the "emergency theory of unemployment" adhered to by the President, which viewed joblessness as an "unexpected accident to be received with surprise, nursed with first-aid methods, and borne stoically until nature has taken its course."

The desirable alternative, Wagner asserted, was to regard enforced idleness as a recurrent event "which can be anticipated, controlled, and prevented"—the approach involved in his Three Bills. "This is the psychological moment to give legal recognition to the principle that it is part of the essential function of government to provide regularity of employment," an objective which was no longer a luxury, "but a necessity if the standard of living is to be maintained and advanced, and the production of our efficient methods given an outlet in profitable consumption." And only in that way could Congress give proper recognition to the "anciently stated first law of nature," which, in its modern context, had become "the right to work." "If we deny our people that right," Wagner concluded, "we have denied them everything. If we fail them in preserving that right, we have failed them in everything." In contrast to 1928, reporters in the press gallery noted, not a single Republican senator rose to challenge the New Yorker when he finished.[11]

At the time Wagner spoke the legislative ice jam blocking further action on his bills appeared unbroken. Nevertheless the growing chorus of protest against the Administration's inaction began to produce a thaw soon thereafter; its progress became particularly noticeable with the recruitment of allies within the President's own camp. In October Hoover had appointed an Emergency Committee for Employment to mobilize the nation's "voluntary" relief efforts for the coming winter. But after a survey of the situation the committee's chairman, Colonel Arthur Woods, was converted to Wagner's view that "a place on the bread line is, after all, an unkind and ungenerous reward" for the country's workers. In November, after the election, Wagner had several meetings with Woods; by the latter part of December Arthur Young of Industrial Relations Counsellors, Inc., an early supporter of Wagner's Three Bills and a personal friend of Woods, was sounding out the colonel regarding the chances for an Administration change of heart on the long-range planning bill. It seems apparent that Woods convinced President Hoover to relent, for in January 1931 he was serving as the President's spokesman in

[11] Wagner speech file, Dec. 11, 1930, RFW Papers; New York *American,* Sept. 6, 1932; *New York Times,* Dec. 12, 1930.

productive talks with the New York lawmaker.[12]

The outcome of the negotiations was a new long-range planning bill that received the Administration's approbation but constituted an almost total victory for Bob Wagner. The revamped measure contained a few "Administration amendments" affecting details. Wagner and his Senate colleagues acquiesced in the questionable contention of the House conferees that the amendments involved "new legislation," necessitating reintroduction of the measure *in toto*, even though some observers maintained that the House spokesmen's strategy was designed solely to afford Congressman George S. Graham, the Republican chairman of the House Judiciary Committee, an opportunity to associate his name with the legislation as cosponsor.

In any event, when Wagner presented S. 5776 to the Senate on January 19 he assured his colleagues that it was practically the same bill that had passed during the last session, and they approved the new version, without a roll call, two days later. The lower house followed suit, on Congressman Graham's motion, on February 2. A week later President Hoover signed the Employment Stabilization Act of 1931; "an admirable measure," he called it, and he was careful to refer to it as "the Wagner-Graham bill." But almost invariably the newsmen, more scrupulous in awarding legislative laurels, reported the event as the signing of "the second Wagner bill." [13]

At the same time there were indications that the Administration might also be coming around to support the third measure in Wagner's trilogy, which would establish grants-in-aid for a coordinated system of federal-state employment exchanges. In December 1930 the President directed his new Secretary of Labor, William N. Doak, to look into the matter as his first order of business; by late January Doak had devised a list of changes he desired in the Wagner bill and was in communication with the New York Senator. This time the negotiations did not proceed so smoothly, however, for Doak's proposals added up to a complete repudiation of Secretary Davis' previous endorsement of the principles involved in Wagner's measure. In place of a grant-in-aid system that would leave actual job-placement work in the hands of state officials—an objective espoused by virtually every group of experts from the President's commission of 1921 on down—the new Secretary of Labor proposed merely a "reorganization" of the existing United States Employment Service which, working with a vastly expanded appropriation, would be free to engage

[12] *New York Times*, Nov. 11, 1930; Samuel Joseph to RFW, Dec. 17, 1930, RFW Papers; 74 *Congressional Record*, 5752.
[13] 74 *Congressional Record*, 2763–65, 3812–17; *New York Times*, Feb. 11, 1931.

directly in placement activities independent of, and perhaps in competition with, the state and local offices. There was no provision for joint employer-employee advisory councils to serve in conjunction with the placement offices—a feature the experts deemed necessary in order to gain for the service the mutual confidence of hirers and workers—nor was there even any provision for placing the service's augmented personnel under the civil service system. "Very frankly," Wagner wrote Doak on February 6, "I am convinced that your proposal does not change my bill, but destroys it."

The officials of the American Association for Labor Legislation and the American Federation of Labor, and others whom Doak summoned to Washington in an effort to garner backing for his substitute bill, agreed with the Senator, and they remained adamant in their support of Wagner's version. Moreover, on February 12 the House Rules Committee, buckling under the nine months of pressure put on it by Wagner's allies in the lower chamber, finally "granted a rule" for House consideration of S. 3060. It was scheduled for debate on Monday, February 23.[14]

Despite the rebuffs he had encountered, Secretary Doak remained undeterred, although he did submit his resignation as a vice-president of the A.A.L.L.! On February 17 he secured from Chairman Graham permission to be heard by the Judiciary Committee. Three days later a Republican majority of the committee agreed to report the Doak substitute as a committee amendment to the Wagner bill, which all but one of them had voted to report favorably nine months earlier. In the raucous floor debate that ensued on the twenty-third, Wagner's supporters assailed the parliamentary legitimacy of the committee majority's action, but they were even more bitter in questioning the motives behind the Administration's last-minute maneuvers. Pointing out that the National Association of Manufacturers was supporting the Doak substitute despite the fact that it was even more "centralizing" and "bureaucratic" than the Wagner bill, Representative La Guardia accused Hoover of pandering to the N.A.M.'s desire to kill *any* employment exchange legislation, since it was unlikely that the Senate would accept the Doak bill by March 4 even if the lower house passed it. Emmanuel Celler and other speakers charged that, at best, the Doak scheme was a shabby eleventh-hour attempt to save face for a do-nothing Administration—"a credit-snatching proposition."

Graham and the Republican leaders made a feeble defense

---

14 RFW Papers: RFW to Doak, Feb. 6, 1931; John B. Andrews to RFW, Feb. 2, 1931; Paul Kellogg to RFW, Feb. 5, 1931; also *Labor* (Washington, D.C.), March 3, 1931.

against the withering attack during their half of the three hours allotted for the debate, but they must have sensed that the tide was running against them as the time approached for a vote. In the end, when Graham moved adoption of the Doak substitute, he was defeated by a vote of 182–84! The result was a remarkable repudiation, in which many Republicans joined, of the President, who had, in the words of one newspaper, "entered the lists with no higher motive to be seen than a disposition to deprive the New York senator of credit." A few minutes later the House passed Wagner's bill, and S. 3060 was on its way to the White House for a disappointed President's consideration.[15]

By the time the Seventy-first Congress expired on March 4, 1931, the legislative branch, if not the Chief Executive, had more than completed action on the entire first installment of Bob Wagner's antidepression program. It had also begun work on the next step that he urged, federal encouragement of unemployment insurance. As in the case of the need for better statistics, employment exchanges, and planning of public construction, the idea of accumulating reserves that would be paid out to unemployed workers during hard times had been the subject of study and discussion all during the 1920s. A few business concerns, anxious to put "welfare capitalism" to work, had actually inaugurated private plans covering their own employees. Meanwhile the American Association for Labor Legislation perfected, and had introduced in several legislatures, a model bill providing a plan for state compulsory unemployment insurance to which employers, employees, and the state governments themselves might contribute.

Bob Wagner, viewing unemployment reserves as the next logical extension of the workmen's compensation principle that he had championed at Albany, sympathized with these early developments in the field of jobless insurance. In an article published in April 1928, for example, just after he had begun pounding at the issue of unemployment in his maiden Senate speech, Wagner observed: "For a long time the total loss of industrial accidents was borne by the poor unfortunates who were injured, until workmen's compensation was conceived and the cost was transferred to the industry where it rightfully belonged." That transfer had also proved a great stimulant to the introduction of safety devices that actually reduced the industrial accident rate, Wagner pointed out. "It may well be," he contended, "that

[15] John B. Andrews to RFW, Feb. 7, 1931, RFW Papers; 74 *Congressional Record,* 5745–77; New York *Evening World,* Feb. 20, 1931.

a similar result would follow if industry were compelled to bear the cost of its seasonal, technological, and cyclical unemployment." [16]

At the time Wagner wrote, few conceived any role for the federal government in the realm of unemployment insurance. The Couzens Committee report of March 1929, while endorsing the reserves concept, considered it a problem for private industry or, at most, the states, to handle. But the onslaught of the depression had stimulated a great deal more thinking about the possibility of ensuring against a repetition of the disaster, and by 1930 New York's junior senator, among others, had become convinced that in some manner the federal government must take a hand in encouraging the reserves experiment. During the spring of that year he and his legislative assistants worked on two alternative methods whereby Washington might be brought into the picture.

The first and more indirect method was suggested to Wagner in a letter from a man he had never met, ex-Senator George H. Williams of Missouri. It involved encouraging the establishment of reserves by private businesses by exempting such funds, and the contributions made to them, from tax liability. The second plan, presented by the A.A.L.L., would create a system of federal grants-in-aid—a favorite device of that organization—whereby the government would match up to one-third of the amounts contributed into compulsory unemployment insurance systems established by *state* law. Dr. Andrews wanted Wagner to introduce the grant-in-aid measure in May 1930, while the Three Bills were still pending, but the Senator pointed out that since opponents were using "the usual 'opening wedge' argument" against these measures, "perhaps it would be inadvisable to frighten away possible support by the introduction of other legislation which my colleagues are not yet ready to follow." Bowing to Wagner's superior experience in the realm of legislative tactics, Andrews accepted the Tammany politician's advice.[17]

Nevertheless, by the time Congress reassembled for its short session in December 1930 Wagner felt that the atmosphere had become favorable for beginning the agitation that would *make* his colleagues "ready to follow." He introduced two unemployment insurance bills, based on both the Williams and Andrews plans, and thereafter the subject commanded almost as much attention in his public utterances as did the Three Bills. Typically, Wagner stressed the human and

[16] Robert F. Wagner, "Sound Policy to Break the Bread Lines," *Independent*, April 14, 1928, p. 353.

[17] RFW Papers: Williams to RFW, May 15, 1930; Andrews to RFW, May 17, 1930; RFW to Andrews, May 28, 1930.

ethical side of the legislation as well as its economic import. Joblessness under modern industrial conditions is not the merited penalty of
the workers' own misdoing, he maintained; rather "It is the resultant
effect of forces beyond their control—forces which the entire industrial and business community has set into motion." It followed, therefore, that if the wage earner was to be protected in his "right to
work," industry must assume "its inescapable moral obligation" of
maintaining the continuity of wages. "It would never occur to a man-
ufacturer," he suggested, "to set his machinery out on the street during depression in the hope that the Red Cross would maintain it for
him until the recovery of business."

But "the present confusion, with its layoffs and its bread lines
and its charitable appeals" did far more social damage than merely
impoverishing and possibly wrecking individual lives, Wagner asserted, as he shifted over to the dollars-and-cents arguments more appealing to economists and businessmen. "It lets loose a destructive
force—curtailed purchasing power—which may bring the entire industrial house tumbling down in a heap of ruins." It all added up to a
failure of proper organization and planning, which could be remedied
in large part by measures such as unemployment insurance. "I prophesy that when we shall have learned to manage our economic affairs in
a more sensible way," the New York lawmaker confidently asserted,
"we shall look back at the present disorder with amazement that a
generation which called itself civilized could be guilty of sustaining
it." [18]

Wagner was realistic enough to realize that his unemployment
insurance measures stood little chance of enactment in the Seventy-
first Congress; the subject was even newer than those involved in the
Three Bills, and powerful groups such as the American Federation of
Labor were still uncommitted to the concept even in principle. His
bills were meant as trial balloons to stimulate discussion. As Bob told
a group of economists and reformers who assembled in Cleveland in
December 1930 for a Conference on Permanent Preventatives of Unemployment: "It is my experience that social legislation does not
pass any sooner than the public is educated to demand it. That process of education," he admonished his audience, "is largely in your
hands." [19]

Yet, as always, Wagner was ready to do his part in promoting the
learning experience, and this time he chose a Senate investigation as
his vehicle. In January 1931 he introduced a resolution creating a

[18] Wagner speech file, Dec. 30, 1930, RFW Papers.
[19] *Ibid.*; William Green to RFW, Jan. 19, 1931, RFW Papers.

three-man select committee to study the operation of unemployment insurance systems, both public and private, at home and abroad. The cooperative Hiram Johnson reported it back favorably from the Commerce Committee, and although the Committee to Audit and Control the Contingent Expenses of the Senate dallied some weeks with the measure, it too released the bill in short order as soon as Wagner entered a motion to discharge the committee six days before the session was due to expire. His colleagues approved the resolution without a roll-call vote: they were taking the New York member at his word now in matters involving the economy, and Wagner himself was gratified that he no longer had to apologize "as was my custom a time not so long ago," for intruding with a discussion of unemployment on the floor of the Senate.

On March 4 the Vice-President appointed Wagner and Republicans Felix Hebert of Rhode Island and Otis Glenn of Illinois as members of the study group. With the assistance of Simon Rifkind, Isador Lubin, and Bryce M. Stewart of Industrial Relations Counsellors, Inc., Wagner laid plans for an exhaustive study of jobless insurance. Offers of assistance flowed into Wagner's office from business executives, insurance companies, labor experts, and social scientists; job-seeking Washington stenographers also addressed their applications for employment with the new committee to the man whom everybody assumed would be its chairman.[20]

It had been a productive legislative season indeed, not only for Bob Wagner but also for all those who were determined to get the wheels of government rolling once again on the path of modern liberalism. Some felt they were witnessing the dawn of a new era of collaboration among enlightened businessmen, labor spokesmen, professional reformers, and forward-looking politicians—the dawn of a new Progressive Era. That was the sentiment expressed by speakers at a "victory banquet" early in April 1931 sponsored by the New York Conference for Unemployment Insurance Legislation. Wagner was particularly delighted with the occasion, for it gave him "a long-sought opportunity" to express his appreciation to the nonpolitician allies who had sustained his fight for unemployment legislation in the Seventy-first Congress. He was glad to acknowledge his indebtedness to them, he declared, for "In the problem of human engineering you are the experts. It is your prerogative to prescribe for us the new economics of social control. There are men in every legislature today who

[20] 74 *Congressional Record*, 1754, 5961, 6451, 7271; files on "Unemployment Insurance, 1931," RFW Papers.

look to you to point the way." That the assembled experts thought they knew who was the chief of those men in Washington is certain, for the banquet program was inscribed "in honor of Senator Robert F. Wagner." [21]

The enthusiasm of the celebrants that night, and of all who looked forward to a new Progressive Era, was nonetheless dampened by the continued obstinacy of the President, whose treatment of "their" measures proved that there was no Teddy Roosevelt in the White House. It was a difficult decision that Herbert Hoover faced when, on February 25, Congress sent him the Wagner employment exchange bill. On the one hand were the increasingly frequent remarks in the press to the effect that, through the efforts of Bob Wagner, the Democrats were "running away with the depression issue." On the other hand were the thousands of letters, telegrams, and petitions favoring the bill that poured into the executive mansion; and there was also the counsel of Colonel Arthur Woods and other members of the President's own Emergency Committee for Employment, who urged Hoover to sign it. Undoubtedly it required real courage, against that caliber of advice, to veto S. 3060, as the President did on March 9—*after* Congress had adjourned and when there was no chance to override the man in the White House.

In an attempt to fend off the anticipated storm of criticism, Hoover issued a statement defending his action on the ground that Wagner's bill would abolish the existing "well-developed Federal employment service," while the new federal-state cooperative system that it envisaged "[could not] be made effective for many months or even years." The President also promised that Secretary Doak would study the matter further and that in the meantime the U.S.E.S. would be expanded and reorganized. But the President's insulating efforts failed, and he was subjected to a blistering heat of denunciation hitherto unprecedented during his term. In a statement asserting that Hoover had "failed every man who is pounding the pavements in search of work," Wagner himself pointed out that his measure contained a provision for a two-year period of adjustment from one system to the other, leaving no hiatus between services. Harvard economist Sumner Slichter denounced the veto message as "one of the most dishonest documents I have ever read." Democratic newspapers called the President's action "despicable" and an illustration of "peanut politics"; they were even joined by journalists who were accustomed to taking Hoover's side. "The President's veto of the Wagner bill . . . was based apparently on a counsel of perfection," de-

[21] Wagner speech file, Dec. 30, 1930, April 8, 1931, RFW Papers.

clared the New York *Herald Tribune*, a Republican journal; "in lieu of a better measure it deserved his signature." "The pocket veto," added columnist David Lawrence, who had no reputation for being overly sympathetic with Democrats, "is going to require a good deal of explanation on the stump." [22]

The disappointment of liberals—and the consternation of some of the President's own friends—reached even greater heights a few days later when, on Hoover's orders, Wagner was deprived of the chairmanship of the select committee on unemployment insurance that had been created by his resolution. According to senatorial custom and courtesy, the author of such a resolution enjoyed the "right" to head the committee if he wished. Bob wanted to be chairman, of course, and in line with his desire, Vice-President Curtis had put his name first in announcing the committee's personnel; Wagner called the first meeting, for March 18, and it took place in *his* New York law office. But when the three men assembled, Senator Glenn informed Wagner that the President now insisted on the chairmanship going to one of the Republicans, and thereupon Glenn and Hebert proceeded to elect the latter to head the group.

Wagner himself remained quiet—after all, his claim to the position rested merely on "the long established and unvarying usage of the Senate"—but others spoke his thoughts for him. "Presidential interference with an independent Senate committee is usurpation," declared the New York *World-Telegram*. "The humble voter can understand cheap trickery when he sees it," chimed in a reporter from the nation's capital, who added that "the long succession of petty Presidential attacks upon the efforts of Senator Wagner . . . have made Washington correspondents as prolific of profanity as a Missouri mule-driver." And more than one editorial page described Hoover's conduct with a phrase that he himself had coined—"playing politics with human misery." [23]

While confidence in the Chief Executive descended to new lows, Bob Wagner's stature mounted ever higher. His articles on unemployment were reprinted in France and Italy; his opinions were quoted in debates in the South African Parliament. Invitations to

[22] *New York Times*, March 8, 9, 1931; New York *Evening Journal*, March 20, 1931; Brooklyn *Citizen*, March 21, 1931; New York *Herald Tribune*, March 9, 1931; Rochester *Times-Union*, March 10, 1931. Slichter's statement is quoted by William E. Leuchtenburg in the Washington *Post*, Aug. 9, 1964.

[23] New York *World-Telegram*, March 19, 1931; article by Washington correspondent Frederick R. Barkley, clipped from an unidentified periodical, RFW Papers; New York *American*, March 23, 1931; Philadelphia *Record*, April 20, 1931; Simon H. Rifkind, interview.

speak were innumerable; he also received, and sometimes accepted, invitations to lead student seminars in economic policy at Princeton and other universities. "Among the notable events of the session which has just ended was the rise of Robert F. Wagner," observed a New York newspaper in March 1931. "There is no clearer, saner, more honest and more generous voice to be heard in the Senate than his." "Mr. Wagner has succeeded," wrote Washington columnist Clinton W. Gilbert, "precisely because he has given more study to modern industrial conditions than any other Senator has. He had ideas on the subject and nobody else did." "Time and again Senator Wagner has proved himself one of the most valuable men in public life," rhapsodized a newspaper in St. Louis. "Except that he was born in Germany, he would be a leading factor in next year's presidential race." [24]

The New York lawmaker had still more ideas in mind regarding the subject on which he had become the Senate's leading expert. And, partly because he could not be deterred from them by the buzzing of a presidential bee in his bonnet, he was destined to play a larger role than ever when the new Seventy-second Congress convened, in December 1931.

[24] New York *World*, July 23, 1931; Syracuse *Herald*, March 10, 1931; St. Louis *Star*, Feb. 23, 1931.

CHAPTER 7

Affirmative Action at Last

WHILE LABOR SECRETARY DOAK carried out the "reorganization" of his United States Employment Service during the summer of 1931 (in the fall the convention of the Association of Public Employment Services officially labeled his efforts a failure),[1] and while Senators Wagner, Hebert, and Glenn went their separate ways in investigating the subject of unemployment insurance, the nation's economy cascaded at a rate even greater than before. Its descent was abetted by economic collapse in Europe, and was accompanied by a federal deficit—approximately $900 million for the fiscal year ending June 30—for the first time since the World War. The Great Depression was entering its darkest phase.

The clouds that gathered in the fall propelled President Hoover to an unprecedented degree of federal antidepression activity. And while parts of his program won widespread acclaim, much of it incensed those who continued to believe in the efficacy of direct government spending as a means of priming the pump and sustaining mass purchasing power. The turn of events in Europe confirmed the President's conviction that "the major forces of the depression now lie outside of the United States," while the appearance of a budget deficit violated the orthodox fiscal principle that held that, except in wartime, the government must balance its income and outgo every year. To these two developments Hoover ascribed the panic that seized America's banking and business communities in September 1931, and

[1] John B. Andrews to RFW, Oct. 19, 1931, RFW Papers.

on the resultant hoarding of capital he blamed the mounting unemployment that ensued. His program therefore embraced steps to restore order to international economic relationships, mainly through a moratorium on reparations and debt payments stemming from the World War; measures to "thaw out" the nation's frozen credit resources so as to get moving again the flow of job-producing investment capital in the private sector of the economy; and a determination to bolster business confidence by returning the federal government to the safe and sane fiscal policy of the balanced budget.[2]

The last-mentioned objective required retrenchment, even to the extent of reducing the salaries of government employees. It meant turning a deaf ear to those who pleaded for vastly enlarged programs of public works or for federal relief appropriations to supplement the dwindling resources of private charities and local governments. Hoover was willing to pay that cost, however, for of all the unhappy events of 1931, it appears that the deficit affected him most profoundly. But as the budget-conscious President drew further away from the advanced doctrines he had endorsed earlier, the dismay of many of his original supporters rapidly mounted. William Trufant Foster and Waddill Catchings, lamenting the Administration's apparent repudiation of the "Hoover prosperity plan" of 1928, acknowledged that "Our failure is complete." "They also serve who only stand and wait," the two economists wrote, "but they serve the cause of Communism."[3]

The significance of Europe's financial crash was not lost on Bob Wagner. "To the American people," he told an audience in September, "has now come the realization that we have been and still are, in company with the other nations of the world, plodding the deep and broad valley of universal depression." He hailed Hoover's debt-moratorium proposal as representing "affirmative action at last," and in 1932 he was supporting measures that foreshadowed the New Deal's reciprocal trade agreements program.

Nevertheless Wagner continued to insist that the primary reason for America's distress was internal: it lay in "forgetting the human equation," in forgetting that while "machines may produce, they do not buy." Nor did the appearance of the federal deficit deter him from his conviction that "under present conditions the only customer who can sufficiently enlarge his requirements so as to give business a

[2] William Starr Myers and Walter H. Newton, *The Hoover Administration: A Documented Narrative* (New York, 1936), pp. 147ff.

[3] Proof of Foster and Catchings syndicated column of Oct. 3, 1931, in RFW Papers.

real spurt is the United States Government, through the inauguration of an ambitious program of necessary public improvements." Only in that way, moreover, could the outright relief dole be avoided; and only in that way might the entire economy "feel the returning vigor and sustaining strength of purchasing power in the hands of the great masses of people." [4]

As he waited in vain during the summer of 1931 for signs that the Administration intended to make vigorous use of the new Federal Employment Stabilization Act, Wagner and his aides formulated a program whereby the New York legislator might once again take the lead in achieving an adequate pump-priming effort. It was unveiled early in September when Wagner called on the federal government to undertake a two-billion-dollar construction program, which, according to his sources, would provide direct employment for one million men and indirect employment for at least another million workers. To the inevitable question "Where is the money coming from?" the Senator supplied a simple, direct answer: "The government can borrow it." [5]

Wagner was not, by any means, the first depression-weary American to advocate deficit spending as a way out of the morass. But the era of Lord Keynes had not yet arrived, and few figures in official Washington had allowed themselves to speak of fiscal policy except in the most traditional terms of balanced budgets. Wagner was helping to break new ground, therefore, when in December 1931, shortly after the convening of the Seventy-second Congress, he introduced Senate Resolution 72, calling on the President to transmit to Congress a two-billion-dollar emergency public works program to be financed by long-term bonds. He was joined a few days later by Senator Robert La Follette, Jr., of Wisconsin, whose bill for a five-and-a-half-billion-dollar bond issue envisaged not only a federal public improvements program but also federal loans to states and municipalities, so that they might press forward with public works and housing programs of their own.

In defending his proposal Wagner, like La Follette, demonstrated his familiarity with most of the then existing arguments in favor of deficit spending as a countercyclical measure. He drew a distinction between the government's "current running expenses," which must be kept within the government's current income, on the one hand, and the proposed public works expenditures on the other. Since the

[4] Wagner speech file, Jan. 16, Sept. 7, Dec. 6, 1931, RFW Papers; *New York Times*, July 24, 31, 1932.
[5] Wagner speech file, Sept. 7, 1931, RFW Papers.

latter represented outlays for *permanent* improvements, which would enlarge the permanent assets of the nation, they need not be met out of the already heavy tax burden: "It is entirely just that future taxpayers should pay part of the cost." Anticipating that the increased employment occasioned by the construction program would augment the government's income from tax revenues, Wagner stated with a special note of modernity that "the problem of balancing the federal budget will be very much simplified, may indeed cease to be a problem, if we succeed in balancing the individual budget of the American family by restoring the breadwinner to a job."

Moreover, since the projects envisaged in his bill would be built at some future time, Wagner maintained that it was only good business sense on the government's part to accelerate their construction so as to take advantage of the prevailing low prices of building materials, of the abundance of labor, and of interest rates that had rarely been cheaper. "Were there in existence a private corporation situated like the federal government, is there anyone," he asked, "who would not agree that it would be the depth of folly if it did not pursue such a course?" A final advantage accompanying a federal construction bond issue, in the view of the New York lawmaker, would be its contribution to that very process of "thawing out" the nation's credit structure that President Hoover was seeking to promote. "The banks are glutted with idle funds that ought to be busy creating employment," he asserted. "It would be a boon to the entire country to cause this frozen capital to flow freely once again in the channels of trade." Everything considered, Wagner concluded that "Never in its history has our government had occasion to borrow money for more economic reasons and for loftier purposes." The only requirement for their realization was that the government should begin to measure the adequacy of its fiscal policies "by the needs of the American people, and not by the artificial restraints of doctrinaire dogmas." [6]

Nevertheless, the traditional ideas that Bob Wagner depicted as "the artificial restraints of doctrinaire dogmas" remained eternal verities as far as President Hoover was concerned. Hoover's conviction was stated in his opening message to Congress: "We can now stimulate employment and agriculture more effectually and speedily through the voluntary measures in progress, through the thawing out of credit, through the building up of stability abroad, through the Home Loan Discount Banks, through an emergency finance corporation and the rehabilitation of the railways and other such directions." [7]

[6] *Ibid.*, Jan. 15, March 26, 1932.
[7] Myers and Newton, *The Hoover Administration*, pp. 150, 156.

Consequently the President concentrated his attention on and got Congress to pass such bills as the one creating the Reconstruction Finance Corporation. A federally chartered corporation, the RFC started out with an initial capital of $500,000,000 subscribed by the government, and was empowered to raise an additional $1,500,000,-000 by issuing its own debentures, which, while guaranteed by the government, did not appear as a direct charge in the federal budget—an ambiguous arrangement compatible with Hoover's illusion that he was on the road to balancing the nation's fiscal accounts. Through loans to deserving banks, insurance companies, and other financial institutions, and to the railroads, the RFC was supposed to help liquify their resources so that they might once again indulge in venturesome and job-producing business activities. The Federal Home Loan Bank Act was designed to do the same thing for building and loan companies and the other credit sources vital to the construction industry. At the President's request, Congress also augmented the capital of the Federal Land Banks, while other Administration-approved measures loosened the restrictions governing the Federal Reserve system. It added up to the most ambitious antidepression program ever undertaken by the government, but it was all based on the assumption that, if assured adequate credit resources, the businessmen of American could by themselves once again get the wheels of industry rolling.

On the whole Bob Wagner supported the President's inflationist program, calling it "a very laudable effort to prevent a serious and irreparable break in our credit structure." During the debates on the Reconstruction Finance Corporation bill in January 1932 he defended the project against both ultraconservative Republicans, who viewed it as a dangerous expansion of government "interference" in the economy, and suspicious progressives in both parties, who denounced it as an undeserved government "handout" to big business. Wagner also voted for some of the tax increases that the President insisted on in the spring, although the New Yorker continued to distinguish between the government's "ordinary" budget, which should be balanced, and the emergency expenditures for relief and construction, which were not in that category. And when the economy drive reached the point of cutting the salaries of government employees, Wagner demurred. The government should be a "model employer," he maintained, and should not indulge in the very type of wage-cutting practices that, all along, the President had urged private businessmen to renounce.[8]

[8] Wagner speech file, Jan. 15, 22, 1932, and *Yea and Nay Votes of Robert F. Wagner, Seventy-second Congress,* RFW Papers.

Moreover, throughout the session, as he hammered away at the need for an ambitious public works program, Wagner amplified his conviction that "the President's recommendations are alone insufficient to deal with the present emergency." "The Administration's view," he complained, "seems to be based on the assumption that men are out of work because banks curtailed the supply of credit. The reverse is the fact," he insisted. "Banks curtailed their credit because so many are out of work. And we do not restore any substantial number of these men to their jobs merely by liberalizing credit." From the beginning Wagner took a firm stand against the so-called "filter down" approach, which at times he identified as "the historical policy of the Republican Party: that government favors should be applied at the top in the hope that in due time the prosperity of those at the top would seep down to those below." [9]

The President's attitude was sincere and based on principle, but it left him open to attack by equally sincere people who contrasted his solicitude for businessmen—and his willingness to afford them financial help from the overstrained Treasury—with his adamant rejection of proposals for injecting purchasing power directly into the hands of the idle masses. With completion of legislative action on Hoover's RFC bill in January 1932, questioning of the adequacy, and indeed the justice, of the President's one-track approach became even stronger. "When adverse circumstances compelled the railroad presidents to come to Washington," Wagner declared in a well-publicized Senate speech on the fifteenth, "we listened attentively to their story. . . . We replied that we would lend them the aid of the Federal Government; that we would lend them money out of the United States Treasury. . . . We did not preach to them rugged individualism. We did not sanctimoniously roll out sentences rich with synonyms of self-reliance. We were not carried away with apprehension over what would happen to their independence if we extended them a helping hand. We followed the same procedure in an effort to strengthen the banking situation." And he reiterated his approval of those steps. "But when millions of Americans, foot weary and heartsick, cry out in despair, 'Give us work,' we suddenly are overwhelmed with devotion for the preservation of self-reliance. We plug our ears to the cry of the multitude while the prophets burn incense upon the altar of rugged individualism, and the fanatics would sacrifice the Nation to preserve its empty slogans." [10]

[9] Wagner speech file, Dec. 6, 1931, and Jan. 15, March 26, April 1, 1932, RFW Papers.
[10] *Ibid.*, Jan. 15, 1932.

Before Wagner found the parliamentary opportunity to open his fight for a public works program, however, an even more pressing issue took the stage away from Administration-approved measures, and that was the question of federal appropriations for outright relief payments—the resort to the "dole." While throughout 1931 President Hoover insisted that private charities, and the local and state governments, were adequately handling the problem of direct relief to the destitute, evidence mounted that such was not the case, and so did the chorus of demands that federal funds be introduced into the picture. Bob Wagner, believing that "it is wiser national economy to expend a thousand dollars to maintain a man on a job, than to expend only five hundred dollars to maintain him in idleness," hoped against hope for an adequate public works program launched in time. As late as November 1931, when William Hodson of the New York City Welfare Council and other social workers urged Wagner to sponsor a direct relief bill, he replied, "I am not at all satisfied that we have even begun to exhaust the possibilities of relief by way of an intensive federal construction program." The importuners thereupon turned to Senator La Follette and to "radical" Democrat Edward P. Costigan of Colorado, and these two men, rather than the New York member, led the early part of the fight in the Senate for a relief bill. But Wagner was not far behind.[11]

The La Follette-Costigan bill of January 1932, drawn up in consultation with Hodson, Allen T. Burns of the Association of Community Chests, and other charity experts, appropriated $375 million for outright federal gifts to the states for relief purposes. The act would be administered by a federal board possessing considerable power to influence the organization, personnel, and policies of the recipient states' relief agencies. The President and his supporters abhorred the proposal. Even the more conservative Democrats shied away from the precedent-shattering idea of inaugurating direct relief grants to the states, while most of the Southerners among them feared that the federal board's powers might interfere with "local customs" in the matter of granting relief—customs that in the South usually worked out to the disadvantage of the Negroes.

Bob Wagner had reluctantly come to share Hodson's conclusion that, given the Administration's negative attitude toward public works, "it hardly seems possible that much relief will come from that source this winter." "No one," declared Wagner in explaining his support for the dole proposal, "took a more determined stand than I

11 *Ibid.*, Sept. 7, 1931; RFW to Hodson, Nov. 7, 1931, Hodson to RFW, Nov. 10, 1931, RFW Papers.

against consigning those out of work to the humiliating experience of charitable relief. . . . It was because we failed to provide work that we are today under the necessity of providing relief." Meanwhile Lowell Limpus, Bob's New York newspaper friend, had been set busy collecting heart-wrenching pictures of the metropolis' bread lines and "Hoovervilles." They became part of the ammunition Wagner used as, in conjunction with La Follette and Costigan, he now set out to convince his colleagues that relief expenditures, like public works appropriations, were "not a proper area for retrenchment." [12]

By the time debate began on the La Follette-Costigan bill on the first of February, however, it appeared that a federal relief program of any sort might be lost due to a dispute over the method of its operation. A large group of Democrats, regarding the La Follette-Costigan measures as one that "provides a new bureau in Washington with dictatorial powers over the states," backed a substitute proposal drawn up by Senators Hugo Black of Alabama, David I. Walsh of Massachusetts, and Robert J. Bulkley of Ohio. It authorized the same appropriation as the original bill—$375 million—but the money would be distributed to the states in the form of interest-bearing *loans* rather than as outright gifts. Since the states would have to pay the money back, the bill's authors contended that there was no need for creating any elaborate federal machinery to supervise and regulate its expenditure. Thus interference with "states' rights" would be avoided. As a lure to rural representatives, the Black-Walsh-Bulkley measure incorporated an additional $375 million emergency grant-in-aid for road construction—a feature that La Follette and Costigan quickly added to their own version.

The debate over the alternative measures raged for two weeks while Administration supporters sat back and gleefully observed the disruption of their opponents' ranks. On February 15 enough progressives joined up with the conservative Republicans to defeat the Democratic substitute, 48–31; the next day enough Democrats voted with the Administration's supporters to beat the La Follette-Costigan bill 48–35. Only the President and his friends profited from the deadlock.[13]

Bob Wagner, who cast his vote for *both* versions of the relief proposal, was perturbed by the impasse. On February 17 he introduced, as S. 3696, a compromise bill that in the preceding weeks he

[12] RFW Papers: Hodson to RFW, Nov. 10, 1931; Wagner speech file, April 1, 1932; Limpus to Simon H. Rifkind, Dec. 31, 1931.
[13] Hugo Black to Franklin D. Roosevelt, undated telegram, FDR Papers; 75 *Congressional Record*, 3939, 4052.

had tried unsuccessfully to get the warring factions to agree on. It authorized the same amounts for relief and road work as the other versions, but provided that the relief money be distributed in the form of *advances*, to be repaid by withholding yearly, beginning in 1937, a portion of the amount that would normally be allotted to each state under the long-established federal grant-in-aid program for road construction. His administrative structure envisioned a *temporary* federal relief board that, while it might set minimal conditions the states had to meet, would not have the sweeping powers envisioned in the La Follette-Costigan measure.

Quite apart from the details of Wagner's proposal (he apparently appropriated the idea of "advances" from an unsuccessful emergency road appropriation bill that Senator Tom Connally of Texas introduced in 1930), was its illumination of the practical approach that he customarily adopted in situations where action seemed about to be strangled in a knotty dispute over "principles." "The most important need is that relief funds be made available," he exhorted in arguing for his substitute; "methods are of secondary consideration." [14]

Senator La Follette's Committee on Manufactures, to which Wagner's S. 3696 was referred, reported the bill favorably at the end of February. Although it failed to provide all the administrative standards that the welfare experts wanted, and that Wagner himself regarded as ideally desirable, the New York lawmaker managed to convince the more doctrinaire La Follette that the compromise measure was the only practical solution in view of the Senate's temper. Thereafter the Wagner bill held the center of the stage in the upper chamber's intermittent discussions of the relief problem.

Moreover, in March Wagner, who had become convinced that the President would refuse to formulate a public works program even if Senate Resolution 47 were pressed to passage, introduced a new bill authorizing a $1.1 billion federal construction undertaking. The new amount was considerably less than the two billion dollars worth of projects Wagner had called for in the previous fall, but it was based on the report of Colonel Donald H. Sawyer, the Director of the Federal Employment Stabilization Board, regarding the number of authorized, planned projects that the federal departments were ready to go ahead with immediately if given the signal. During April copies of the bill—together with a special query regarding the wisdom of its deficit financing provision—went out to the list of economists maintained by Simon Rifkind; their replies, which Wagner periodically en-

[14] 75 *Congressional Record*, 4113; also RFW Papers: files on "Relief and Construction Act, 1932"; Wagner speech file, Feb. 15, 1932.

tered in the *Congressional Record*, were overwhelmingly favorable.[15]

Meanwhile President Hoover seemed to remain oblivious to pleas for more affirmative government action. On May 5, in a special message to Congress, he delivered a blistering attack on the "spenders," reiterating his demands for governmental economy and tax increases so that the budget might be balanced. The White House and Capitol Hill seemed to be at loggerheads.

The leading figures in both branches of government knew, however, that the grumbling across the country against the apparent inability of *any* of "the politicians" in Washington to effectively lead the nation, bode well for none of them. An indication that the Senate Democrats intended to make one last try to seize the initiative, or at least to "smoke out" President Hoover, came on May 11 when Minority Leader Joseph T. Robinson of Arkansas took the floor for a speech billed as a reply to Hoover's tongue-lashing the previous week. After pledging the Democrats to cooperate in the Chief Executive's efforts to balance the normal budget, Robinson pleaded with the President to relent, on his part, to the extent of approving a special $2.3 billion bond issue to finance relief loans to the states, a federal public works program, and federal loans to states and municipalities for construction programs of their own.[16] To the surprise of many observers Hoover responded to the minority leader's overtures—"the greatest reversal of position by the President since the depression began," one newspaper termed it—and the next day Robinson was invited to the White House to canvass the situation. On the thirteenth the Senate Democratic Conference established a subcommittee charged with preparing a bill that would satisfactorily combine the Democrats' own program with the Administration's counterproposals. Its members, besides Robinson, were Bulkley of Ohio, Thomas J. Walsh of Montana, and Key Pittman of Nevada; Bob Wagner was its chairman.[17]

The next few weeks were undoubtedly the busiest that Wagner had yet encountered in his long legislative career as, in the Democratic subcommittee, the Banking and Currency Committee, on the

[15] 75 *Congressional Record*, 4906, 5956–58, 10309–39; Wagner speech file, March 14, 1932, and files on "Relief and Construction Act, 1932," RFW Papers.

[16] That the Democrats were working on a new formula might have become obvious to newsmen two days earlier when Bob Wagner issued a press release giving his suggestions for the forthcoming Democratic national platform. To his now-familiar calls for federal relief and construction appropriations Wagner added the new point of federal loans to finance state and local construction projects. The latter proposal, adapted of course from the La Follette bill of December, was penciled into Wagner's prepared statement, apparently at the last minute and in accord with the most up-to-date deliberations among the Senate's Democratic leaders (Wagner speech file, May 9, 1932, RFW Papers).

[17] *New York Times*, May 6, 12–14, 1932; St. Louis *Star*, May 13, 1932.

floor of the Senate, and then in conferences with the House, he strove to guide to enactment a compromise bill that would at least make a start in the direction he had been urging the government to take. In his conversations with Robinson the President indicated that he would approve of *lending* $300 million to the states for their direct relief activities, and another billion or so of loans for revenue-producing, self-liquidating public works such as toll bridges and tunnels. But he wanted the entire operation to be directed and financed by the RFC, which would be authorized to issue additional debentures, rather than by a federal bond issue; furthermore, he wished to have the RFC empowered to make loans to private businesses of *all* sorts for "repro-ductive" enterprises that they could not finance through regular bank-ing facilities. The President also reiterated his opposition to a federal public works program; he wanted no part of the "extraordinary budget" idea that Bob Wagner had helped popularize, for in the Ad-ministration's eyes that was "an unsound device." [18]

Wagner and his Democratic cohorts readily acquiesced in Hoover's preference for indirect RFC financing of the relief and con-struction loans to the states, even while recognizing it as a continu-ation of the "fiction" that the Republicans were bringing the govern-ment's budget into balance. When, during the floor debates on the compromise bill, irate progressives railed against this concession to the President's wishes, Wagner interjected that "we are talking about form, which does not interest me very much."

The Administration's desire to open up the RFC's credit facili-ties to businessmen in general, however, presented a thornier prob-lem. The suggestion, which had been part of Hoover's original recom-mendations in December, was rejected by Congress in the passage of the RFC act; neither the Democrats nor the progressive Republicans had been willing to entrust to the Administration that immense au-thority, with all its possibilities for favoritism and political manipula-tion. Much of that distrust still persisted in the spring, especially in view of a rumor—which turned out to be fact—that a large propor-tion of the RFC's resources had been used to support a Detroit bank in which General Charles G. Dawes, the former Republican Vice-President whom Hoover had appointed to head the agency, had a direct interest. In conformity with Congressional opinion, therefore, Wagner's bill extended RFC borrowing privileges only to private businesses that were engaged in the construction of self-liquidating facilities "devoted to a public interest," such as water works, docks, and limited-dividend housing projects.

On the final question in dispute, regarding a direct federal public

[18] *New York Times*, May 13, 14, June 3, 1932.

works program, Wagner was as determined as the President, and the bill he introduced on behalf of the Democratic subcommittee on May 25 enumerated the specific projects—all of which had received prior Congressional authorization and comprised part of Colonel Sawyer's "ready to go" list—that the government should undertake immediately and pay for by issuing long-term bonds. The program that Bob envisaged was now whittled down to $500 million, however, and more than one-third of that amount was to go for road construction.[19]

Hundreds of hands went into the formulation of Wagner's S. 4755—the Emergency Relief and Construction Act of 1932. For weeks Bob had been in daily consultation with senators, congressmen, and Administration officials; with social workers and welfare experts concerned particularly with the bill's relief provisions; with city officials and with groups such as the American Society of Civil Engineers, the American Waterworks Association, and the American Institute of Steel Construction, all of whom were deeply interested in provisions for encouraging local public works construction; with the heads of government bureaus, who furnished him the figures for a feasible federal public works program; and with economists throughout the country, who supplied arguments and statistics for repelling the Administration's anticipated attack against the proposed federal public works bond issue.

When the finished product was unveiled, congratulations and endorsements flowed into Wagner's office from every conceivable source: from General Electric's Gerard Swope and Sanford E. Thompson, the president of the Taylor Society; from the director of the American Legion's National Employment Commission; from Walter White of the N.A.A.C.P. and from the Board of Directors of the National League of Women Voters; from businessmen, labor leaders, social workers, and economists beyond number. The newspapers reported the White House as generally satisfied with the measure—except for its federal public works provision—while Walter Lippmann told his readers that "the Wagner Bill is as statesmanlike an adjustment of conflicting opinions as we are likely to see," and one that provided "a golden opportunity for prompt national cooperation." [20]

The Senate took up the relief and construction bill on June 18, and during the next six days Wagner, the measure's floor general,

[19] 75 *Congressional Record*, 11081ff., 12519; Wagner speech file, May 25, 1932, RFW Papers. On the Dawes matter see Arthur M. Schlesinger, Jr., *The Crisis of the Old Order, 1919–1933* (Boston, 1957), p. 238.
[20] Files on "Relief and Construction Act, 1932," RFW Papers; *New York Times*, May 21, 1932; New York *Herald Tribune*, May 27, 1932.

labored incessantly to pilot his handiwork to enactment. (After the third day of debate a number of senators appealed to Wagner to spare them from what was becoming a steady diet of night sessions. Bob, realizing that not everyone had profited from the experience in marathon legislating that he had absorbed at Albany, relented somewhat on behalf of his less robust colleagues.) The section of the bill authorizing the RFC to lend $300 million to the states for relief purposes was approved with little difficulty, although a handful of ultraconservative Republicans refused to abide by even President Hoover's endorsement of that indirect form of federal "dole." "The historian of the future," intoned Pennsylvania's Senator David A. Reed, "who writes, perhaps, upon the decline and fall of the American Republic, will point to today as one of the milestones upon the road to the disintegration of this Government." Unfortunately for the cause of orthodoxy, only seven other members stood with Reed in defense of what they chose to regard as "the sacred laws of economics." [21]

With respect to the other sections of the bill, however, Wagner had to parry a multitude of amendments that would either strip it of its usefulness, or so broaden its content as to invite a veto from the White House. Democratic Senator Millard Tydings of Maryland, who denounced federal financing of local and private construction activities as "state socialism, state communism," sought unsuccessfully to strike out of the measure every section except the roadbuilding one. Speaking for the Administration, on the other hand, was Senator George H. Moses of New Hampshire, who entered a motion to remove the federal public works program—Wagner's favorite provision. But in an impressive vote of confidence in the bill's author, the Senate rejected Moses' amendment 57–19.

Equally troublesome were the amendments offered by the members of the progressive contingent, most of which involved spending more money than anyone believed the President would approve. The colorful and somewhat eccentric Senator Henry Ashurst of Arizona, for example, wanted the RFC to lend money to Indians living on the plains reservations, accepting their handmade blankets as collateral. John H. Bankhead of Alabama proposed that the lending agency finance a "back to the soil" movement that would return unemployed city workers to the farms from which they had migrated, an idea that would be revived by some New Dealers in the near future. Senators like La Follette, Costigan, Norris, and J. Hamilton Lewis of Illinois— the latter resplendent in his pink whiskers, purple trousers, yellow

---

[21] 75 *Congressional Record*, 12533. The Senate debates on the Emergency Relief and Construction Act of 1932 may be followed in the *Record*, Vol. 75, beginning at p. 13341, or in the newspapers beginning June 18, 1932.

waistcoat, and faun-colored cutaway—complained that Wagner's bill was too modest, and La Follette offered his long-pending $5.5 billion bond issue measure as a substitute.

Wagner sympathized with many of these voices on the left. "However, I have a practical question in mind," he invariably stated. "I really want to see legislation enacted. Even though it might not go to the limit to which I would like to see it go, and though it might not be quite as adequate as I would like to see it, I am praying for a start somewhere, and I do not want to be in a position of advocating legislation which I am told ahead of time will not be approved." [22]

In the end Bob's legislative generalship carried the day: not a single floor amendment that he opposed, whether from the left or from the right, was added to the measure. The bill the Senate adopted on June 24 was, in all essentials, the one Wagner had introduced a month earlier.

Still, there was the lower house of Congress to contend with. There Representative John Nance Garner of Texas, who assumed the speakership when the Democrats took control of the House in 1931, had not hitherto distinguished himself in the field of antidepression legislation. By the spring of 1932 Garner entertained presidential aspirations, however, and in June he hastily put together a relief and construction bill that differed from the Senate measure mainly in that it opened the RFC's coffers for loans to "any person"—which meant not merely states and corporations but every individual in the country. President Hoover vowed to reject any bill embodying that "pork barrel" provision, but the lower chamber passed it nonetheless. When Wagner together with Senators Peter Norbeck of South Dakota and Smith W. Brookhart of Iowa entered into conference with their House counterparts to iron out differences, they found the congressmen so determined in their support of the Speaker that they were forced to give in. The bill, including Garner's pet scheme, went to the White House on July 9; as expected, Hoover immediately vetoed it.

During the next two weeks Wagner and the other more realistic leaders of both houses labored furiously to undo the damage. The House finally agreed to remove Garner's monkey wrench from the machinery and on July 21 the President set his signature to a relief and construction bill that had been in gestation since December. "Naturally," commented Wagner in a brief statement, "I am gratified." [23]

[22] 75 *Congressional Record*, 13352.
[23] *Ibid.*, pp. 14944ff; *New York Times*, July 12, 22, 1932; Wagner speech file, July 23, 1932, RFW Papers.

Nevertheless, Wagner could not regard the act, as signed, a complete victory—"so rocky has been its road." Especially disappointing to him was the fact that in the closing stages of the battle, and despite the Senate's overwhelming concurrence in his position, he had been forced to yield to presidential pressure with regard to his cherished federal public works program. Unable to excise that provision entirely from the bill, the Administration wrung from Wagner the concession that the works should be financed by regular Treasury methods rather than through a special bond issue, and exacted the even more damaging stipulation that any particular project should not be launched if, according to the Secretary of the Treasury, the money to finance its prosecution was not available and could not be borrowed on reasonable terms. Wagner feared, with good reason, that the surrender sounded the death knell for the energetic type of pump-priming federal construction program that was needed.

But despite the major blemishes that marred the Emergency Relief and Construction Act of 1932, its historical significance was great. For the first time, however indirectly, the federal government committed itself to a positive role in providing outright relief for the unemployed and, despite a myriad of qualifications, to the stimulation of a public works program that far overshadowed any previous effort. In the words of its principle author, the act "wrote into law the position which I have continuously maintained: that modern unemployment is a consequence of national developments which must be dealt with, not as a purely local concern, but as a national problem." The New York lawmaker could also take pride in the fact that the legislation was popularly referred to as the Wagner Act—"a rare honor," said *Time*, "for a Democrat in a Republican Senate." "The Wagner bill is not miscalled," added *The New York Times*, for it was the Empire State's junior senator who, "diligent, consistent, and conciliatory . . . did the most to persuade the Senate, the Treasury, and the President of its wisdom." A more westerly newspaper, with greater justice, joined La Follette and Costigan with Wagner as the senators who, "it may be said without hesitation, forced a showdown and won." [24]

The St. Louis *Star* feared, however, that, as in the past, while "the pioneers do the fighting, the resisters reap the reward." And surely enough, President Hoover and other Administration spokesmen moved swiftly to claim for themselves whatever political benefits might flow from enactment of the new antidepression law. In a

[24] Wagner speech file, July 23, 1932, RFW Papers; *Time*, July 11, 1932, p. 4; *New York Times*, undated clipping in RFW Papers; St. Louis *Star*, May 13, 1932.

statement following Senate passage of the measure Hoover congratulated the lawmakers on adopting "the major provisions"—relief and
construction loans to the states—"for which I have been contending";
he neglected to mention, of course, that he had been "contending"
for them for little more than a month. During the fall election campaign Republicans even claimed credit for the construction work due
to be launched under the Act's federal public works section, which
they had done so much to scuttle; in a Cincinnati speech Hoover
himself pointed to the prospective construction of a new post office in
that city as one of his measures for fighting the depression!

But the pioneers did reap the harvest in November, and the resisters reaped only a whirlwind. The election returns signified that a
great many Americans concurred in Bob Wagner's verdict on the
President's role in the precedent-shattering legislative session of 1932.
"It may well be," Wagner told his weary Senate colleagues as they
brought their labors to an end, "that within the silence of his own
heart [the President] approved of legislation for relief of the country
from the blighting effects of unemployment. If so, he very effectively
concealed his purpose from Congress until after every item which
constitutes the relief and construction bill had already been proposed
in this body." [25]

The legislative business of Congress carried well into the beginning of the political season of 1932; by the time the lawmakers adjourned in July the Republicans had renominated President Hoover
for a second term, and the Democrats had already picked their man to
make the race against him. Bob Wagner, whose rooms in Chicago for
the Democratic national convention were reserved as early as March,
was forced to miss the fireworks, a development he must have viewed
as a blessing. For as it turned out, the fireworks involved an explosion
between two of Wagner's closest friends, Al Smith and the man who
succeeded him as chief executive at Albany, Franklin D. Roosevelt.

After his defeat in 1928 Smith told his associates he would never
run for the presidency again, and thereafter Wagner, along with
others such as James A. Farley and Herbert H. Lehman, devoted
themselves to promoting Governor Roosevelt's ambitions. In the fall
of 1929, for example, Bob readily agreed to introduce a Senate resolution that would compel the Federal Power Commission to cooperate
with a Roosevelt-sponsored investigation of public utility corporations
in the state of New York; Louis McHenry Howe elatedly reported to

[25] St. Louis *Star*, May 13, 1932; *New York Times*, June 25, 1932; Wagner
speech file, June 25, Oct. 31, 1932, RFW Papers.

the governor that Wagner had invited him down to Washington to discuss "how we can squeeze the last ounce of publicity out of it." [26]

By the spring of 1932, however, and for reasons that his biographers still debate, Smith decided that he would like to make another run for the White House. Smith's decision put all of New York's Democratic leaders on the spot, and for none of them was the predicament more embarrassing than it was for Bob Wagner. When, at a Jefferson Day dinner in the spring, Smith "took off his coat" and accused Roosevelt of resorting to demagogic tactics in his bid for nomination, Wagner made himself scarce at the partying that followed the banquet so as to dissociate himself from the former governor's attack. On the other hand, when newspapers carried the rumor that the Senator would present Roosevelt's name to the Chicago convention, Smith was furious; in deference to his fellow East Sider's feelings, Wagner turned down the honor of nominating the man destined to become one of the nation's greatest Presidents.

Wagner's relations with both contenders dated back to the early years of the century, and he regarded both of them as progressives; he therefore refrained from any public participation in the fray, and his legislative duties in Washington afforded him a good excuse for doing so. But although his bonds of personal friendship were stronger with Al than with "Frank," Wagner had concluded that it would be wiser for the Democrats to avoid possible resurrection of the discreditable "issues" that had swamped Smith's candidacy four years earlier. The convention concurred in his private judgment, Roosevelt made the race, and in subsequent years a soured Al Smith moved further and further away from New Deal policies that were akin to those he had espoused at Albany. Yet through it all Bob and Al, despite frequent and heated arguments over public affairs, preserved the bonds of personal affection that earlier had linked them so closely together. When Smith died in 1946, it was Wagner who filed his will for probate.[27]

The Democratic state convention at Albany early in October presented Wagner with another political crisis, for it confronted him with the prospect of being drafted for a gubernatorial nomination that he did not want. The conclave provided the backdrop for a temporary reconciliation between Roosevelt and Smith, and among the objectives for which they worked in common was the nomination of

[26] RFW to Jack Bell, March 10, 1932, RFW Papers; Jeremiah T. Mahoney, interview; James A. Farley, *Behind the Ballots* (New York, 1938), p. 78; Howe to Roosevelt, Sept. 24, 1929, FDR Papers.

[27] Interviews with Howard Cullman, Jeremiah T. Mahoney, and Francis J. Quillinan, who was Wagner's law partner and Smith's son-in-law; RFW to Walter White, June 22, 1932, RFW Papers.

Roosevelt's lieutenant governor, Herbert H. Lehman, to be his successor. But the leaders of Tammany Hall and of the Brooklyn Democratic machine, anxious to reassert their authority, resisted. Unable to come up with any other attractive candidate of their own as an alternative to Lehman, the machine leaders at the last minute seized on a plan that Jim Farley, Roosevelt's manager, considered "a really smart piece of strategy." They suggested as a "compromise" that Lehman be sent to the Senate and that Wagner be drafted for the gubernatorial nomination. "There was no doubt," Farley recounted later, "that a vast majority of the delegates were ready to flock to [Wagner's] standard if the plan wasn't halted in rapid-fire order."

On his part, Wagner agreed that Lehman deserved the governorship; he himself was anxious to stay in the Senate, and he shared the sentiments of a friend who advised him that "Governors come and go—maximum sentence generally four years. Usually forgotten in four months." [28] When he arrived in Albany, therefore, Bob was determined to resist the pressure of the dissident leaders to gain his complicity in their plan. For a while he went to the extreme of "holing up" in an out-of-the-way hotel so as to avoid even the physical possibility of their overtures! So great did the threat to party harmony become, however, that toward the end Jim Farley felt Wagner to be on the verge of consenting to the draft. That contingency was avoided when Lehman, summoning up all his courage just an hour or so before the convention was scheduled to open, told a smoke-filled room full of Tammany and Brooklyn leaders that he would under no circumstances accept nomination to the Senate. Fearing to create a scene on the floor of the convention, the insurgents finally backed down; a short time later the delegates nominated Lehman for the governorship, and Wagner, his face wreathed in smiles, accepted renomination to the United States Senate. [29]

Following a brief vacation in the Adirondacks, Wagner embarked in the fall on the kind of strenuous campaign for which he had become noted and which usually caused the slightly built Simon Rifkind to lose ten or more pounds. In his speeches Wagner concentrated on the six-year history of his efforts, against Administration

[28] Farley, *Behind the Ballots*, p. 174; Charles Fleisch to RFW, May 12, 1932, RFW Papers.

[29] Farley, *Behind the Ballots*, pp. 174–176; Allan Nevins, *Herbert H. Lehman and His Era* (New York, 1963), pp. 127–131; interviews with Simon H. Rifkind, Isador Lubin, and Warren Moscow, who was for many years a political reporter with *The New York Times*. Rifkind and Lubin, who were at the convention with Wagner, deny that the Senator ever weakened in his determination to resist being drafted for the governorship. According to Rifkind, Wagner regarded the governorship as "a pip-squeak job."

opposition, to inaugurate antidepression measures by the federal government. Sometimes, in the heat of political battle, Bob indulged in
overstatement, as when he characterized Hoover's approach to the
depression as an adherence to "blind traditionalism." That was an in-
justice to the President, whose policies had gone a long way in breaking with the past. And although Wagner sometimes pointed out that
emphasis on balancing the budget might endanger "the humane part
of government, which in my judgment has been neglected too much,"
at other times he made the unalloyed promise that his party's victory
would bring a change "from the Republican policy of deficits to a
policy of balanced budgets and reduced government expenditures."
His neglect on such occasions to mention the distinction that he usually made in Senate debates between the government's ordinary expenses and its emergency, antidepression expenditures was a serious
sin of omission from the standpoint of those who view election campaigns as media for mass education. But in committing it Wagner was
joined by those who wrote the Democratic platform and by virtually
every Democratic candidate from Roosevelt on down.[30]

Wagner was at his best when, moving beyond the more immediate issues of relief and recovery, he dwelt on his vision of the better
future that a Democratic victory would help bring about—that is, on
the need for reform. Complaining that "too many feel that our objective is limited to a return to the conditions prevailing in 1928 and
1929," which underneath their tinsel were themselves symptomatic
of a diseased social condition, Wagner condemned President Hoover's
failure to realize that the events of the last three years had produced
"a spiritual reawakening" in America. "He continues to live in his
little world of radios, telephones and automobiles," said Wagner on
one occasion, "which he uses as the yard-stick of our progress." But
"of what use," the Senator asked again and again, "are material resources and scientific resourcefulness, all our equipment, our enterprise, and our efficiency, if the sum total of human happiness enjoyed
by our people—*all* our people—be not increased thereby?" The time
had come, the New York Senator insisted, "to go forward to the conquest of the present-day economic frontiers as zealously and as successfully as the early pioneers conquered the physical frontiers, and the
men of the Revolution the political frontiers."

Throughout the campaign Wagner emphasized the larger social
needs of the nation without whose fulfillment there could be no "real
freedom" for Americans under modern conditions: "a progressively

[30] Simon H. Rifkind, interview; Wagner speech file, Oct. 17, 19, Nov. 1,
1932, RFW Papers.

increasing degree of regularity of employment," "some degree of economic security," "proper housing," "adequate professional care and hospitalization," the eradication of child labor, vocational training, "the shorter work day as a necessary corollary of the increasing productivity of labor," "the right to bargain on terms of equality for our place in the economic world," "a reasonable amount of leisure." It was a lengthy catalogue, going far beyond the objectives encompassed in the "Wagner bills" introduced thus far. And it indicated that, given the chance, the junior senator from New York would in the future attempt to induce the government to assume an even larger role in the nation's quest to guarantee the "real freedom" of security and opportunity demanded by the new frontier. For, as Wagner told one audience, "To preserve and enhance this freedom, and to bring it to a realization in richer lives, in expanded existence and nobler character—that I regard as the primary function and purpose of government." [31]

Despite many requests for appearances elsewhere, Wagner confined his campaign activities to New York State. He was a candidate for reelection himself, and even though virtually no one conceded his opponent a chance, Wagner "ran scared" as usual. He needn't have, for on election day he received more than 2.5 million votes compared to Republican George Z. Medalie's 1.75 million. His victory margin of 781,719 votes exceeded Roosevelt's New York plurality over Hoover by nearly 185,000, and as far as Simon Rifkind could determine, it established a record in senatorial elections throughout the nation's history. "The re-election of Senator Wagner," declared *The New York Times*, "was based on personal merit and solid achievement. For the splendid endorsement he has now had from his own State, the nation itself should be grateful." [32]

[31] Wagner speech file, 1932 campaign, *passim*, RFW Papers.

[32] Philip Levy to Simon H. Rifkind, Sept. 29, 1938, RFW Papers; *New York Times*, Nov. 10, 1932. For official election returns see New York (State) *Legislative Manual,* issued annually at Albany.

CHAPTER 8

The Key Man in Congress

THE DEMOCRATIC SWEEP in the fall of 1932 established the fact that New York's junior senator would be one of Washington's most important figures after March 4, 1933, and the capital's newsmen undertook to acquaint their readers with him. "He is a widower," explained one columnist, "lives in the most exclusive hotel in Washington, and is active socially. He is immaculately groomed at all times, is short—a bit rotund—has iron gray hair and is in a perpetual good humor. He is one of the most approachable men in the Senate. He is 'Bob' to his friends, and those who know and admire him refer to him in this manner."

Time's thumbnail sketch painted a similar portrait: "In appearance he is short, thick-set, broad-faced." ("His expansive, ruddy Teuton countenance has a bartender's veracity," was the way another writer expressed it.) "He dresses smartly in grays and browns. From his watch chain dangles a Phi Beta Kappa key. He smokes cigars. His command of language is good, but his diction has still a touch of the Tammany East Side ('woik,' 'goil'). Because he is mild, friendly, approachable in manner, his popularity with the press gallery is great." [1]

Thus it would appear that the years had not changed Bob Wagner very much from the man whom Albany correspondents described two decades earlier. Certain physical characteristics had become more pronounced: the firm mouth that had a way of drooping at the cor-

[1] Clipping from an unidentified St. Louis newspaper, *ca.* 1932, RFW Papers; *Time*, July 11, 1932, p. 4; New York *Telegram*, Feb. 19, 1931.

ners when he was in a serious mood, the prominent lower lip that protruded noticeably at such times, and the strong chin that "would suggest a contentious nature if the heavy-lidded blue eyes were not so mild and friendly." He also had a weight problem, which his penchant for midnight snacks—usually in the form of tartar steaks— didn't help; an incipient bald spot, which cooperative barbers managed to keep under cover, bothered him too. But withal the inner man remained unchanged, and a writer in the 1930s listed virtually the same catalogue of Wagnerian "assets" that an Albany newspaper cited in 1913: "fundamental honesty and sincerity . . . a rugged constitution, an easy, urbane manner . . . vast capacity for work . . . humility." [2]

That quality of humility, "one of Wagner's most engaging traits," went a long way in accounting for the fact that, despite his importance in the nation's lawmaking circles, he remained "a blurred and shadowy figure" in the public eye. "An unassuming man," noted one observer, "sincere and unaffected, he has neither the desire nor the talent for self-exploitation." He lacked the flair of showmanship that friends like Al Smith, and senatorial colleagues like Huey Long and J. Hamilton Lewis, possessed to a consummate degree. He had no real or contrived eccentricities to capitalize. "He never plays to the galleries, and he abhors the tawdry insincerities of the vote-catcher." The truth was, as more than one reporter concluded, "that Wagner does not put on a good show." Some of Bob's colleagues, Senator Burton K. Wheeler, for instance, thought that a very odd thing indeed, considering that Wagner had been bred as a Tammany politician. [3]

There had been times during his Albany career when Wagner was more bumptiously aggressive, as when the Republican majority leader there accused him in 1915 of turning the State Senate into a Punch and Judy show. But it would appear that even then Wagner's adoption of "gymnastic" debating techniques was something of a forced posture. Throughout his life his personality was marked by a basically conservative, self-conscious shyness; Senator Henry Ashurst, after half a century in the game, commented that he had never seen "such a sensitive man in politics." Why, Wagner would actually *blush,*

[2] *New York Times,* July 9, 1932; John C. O'Brien, "Robert F. Wagner: Pilot of the New Deal," in J. T. Salter, ed., *The American Politician* (New York, 1938), p. 114; interviews with Jeremiah T. Mahoney and Theodore Granik, a lawyer and publicist who was a companion of Wagner's, particularly on campaign trips.

[3] O'Brien, "Robert F. Wagner," pp. 109, 114; Burton K. Wheeler, interview.

Ashurst added, if in the course of debate on the Senate floor he made a slip of some kind or mispronounced a word! [4]

In any event, age and his years of service as a "calm judge" ended any tendency that Wagner might have been developing toward flamboyance and dramatics. Far more important was his perception of the inner workings of the legislative machinery as it operated in the United States Senate. He was not the spokesman for his party's delegation there, and even if he had been, there was no Charles F. Murphy to crack the whip and force recalcitrants into line behind a prearranged party program. The Senate was a collection of ninety-six individualists, and even the Democrats represented widely different sections, classes, and interests. There could be no bulldozing, and "early in his first term he abandoned the idea that the way to be effective was to make two or three speeches a week."

To a reporter the socially conscious New Yorker once acknowledged that it was harder to get things done in Washington than at Albany, "because what can a man do to convert a lot of traditional thinkers who get up, stick their hands under their coat-tails and dilate on the way their fathers and grandfathers used to live?" In the end, of course, Wagner—"the one real product of life in a modern crowded city in the Senate," a journalist called him in 1931, "the first thoroughly urban member of the Upper House"—made a lot of converts. How did he do it, this "small, stocky, inconspicuous, gray-haired senator, who moves toward his objectives as irresistibly as a glacier?" [5]

The first secret of Wagner's success lay in his determination to limit his legislative program to manageable proportions. "He concentrated his energies upon a few subjects," *The New York Times* once wrote, "and became an authority to whom the whole country looked." He was no legislative gadfly. While some of his colleagues regarded themselves as "experts" on every topic under the sun—and even more senators have adopted that pose since his time—Wagner prudently chose almost at the outset to center his attention on the problem of promoting economic and social security in an industrial, urban age. But even so, he adhered rigidly to his resolve never to overextend his lines, and on more than one occasion during the 1930s he turned down requests that he sponsor antidepression or social-reform bills with which he sympathized, simply because he was already too busy to give them the kind of painstaking legislative care they de-

[4] Henry Ashurst, interview.
[5] O'Brien, "Robert F. Wagner," p. 115; Owen P. White, "When the Public Needs a Friend," *Collier's*, June 2, 1934, p. 60; Syracuse *Herald*, March 10, 1931; Beverly Smith, "Thanks to Brother Gus," *American Magazine* (Dec. 1939), p. 83.

served. The men in the Senate press gallery knew, we are told, that "Wagner always comes through with one or two big bills each session," and they knew also that "He never scatters his fire." [6]

Next there was the New York lawmaker's well-known willingness to accept—indeed, his reliance on—tutoring from those whose intellectual endowments, or at least expertise, exceeded his own. "He is not brilliant," those who wrote about him frequently said, but "he is eager to learn from anyone who knows more about a subject than he does." In these early years he relied a great deal on Simon Rifkind, who *was* brilliant. But Rifkind, too, considered himself only an amateur in economics; his main function was to serve as a contact in bringing into his boss's purview the thinking of the most advanced social science experts. Isador Lubin ("Doc" to the Senator) was another collaborator in that process. All three men enjoyed "picking other fellow's brains"; authorities like William Trufant Foster, and others who would later become authorities, such as Paul H. Douglas, were frequent visitors in Wagner's office. There was an active correspondence between Wagner's staff and specialists throughout the country, while groups like the American Association for Labor Legislation, the League of Women Voters, and the Russell Sage Foundation kept the New York Senator well supplied with reports of their studies and recommendations. "No member of Congress makes more frequent use of the research facilities of the Brookings Institution," wrote one observer; the same report might have been made by officials of the Legislative Reference Bureau, the Bureau of Labor Statistics, and other governmental agencies that Wagner's office constantly "pestered." [7]

Frequently, the end result of that study and research was the introduction of another "Wagner bill." The origin of the measure might sometimes be traced to an outline, scribbled in Wagner's handwriting, on a piece of Shoreham Hotel stationery or on the back of a letter (that went unanswered) from a constituent. Before it found its way into the legislative hopper, of course, the measure went through numerous revisions and refinements; as in the old days at Albany, Wagner scrutinized each word in the draft to make sure it would "hold water." Such periods were excruciating ones for Simon Rifkind

[6] *New York Times*, Nov. 10, 1932; O'Brien, "Robert F. Wagner," pp. 114–115; interviews with Simon H. Rifkind, Isador Lubin, Leon H. Keyserling, and others. For an incisive description of Wagner's character and legislative techniques see also Leon H. Keyserling, "The Wagner Act: Its Origin and Current Significance," *George Washington Law Review* (Dec. 1960), pp. 119ff.

[7] Smith, "Thanks to Brother Gus," p. 83; O'Brien, "Robert F. Wagner," p. 115; interviews with Simon H. Rifkind and Isador Lubin.

and the bill-drafting experts whom he consulted in the Senate's Office of Legislative Counsel. But they were trying times for Bob Wagner too, and we have the word of people who knew him well that, unlike those (including Franklin Roosevelt) who were able to leave their public business outside the bedroom, Wagner sometimes spent sleepless nights worrying about the wording of a bill or the phrasing of a resolution. He was deeply afflicted with what the reporters called a "Teutonic passion for thoroughness." [8]

The same meticulous care went into building the case Wagner would present for his bill at committee hearings. He knew that this stage of the legislative process, behind closed doors, and *not* the open debate on the floor of the chamber, was usually the crucial one in the life, mutilation, or death of a proposal. He oversaw the prearrangements for it—the assembling and rehearsing of witnesses, the preparation of statements and briefs, the moves to counter the anticipated arguments of opponents—with all the care and finesse of a theatrical producer. And always the emphasis was on the presentation of "facts," the kinds of evidence, statistics, and case histories that, years earlier, had swept away opposition to the Triangle Commission's recommendations. It was in the committee room itself, we're told, that Wagner was at his best. "He is affable, intent, patient, persuasive," one reporter wrote. "He never tires of answering questions, never impugns the motives of his opponents. At the same time, as fast as the committee's digestion permits, he pours in the facts." [9]

Of course speech-making, in the Senate and in other public forums, was a necessary adjunct to the lawmaking process, and the fact that this was so occasioned many other uneasy moments for Wagner and for Simon Rifkind, who served as his "ghost." A Wagner speech (or an article for publication) normally originated in an outline, composed by the Senator, of what he wanted to say; it was up to Rifkind to devise the manner of saying it. But the ghost had a strict taskmaster, and his handiwork stood rigid inspection before Wagner consented to make Rifkind's words his own. There were two main tests that the Senator applied: one, as might be expected, was factual accuracy—the verification of a single paragraph in the text might send Rifkind to the telephone for a score of calls to the experts; the other test centered on clarity, for Wagner had no use for "high-flown" or pedantic language. Time and again Rifkind encountered a stern

[8] Marguerite Cummins Hayes, interview; O'Brien, "Robert F. Wagner," p. 115. The outlines and successive drafts of numerous Wagner bills are preserved in the RFW Papers.

[9] Smith, "Thanks to Brother Gus," p. 84. Materials relevant to committee hearings on various Wagner bills are to be found in the RFW Papers.

"What does this *really* mean?" followed by an admonition to simplify the passage in question.

The finished product of their labors (Rifkind recalled that one speech went through fourteen drafts) was never a flowery oration, and Wagner seldom "packed the galleries" the way a Huey Long did periodically. But his Senate colleagues "always give him a respectful hearing," the men in the press section noted, and the verdict that the Baltimore *Sun's* Frank R. Kent passed on the content and style of Wagner's maiden speech held true for the New Yorker's oratorical efforts throughout his career in Washington. "His speech," Kent wrote on March 9, 1928, "was the speech of a careful, conservative man who makes sure of his facts before presentation, and bases his conclusions on them.[10]

Over the years, however, Wagner spent only the barest minimum of time in the Senate chamber making speeches or listening to those of others. "He relies on his persuasiveness in the cloak room more than on debate on the floor to win support for his measures." "He likes and respects his colleagues," wrote another analyst of Wagner's legislative technique, "and they return the compliment, which helps a lot."

On the point of Wagner's charm and tactfulness the evidence is overwhelming: one colleague thought he summed it all up by remarking to news commentator William Hard, as early as 1929, "I can't believe he is a Tammany man." In large part Bob's pleasant demeanor toward his senatorial peers was a natural reflection of his personality, and he manifested the same manner in his relations with friends, newspapermen, and even strangers. Yet when he had an important bill pending, his ingratiating qualities seemed to activate themselves, perhaps unconsciously, to the point where they became a potent element in the lawmaking process. Simon Rifkind remembers being "fascinated" by the "transformation" Wagner underwent at those times, and he marveled at the dexterity with which his boss carried out his part, "like a great actor who has absorbed a role." The New Yorker would become unusually sociable with his colleagues and uncommonly solicitous about their affairs, inquiring of the key figures about everything ranging from bills they themselves had introduced to the status of their golf scores. Certainly these were the arts of the politician, and Wagner's absorption of them had begun early; by the

[10] Simon H. Rifkind, interview; Wagner speech files, *passim*, RFW Papers; O'Brien, "Robert F. Wagner," p. 115; Baltimore *Sun*, March 9, 1928. With characteristic directness, former President Harry S Truman informed the author in an interview that "When Bob Wagner got up to speak, you knew that you were going to hear the facts, and not a lot of bull shit."

1930s he had become, in Rifkind's words, "a virtuoso, masterfully employing every proper technique" available in the process of winning the friendship and good will of his fellow senators.[11]

That Wagner won his way into the Senate's "inner circle" is beyond doubt; that he did it so quickly is remarkable. As early as 1929, when Frances Perkins made her first appearance before a Senate committee in favor of a Wagner bill, she was "amazed" at the deference that New York's junior senator already enjoyed at the Capitol. A few months later Frederic William Wile, the Washington *Star*'s political columnist, noted that "Wagner is one of the few—the very few— newcomers to the United States Senate in recent years who have speedily made places for themselves on the Hill. He now commands genuine respect there." If there existed in those days the sort of Senate "club" that William S. White has written about—a select group of "insiders" whose word carried much greater weight than that of senators who were mere "outsiders"—Bob Wagner was admitted to it in his first term. And that was another reason why so many Wagner bills became laws.[12]

Despite all the factors working in his favor, however, it often took a long time for Wagner's ideas to be put on the statute books. And here another of the Senator's traits, persistence, came into play. "Opposition does not discourage him," newsmen wrote, and they quoted with approval his own ascription of his achievements to "plodding." Despite the zeal with which Wagner believed in the measures that he sponsored—when S. J. Woolf interviewed him on the relief and construction bill in 1932, Wagner's hand struck the glass plate covering his desk so repeatedly and forcefully that the reporter feared it would "fly into splinters"—patience and tenacity were the virtues that he counseled his supporters to follow. He believed that dogged determination, plus a pragmatic willingness to compromise, to take half a loaf rather than nothing, and just to "get the camel's nose under the tent" as a beginning, were the tactics that would bring ultimate success. And more often than not, they did.[13]

The importance of one other element in any description of Wagner's effectiveness as a lawmaker deserves reiteration, and that was the role played by those individuals and groups who, for altruistic, self-

[11] O'Brien, "Robert F. Wagner," p. 115; Smith, "Thanks to Brother Gus," p. 84; text of radio broadcast by William Hard, Nov. 25, 1929, in RFW Papers; Simon H. Rifkind, interview.

[12] Frances Perkins, interview; Washington *Star*, Aug. 4, 1930; William S. White, *Citadel: The Story of the United States Senate* (New York, 1957).

[13] O'Brien, "Robert F. Wagner," pp. 114–115; *New York Times*, July 9, 1932.

interested, or mixed reasons, applied grass-roots pressure on behalf of the progressive measures he introduced. Some observers, Senator Henry Ashurst among them, thought that was all there was to it. "If a Wagner bill failed to pass on the first try, or the second or the third," the Arizona senator related, "he or its backers would cause letters to be sent out to important constituents of those who had voted no. Next time around Wagner would rise, be recognized, and call up the bill. Everybody expected a speech, but he'd just have the bill's first paragraph read, and move passage. Some of its previous opponents would change their votes, and eventually it would pass. Wagner then retired to obscurity, to start work on another bill."

It wasn't that simple of course. But certainly, as indicated earlier, Wagner appreciated the debt he owed to a vast network of behind-the-scenes supporters. He actively solicited their help, and advised them in the ways to make it most effective. At times the complexity and scope of their operations even became embarrassing to the Senator, as when, during the 1930 campaign for his Three Bills, an enthusiastic constituent and admirer urged him to take the initiative in raising funds to finance a wide-scale propaganda campaign for the measures. Wagner's answer was symptomatic of his sensitive code of ethics: "I have been somewhat in doubt as to the exact limits that propriety sets upon my own efforts in securing the organization of support in behalf of the legislation, especially when it assumes such proportions that funds are necessary for its conduct." His chagrined correspondent quickly agreed with the implicit suggestion that someone else take the initiative in that direction. But after all, those letters that made such an impression on Senator Ashurst did cost money, and certainly, therefore, the funds expended over the years by numerous groups such as the A.A.L.L., the League of Women Voters, labor unions, and the N.A.A.C.P. on behalf of measures for which Bob Wagner stood as legislative spokesman deserve to be mentioned. (And so do the much larger amounts spent by his opponents!) [14]

Thus read the prescription for success as a lawmaker developed by Bob Wagner on the basis of experience dating back to his early days in the New York legislature. It's evident that the Senator depended on a lot of people—ranging from progressive-minded individuals who contributed dollars, to groups like the Consumers' League, through a whole assortment of "experts"—and he depended particularly on Isador Lubin and Simon Rifkind. Indeed, some people, observing that dependence at close range, wondered whether the Sena-

[14] Henry Ashurst, interview; RFW to Samuel Joseph, Nov. 29, 1930, RFW Papers.

tor "does anything for himself," and whether he really deserved any credit at all for what passed as "Wagner bills." That question suggested itself to Milton Handler, a young lawyer and friend of Simon Rifkind's, who in the early days of the New Deal joined the trek to Washington and was thus able to view Wagner's mode of operation from a "ringside seat." But years later Handler learned for himself the degree to which "important" and busy men must rely on the assistance of others. He realized then that he had earlier formed a distorted impression of the Senator's role, and he aptly enumerated Wagner's own vital contributions to his legislative reputation as follows: "First, his ingrained, humanitarian, progressive philosophy; second, his uncanny capacity to recruit good men to do the detail work for him; third, his masterful ability to maneuver bills through the legislative mill; and fourth, and most important of all, his willingness and determination to stick to his basic convictions through thick and thin—in a word, his 'guts.' " [15]

Many congressmen have followed formulas different from Wagner's; a good many of them have gotten much more publicity; and a few have also earned reputations as the progenitors of significant pieces of legislation that have vitally affected the nation's course. Yet of no other modern American lawmaker can it be said, as one journalist wrote of Wagner during the 1930s, that "whether you like his laws or deplore them, he has placed on the books legislation more important and far-reaching than any American in history, since the days of the Founding Fathers." [16]

Wagner's proposals were important and far-reaching, of course, precisely *because* they seemed to run counter to the doctrines of individualism and *laissez faire* usually ascribed to the founding fathers, and especially to those among them whom Wagner's own party had enshrined. He was conscious of that, and conscious too of the firm hold "the old slogans" had on the popular imagination. Again and again, particularly in addresses before gatherings of Democratic partisans, he strove to justify his deviation from the Jeffersonian phrases traditionally dear to the hearts of Democratic orators. Insisting that those who placed their faith in a return to "the fundamentals of the Fathers of the Republic" were unrealistic, Wagner maintained that the nature of the major issues facing the American people in the twentieth century had changed radically since the time of the revolutionary generation. That generation's problems had been essentially

[15] Milton Handler, interview.
[16] Smith, "Thanks to Brother Gus," p. 42.

political—"security against the arbitrary action of a sovereign, freedom of speech, freedom of the press and religion, and personal participation in government"—and "the foundations which they built . . . are still firm and true."

But in the intervening decades, and particularly since the Civil War, Wagner maintained, the effects of industrialism had remade the nation economically and socially; the major task of its people now must be "to translate the virtues, aspirations and ideals of a rural people so as to serve in the development and progress of an urban people." That readjustment might well necessitate considerable broadening of the functions of government. "But where in industry, in commerce, or even in agriculture," Wagner asked, "do we find conditions and methods today which duplicate those of one hundred years ago? Is it not folly to assume that the whole economic structure of the country can change without involving some adjustment in government?" To Wagner the conclusion seemed inescapable: America must stop attempting "to live in a twentieth-century world with the ideals of a world that has long since disappeared." [17]

But if Wagner rejected the approach of those who futilely sought answers to modern problems in "the formulas of the distant past," he was equally scornful of impatient utopians who "riveted their eyes solely upon the distant land of their dreams," of those who "hope for a Napoleon to give them the spurious efficiency of despotism," and of "the radical who would remake us overnight." While insisting that capitalism must mend its ways and that "business stability, steady employment, and reasonable security can, very much like good health, be purchased for the price of planning, foresight, and preventive action," he was equally determined that reform be achieved through "cooperation between equals, not regimentation." "We do not want that kind of security which will close the avenues of opportunity to the enterprising and the daring," Wagner stated on another occasion. "We do not want the kind of stability which will stall the business machinery of the country. We do not want the steadiness of poverty and idleness. The goal to be achieved is not inertia, but equilibrium." [18]

Nevertheless, mindful that the distress produced by depression was unleashing revolutionary tides of unrest among masses of disillusioned people both at home and abroad, Wagner warned: "If we would conserve this civilization we must take the initiative. We cannot wait until others who see in it nothing of value tear it up by its

[17] Wagner speech file, Jan. 18, 1930, April 8, June 7, 1931, an undated speech prepared during the summer of 1931, and Nov. 24, 1931, RFW Papers.
[18] *Ibid.*, April 8, Sept. 1, 1931, and July 4, Oct. 18, Nov. 6, 1932.

roots. The next move is ours."

What was needed was not an entirely new order but "a more precise and more humane organization of the existing order." The steps to be taken in that reorganization could not be determined with exactness at the outset, for "in the large effort to ameliorate social conditions, and to introduce order into economic life, there are no fixed and ultimate goals. The goal posts of today become the sign posts of tomorrow." But from the standpoint of 1931, Wagner felt that the direction in which the beginning must be made was clearly visible: "A steadily increasing measure of security, a steadily rising standard of living, a steadily lengthening period of leisure well spent, a never ending increase in the value and nobility of life—we can do no better than to devote ourselves without stint to make that the history of our country." And time and again, in a score of variations, he reiterated that "the method we should adhere to is to accept nothing as final simply because it is old; to reject nothing as undesirable simply because it is new, but rather by the process of continual testing, to preserve the best of yesterday and improve it with the best of today." Though that process might outrage the reactionary who regarded the past as untouchable, "we must have no sacred white elephant." Rather "piece by piece, section by section," the better world of the future must be contrived "out of the very world we live in, by introducing order where chaos now reigns, by subjecting to plan what now moves haphazardly." [19]

Despite the tones of down-to-earth realism that permeated Wagner's liberalism, his words were strong medicine indeed for many of his colleagues during his first term as a senator. Right-wing Republicans regarded them as rank heresy, of course, and never tired of expressing amazement, as Hiram Bingham did during debate on the unemployment exchange bill, that such measures as Wagner's should emanate from a member of "the states rights party." And although insurgent Republicans like Robert La Follette and "radical" Democrats like Edward Costigan concurred in Wagner's sentiments, they were at all times a small minority of the Senate, and incapable by themselves of enacting progressive programs. Moreover, while Wagner valued their friendship and welcomed their support for his measures, his strong sense of party loyalty inhibited him from casting his lot irrevocably with theirs; in 1931, when George Norris called a series of meetings in an attempt to forge a bipartisan progressive bloc of independents in Congress, Wagner declined to attend. He insisted on

[19] *Ibid.*, April 8, June 7, 1931, and Oct. 18, 22, 1932; Robert F. Wagner, "Danger Ahead! A Frank Warning," *Liberty*, July 23, 1932, pp. 6–9.

working primarily through his own party and on making it the main
instrument of leadership toward "the ever-widening horizon" of
social betterment, even though that involved the necessity of con-
verting to his way of thinking some of its leading statesmen who, almost as much as the conservative Republicans, were given to "piously
uttering the ancient slogans." [20]

It was in this process of readying the "respectable" senatorial
Democrats for the task of reform they would soon be called on to
shoulder that Bob Wagner performed his most notable *political* service during the Hoover years. Through instruction, through his sincerity, and through persistence Wagner helped convince his more conservative Democratic brethren—even some of the Southerners among
them—that "we cannot find the answers to our modern problems in
the locker of history, no matter how fervently we search." They came
to trust his knowledge and judgment on industrial problems, and
gradually accepted his admonition that "The traditions we cherish
cannot endure in a world . . . distracted by hunger." His command
of the political arts, and particularly his pragmatic willingness to settle
for less than the ideal, enabled him to begin bridging the gap between
the Senate's regular Democrats and its progressive insurgents—between the men to whom party ties bound him and those with whom
he was identified ideologically—and to weld them into an effective,
working majority. Perhaps it was for this reason that during the relief
debates of 1932 the Peoples' Lobby, an organization of advanced reformers presided over by John Dewey, cited Wagner as "the key man
in Congress." [21]

In short, between 1927 and 1933 Bob Wagner played somewhat
the same role in the United States Senate as he had much earlier in
the New York legislature, namely, that of helping to bring the Democratic party abreast of the twentieth century. Of course, on the national level the swift movement of dire events in the Great Depression
aided in that process, and soon the leadership of Franklin Roosevelt
would help carry it further. But it was important to the cause of modern liberalism that a man of unimpeachable party loyalty, and a member of the Senate "club," had been available early to proclaim that
"The Democratic Party can well afford to plead guilty to the charge
. . . that we are dreamers." For, as Wagner asserted, "If a govern-

[20] RFW Papers: RFW to Minna L. Ruppert, March 10, 1931; Wagner
speech file, April 8, 1931, and Oct. 29, 1932.
[21] Wagner speech file, April 8, 1931, RFW Papers; Wagner, "Danger
Ahead!," p. 6; copy of Peoples' Lobby press release, dated April 18, 1932, RFW
Papers.

ment or a people is to progress, its goal must ever be a little beyond its reach." [22]

Wagner's deep involvement in the political and ideological reformation that began to affect Washington in the early years of the Great Depression left him little time for attending to the routine chores that accompanied his office as a senator and his profession as a politician. He was just as well pleased, for such matters as answering mail or arranging "favors" left him cold. "I could answer a hundred letters a day, and do three favors," he once remarked to Simon Rifkind, "and what would it mean? One hundred and three votes. Why not concentrate on the big things that affect millions?" The reporter who singled out Wagner's "sure sense of the difference between the trivial and the important" as a contributing factor to his stature knew the man well.[23]

As the more prominent of the two senators from the nation's most populous state, Wagner probably received more mail than any of his colleagues, averaging a thousand letters a day. Even though his staff grew—Simon Rifkind acquired a secretary of his own, and two, three, and then four typists were brought in to assist Minna Ruppert —they found it difficult to keep up with the deluge as more and more Americans turned toward the Capitol with their hopes, their fears, and their demands. Sometimes the letters were merely heartfelt notes of congratulation and encouragement. "I wish to God we had more Sen. Wagners in the world," wrote a Brooklyn housewife in 1932; "I feel the needy would have less to worry about." "If it were not for the honest, fearless men in our legislative halls, such as Borah, Johnson, Norris, La Follette, and yourself," stated an unemployed Sacramento railroad worker, "we would be forced to resort to violence, and revolution would be the outcome." From Philadelphia a landlord congratulated Wagner on "the excellent efforts put forth by you in behalf of an improvement for the laboring man which will, in fact, benefit conditions for all of us . . . If conditions keep on the way they are," added this property-owning correspondent, "we will all become reds." "I should be glad if you would write some more talks in the paper," said the wife of an Illinois miner who was on public relief, "and let the world know it is a job these men want and not charity." And a civil engineer of twenty years experience who had suddenly lost his position was happy that "There are a few in Congress, like your-

22 Wagner speech file, Sept. 26, 1932, RFW Papers.
23 Interviews with Simon H. Rifkind and Minna L. Ruppert; New York *World*, July 21, 1930.

self, who can force aside other business to support the main pillars of the temple." [24]

More often than not, however, the Senator's correspondents wanted something: passage or defeat of a particular bill; an appointment to discuss personal problems, a "business deal," or "a scheme to surely end the depression"; a job; a loan of money; an appointment to Annapolis; or intercession with the proper government bureau to arrange for a pension increase, an immigration visa, a patent on an invention, or a tariff adjustment. Such requests fell primarily into Minna Ruppert's province. On the "really tough nuts" (referring to both problems and persons) she sought Simon Rifkind's help; *very* rarely did she carry them to "the Boss" himself. With skill, tact, and diplomacy she handled even the oddest situations: the constituent who, having been told that a rapid change in barometric pressure might restore his hearing, wanted the Senator's secretary to arrange a ride for him in an Army airplane; the 106-year-old Indian chieftain seeking a letter of introduction to the President, who promised to make Miss Ruppert a princess of his tribe; a pension seeker, calling in person, who presented her with a handful of "mushrooms" he'd "just picked on the Capitol grounds." Within a short time Miss Ruppert, like her employer, made a name for herself in Washington; with numerous contacts in the Veterans Administration, Immigration Office, and other governmental bureaus, she became known as one of the best "fixers" on the Hill. Her devotion, and that of the others on Wagner's efficient staff, helped immeasurably in making it possible for the Senator to concentrate on "the big things." [25]

Not that Miss Ruppert, or anyone else connected with Wagner's office, was expected to "fix" anything that savored of impropriety. In his capacity as a lawyer, Wagner, according to Simon Rifkind, on more than one occasion turned down attractive retainers of $25,000 or more simply because "something about the case disturbed him"; in his capacity as a senator, he adhered to the same strict code of ethics. "He guards his reputation carefully," Washington reporters knew. And so did those constituents who received back by return mail the "presents" sent Wagner in gratitude for favors done, ranging from hundred-dollar contributions to the Democratic party's campaign funds down to billfolds and even cigars intended for the Senator's

[24] RFW Papers: Christine Austin to RFW, July 18, 1932; John D. Bowler to RFW, Nov. 11, 1931; Emanuel Kline to RFW, March 11, 1930; Annie Maggs to RFW, Jan. 25, 1931; H. P. Wilson to RFW, April 4, 1930.

[25] Minna L. Ruppert, interview; Minna L. Ruppert to Jacob Leventman, Sept. 6, 1932, and Minna L. Ruppert to Marguerite I. Cummins, Feb. 15, 1928, RFW Papers.

personal use. Every employee in his office was under orders to reject gifts, regardless of their value; the rule was irksome at times, as Wagner's assistants watched their counterparts in other offices dividing up the largesse their employers freely accepted—everything from crates of oranges presented by a fruit growers' association to dresses and handbags bestowed by garment-industry lobbyists. On very rare occasions Wagner relented a bit, as when a case of caviar arrived from one of his admirers; the Senator allowed each of his girls to keep one jar as a "sample." The rest was packed up and shipped back whence it came![26]

According to those who knew him best, political corruption was one of the few things, along with unemployment, about which Wagner could become openly and emotionally upset. And on one occasion, at least, his sensitivity on that subject had unfortunate consequences. In August 1930, while Bob was en route from Europe aboard the *Bremen*, news broke of the disappearance of his legal associate, Joseph Force Crater. Since Crater had had connections with politicians less circumspect than Wagner, metropolitan dailies were full of rumors that the mystery of his whereabouts involved wrongdoing of one kind or another. When newsmen met him at the dock to seek his opinion Wagner, lacking any briefing on the situation, made light of his relation to Crater and denied the commonly held notion that they were law partners (a denial that, technically, was correct).

Some interpreted the Senator's attitude as a repudiation of his friend. Actually it reflected his own disillusion; that evening Wagner's niece, visiting his apartment, found him "boiling mad" and disconsolately musing about "what a dirty game politics is," all the while whacking a golf ball about the living room with such forceful strokes that she "feared for the furniture." Two days later he called in the newsmen and gave a more charitable analysis of the Crater mystery, which remains unsolved to this day. Wagner's original attitude was unfair to Crater, for it has never been proved that his disappearance involved anything unsavory. The only excuse that might be offered for Wagner is that it represented the response of one who, possessing "imperturbable integrity" himself, was sometimes inclined to judge rashly the conduct of others.[27]

Even more repugnant to Wagner was the undoubted miscon-

[26] Interviews with Simon H. Rifkind, Minna L. Ruppert, and Edythe Griffinger (Rifkind's secretary); New York *Telegram*, Feb. 19, 1931; RFW to John E. Judge, Dec. 14, 1927, and RFW to Morris Sisskind, Dec. 11, 1930, RFW Papers.

[27] Interviews with Simon H. Rifkind and Claire Dittrich Denzer; New York *Telegram*, Feb. 19, 1931.

duct of those who had assumed control of New York City's Democratic organization by the early 1930s. Following Charles Murphy's
death in 1924 the leadership passed to George Olvaney, who was
thought to be a representative of the New Tammany. But Olvaney
proved inept, and when he yielded up his office in 1929 a coterie of
district leaders, feeling inhibited by the organization's recently acquired air of respectability, determined to choose a boss who would
sanction a return to "the good old days." Three of Tammany's "Big
Four"—Wagner, Smith, and Surrogate James A. Foley—tried to
withstand the tide of reaction, but the fourth, Mayor James J.
Walker, was inclined to side with the district leaders. In an attempt
to head off the insurrection, Smith and others pleaded with Wagner
to accept the leadership himself, but Bob was in no mood to step
down from the United States Senate to assume the picayune yet nerve-
shattering worries that went with bossing the Hall. In the end the
district leaders had their way: John F. Curry occupied the seat of
power on Fourteenth Street, and under him and Jimmy Walker—
whose flippant attitude toward both his public and private responsibilities was a vast disappointment to those who earlier expected much
of him—the "good old days" began to return.[28]

In 1930 fumes of scandal, involving charges of selling offices and
judgeships, were already beginning to seep through the insubstantial
seams of the city administration. In his keynote speech at the Democratic state convention that fall—a speech that New York newspapers
published in full under the caption, "Wagner Demands Democrats
Read Office Buyers Out of the Party"—Bob outspokenly condemned
those party officials who were "found wanting in honor or derelict in
duty." As the record of corruption was unfolded in the next two years,
leading finally to Walker's resignation, Wagner lifted not a finger to
ease the burden of the miscreants. Some of them accused the Senator
of "running out" on the organization and threatened reprisals. There
were even rumors that the disgruntled elements in the Hall might try
to block him from the ticket in 1932; but such talk quickly evaporated
as Wagner's stature in the public's estimation rose even higher that
year. When the 1933 municipal election proved disastrous for Tammany and inaugurated the memorable Fusion regime of Fiorello La
Guardia, Wagner was secretly satisfied with the result. Nevertheless,
even in that year he gave nominal support to the Democratic nominee, and thereby maintained his party regularity. He would never re-
linquish that loyalty, nor his fervid hope that Tammany might again
live up to the full meaning of what he considered it—"the cradle of

[28] *New York Times*, March 24–April 24, 1929.

modern liberalism." By 1937 it appeared that the Hall might be returning to the right path, for that year its leaders spearheaded the drive to conscript Tammany's Number One liberal, Bob Wagner himself, to run against the equally liberal La Guardia. Once again Wagner declined to be drafted, but he was able to join with enthusiasm in campaigning for the man who did make the unsuccessful race against the Little Flower—Jere Mahoney.[29]

Perhaps Wagner should have intervened more forcefully than he did in the managing of Tammany Hall during the 1920s and 1930s. The rank-and-file braves admired him, and his word carried great weight. In 1928, for example, a distraught district leader named Dan Finn could think of no fairer way of disposing of a squabble between two of his women lieutenants, both of whom wanted "to run the news-stand at the foot of Liberty Street" in his bailiwick, than by referring it to his United States senator for adjudication.[30] But as Wagner became increasingly involved in "the big things" at Washington, the peculiar problems of Dan Finn, and of the metropolis as a whole, receded from view. During his first term his office maintained a file on "New York City Affairs," but thereafter that practice was abandoned. As mentioned before, Wagner had a realistic conception of the scope of a man's effectual attention, and in his system of priorities the problems of his city—though he loved it dearly—took on an inferior rank. Had it been otherwise, Tammany Hall and the people of New York would have been the gainers, but the nation as a whole would have lost.

Wagner remained deeply attached to the social pleasures of his "home town" nonetheless, and even during Congressional sessions he returned there on weekends whenever he could. An enthusiast for the infant industry of air travel, Wagner announced shortly after his first election that he intended to commute between New York and Washington by plane. He tried it a few times, but as his New York secretary, Marguerite I. Cummins, informed Minna Ruppert a short while later, "I think we have persuaded him that life is still very dear."

Thereafter the Senator usually took the Friday afternoon train from Washington; a telegram to his Yorkville housekeeper signaled her to lay out the formal attire he would wear that evening to the Metropolitan Opera House. (On weekends when Wagner couldn't

[29] New York *Evening Post*, Sept. 29, 1930; *New York Times*, June 18, 1932; New York *Daily News*, July 26, 1932; O'Brien, "Robert F. Wagner," pp. 112–113; Jeremiah T. Mahoney, interview.

[30] Daniel E. Finn to RFW, July 28, 1928, RFW Papers.

make it up from Washington, "Ma" Cummins faced a minor political crisis in deciding who, of many petitioners, should get to use the Senator's season tickets for the evening's performance.) Saturdays usually called for a visit to local Tammany headquarters in Yorkville, followed perhaps by a round of golf at Oakland, a ball game viewed from Colonel Jacob Ruppert's box at Yankee Stadium, or maybe a visit to Staten Island, where Wagner's companion, Congressman Anning Prall, always promised "a real wet time." Occasionally Wagner used the facilities of clubs he belonged to, such as the Manhattan Club and the Lambs; there was also a select fifteen-member group dubbed the "Black Sheep," whose room at the New York Athletic Club boasted "a radio, victrola, card tables, bathrobes, slippers" and—still in the era of Prohibition—"corkscrews, bottle openers, and a locker for each member." [31]

Sunday mornings Wagner usually worked on legal and political business, beginning at 7:00 A.M.—and eventually Marguerite Cummins got used to early Sabbath rising. But Sunday evening was poker night, often at the home of Francis J. Quillinan, who was Al Smith's son-in-law as well as Wagner's law partner; sometimes the locale shifted to the Tiger Room, the sumptuous private club maintained by millionaire contractor William F. Kenny. At these sessions not only the cards but also the conversation must have been interesting—even historic, if it had been recorded—for in addition to the regulars who participated, like Wagner and Smith, there were such occasional interlopers as Herbert Lehman and Governor Franklin Roosevelt. (The Wagner-Smith poker games, famous in New York political lore, continued throughout the 1930s, but with Smith turning ever more bitterly against the New Deal, fewer and fewer hands got to be played as the political arguments between Bob and Al grew hotter and hotter. Uninitiated bystanders sometimes feared the two men would come to blows; by the end of the evening, however, liquid spirits plus the good spirits invoked by reminiscences of times past invariably restored amicability as the two old cronies, arm in arm, made their unsteady exit.)

Bob found it hard to tear himself away from these gatherings, even as the hour neared for departure of the midnight train he was due to take back to Washington. That sometimes necessitated a phone call to Pennsylvania station; and as irate passengers grumbled about the railroad's failure to keep on schedule, few except the station master and the engineer knew that the train was being delayed so that a United States senator, unable to resist the appeal of "just one more

[31] *New York Times*, Oct. 3, 1927; also RFW Papers: Cummins to Ruppert, May 1, 1928; RFW to Thomas C. Brown, May 9, 1928; Warren C. Fielding to RFW, March 4, 1929; also Marguerite Cummins Hayes, interview.

hand," might reach his desk at the Capitol in time for Monday morning appointments![32]

In Washington, too, Wagner enjoyed abundant opportunities for social diversion when time and his work-driven conscience permitted. The Senator, like many of his colleagues, belonged to the Columbia Country Club, which became his favorite haunt for mixing business and pleasure over the dinner table. He also frequented the other fine restaurants of the city, among which the Occidental and Harvey's were then accounted the best. There were race tracks nearby, and in those days the Washington Senators still put on a pretty good ball game. On some evenings tourists, if they made their way to the Shoreham Hotel, might even observe New York's junior senator keeping step in the conga line.

Because he was a widower, Wagner was a favorite guest of Washington hostesses, and the innumerable invitations to parties and dinners were more than he could cope with. In this period he attended a good many such affairs—another circumstance that presented "Ma" Cummins with minor crises at times. On more than one occasion, in response to an urgent telegram from Washington, she made her way to the Senator's Yorkville apartment and thence to the railroad station, where she delivered a package to the engineer of a train due to arrive in the capital early that evening. At the end of the run a boy sent by Miss Ruppert waited to rush the parcel to the Senator's hotel suite. And later that night Wagner would appear, dapper and resplendent, at some gala affair, wearing the favorite diamond cuff links or shirt studs or the gold watch chain he'd left in New York the previous weekend.[33]

If any of Washington's unattached ladies had serious designs on this particular one of the city's more eligible males, however, their hopes eventually grew feeble. Soon after his second term began, Wagner's name was linked romantically with that of an attractive New York widow named Ruth Tennant. She had been married to a man Wagner knew well, a former editor of the New York *World*. The Senator and Mrs. Tennant were seen together frequently during the time he spent in New York, and in 1935 Ed Sullivan's column rumored that marriage was in the offing. But perhaps for reasons that only a fifty-eight-year-old widower could understand, Sullivan's prediction never came true.[34]

A possible reason for Wagner's shunning of matrimony after he

[32] Interviews with Marguerite Cummins Hayes and Francis J. Quillinan; Howard Cullman to RFW, Dec. 16, 1930, RFW Papers.
[33] Interviews with Marguerite Cummins Hayes and Minna L. Ruppert.
[34] New York *Daily News*, Nov. 18, 1935.

became a senator was that whatever need he may have felt earlier to
add a woman's hand to his own in the raising of his son no longer
existed. In 1929 young Bob entered Yale. During the next four years
the boy provided Wagner with some of the usual, and a few unusual,
parental headaches. There was the time after a football game when "a
drunken Dartmouth alumnus" crashed into Bobby's car and "bent
things up pretty badly"; there were the letters that asked the busy
Senator to contribute articles to the *Yale News*, bearing postscripts
reading "Please oblige as soon as possible, Dad, as a personal favor";
and there was the request that Wagner help arrange an exhibition
baseball game between Yale and the New York Yankees, to which the
Senator responded with a personal letter to Colonel Jacob Ruppert.[35] But his son also provided Wagner with a more than sufficient
share of occasions for the swelling of parental pride: selection as manager of the Yale baseball team, for example, and the winning of a
coveted "Y"; election to Key and Scroll, the college's honor society;
graduation, and admittance to one of the best law schools.

By the end of his first term in Washington, then, Bob Wagner's
son was a young man and a credit to the parent who had raised him
alone since his tenth year. The relationship between the two Wagners
ripened into something more than that of father and son, for they
had become affectionate friends. Frequently they converged on New
York City, one from the north and the other from the south, for a
weekend of theater-going and talk. During fall election campaigns
Wagner allowed his son to travel with him whenever it could be arranged. And when the Senator managed to find time enough for a
vacation, it was more than likely that his companion would be Bob,
Junior.

As the tempo of affairs increased at Washington, Wagner found
it ever more difficult to enjoy extended vacations. He went to Europe
in the summer of 1927 and again in 1930 and spent several weeks in
Canada in 1931. But the special session of 1929 forced cancellation of
his plans to tour the Continent that summer. "I can easily get along
without the cathedrals and the galleries," he lamented to a friend,
"but how cruel to deprive me of the beer!" The respite that Wagner
hoped for following the arduous election campaign of 1932 also had
to be postponed, for a week after the votes were counted the chairman of the Senate Foreign Relations Committee, of which Bob had
become a member, convened hearings on the pending St. Lawrence
Seaway treaty. A month later the lame-duck session of the Seventy-

[35] RFW Papers: Mac Williamson to RFW, Nov. 18, 1931; Robert I. Stev-
enson to RFW, March 2, 1931; RFW to Jacob Ruppert, Feb. 8, 1933.

second Congress opened, and once again Wagner was plunged into work that kept him occupied from dawn until dusk.[36]

During the four-month interregnum between Franklin Roosevelt's election and inauguration the depression reached its nadir, while the attendant human misery reached its highest point. "We are not in a mere business recession," Wagner told his colleagues in February, "we are in a life and death struggle with the forces of social and economic dissolution." At the outset of the session Minority Leader Joseph T. Robinson put Wagner in charge of employment and relief measures for the Democratic Senate Conference; significantly, his assistants were the "radical" Edward P. Costigan and the conservative Southerner, Tom Connally of Texas.[37]

The trio devoted its main efforts to refurbishing the Emergency Relief and Construction Act of the previous July, which, in Wagner's estimation, the Hoover Administration had tied up "with mile upon mile of red tape." By the end of December not a single one of the federal public works projects enumerated in that measure had yet been put in actual process of construction; Wagner's earlier misgivings about making their prosecution discretionary with the Administration appeared fully justified. Several governors publicly attacked the RFC's parsimonious attitude in carrying out the section of the act that authorized relief loans to the states. At the same time, municipal officials and private builders alike, anxious to secure loans for "self-liquidating projects devoted to a public use," complained about the RFC's slowness in processing applications and the unduly high interest rates charged on the few loans that were finally approved. "The personnel of the R.F.C.," wrote the president of one company, "are evidently endowed with userers' minds, intent on discouraging borrowers." "It must be that they are more anxious to earn money than to render relief," wrote another, "which is not the purpose of the act at all." Wagner concurred in those sentiments. "Those of us who conceived of the Relief and Construction Act as a great undertaking to assist in business revival through the provision of employment," he told the Senate, "have seen our expectations frustrated by a mechanical interpretation and bureaucratic application of the law." "A pump," he warned, "cannot be primed with an eyedropper." [38]

Wagner's bill to amend the Emergency Relief and Construction

[36] RFW to August Zinzer, July 19, 1929, and RFW to M. William Bray, Nov. 14, 1932, RFW Papers.

[37] 76 *Congressional Record*, 4315; Robinson to RFW, Dec. 15, 1932, RFW Papers.

[38] RFW Papers: Wagner speech file, Oct. 9, Dec. 19, 1932, and Feb. 24, 1933; Charles V. Bossert to RFW, Dec. 16, 1932; Joseph T. Losee to RFW, Feb. 28, 1933.

Act, introduced early in January 1933, made no further reference to federal public works. He still insisted that they were of utmost importance, but in view of President Hoover's implacable hostility, he believed that "we can more successfully formulate such a program under the auspices of the new administration." The bill doubled the original $300 million authorized for relief loans to states, however, and it also simplified the "pauper's oath" certification that the RFC had been requiring supplicant governors to make. The requirement that public works, and private works devoted to a public use, be self-liquidating in order to be eligible for RFC loans was dropped; instead, it was necessary for such works only to be found "needful and in the public interest." Among several other technical adjustments proposed in the bill was one that would place a ceiling on the interest that the RFC might charge.[39]

When the latest Wagner bill reached the Senate floor in the middle of February, once again its author had to fight off attacks from both the right and the left. Conservatives like Democrat Carter Glass of Virginia and Republican Simeon D. Fess of Ohio, who charged that the government was being turned into a "wet nurse," wanted to abolish the RFC altogether; but these extremists were a small minority indeed by now. On the other hand, when Senator La Follette reopened the issue of extending federal relief aid to the states in the form of outright grants, rather than as loans, Wagner reiterated his position for the benefit of the Senate's more intransigent liberals. "I do not want the *Record* to show that the Senator from Wisconsin and I differ upon any of these efforts," he declared, but "I do not want to indulge in pure futilities. I do not see that it gets bread to the destitute to stand for some so-called principle . . . if, in the end, by pursuing that policy, we invite a veto and the hungry get nothing." The Senate preferred Wagner's pragmatic liberalism to La Follette's unyielding approach by a vote of 44–28; and on February 20 it approved Wagner's measure, virtually as introduced 54–16.[40]

By now the life of the Seventy-second Congress was expiring, however, and when it adjourned for the last time on March 4, Wagner's bill was still pending in the House of Representatives, unacted on. Still pending in the Senate were other measures that he had introduced during the hectic year 1932 while the fight over relief and construction occupied the center of his, and the nation's, attention:

[39] 76 *Congressional Record*, 1401, 4320; files on "Relief and Construction Act Amendments, 1933," RFW Papers.

[40] The Senate debates on amending the Emergency Relief and Construction Act in February 1933 may be followed in the *Congressional Record*, Vol. 76, beginning at p. 4314, or in the daily newspapers of February 17–21, 1933.

the latest version of his federal-state employment exchange scheme; his minority report and recommendations as a member of the Senate select committee on unemployment insurance; a bill, introduced in March 1932, to create a system of old-age retirement insurance for railroad workers; a resolution calling for Senate investigation of "peonage" conditions allegedly suffered by Negro laborers on the Mississippi River flood-control project (conditions that Walter White and the N.A.A.C.P. had sought, futilely, to have the Hoover Administration correct for a year or more); and a measure that would legalize the sale of beer and wine. All these Wagner proposals were forerunners of the New Deal that was about to begin as Franklin Roosevelt took the oath of office, and they were indicative of the groups that would benefit from New Deal policies—the destitute, the unemployed, businessmen shorn of orders and customers, the elderly, exploited minority groups, and yes, even those who yearned to take a legal drink.

And while Americans appropriately looked to the new President to provide leadership in the quest for a better day—"He is the great reliance in this dark hour of national moratorium," declared even the ultra-Republican Boston *Transcript* on the afternoon of March 4— keen observers of the Congressional scene realized also that the most strenuous and productive phase of Robert Wagner's legislative career was about to begin. "I feel you must know how happy I am and how sure I am," Lillian Wald of the Henry Street Settlement House wrote Wagner, "that . . . when Mr. Roosevelt enters the White House, your position in Washington and in the Senate will make many measures possible. I follow you with pride," added the veteran social reformer, "and I feel that, distressing as are some of the obvious taints in our party politics, courageous men like you who have training and the sense of values will push us on." [41]

[41] Boston *Transcript*, March 4, 1933; Wald to Wagner, Oct. 13, 1932, RFW Papers.

CHAPTER 9

The Need for Planning

THE ASSORTED NEW DEALERS who poured into Washington in March 1933 and in the months and years thereafter, from Franklin D. Roosevelt on down, were united in objectives. Their aims, as Robert F. Wagner once explained, were "first to see that the hungry are fed, but second and more important, to see that men are reemployed, and third, to prevent a recurrence of so prolonged a depression as the one we are now experiencing." But when it came to the question of precise means for achieving the common objectives of relief, recovery, and reform, agreement ended. The President, who brought no over-all plan of his own to Washington, picked and chose in his pragmatic way from among the proposals presented by competing brain trusts, congressmen, and pressure groups, and fashioned from them a program—a New Deal—that was "highly experimental, improvised and inconsistent." [1]

Of course, after the domestic New Deal came to a close in the late 1930s a *post hoc*, or residual, "philosophy" began to be discernible behind its gyrations. Historians and economists pieced it together

---

[1] RFW to Joseph Berran, Aug. 24, 1932, RFW Papers; Leon H. Keyserling, quoted in Arthur M. Schlesinger, Jr., *The Age of Roosevelt: The Politics of Upheaval* (Boston, 1960), p. 691. The best one-volume treatment of the New Deal is William E. Leuchtenburg's *Franklin D. Roosevelt and the New Deal: 1932–1940* (New York, 1963). Schlesinger's several volumes of his *The Age of Roosevelt* (Boston, 1957 and after) are excellent. See also James MacGregor Burns, *Roosevelt: The Lion and the Fox* (New York, 1956), and Dexter Perkins, *The New Age of Franklin Roosevelt: 1932–1945* (Chicago, 1957).

in their writings and lodged it in their textbooks; gradually some of them made it seem as though it had all been "planned that way," which was a gross oversimplification. Nevertheless, what they depicted was another age of reform in which the federal government, taking its cue in many respects from precedents established in the Progressive Era, assumed a much greater role in the economic and social life of the nation. It shouldered the main responsibility for stabilizing the national economy through various countercyclical devices; it regulated business, and particularly big business, more than ever before; and it adopted measures designed to promote a sense of security by removing some of the risks that had formerly burdened businessmen, property owners, consumers, farmers, and the urban working class during the earlier regime of rugged individualism.

Not that Washington undertook to regulate and guarantee *everything*, however, for that would be a form of state socialism too foreign to the American tradition. Instead, after providing minimum standards of public control and security, it left much to the operation of the free market, free enterprise, and private bargaining between the nation's various interest groups. But in order to prevent one interest from overwhelming the others, as happened in the era of big-business domination during the 1920s, the government encouraged and helped make feasible collective action on the part of disadvantaged groups, such as the farmers and labor. Thus there emerged in the private sector of the economy a network of "countervailing powers" whose operations, in conjunction with the government's own minimal direct activities, would help guarantee equality of opportunity and equal justice for all Americans. The end result of the New Deal, then, was the creation of the "mixed economy," the "welfare state," or the system of "people's capitalism," which, by the mid-1950s, even most Republicans had come to accept, and which most Americans by then regarded as a viable answer to the challenge of foreign totalitarianisms.[2]

That the system just described constitutes the enduring legacy of the New Deal is beyond contention. But to imply that the chief New Dealer and his sets of Administration brain trusters "planned it that

---

[2] See John Kenneth Galbraith, *American Capitalism: The Concept of Countervailing Power* (Boston, 1952); Arthur M. Schlesinger, Jr., *The Vital Center: The Politics of Freedom* (Boston, 1949); Massimo Salvadori, *The Economics of Freedom: American Capitalism Today* (Garden City, N.Y., 1959); Adolf A. Berle, *The 20th Century Capitalist Revolution* (New York, 1954); Russell W. Davenport *et al.*, *USA: The Permanent Revolution* (New York, 1951); Frederick Lewis Allen, *The Big Change: America Transforms Itself, 1900–1950* (New York, 1952).

way," or that the outcome followed a neat and logical pattern of evolution through a First New Deal and then a Second New Deal between the years 1933 and 1939, is wide of the mark. More accurately, that legacy could be viewed as the distillation that emerged out of what one "inside observer" of the Roosevelt Administration described as "a great cacophonic kind of symphony of wails and cries and voices from all quarters about doing this this way and that that way"—a symphony created by what another insider has called "a great array of thinkers and doers of all kinds." Roosevelt himself conceded the indecision regarding the proper routes to take that marked the beginning of his term in office. "There are about 350 plans here in Washington, public and private," he told reporters at a press conference in the spring of 1933. "I should say they are still coming in at the rate of 25 or 30 a day." And in large measure the confusion that characterized the hectic First Hundred Days of the New Deal continued throughout its life.[3]

Within the New Deal "family" that gathered in Washington in the spring of 1933—the informal brain trusters, Administration officials, and congressmen with whom Bob Wagner now had to deal— most of the profound differences of approach that were to wrack the government during the ensuing years were apparent almost from the outset. There were internationalists like Secretary of State Cordell Hull, who sought to bring about recovery through cooperation with other nations in attempts to stabilize the world economy and who entertained high hopes for the World Economic Conference scheduled to meet in London in June. On the other hand were the economic nationalists like Rexford G. Tugwell, Raymond Moley, and George Peek, who insisted that the United States remain free of foreign entanglements so as to be able to adopt whatever trade and monetary policies might be deemed necessary for domestic purposes. ("In my judgment," Wagner declared on the floor of the Senate late in April, "the fate of civilization as we know it depends upon the degree of economic disarmament which the World Economic Conference accomplishes." Later in the year, after the Tugwell-Moley-Peek policies prevailed and the President had sabotaged the conference, Wagner commented to a friend that "We're in a mess. We've all gone nationalistic.")[4]

Then there was the chasm between the inflationists and the "sound money" men in Democratic circles; between heirs of the Pop-

[3] Boris Shishkin, "Reminiscences" (Oral History Research Office, Columbia Univ., 1957), pp. 760–761; Leon H. Keyserling, quoted in Schlesinger, *The Politics of Upheaval*, p. 690; transcript of press conference, May 5, 1933, FDR Papers.

[4] 77 *Congressional Record*, 2513; RFW to Dorothy Straus, Dec. 18, 1933, RFW Papers.

ulists like Senator Elmer Thomas of Oklahoma, who viewed the issuance of greenbacks and monetization of silver as the sure cure of all
the nation's ills, on the one hand, and conservatives like Director of
the Budget Lewis Douglas, who regarded any deviation from the gold
standard as marking the approach of "the end of Western civilization." (When Congress in April adopted the Thomas amendment
to the agricultural relief bill, granting the President discretionary
power to invoke a variety of inflationist devices, Wagner spoke,
guardedly and skeptically, in its favor. "It is safe to assume that
the pending amendment will not accomplish all the miracles which
some of its advocates proclaim," he told his colleagues, "and I am
certain it will not spread the general havoc which its opponents pro-
fess to dread." On the whole, economists and historians have since
rendered a similar verdict on the rather quixotic monetary experiments that Roosevelt indulged in during 1933 and 1934.) [5]

Even more significant was the deep-seated rural-urban split
within the ranks of the New Dealers. A good many of them continued to regard the plight of agriculture as the root problem of the
depression, and they considered efforts to raise farm prices and to
restore a long-lost "balance" between the agricultural and industrial
sectors of the economy as the front line of the recovery campaign.
The farm bloc in Congress was still very strong, and, oddly enough,
many of the city-bred intellectuals who surrounded Roosevelt—
enamored perhaps of the history-book portrayal of the embattled
farmer as the hero of American liberalism in the past—shared that
rurally oriented approach to the restoration of prosperity. Even such a
sophisticate as Columbia Professor Rexford Tugwell, who later bore
the brunt of the attack on the New Deal as a "radical working-class
movement," once confessed that "Since my graduate-school days I
have always been able to excite myself more about the wrongs of the
farmers than those of urban workers." [6] To an extent the President,
too, affected perhaps by his Dutchess County background, shared
those sentiments.

At the outset, then, relatively few New Dealers, in Congress or in
the Administration, believed with an intensity equal to Bob Wagner's
that farm prices, like all others, could be raised in a way productive of
real prosperity only by stimulating "an effective demand for commod-
ities created through the resumption of investment and restoration of
employment" in the industrial sector of American society.[7] A few,
such as Senators La Follette, Costigan, and David I. Walsh of Massa-

[5] 77 *Congressional Record,* 2512.
[6] Quoted in Leuchtenburg, *Franklin D. Roosevelt,* p. 35.
[7] 77 *Congressional Record,* 2512.

chusetts, were at his side, but the urban areas of the country were grossly underrepresented in Congress. Some others in Roosevelt's inner circle, like Secretary of Labor Frances Perkins, concurred in Wagner's analysis. But their relative disproportion meant that, during the gestation period of the Hundred Days program, the New York Senator's pleas for a huge public works program and other measures designed primarily to benefit industry and its workers received much less attention, initially, than did the proposals for a farm program that the President presented to Congress as early as March 16.

Of course, another reason for the new government's hesitancy in undertaking public works was the dispute over fiscal policy that divided the Roosevelt Administration between "spenders" and "budget balancers" throughout its duration. Advisers like Lewis Douglas and Bernard Baruch viewed Roosevelt's campaign pledge to reduce government spending as the most essential element in the candidate's program. Within a week of his inauguration the President, in conformance with that promise, submitted to Congress an economy act providing for severe cutbacks in veterans' pension payments and government salaries; and conservatives regarded that as just the beginning of retrenchment. Wagner voted for the President's bill, but it was with "heaviness in my heart," he told the Senate, for its philosophy did violence "to convictions which have become an inseverable part of my very being." [8] He made it clear, furthermore, that his vote was intended only to preserve the credit rating of the government so that it might remain in a position to borrow the funds necessary to finance the huge construction and relief measures that, he insisted, it must soon undertake. Out of sheer necessity the Chief Executive disappointed the fiscal conservatives many times thereafter—Douglas, exasperated by mounting deficits, resigned in 1934—even though Roosevelt remained one of them at heart. In any event, the running battle between the Wagners, La Follettes, and later the professional Keynesians, on one hand, and, on the other, people like Douglas and Henry Morgenthau, Jr.—whose fiscal views were sometimes reminiscent of Herbert Hoover's—constituted one of the most disruptive, and important, points of debate during the New Deal era.

Nor did there exist in Washington during that period anything like unanimity regarding the form that the government's relation to the business community should take. Powerful and strident voices, like those of William E. Borah, Wheeler, and Huey Long in the Senate, remained steeped in the rhetoric of Populist days and called

[8] *Ibid.*, pp. 341–342.

for vigorous enforcement of the antitrust laws so as to break the hold of big-business monopolists; nearly all of the early brain trusters, however, had come to accept the trend toward oligopoly as something virtually inevitable, and they viewed any attempt to return to a pristine regime of small-scale competition as being not only futile but malicious. Most of them envisioned some scheme of government-business cooperation as a means of promoting recovery, stability, and efficiency; they would subscribe to Wagner's earlier dictum that the path to a better future lay in "subjecting to plan what now moves haphazardly." But even on this point vital differences of approach were discernible, for while Raymond Moley and others were apparently ready to concede businessmen the role of "senior partners" in the cooperative arrangement, Rex Tugwell and those who were more skeptical of the idea of business self-government wanted to reserve that role for the government's own representatives on the coop's board of directors.

Finally, there was among the "planners" an even more basic disagreement involving the reasons *why* more "planning" of the national economy was necessary, and the purposes for which it should be done. It had become the custom in some circles of economic theorists and among many of Roosevelt's entourage of advisers to speak darkly of America in terms of economic "maturity" and "saturation." According to this view, the closing of the frontier, birth-rate statistics that seemed to portend an incipient population decline, and an apparent lack of new inventions and industries awaiting development meant that the era of rapid economic growth spanning the preceding one hundred years had come to an end; indeed, in the new era of stagnation that was beginning, some forecasters hinted despondently, the country might be consigned to a condition of "permanent depression." Greater planning had become necessary, therefore, for the sake of more carefully administering the existing and limited store of economic resources; in the formulations of some pessimists, the system envisioned portended an economy of "planned scarcity."

Of a quite different order was the concept of "planning for abundance" that underlay Bob Wagner's frequent calls for substituting "mastery" in place of "drift." As early as April 1931 the New York Senator was pointing out that "Before this depression began we fell into the grievous error of thinking in terms of *maintaining* the American standard of living, instead of *lifting* it," with the result that even in the heyday of "Coolidge prosperity" millions of citizens existed at the poverty level. Confident that by conscious effort—directed, perhaps, by "an economic general staff"—the nation could materially lift its entire standard of living, Wagner called for a bold undertaking to increase the average annual income of those gainfully employed by one thousand dollars during the next six years. That effort would necessitate raising the national income by forty billion dollars and would impose on American industry the burden of satisfying an additional demand for that amount of goods and services, but it would be a burden "under which business would thrive" and unemployment would virtually disappear.[9]

During the 1932 campaign, while even the buoyant Franklin Roosevelt sometimes uttered the dismal forecasts of his "stagnationist" counselors ("Our task now," he declared in his famous Commonwealth Club speech in San Francisco, "is not discovery or exploitation of natural resources, or necessarily producing more goods"), Wagner kept reiterating his demand for planned, deliberate exploitation of the new frontiers afforded by the beckoning prospect of enlarging "the wellbeing of the great body of the American people." "[It] is for us not only a moral obligation," Wagner wrote in a national magazine in October 1932, "it is an economic necessity. It is not only that we should do it; we must, or we shall be crushed under our own abundance." He went on to list a number of specific projects that might be undertaken in the campaign, and included in the catalogue was the admonition that "About a third of the population must be rehoused if the minimum requirements of an American home are to be met." [10] That was more than four months before Franklin Roosevelt entered the White House and more than four years before the 1936 speech in which the President pointed to the one-third of the nation that was "ill-housed, ill-fed, and ill-clothed!"

In the end the outlines of what historians now describe as the permanent legacy of the New Deal, and as today's welfare state, adhere more closely to the positions that Bob Wagner held on the various points of dispute within the New Deal family than to those held by his opponents. But Wagner's triumphs were not easily won, for the President and influential members of the Administration—sometimes even those whom Wagner counted on most—were not always on his side at the outset. Then, too, ideological conflicts were often complicated by personality clashes as important figures, in the bureaucracy and in Congress, strove to preserve the integrity of their prerogatives and their "empires." Even Wagner, whom other New

[9] Wagner speech file, April 8, 1931, RFW Papers.
[10] Arthur M. Schlesinger, Jr., *The Age of Roosevelt: The Crisis of the Old Order, 1919–1933* (Boston, 1957), p. 425; Robert F. Wagner, "The Problem of 25,000,000," *New Outlook* (Oct. 1932), pp. 35ff.

Dealers sometimes described as "very genial . . . and exuding good will and amiability," or as "a nice gentlemanly person who didn't like to offend anybody," was forced to engage in several of these scrapes, and he came off with a goodly number of scalps to his credit.[11]

That so much of what is remembered about the New Deal bears Wagner's imprint is a tribute to the resourcefulness with which he fought both his ideological and fratricidal battles during the depression era. Though he continued to remain "a blurred and shadowy figure" in the public eye, close observers of the governmental scene during that turbulent decade were aware of his power, and newspapermen gave him such titles as "Legislative Pilot of the New Deal." "The New Deal owed as much to Robert Wagner as to Franklin Roosevelt," reminisced an intimate of the Administration years later, "and that is not meant to take away anything from the President, whom I dearly loved." "He was about as influential a person as there was," declared another. "I've often said that I can't think of another man whose . . . work is more deeply imbedded in American life than Senator Wagner's." [12]

A good many of the "350 plans" for industrial recovery that Franklin Roosevelt referred to during the First Hundred Days found their way to Bob Wagner's Senate office. Some were routed there by Administration officials since, sometime after his election, the President-elect had designated Wagner "chief planner" as far as Congress was concerned. Scores of others were submitted by citizens scattered across the country. The latter—Simon Rifkind started collecting them soon after Wagner's emergence as the Senate's foremost expert on economic affairs—ranged from sober, elaborate proposals, drawn up by business leaders like Gerard Swope of General Electric, to crackpot schemes that would cure the depression by destroying all buildings more than twenty years old, taxing machinery out of existence, forbidding women to work, eliminating the evil effects of "drugs and occultation" in American life, or "Applying Birth Control to Unemployment." Other correspondents submitted intimations of plans that were "too secret" to risk divulging in the mail—the Senator would have to make a personal appointment with their proponents—and there was even "A Plan to Protect Against Plans of Economic Relief," submitted by two of Wagner's New York constituents! [13]

[11] Boris Shishkin, "Reminiscences," p. 503; Thomas I. Emerson, "Reminiscences" (Oral History Research Office, 1953), p. 321.

[12] Anna M. Rosenberg, interview; William H. Davis, "Reminiscences" (Oral History Research Office, 1958), p. 53.

[13] Files on "Unemployment Plans, 1930–1933," RFW Papers.

Wagner's own recovery program in March of 1933 continued to be based on initiation of massive public construction: "that is the keystone of recovery," he insisted again and again in the Senate. But by now he had also become deeply interested in formulating some means whereby industry, integrating itself under governmental supervision, might stabilize itself, create employment opportunities, and end the orgy of cutthroat competition that was dragging wages, hours, and working conditions down to pitiable levels. The President had also directed others in his own inner circle, such as Raymond Moley and New York financier James P. Warburg, to look into similar proposals, but so varied was the advice he received that by early April Roosevelt—though not Wagner—concluded that action along those lines was not feasible. Not for the present, at least. Moreover, for a while during his first month in office it even appeared that the President was opposed to undertaking a massive public works spending program. Wagner, La Follette, and Costigan, and some Cabinet members like Frances Perkins, pressed their pump-priming views on the Chief Executive, but the voices of budget balancers like Lewis Douglas were difficult to countervail.[14]

In the meantime, therefore, the President and most of his spokesmen on Capitol Hill concentrated on moves designed to cope with some of the more glaring problems of relief and reform confronting the virtually prostrate nation. It took Congress just one day, the first of the special session that convened on March 9, to rush to passage the Emergency Banking Act submitted by the White House. The measure established procedures for reopening and reorganizing America's banks, whose doors had been closed since the day following Roosevelt's inauguration; later in the session Congress approved the Glass-Steagall Act, which instituted further reforms in the banking system and marked the beginning of federal insurance of depositors' accounts.

By the end of March the President had asked Congress for federal regulation of securities issues also. Its path smoothed by the sensational exposure of Wall Street irregularities brought to light not long before by a Congressional investigation, the Administration's bill won quick passage a short time later. (In connection with the proposed Securities Act of 1933, Richard Whitney, the president of the New York Stock Exchange, presented himself one day at Bob Wagner's office to protest the government's "persecution" of respected financiers. "I am here speaking for the people of New York," Whitney started to say following the introductions, but before he could get

---

[14] 77 *Congressional Record*, 342; Wagner speech file, March 20, 1933, RFW Papers; Leuchtenburg, *Franklin D. Roosevelt*, pp. 52, 55.

any further Wagner interrupted him with unaccustomed rudeness. "What did you say?" the Senator asked, and the representative of Wall Street repeated himself. "If that were true," Wagner rejoined from behind his desk, "I'd not be sitting where I am right now.")[15]

While Congressional liberals voted for the President's Economy Act of March 1933 only with "heaviness of heart," as Wagner expressed it, most of them lent more avid support to another Administration measure, which was designed in part to help balance the government's budget and at the same time to redeem another Democratic campaign pledge of 1932. On March 13 Roosevelt asked for modification of the Volstead Act, pending ratification of the repeal amendment, so as to legalize—and tax—3.2 percent beer. Within a week jubilant wets in both houses subdued the protests of ardent Prohibitionists making their last stand, and the bill that the President signed on the twenty-second authorized not only beer but light wines as well. On April 7 America's twelve-year "legal" thirst ended; New York's junior senator gladly did his share to help celebrate the event.

In a much soberer mood Congress received Roosevelt's message on March 21 dealing with the subject of relief. In the previous months all but eight states had been forced to borrow relief money from the RFC under the terms of the Relief and Construction Act of 1932, and it was estimated that the funds available under that legislation would be exhausted by the end of six weeks. The new President therefore advocated a three-pronged attack on the relief problem: creation of a Civilian Conservation Corps to provide noncompetitive employment on public works that could be quickly set in motion, primarily in the national parks and forests; establishment of a Federal Emergency Relief Administration to dispense $500,000,000 in relief *grants* to the states and to supervise their expenditure; and inauguration of "a broad public-works labor-creating program." While the third point in the President's message represented a special victory for Wagner and other spenders in administration circles, it was tempered by Roosevelt's comment that "the many projects suggested and the financial questions involved" were still under study, and that he was not yet ready to submit a definite public works proposal.

At the conclusion of the President's message Senate Majority Leader Joseph T. Robinson, on behalf of himself and Wagner, introduced the CCC bill. A week later Wagner, for himself and Senators La Follette and Costigan, introduced the measure setting up a Federal Emergency Relief Administration.[16]

[15] Kenneth P. Steinreich, interview.
[16] 77 *Congressional Record*, 650–651, 860.

Since December members of Roosevelt's brain trust had been in contact with Wagner, La Follette, and Costigan regarding the relief program, and it soon became evident that the Conservation Corps was the new President's pet project. As governor he had set thousands of unemployed youths to work in the state's forest preserves, and during the presidential campaign he had talked of employing a million men in a similar national undertaking. (In his Labor Day speech of 1931 urging a two-billion-dollar public works program Wagner, too, had pointed out that "There are large federal zones which require reforestation.")

When the Robinson-Wagner bill reached the hearing stage before the Senate Labor Committee, however, labor leaders and spokesmen for liberal organizations like John Dewey's Joint Committee on Unemployment protested that the corps idea smacked of conscription and militarism and that the $30 a month pay scale envisioned for the corpsmen would further depress wage standards in private industry. Wagner helped devise changes that eliminated some of the bill's objectionable wording, and he assured William Green of the A. F. of L. that the measure did not contemplate a form of "Hitlerism." Also useful in converting the doubters was a letter that Wagner received from a group of volunteers at Camp Bluefield, one of Roosevelt's New York state reforestation centers. "We here received a new lease on life," two hundred signers asserted, "a restoration of our morale, and actual gain in weight averaging ten pounds." On the last day of March the President signed the CCC bill, and one of the New Deal's most successful relief experiments was launched. During the next ten years 2.5 million young men served in the corps, and most of them readily concurred in the Bluefield boys' evaluation of their experience.[17]

S. 812, the Federal Emergency Relief Act of 1933, authorized an appropriation of $500,000,000 for relief grants to the states, and, in line with the thinking of social workers and relief experts, it vested in the administrator considerable authority to supervise the states' disposal of sums received. While Southern Democrats now generally acquiesced in this new departure, Republican conservatives denounced the latest "Wagner bill" as representing the type of legislation "which increases the lack of confidence" among businessmen. "This is permitting our hearts to overcome our judgment," admonished Ohio's Simeon D. Fess, who regretted that "Uncle Sam is looked upon as a

[17] RFW Papers: Wagner speech file, Sept. 7, 1931; Henry Morgenthau, Jr., to RFW, Dec. 10, 1932, and Feb. 27, 1933; files on "Civilian Conservation Corps, 1933."

Santa Claus to give alms." But so desperate had the relief problem become that in the Senate only sixteen others joined Fess in voting against "the dole." A short time later President Roosevelt signed S. 812; Harry Hopkins, who was to become one of the New Deal's most serviceable lightning rods, arrived in Washington; and the biggest relief undertaking in the nation's history got under way.[18]

Almost as distressing as the plight of the unemployed was the situation faced by millions of mortgage-laden property owners in the United States—both farmers and homeowners—as a result of the depression. While farm income in 1932 was reduced to less than one-third of the 1919 figure, farm indebtedness remained almost stable and hence had become many more times burdensome. During the twelve months preceding Roosevelt's inauguration there were forty-one forced sales per thousand farms, and the foreclosure rate rose even more drastically thereafter. In some country areas sheriffs armed with eviction notices found themselves in danger of physical harm at the hands of a victim's irate neighbors; in Congress the proposals for relief voiced by the more radical members of the farm bloc on the Senate's Agriculture Committee bordered on outright repudiation of farm indebtedness. But the Administration preferred to entrust its own mortgage-relief program to the more conservative Banking and Currency Committee, and, ironically enough, in the middle of March the Senate's "most thoroughly urban" member, Bob Wagner of New York's East Side, found himself chairman of a subcommittee charged with guiding Roosevelt's rural-credits legislation to enactment.

The bill itself had been drafted by officials in the Department of Agriculture. But during the committee hearings, on the floor of the Senate, and in conferences with the House, the measure's fate was entrusted to Wagner's legislative know-how. He did a good job withstanding attacks from both the right and the left, and, as finally enacted, the bill adhered closely to the specifications laid down in the President's program. The act augmented the capital of the Federal Land Banks so that they might relieve hard-pressed creditors of mortgages they could no longer afford to carry; established a five-year moratorium on principal payments due on mortgages assumed by the Land Banks; authorized the Farm Credit Administration to make loans directly to farmers to refinance their mortgages or recover properties recently foreclosed; and provided the government with tools whereby

<hr />

[18] 77 *Congressional Record*, 1035ff; files on "Federal Emergency Relief Act, 1933," RFW Papers. See also Edward Ainsworth Williams, *Federal Aid for Relief* (New York, 1939), *passim*; Lewis Meriam, *Relief and Social Security* (Washington, 1946), *passim*.

it might bring about a general reduction of interest rates in the farm-mortgage field. During the next eighteen months government agencies aided, one way or another, in refinancing a fifth of all farm mortgages.[19]

The depression had a blighting effect on urban homeowners too, and by the early part of 1933 the foreclosure rate exceeded a thousand homes a day. The Hoover Administration's Home Loan Bank Act had proved ineffective, and in March Bob Wagner expected to head the Banking and Currency subcommittee that would handle the home-mortgage relief program then being formulated by New Deal officials. But by the time the Administration's measure reached the Senate in May Wagner was preoccupied with other legislation, and Senator Robert Bulkley of Ohio was put in charge. Modeled after the farm-mortgage relief act, the bill created a Home Owners' Loan Corporation empowered to make direct loans to property owners in order to refinance mortgages or recover foreclosed homes. The corporation might also assume mortgages by exchanging its bonds with creditors, a procedure that usually resulted in lower interest rates and a longer amortization period for the mortgagee.

As reported by the Banking and Currency Committee, however, the Home Owners' Loan Act of 1933 provided no moratorium on principal installments due on mortgages acquired by the corporation, a divergence from the farmers' relief act that disturbed Wagner. During Senate debate on the measure the New York Senator offered an amendment providing for a three-year moratorium on such payments. It was adopted, survived the conference committee, and became part of the bill that the President signed in June. Wagner's contribution to the Home Owners' Loan Act—which eventually benefited one out of every five mortgaged urban homes in the nation—reflected his growing determination that the New Deal must treat city dwellers at least as well as their country cousins.[20]

While the relief and reform measures enacted during the Hundred Days were expected to be conducive to economic recovery, their contribution toward that objective was peripheral; the goal of reviving industry and agriculture to self-sustaining life required major efforts along other lines. Conforming to the rural bias that pervaded his general staff, Roosevelt moved in the direction of stimulating recovery by

[19] Files on "Farm Relief Legislation, 1933," RFW Papers; 77 *Congressional Record*, 1984ff; Leuchtenburg, *Franklin D. Roosevelt*, pp. 51–52.

[20] RFW to D. E. McAvoy, March 22, 1933, and files on "Home Owners' Loan Act, 1933," RFW Papers; 77 *Congressional Record*, 4974ff, 4978, 4989, 4995, 5229–32. See also Leuchtenburg, *Franklin D. Roosevelt*, p. 53.

proposing an ambitious farm program, which he laid before Congress on March 16. Through a system of acreage restrictions and benefit payments of several types, the plan aimed at raising the farmer's income to a "parity" level that would give him the same purchasing power he had enjoyed in the relatively prosperous period before the First World War. Earlier, when similar schemes were proposed by the farm bloc in the Seventy-second Congress, Wagner and other city-oriented representatives had expressed doubts about their desirability, doubts based in part on recognition that farm-price legislation inevitably meant a higher cost of living for their urban constituents. But in the spring of 1933, under the threat of a "strike" in the farm belt and in response to the Administration's pleas, most of the big-city spokesmen in Congress went along with Roosevelt's project. When the Agricultural Adjustment Act passed the Senate, only one member who could be classed as an urban liberal cast a negative vote.

Still, when Bob Wagner sought to explain the farm program to his own constituents, placing it in the context of his familiar dictum that under modern economic conditions "there can be real security for none unless there be ample security for all," the effect was far from convincing in some quarters. "My wife became so incensed at your advocacy of raising farm prices," wrote a New York City listener, "that she was ready to take off her shoe and smash the radio. Why it is necessary for you . . . to take up arms in favor of states that only contain farmers who have always been Republicans, is beyond my comprehension." [21]

In the meantime Wagner and like-minded individuals in Congress and in the executive branch continued their campaign to turn the Administration's efforts in the direction of industrial as well as agricultural recovery. On March 20 Wagner reintroduced his bill, which had died in the House the previous month, to amend the Relief and Construction Act of 1932 in ways that would step up the tempo of RFC loans to local public works and to private undertakings devoted to public use. At the same time he was in almost daily contact with the heads of federal construction agencies and with other congressmen, compiling an agenda of feasible projects that might go into a *federal* public works program. The President's reference to such an undertaking in his relief message on March 21 encouraged New York's Senator and other spenders, such as Senators La Follette, Costigan, and Bronson Cutting of New Mexico, who had already jointly introduced a bill calling for a six-billion-dollar building program. But

[21] 77 *Congressional Record*, 2562; John J. White to RFW, April 14, 1933, RFW Papers.

in mid-April Roosevelt was still noncommital in parrying the insistent questions regarding the government's public works plans put to him by reporters at his press conferences. "I have not talked about it at all yet," he told the newsmen as late as April 14.[22]

By that time, however, the Administration's lethargy concerning an industrial recovery plan had received a severe jolt, and much more than a federal construction program now seemed in the offing. The event that triggered the President into action was the Senate's passage, on April 6, of a bill that would bar from interstate commerce articles produced in any establishment where workers were employed more than five days a week or six hours a day.

The movement for reducing hours as a means of spreading employment dated almost from the beginning of the depression; even before that, Wagner had urged it as a way of combating technological unemployment. During the 1932 campaign Wagner endorsed the Pittman-Crosser bill calling for the establishment of a six-hour day in the railroad industry (which was clearly subject to federal regulation), although he had doubts regarding the constitutionality of any federal measure that sought to control the hours of work in manufacturing establishments. But the adverse record of Supreme Court rulings failed to deter Senator Hugo Black of Alabama, who, in December 1932, introduced the general Thirty Hour bill. Hearings were held in January; labor leaders and the American Legion endorsed the measure; and William Green of the A. F. of L. threatened that labor might stage a general strike to secure its enactment. When the measure reached the Senate floor early in April it seemed likely to pass, despite the fact that the President regarded it as being too rigid, as well as unconstitutional. A last-minute Administration amendment that would raise the hours limitations to 36 per week and 8 per day was beaten, however, and 53 senators, including Bob Wagner, overwhelmed the bill's 30 opponents.[23]

Fearful that the Congress might enact "recovery" legislation that he viewed with disfavor and for which, moreover, the Administration

[22] Transcript of press conference, April 14, 1933, FDR Papers; files on "Relief and Construction Act Amendment, 1932–1933" and "National Industrial Recovery Act, 1933," RFW Papers.

[23] Wagner speech file, Sept. 5, Oct. 18, 1932, RFW Papers; *Labor* (Washington, D.C.), Sept. 27, 1932; RFW to Herbert H. Maass, March 24, 1932, RFW Papers; Hugo Black, interview. Good accounts of the influences and events leading up to formulation of the New Deal's ambitious National Industrial Recovery Act of 1933 are given in Leuchtenburg, *Franklin D. Roosevelt,* pp. 55ff; Arthur M. Schlesinger, Jr., *The Age of Roosevelt: The Coming of the New Deal* (Boston, 1959), pp. 87ff; Irving Bernstein, *The New Deal Collective Bargaining Policy* (Berkeley and Los Angeles, 1950), pp. 29ff.

could not claim credit, Roosevelt now moved swiftly to head off the "revolution boiling up from the bottom." He put to work a Cabinet committee that, in collaboration with Wagner, eventually formulated a 3.3-billion-dollar Administration-approved public works program. He also commissioned Raymond Moley to look again into the plans that were floating around Washington for "business self-government," for relaxation of the antitrust laws, and for stabilization of wages and hours and working conditions. By the last week of April Moley had deputized General Hugh Johnson, a veteran of 1918's War Industries Board, and Donald Richberg, an attorney for the railroad unions, to come up with a workable scheme of government-business partnership. And at the same time Roosevelt lent new encouragement to Bob Wagner, who, for many months past, had been engaged in the quest that Moley, Johnson, and Richberg were now undertaking.

As early as the spring of 1931 Simon Rifkind, at the Senator's suggestion, had begun studying the possibly deleterious effects of the nation's antitrust tradition on such matters as economic stabilization, industrial competition, and labor conditions. In December of that year Wagner suggested that the forthcoming Congress launch an intensive investigation of the subject. (President Hoover made the same recommendation a few days later in his State of the Union message, but it went unheeded.) During 1932 Milton Handler, a friend of Rifkind's who was a specialist in antitrust law, made another study for the Senator; during the fall campaign Wagner discussed the matter with fellow lawyers in New York, although he had not yet concluded what ought to be done. By November the Senator was giving serious attention to "planning" proposals, such as those submitted by industrialists Gerard Swope and Rudolph Spreckels, that might help put an end to industrial instability, cutthroat competition, price deflation, and oppressive labor conditions.[24]

By the time of Roosevelt's inauguration industrial coordinating schemes of one sort or another had also won the support of such diverse proponents as the National Association of Manufacturers, the U. S. Chamber of Commerce, the National Progressive Conference, and such labor leaders in competition-ridden industries as John L. Lewis and Sidney Hillman. Especially appealing to Wagner was a

[24] RFW Papers: Simon H. Rifkind to the Director of the Legislative Reference Service, Library of Congress, April 1, 1931; Wagner speech file, Dec. 6, 1931; William Church Osborne to RFW, Nov. 11, 1932; Alexander Levene to Simon H. Rifkind, Nov. 25, 1932; Samuel L. Kuhn to RFW, Dec. 20, 1932; files on "Unemployment Plans, 1932–1933" and "National Industrial Recovery Act, 1933"; also interviews with Simon H. Rifkind and Milton Handler.

proposed National Economic Recovery act drawn up by Harold Moulton, the head of the Brookings Institution, and Meyer Jacobstein, a Brookings economist who had formerly represented the Rochester district in Congress and who was a close friend of New York's junior senator. Early in April 1933 the Moulton-Jacobstein plan became the focal point of Wagner's thinking. Toward the middle of the month, a short time after the Senate passed the Black Bill, Arthur Krock of *The New York Times* had lunch with Wagner, and, as the journalist recalled later, the Senator told him "all about NRA." [25]

According to Krock, the President was somewhat disturbed by Wagner's volubility with newsmen. At any rate, during several more weeks Roosevelt's press conference answers to questions about "the partnership with industry bill" were guarded and vague. Nevertheless, by the twenty-second of April the President had given Wagner the go-ahead signal to prepare a concrete piece of legislation, and on that date the Senator issued invitations to a series of conferences that got under way in his office on the twenty-fifth. Besides Moulton and Jacobstein, the members of "the Wagner group" included Fred I. Kent of the Bankers Trust Company in New York; Virgil D. Jordan of the National Industrial Conference Board; James H. Rand, Jr., of Remington-Rand; trade association attorney David L. Podell; industrial economist Malcolm C. Rorty; W. Jett Lauck, an economist with the United Mine Workers; and Representative Clyde Kelly of Pennsylvania, who had earlier sponsored legislation designed to stabilize competitive practices in the coal industry.

Following the first meeting Wagner delegated the task of drafting a bill to a subcommittee composed of Moulton, Podell, and Lauck, and on the twenty-ninth of April *The New York Times* carried an outline of their tentative proposal. It called for relaxation of the antitrust laws so that trade associations in industries "affected by a public interest" might, under the supervision of a federal board, draw up codes to regularize production, pricing, and competitive practices. The measure also called for regulation by the national board of wages and hours of labor on a flexible, industry-by-industry basis and for a guarantee of labor's right to organize and bargain collectively free of employer interference—a provision that had been included in Congressman Kelly's earlier legislation pertaining to the coal indus-

[25] RFW Papers: Sidney Hillman, "A Proposal for Labor Boards as an Essential in the Emergency," in Henry Moskowitz to RFW, April 12, 1933; Meyer Jacobstein to RFW, April 5, 1933; files on "National Industrial Recovery Act, 1933"; also Arthur Krock, "Reminiscences" (Oral History Research Office, 1950), p. 24.

try. As might be expected, the Senator saw to it that the bill also made provision for a federal public works program.[26]

In the meantime the activities of the Wagner group were duplicated in the executive branch. The office of Undersecretary of Commerce John Dickinson served as headquarters for the exchange of "planning" ideas among such figures as Rex Tugwell, Frances Perkins, and Jerome Frank, who was counsel to the new Agricultural Adjustment Administration. Wagner established liaison with this circle early in May, and during a series of conferences at the Commerce Building the Senator was especially impressed with the contributions of a young lawyer on Frank's staff named Leon Keyserling. Within a few days Dickinson and Frank, at least, had merged forces with Wagner. Moreover, the Senator had recruited Keyserling as a replacement for Simon Rifkind, who was due to leave Washington at the end of the special session to become a full partner in Wagner's New York law firm.

Next came the task of integrating the Wagner-Dickinson bill with the one that Hugh Johnson and Donald Richberg had presented to the President. During the next two weeks meetings and negotiations seemed interminable; on May 10, following an unproductive meeting at the White House, the President ordered Wagner, Dickinson, Johnson, Richberg, Perkins, Tugwell, and Budget Director Lewis Douglas to "lock themselves in a room" until they could come up with a common proposal.

All during this time Bob Wagner stood guard over the provisions of his draft that seemed to him especially important. Lewis Douglas, for example, made one last effort on behalf of fiscal orthodoxy by proposing to eliminate the 3.3-billion-dollar public works program, but Wagner and allies like Frances Perkins stood firm and had their way. Under the prodding of the National Association of Manufacturers various attempts were made also to soften the guarantee of collective bargaining that had found lodgment as Section 7(a) of the evolving bill. At one point Wagner even had to deliver an ultimatum: "No 7(a)," he told the conferees, "no bill"—and the disputed passage remained intact.

In only one feature, in fact, did the finished product diverge significantly from the Wagner group's original draft: while it had envisaged applying the "codes of fair competition" device only to major industries like steel and automobiles, the final version would attempt to

[26] Transcripts of press conferences, April 14, May 5, 10, 12, 1933, FDR Papers; RFW to Fred I. Kent *et al.*, April 22, 1933, RFW Papers; interviews with Simon H. Rifkind and John L. Lewis; *New York Times*, April 29, 1933.

codify all industries involved in interstate commerce. Wagner resisted the more grandiose scheme, feeling that it might endanger the experiment's success both constitutionally and administratively, but at General Johnson's insistence the conferees finally agreed to follow the more ambitious path. That it led into the thickets Wagner had foreseen became evident later when the NRA bogged down in efforts to extend the business-government partnership idea to burlesque theaters, the dog-food industry, and poultry markets.[27]

When Wagner introduced the Administration's industrial recovery bill on May 17, therefore, following the reading of a presidential message outlining its contents, he had his fingers crossed, at least in a figurative sense. He harbored no doubts about the desirability of the bill's public works program, of course, about its guarantee of labor's right to collective bargaining, or about the need for somehow stabilizing wages and hours. Nor, for the time being, did these provisions occasion much concern in the halls of Congress. Yet the means proposed for achieving the last-mentioned objective involved considerable risk since they entailed suspending the antitrust laws and conferring on business rights of self-government that might result in price-fixing and production-limiting agreements as well as better working conditions. And it was this aspect of the measure that commanded the lion's share of attention during the monumental debate that began June 7 when the Senate took up S. 1712.[28]

Insisting that the antitrust laws should be strengthened and ruthlessly enforced rather than relaxed, Senator William E. Borah of Idaho led the attack for those who believed that the NRA scheme represented a victory for big business and consequently a defeat for the small entrepreneur and the consuming public. The largest units in every industry would inevitably dominate the code-making process, Borah asserted, and thus the interests of smaller competitors and of consumers would be left to the tender mercies of the giants. He envisioned a situation where even the government's administrators, charged with policing the codified industries, would most probably be selected from the ranks of big business itself; in the end, therefore, the monopolists would end up dominating their own "regulators," as

27 Files on "National Industrial Recovery Act, 1933," RFW Papers; interviews with Simon H. Rifkind, Leon H. Keyserling, John L. Lewis, and Frances Perkins; Boris Shishkin, "Reminiscences," p. 482; Rexford G. Tugwell, "Reminiscences" (Oral History Research Office, 1950), pp. 47ff; Schlesinger, *The Coming of the New Deal*, pp. 96ff; Bernstein, *The New Deal Collective Bargaining Policy*, pp. 32–33.

28 77 *Congressional Record*, 3549–50, 5151ff. For Wagner's interpretation of the recovery act see also Robert F. Wagner, "Planning in Place of Restraint," *Survey Graphic* (Aug. 1933), pp. 395ff.

always. The net result of it all would be "ultra-concentration of wealth" and an end to traditional freedoms. For, in any event, according to the Idaho statesman, governmental attempts to avoid the dire consequences that he foresaw could only lead to a degree of federal bureaucracy, control, and censorship incompatible with the American system. "Shades of Stalin!" Borah proclaimed at one point. "Stabilization, what crimes are to be committed in thy name!"

Bob Wagner was fully cognizant of the dangers his colleague dwelt on and of the fact that his bill involved modification of traditional attitudes toward business concentration. "The bill is frankly an experiment," he reminded the Senate, "designed to last not more than two years." Its single objective, in Wagner's eyes, was "to speed the restoration of normal conditions of employment at wage scales sufficient to provide a comfort and decency level of living," a level that appeared unobtainable under the conditions of cutthroat competition that the inherited antitrust philosophy spawned.

In the forty years of their existence the antitrust laws had failed completely to check the constant growth in the size of business units, Wagner maintained, for the simple reason that the trend toward bigness was the inevitable result of advances made in science, technology, and the modes of production. "Any attempt by law to arrest this sweep would have been like Canute trying to roll back the sea"; and yet, beginning with the Sherman Act of 1890, the American people had attempted to do just that by employing methods that were based not on a twentieth-century economic philosophy but on "the abstract theories of Adam Smith's *Wealth of Nations*, published in 1776." And while failing to achieve their imagined objectives, the Sherman and Clayton acts, "as in the case with most laws which are out of touch with the times," produced unlooked-for side effects that injured the very groups the laws sought to protect—the small enterpriser, the consumer, and the laborer. "Since the law frowned upon the mutual association of independent groups, business expanded in size by ruthless and predatory practices . . . which bore heavily upon the small enterprise," Wagner asserted. The small businessman, barred from cooperating with others of his kind and thus deprived of his only weapon against larger opponents, was forced into "the wrong kind of competition against other smaller men, a competition that was wasteful, blind, and destructive" and that extended to "degrading the position of the wage earner and cheating the consumer."

Such were the practical effects of "the acceptance of competition as a fetish" that Wagner portrayed in a speech constituting an incisive analysis of the country's recent economic history. The industrial recovery bill, in his view, would further the original objectives of the antitrust laws—protection of small business, consumers, and the workers—but it would do so by applying twentieth-century methods. "It must be stated in the strongest terms that the bill does not abolish competition," Wagner asserted; "it purifies and strengthens it." By making competitive practices "constructive rather than ruinous," and by permitting cooperation among businessmen large and small for the sake of greater stability and industrial progress, the measure would confine competition "to honorable bids for the market and real gains in efficiency" rather than allowing it to extend to labor- and consumer-debasing tactics. In that way Americans would begin to face up to the real problem of their modern industrial economy, "the problem of utilizing the wealth-creating possibilities of large size in such a way as to help everyone," which the antitrust philosophy, by quixotically concentrating attention on the matter of size alone, had obscured. "The task is not to check efficiency," Wagner pleaded, "but to reap its full benefits."

Viewed in that light, which was the perspective on which Wagner, at least, if not others in Administration circles, insisted, the measure was not designed to curtail production, as some of its opponents charged. "It is a measure to expand trade and commerce," the New Yorker averred, "by removing the barriers which have caused factories to close and men to walk the streets in idleness." As to the danger that business might abuse the powers conferred on it, the bill's sponsor conceded that they were real enough. But "when it is administered with the humane sympathies, level-headed judgment, and splendid valor which the President has shown in all his actions," Wagner proclaimed—again, perhaps, with his fingers crossed—"it will be a powerful factor in bringing order and health into the economic life of the American people."

On the whole the Senate's debate on the recovery bill was conducted on an unusually high plane. For sustained periods Wagner matched wits with Borah, one of the most distinguished lawyers in the chamber, in discussions of the constitutional phases of the legislation; to one reporter their exchanges indicated that "at least some semblance of the golden days of statesmanship still remains." [29] As always, Wagner remained calm and courteous as, in response to numberless questions, he repeated his interpretation of the bill's meaning. He listened patiently also while Huey Long delivered a long tirade against the Roosevelt Administration and while, more thoughtfully, Hugo Black suggested that government limitation of profits might be

[29] Undated clipping from the Washington *Star* (June 1933), RFW Papers.

a necessary corollary to the great powers conferred on corporations by the measure. On only two occasions did Wagner's temper show signs of flaring. When antitruster Burton K. Wheeler made a cutting reference to "these professors . . . who are working out these bills," Wagner responded that "there were no professors drafting this legislation"—which wasn't quite true. And when Huey Long, while praising Wagner's record in the field of social legislation, asserted that in the present instance his "good friend from New York" had been "taken in" by the "crowd across the mahogany table who have been working around here trying to get rid of the anti-trust laws," Bob was on his feet in an instant. "Mr. President, I assure the Senator, because I notice his interest in my welfare, that so far as my contribution to such legislation is concerned, it is not an overnight thought," Wagner retorted. "I have been thinking of it for years. I do not think we will ever have industry in order until we have nationally planned economy, and this is the first step toward it. It is not a recent conversion at all," he concluded—and that assertion *was* the exact truth, as most who heard him recognized.

The House had passed the recovery bill quickly, and by the overwhelming vote of 325–76, just a few days after its introduction; in the end, and after more extended consideration, the Senate followed suit on June 9, but by a much closer tally. "History probably will record the National Industrial Recovery Act as the most important and far-reaching legislation ever enacted by the American Congress," President Roosevelt declared in signing the measure on June 16. That its public works section would provide some employment relief, and that the bill's provisions as a whole would promote some degree of economic recovery, seemed assured. But whether the NRA "government-business" partnership scheme would take its place as a permanent reform remained to be seen. "It is a challenge to industry," the President added in his statement, indicating that he, like the Act's sponsor, was keeping his fingers crossed.[30]

Thus ended the First Hundred Days that began the New Deal's transformation of the American way of life. Never had the nation witnessed such a precedent-shattering display of legislative action. Not only had a many-pronged attack on the depression been launched but a series of other ambitious measures, long-frustrated by the conservatism of previous Republican Administrations, had received federal sanction. Senator George Norris saw a dream come true when Congress enacted the bill creating the Tennessee Valley Authority.

[30] Schlesinger, *The Coming of the New Deal*, p. 102.

And toward the end of the session, almost unnoticed, Congress approved Bob Wagner's bill establishing a cooperative federal-state system of employment exchanges; the original Three Bills program, now so outdated, had nevertheless been completed. In a fitting gesture Secretary of Labor Frances Perkins appointed Wagner vice-chairman of the new agency's Federal Advisory Council, and the revivified United States Employment Service was soon on its way to becoming an indispensable part of the American industrial scene.[31]

It had been a hectic time for everyone in Washington. During the first week of May, while engaged in working out the complex details of the industrial recovery bill, for example, Bob Wagner also served as a conferee on both the Federal Emergency Relief Act and the Securities Act at the same time. In July, therefore, while General Hugh Johnson set about the task of codifying the nation's industries and drumming up public enthusiasm behind the Blue Eagle emblem adopted by the National Recovery Administration, Wagner sailed for Europe. A trip to his native land might not be so pleasant now (in a Senate speech on June 10 Wagner had already called on the German people to repudiate the Jew-baiting tactics of the Nazi leaders then coming to power), but he wanted to see for himself how the old country had fared during the depression that had brought a New Deal to America. And in any event, an ocean voyage, as Wagner frequently testified, afforded the best means of relaxation that he had ever found.[32]

The Senator's vacation abroad was short-lived, however, for back home the National Recovery Administration that he had helped establish soon encountered difficulties. Not only did the construction of industrial "codes of fair competition" prove to be a tremendously complex operation, but almost immediately additional complications began to arise under the hitherto little-noticed Section 7(a) of the recovery act. That provision, guaranteeing the right of employees to organize and bargain collectively in codified industries, had been hailed by William Green as labor's Magna Charta, while John L. Lewis compared it with the Emancipation Proclamation. But the labor leaders' view of the matter soon clashed with the determination of some employers, as voiced by the N.A.M., to "fight energetically against any encroachments by Closed Shop labor unions."

Conflicting interpretations of Section 7(a), of the legitimacy of the "company union" device, and of related questions overwhelmed General Johnson and his harried Recovery Administration staff as the

[31] RFW to Frances Perkins, June 24, 1933, RFW Papers.
[32] 77 *Congressional Record*, 5589–90; Claire Dittrich Denzer, interview.

summer progressed, and a rash of strikes aimed at securing labor's "rights" under the recovery act ensued. Early in August the members of both the Labor and Industry Advisory boards that Johnson had attached to his Administration asked for creation of a National Labor Board to consider and adjust differences of interpretation of Section 7(a); to serve as its chairman they suggested Senator Wagner. The President acquiesced, a cablegram was dispatched to Europe, and soon Bob Wagner was on his way home to assume his new post.[33]

Wagner's unanimous "nomination" to head the new Labor Board signified the confidence that industrialists like Gerard Swope, Alfred P. Sloan of General Motors, and Henry I. Harriman of the U. S. Chamber of Commerce—members of NRA's Industrial Advisory Board—placed in the New York Senator's competence and integrity. Yet Wagner's service in his new capacity was to possess even greater significance, for it initiated a further step in the evolution of his thinking regarding labor's rightful place in American life. Soon it would put in process the formulation of *the* "Wagner Act"—the one that was to play the most significant part of all in reshaping the nation's industrial system.

[33] "The N.R.A. at Grips with the Labor Problem," *Literary Digest*, Aug. 19, 1933, p. 5; John L. Lewis, interview; Schlesinger, *The Coming of the New Deal*, pp. 136ff; Bernstein, *The New Deal Collective Bargaining Policy*, pp. 57–58.

CHAPTER 10

A Long Road

WHEN I FRAMED the National Industrial Recovery Act and steered it through Congress," Bob Wagner wrote in September of 1933, following his return from Europe, "I felt that the greatest victory in my war against human misery had been achieved. I am even more confident now." By that time a Public Works Administration, with $3.3 billion at its disposal, had been established, with Secretary of the Interior Harold Ickes at its head. Hugh Johnson had supervised the drawing up of codes of fair competition for the nation's ten leading industries; thousands of other employers had subscribed to the President's "blanket code," fixing a twenty-five-cent-per-hour minimum wage and the forty-hour week, as a stopgap expedient pending separate codification of the lesser industries. Certainly the people experienced an immense psychological uplift, and as production figures, stock prices, and other indices showed improvement, some even assumed that the depression was all but licked. As usual, however, Wagner was more cautious. "No danger could be greater," he warned, "than a failure to realize that the fight against poverty and unemployment has just begun. . . . I have every confidence in ultimate success, but I should deplore a premature cry of triumph. We must soberly face the future." [1]

[1] Robert F. Wagner, "The Fight Has Only Begun," *American Magazine* (Nov. 1933), pp. 14ff; Jack F. Isakoff, *The Public Works Administration* (Urbana, Ill., 1938), *passim*; William E. Leuchtenburg, *Franklin D. Roosevelt and the New Deal: 1932–1940* (New York, 1963), pp. 64ff; Arthur M. Schlesinger, Jr., *The Age of Roosevelt: The Coming of the New Deal* (Boston, 1959), pp. 103ff.

The evidence that stern tests lay ahead for the New Deal wasn't hard to find among the communications that flowed across Wagner's desk, either in the Senate Office Building or on the third floor of the Commerce Building, where he functioned as chairman of the National Labor Board. There were numerous complaints, for example, regarding Ickes' slowness in getting public construction started; the situation was no better now than in the Hoover years, asserted Father John O'Grady of the National Conference of Catholic Charities, "and at the present pace we simply are not going to have any worthwhile public works program." [2]

Even more prolific of trouble were General Johnson's codes of fair competition, for in their construction every one of the roadblocks forecast by Senator Borah—domination by big business, price-fixing, production limitations, and neglect of the small businessman, laborer, and consumer—gave rise to complaints. Typifying the complex of dissatisfactions that clustered about virtually every one of the "industrial self-government" agreements was the four-page memorandum Wagner received from an NRA official listing the objections that were holding up promulgation of the silk textile industry's code: the manufacturers insisted that the producers of their synthetic competitor, rayon, be placed under the same code; labor was so dissatisfied with its wage and hour provisions that they had already gone out on strike; "commission houses object to trade practices as written"; "silk salesmen want consideration in the code"; "the Consumers Advisory Board also objects to trade practices as written," and in this "they are also joined by the National Retail Dry Goods Association." All of which leaves one wondering just who, if anybody, was satisfied with the scheme!

Yet Wagner did not need to rely on Recovery Administration officials themselves to tell him of their woes, for his office, and those of his Congressional colleagues, soon became centers for relaying thousands of complaints to NRA headquarters in Washington. "The task of reconciling the interests of businessmen with the interests of the public at every point will strain the capabilities of the administrators to the uttermost," Wagner declared in November. Developments in the ensuing months more than bore out the truth of that prediction.[3]

[2] Rev. John O'Grady to RFW, Aug. 23, 1933, and files on "Public Works Administration, 1933–1934," RFW Papers.

[3] W. E. Walter to RFW, Sept. 14, 1933, and files on "National Industrial Recovery Act, 1933–1934," RFW Papers; Wagner, "The Fight Has Only Begun," pp. 14ff. For the working of the NRA code experiment in practice see Leuchtenburg, *Franklin D. Roosevelt*, pp. 67ff; Schlesinger, *The Coming of the New Deal*, pp. 107ff; Leverett S. Lyon *et al.*, *The National Recovery Administra-*

Throughout the swirl of charges and countercharges that enveloped the New Deal's industrial recovery program in late 1933 and 1934 Bob Wagner kept his attention riveted on what he regarded as the one critical set of factors: the extent to which the program created jobs and increased wages, thereby augmenting mass purchasing power, so that consumption could be brought more in line with the nation's productive capacity. Again and again he insisted that speed was essential in the administration of the public works appropriation. In October he was privately critical of Ickes' dilatoriness, and only a sudden improvement in the administrator's performance persuaded the New York Senator to delete public criticism from a speech he delivered late in the month. Wagner was gratified when, in November, the President diverted some of the PWA's money to a new Civil Works Administration, run by the more energetic Harry Hopkins. By the middle of January Hopkins had put four million men to work on light public works in contrast to the one million given employment by PWA enterprises.[4]

In February, however, Roosevelt gave in to the dunning of budget-conscious Lewis Douglas and ordered that the CWA be wound up by May 1; Hopkins, reluctant but loyal, asked Congress for a mere $950,000,000, designed to last until the terminal date. On the floor of the Senate a small group of liberals tried to raise the appropriation to $2,500,000,000, so that the CWA might remain in business indefinitely, and Wagner, armed with figures indicating that at least ten million men were still without jobs in private industry, helped lead their fight. Nor did arguments to the effect that "Certainly Mr. Hopkins must know what the task is" deter him. Confident in his own analysis of the situation, Wagner insisted that "whether he wants more or not, he needs more, if we are to take care of the unemployed and avoid another recession. . . . I cannot see any other answer for it except that he indulges in an optimism which I cannot share." Pointing out that the index of industrial production had risen much faster than the index of payrolls, Wagner maintained that only "the steady flow of federal funds . . . into the pockets of consumers" could make up for the looming gap between output and consumption until private business itself had absorbed the unemployed. "It is imperative that public expenditures should continue to serve as a balance

---

tion (Washington, 1935), *passim*; Charles Frederick Roos, NRA *Economic Planning* (Bloomington, Ind., 1937), *passim*.
    [4] Leon H. Keyserling to Simon H. Rifkind, Oct. 10, 1933, RFW Papers; Leuchtenburg, *Franklin D. Roosevelt*, pp. 121–122; Schlesinger, *The Coming of the New Deal*, pp. 269ff.

wheel," he urged. "This is the only safeguard against a relapse." [5]

For the time being, however, the budget balancers had their way, and the spenders' amendment went down to a resounding 58–10 defeat. But Wagner continued to insist that the wisdom of public-employment measures like the PWA and the CWA had been "more than vindicated." His fight for bigger and better public works programs went on, and it would meet with somewhat more success when the President was in a less conservative mood than the one that beset him in 1934.[6]

Convinced that "the New Deal has accomplished too much to fear destruction by its enemies," and that "it can suffer only if its friends clothe it in perfection and scorn the advocates of improvement," Wagner remained equally rigorous in measuring the performance of the NRA's "codes of fair competition" by the yardstick of their contribution toward improving employment, wages, and consumer purchasing power. "Will the united strength of businessmen be used primarily to extract the last ounce of profit . . . ? Will the gains made by the elimination of competitive wastes be pocketed by a few huge concerns?" he challenged in a radio speech on October 18, 1933. "These problems must be solved by industrial leaders in such a way as to justify the confidence which the Recovery Act imposes," he warned.[7]

From the outset Wagner maintained that price-fixing agreements sanctioned by the codes should not go beyond the bounds of establishing minimum wages or, at most, prohibiting the cutthroat practice of selling below the cost of production. And while agreeing that temporary limitations on production of certain articles in some of the codes might be justified to relieve a glutted market, Wagner insisted that "the recovery program certainly contemplates that productive effort shall *not* be withheld for selfish personal reasons." "I am not a scarcity economist," the New York Senator reiterated time and again. "In the vast majority of cases I believe that the long-range task is not to limit production, but to produce as much as possible and to distribute the products widely and equitably." [8]

Assessing the NRA's first-year record in a Senate speech on May

[5] 78 *Congressional Record*, 2162ff, 2179ff; Leuchtenburg, *Franklin D. Roosevelt*, pp. 122–123; Schlesinger, *The Coming of the New Deal*, pp. 276–277.
[6] 78 *Congressional Record*, 2195; RFW to Arthur Brandt, Dec. 18, 1933, RFW Papers.
[7] 78 *Congressional Record*, 9333; Wagner speech file, Oct. 18, 1933, RFW Papers.
[8] 78 *Congressional Record*, 9334; also RFW Papers: Wagner speech file, Oct. 18, 1933, and Oct. 30, Dec. 20, 1934; RFW to Herve Schwedersky, July 18, 1933; RFW to William Bourossa, Oct. 18, 1933.

23, 1934, Wagner remained convinced that "the underlying method of approach of the recovery program is sound," but he conceded the existence of a pressing need "to prevent its instrumentalities of control from falling into the hands of selfish groups." He found grounds for concern in the report issued shortly before by the National Recovery Review Board established by the President under the chairmanship of Clarence Darrow, which contained evidence that price-fixing, production quotas, and other monopolistic practices were being employed by big business in ways detrimental to the interests of small business and the consuming public. There was "a good deal of force" too, Wagner believed, in the widespread complaint that the Recovery Administration itself had come to be composed preponderantly of men whose personal connections made them partial toward the business element in the government-business-labor-consumer "partnership."

"If Government is going to participate in economic affairs, an independent and unhampered public service should be developed for this purpose," Wagner warned. It couldn't be done overnight, he admitted, "because the trained personnel does not exist," but certainly "we should turn our efforts in that direction." For, all in all, though the NRA program had yielded favorable results in terms of recovery, "it has fallen far short of reform." "Its greatest potentialities are still unexplored and await further action," Wagner added. "The road to be traveled is still a long one."

Particularly disturbing to Wagner was the mounting evidence indicating that the industrial working force was failing to share proportionately in the recovery upswing. For while production figures, prices, corporate profits, and executive salaries showed improvement after June 1933, wages lagged behind. "The increase in the real income of the entire wage-earning class has been due to re-employment rather than to improved individual standards," Wagner observed in the spring of 1934. "The individual worker employed full time is earning less today than he did last March." And since "permanent prosperity is a vain hope while workers do not receive enough to buy the goods which they produce," that maladjustment constituted, in Wagner's view, the point at which the New Deal's program "seems in greatest need of immediate improvement." [9]

The failure of the workers' share of the increased national income to rise proportionately could be accounted for, in part, by the unsatisfactory standards of wages and hours established in most of the

[9] 78 *Congressional Record*, 9333ff. On the Darrow Report see Schlesinger, *The Coming of the New Deal*, pp. 132–134.

NRA codes, and as early as December 1933 Wagner was asserting that minimum wages must be higher and hours of work must be cut still further, "even if it requires a definite mandate of Congress to produce these results." Still more alarming, however, was the failure of wage rates in the upper wage brackets to show any improvement; indeed, the minimums set by the codes were looked on by some employers as the *maximums* they need pay to any of their workers regardless of skill or experience. "As a result," Wagner told a meeting of code authorities in Washington on March 5, 1934, "there has been some tendency for rises in the lower brackets to be counteracted by reductions in the upper ones. This is a serious evil," he added, "for prosperity can be neither attained nor preserved by making workers share with workers." [10]

But if profits and wages were to be brought into balance short of reliance on a totalitarian degree of governmental dictation—a method that Wagner unequivocally rejected—then it had to be achieved through "a partnership for economic reconstruction" between business and labor. "The present emergency has justly called forth exceptional activities by government," he had declared in the summer of 1933. "But the long permanent climb is the job of industry itself—of employers and employees, bending their energies to the task with an increasing measure of cooperation." The only feasible basis for such cooperation, Wagner insisted, was equality of bargaining power between the two parties. "Industry's newly won right to unite must be matched by labor's right to bargain collectively," he maintained in justifying the inclusion of Section 7(a) in the Recovery Act, for "only a well-organized labor group can equal the forces of cooperating businessmen and bring about justice and security for everyone." "The attempts of the government to balance conflicting interests and insure fair treatment to all must fail," Wagner asserted on another occasion, "unless every group is united in the presentation of its legitimate claims."

In the first months of 1934, as the efforts of the National Labor Board to protect labor's right to organize encountered increasing resistance, Wagner feared for the success of the Administration's recovery and reform program. New legislation, reinforcing the guarantees of Section 7(a), was needed, he had decided, if the New Deal was to preserve "the basic conditions of fairness and freedom which will allow industry and labor to handle their own problems." Only through such action, he told the code authorities conference in

10 A. L. Warner, "Legislative Prophet of the New Deal," *Literary Digest*, Dec. 16, 1933, p. 6; Wagner speech file, March 5, 1934, RFW Papers.

March, could the New Deal prevent a return "to the uneven prosperity of the 1920's, with its poverty, its uncertainty, and its seeds of
recurrent depressions." [11]

From its inception the National Labor Board created by the President in August of 1933 operated under the vaguest of commissions as
to its jurisdiction, procedures, and enforcement powers. Not until
mid-December, one week before the agency's status faced its first test
in court, was its existence formalized by the issuance of an executive
order. Not until late in October had Wagner and the other original
members—Leo Wolman, William Green, and John L. Lewis representing labor, and Walter C. Teagle, Gerard Swope, and Louis E.
Kirstein representing industry—even received official White House
letters of appointment! But from the outset the body interpreted its
duties liberally: it offered its services to mediate and arbitrate all sorts
of labor disputes, and, when the parties failed to agree, it rendered
"decisions." Eventually nineteen regional boards, manned by unpaid
volunteers, were established, and the Washington board reserved its
attention for the toughest cases.[12]

Wagner hoped that his tribunal might come to be viewed as a
"supreme court" of labor relations (he even provided its hearing
rooms in the Commerce Building with the sort of black velvet wall
hangings usually found in courtrooms) that would evolve a body of
labor "common law" relevant to the whole New Deal recovery and
reform program. He acknowledged that the board "can not force a
single person to appear in Washington" and that its success depended
on the willingness of employers and employees alike to cooperate and
compromise. "Each must discard the old-fashioned notions that gains
are achieved by harrowing conflicts, that competition is the life of
trade, and that the success of one party can result only from the defeat of the other," Wagner exhorted. The lockout and the strike,
while either might be justified "by an extreme situation," should be
abandoned as instruments of first resort; instead, recourse should be

[11] 78 *Congressional Record*, 9335, 12017; Wagner speech file, Sept. 18,
1933, RFW Papers; Wagner, "The Fight Has Only Begun," pp. 14ff.
[12] FDR Papers: Homer T. Cummings to Cordell Hull, Dec. 16, 1933; Marvin McIntyre to RFW, Oct. 26, 1933; also files on "National Labor Board,
1933–1934," RFW Papers; interviews with Simon H. Rifkind, Leon H. Keyserling, Jeremiah T. Mahoney, John L. Lewis, and Philip Levy (an attorney with
Wagner's labor board who, in 1937, succeeded Keyserling as the Senator's administrative assistant). On the organization and operations of the National Labor
Board see Lewis L. Lorwin and Arthur Wubnig, *Labor Relations Boards* (Washington, 1935), *passim;* Irving Bernstein, *The New Deal Collective Bargaining
Policy* (Berkeley and Los Angeles, 1950), pp. 58ff.

had to the arbitral and adjudicatory facilities of the Labor Board. Only in that way could the New Deal's "tremendous experiment in cooperation" be made to work.[13]

For a while all seemed to go well. The board's decisions were usually unanimous, and enough employers and labor leaders seemed to have caught the conciliatory spirit to keep the agency's personnel extremely busy; on more than one occasion, according to Wagner's own testimony, he was up until dawn working on labor matters before going to his regular Senate duties in the morning. Within six months the board and its regional branches handled 1,818 cases involving 914,000 workers; 480 strikes had been settled, and 197 more had been averted.

But good as the record appeared, it wasn't good enough, and as the spring of 1934 approached, more labor strife loomed ahead than before. At the root of the problem lay a deep-seated conflict over the meaning of the guarantee in Section 7(a) that "employees shall have the right to organize and bargain collectively through representatives of their own choosing." To a good many employers a single-plant employee representation plan, or company union, even if initiated, encouraged, or financially supported by management, constituted compliance with the Recovery Act's edict; to labor leaders and to most liberals the company union was anathema. Three-quarters of all the disputes handled by the National Labor Board involved charges of employer interference with workers' organizational activities or refusal to bargain with outside unions claiming to speak for the work force; and that fact, Wagner informed the President in February 1934 represented the most "disquieting aspect" of the labor situation. It also represented the thorniest problem the board had been called on to handle and the one that eventually led to its virtual disintegration.[14]

It was not surprising that, under Wagner's leadership, the Labor Board's own interpretation of Section 7(a) leaned heavily toward the version espoused by labor and liberal spokesmen; more remarkable, perhaps, was the degree to which the industry representatives concurred in the chairman's position. The board ruled, for example, that membership in an outside union might not be used as the basis for discharging an employee, and in several cases it ordered that workers thus discriminated against be reinstated in their jobs. The board also held that a company union, if dominated by the employer, consti-

[13] Wagner speech file, Oct. 3, 18, 1933, RFW Papers; S. J. Woolf, "Wagner Foresees a New Industrial Day," *New York Times Magazine*, Nov. 12, 1933.
[14] RFW to J. B. Mayer, Jan. 16, 1934, RFW Papers; RFW to FDR, Feb. 21, 1934, FDR Papers.

tuted interference with the workers' right to self-organization. In order to resolve disputes involving a contest between a company union and an outside union, it seemed natural to Wagner that the NLB should resort to a secret ballot to determine the wishes of the employees involved, and ninety-seven such elections took place under board supervision during its first six months of existence. The bargaining agent selected by a majority of those voting in the election was to represent all the workers in the unit—"a democratic principle," declared Wagner, "which is followed in every business and in our governmental life." Employers had a duty to confer and bargain in good faith with employee representatives thus chosen, the board ruled, and it recommended that any agreements arrived at through such negotiations be reduced to a written contract.[15]

During the fall and winter of 1933 a number of disputes were settled by application of the NLB's formula, but at the same time the devotion of some employers to the company union device grew fonder than ever. In December the Weirton Steel Company and the Budd Manufacturing Company, in two important cases, refused to abide by board decisions or to allow representation elections under NLB auspices, and their impunity strengthened the determination of recalcitrant employers generally.

Equally detrimental to the board's effectiveness was the attitude of National Recovery Administrator Hugh Johnson and his General Counsel, Donald Richberg, on whose cooperation the board relied for enforcement of its orders. Unlike Wagner, who firmly believed that "until the promises made by the Recovery Act are given definite meaning, we can not have happy and contented workers," Johnson and Richberg viewed strikes strictly as impediments to business revival. They were to be settled as quickly as possible, under whatever formula would best serve to "get the men back to work"—regardless, apparently, of the rights and wrongs involved in the dispute. Consequently those two officials were much more lenient in their tolerance of company unions than were the majority of the NLB. In place of the principle of majority rule, for example, they tended to favor a system of proportional representation that would allow employers to bargain with minority company unions as well as with an outside union chosen by most of the workers. The Johnson-Richberg position was reflected in the NRA's extreme hesitancy to use the sanctions prescribed in the Recovery Act against employers who flouted the Labor Board's decisions, and thus the board found itself impotent.[16]

[15] Wagner speech file, May 31, 1934, RFW Papers.
[16] *Ibid.*, March 5, 1934; Leuchtenburg, *Franklin D. Roosevelt*, pp. 107–108;

As opposition from businessmen and from within the ranks of the Roosevelt Administration itself thus whittled away at the NLB's status, Wagner despaired of turning it, under its existing constitution, into a supreme court of labor relations; late in December 1933 there were rumors that he was about to resign as its chairman. But the President, despite advice from prominent businessmen such as Charles R. Hook of the NRA's Durable Goods Industries Committee to the effect that "it would be tremendously advantageous to your program if Mr. Wagner could be induced to resign," prevailed on the Senator to stay. In February 1934 he even issued another executive order specifically authorizing the NLB to conduct representation elections on the basis of majority rule.[17]

Nevertheless, Roosevelt continued to view the formulation of a labor policy as a secondary problem, and, unlike Wagner, he failed to recognize the connection between free unions and collective bargaining on the one hand and wages, purchasing power, and recovery on the other. Thus he failed to intervene when, in public statements during the month of February, Johnson and Richberg virtually repudiated the principle of majority rule. Moreover, in March, when a representation dispute wracked the important automobile industry, Roosevelt allowed the General to work out an agreement that not only provided for proportional representation but also created an Automobile Labor Board independent of the NLB. Shorn of presidential support for its principles, and also of an important area of jurisdiction, the Labor Board sank into virtual disuse. Thereafter its chairman performed his administrative duties perfunctorily, for he had already turned his primary attention back to the legislative mill.[18]

As early as December 1933 Wagner was telling newsmen that Section 7(a) needed to be clarified and strengthened through amendment. By the end of that month he had his new assistant, Leon Keyserling, at work on the project. In January there were conferences with Green, Lewis, and officials of the Labor Department. During February successive drafts of the bill were hammered out, and on March 1 the New York Senator introduced his "Labor Disputes Act of 1934."[19]

Schlesinger, *The Coming of the New Deal*, pp. 145ff; Leon H. Keyserling, interview.

[17] Transcript of press conference, Dec. 29, 1933, and Charles R. Hook to Hugh Johnson, March 8, 1934, FDR Papers.

[18] Bernstein, *The New Deal Collective Bargaining Policy*, pp. 59–60; Sidney Fine, *The Automobile Under the Blue Eagle* (Ann Arbor, Mich., 1963), *passim*.

[19] New York *Evening Post*, Jan. 2, 1934; 78 *Congressional Record*, 3443ff; files on "National Labor Relations Act, 1934," RFW Papers; Leon H. Keyserling

The measure destined to be the forerunner of the Wagner Act proposed to create a permanent National Labor Board armed with subpoena powers and the authority to enforce its orders directly through the federal district courts; in effect the board would have equal footing with the Federal Trade Commission and the government's other independent regulatory agencies. It might engage in mediation and arbitration of labor disputes affecting interstate commerce; settle representation cases by certifying appropriate bargaining agents; and issue cease-and-desist orders against employers who indulged in such "unfair labor practices" as discriminating against union members, interfering with the workers' right to organize, creating and supporting a company union, or refusing to recognize and deal with representatives chosen by their employees and certified by the Labor Board. The ingredients that went into the bill were obviously derived primarily from the experience of Wagner's own board. While labor leaders and Labor Department spokesmen contributed some suggestions, the legislation itself was drafted in Wagner's office. Keyserling was in charge, and for technical assistance he relied on certain members of the NLB's staff—General Counsel Milton Handler, Executive Secretary William M. Leiserson, Philip Levy, Benedict Wolf, and William G. Rice, Jr. But not a single essential idea went into the measure, Keyserling has testified, without the Senator's explicit approval, and on introducing the legislation Wagner specified that it "reflects only my own views" and not those of any other public official.

Although Wagner insistently repeated that his bill was designed to promote labor-management cooperation, and thus to foster both economic recovery and industrial peace, its reception was anything but tranquil. Labor leaders and most liberals were for the measure, of course, and so were the thousands of workers who informed Wagner, sometimes anonymously, of their feelings—"I'd give a year of my life to be able to sign this letter," wrote an employee in a company-union plant, "I'm ashamed, I can't afford to take the chance." But industrialists like Ernest G. Draper, who endorsed the bill, and Charles Edison, who scorned the narrowness of businessmen "who seem to

---

Papers (in Mr. Keyserling's possession, Washington); interviews with Leon H. Keyserling, Simon H. Rifkind, Philip Levy, Milton Handler, John L. Lewis, Frances Perkins. On the origin, formulation, and principles of what was to become *the* Wagner Act, see Leon H. Keyserling, "The Wagner Act: Its Origin and Current Significance," *George Washington Law Review* (Dec. 1960), pp. 199ff; Leon H. Keyserling, "Why the Wagner Act?," in Louis G. Silverberg, ed., *The Wagner Act: After Ten Years* (Washington, 1945), pp. 5ff; Bernstein, *The New Deal Collective Bargaining Policy*, pp. 60ff.

be afraid that labor might draw a few aces in the New Deal," were hard to find.

At the Senate hearings before David I. Walsh's Education and Labor Committee that began in the middle of March, spokesmen for business presented a virtually united front against the New York Senator's proposal. The plan was unconstitutional, they argued; moreover, it would impede recovery by fomenting strikes, create a labor union monopoly inimical to industrial freedom, and destroy "the happy and peaceful relationships" that had grown up under existing company-union plans.

But the arguments presented by James Emery of the National Association of Manufacturers and his colleagues at the Senate hearings were mild and restrained compared to the flood of propaganda that many companies unleashed through public media, letters to stockholders, and handbills distributed to workers at the factory gates. "This extraordinary bill would place the A. F. of L. in control of every manufacturing industry," the Laclede Steel Company of St. Louis informed its share-owners. "It foments class warfare by forcibly aligning class against class," declared a trade association that deluged members of Congress with letters of protest. The Associated Industries of Oklahoma, in full-page newspaper advertisements, lamented that the bill "prohibits the practice of Christian brotherhood. It puts loyalty to labor unions above loyalty to God. This measure, in effect, would out-Stalin Stalin, out-Soviet the Russian Soviets, and create a despotism." "Vicious" seems to have been the favorite word used to describe the newest Wagner bill in such attacks; nor, this time, did its sponsor completely escape personal criticism. "If he had had thirty years of business experience in place of thirty years of political experience," declared the president of the Goodyear Rubber Company in a radio address, "I might feel differently about accepting his leadership." To an industrial publication in New Hampshire Bob Wagner represented nothing less than "the leftist Left in the left wing of all Demo-Socialists in the legislative, executive, and judicial departments at Washington." [20]

Wagner had been prepared for business opposition to his bill, of

[20] Boris Shishkin, "Reminiscences" (Oral History Research Office, Columbia Univ., 1957), p. 751; also RFW Papers: Ernest G. Draper to RFW, June 4, 1934; Charles Edison to RFW, June 5, 1933; Leon H. Keyserling to George Mitchell, March 7, 1934; files on "Responses to the National Labor Relations Act, Pro and Con, 1934"; also Leon H. Keyserling Papers; U. S. Senate, 73rd Cong., 2nd Sess., Committee on Education and Labor, *Hearings on S. 2926: To Create a National Labor Board* (Washington, D.C., Govt. Printing Office, 1934), *passim.*

course, if not for the vituperativeness of some of it. He was less prepared, however, for the reception it met in Administration circles. In
her testimony before Walsh's committee Frances Perkins was ambivalent in her endorsement of the measure; her main concern seemed to
be to have the new board located within the domain of her Labor
Department rather than to enjoy independent status. (Some attributed Miss Perkins' indifference to what they alleged to be her "typical" middle-class social worker's perspective—a deep desire to do
something *for* labor, but relative insensitivity to the idea of labor,
through organization, doing something *for itself*. It should be pointed
out, however, that many social workers supported the organized labor
movement and Wagner's bill enthusiastically.) Hugh Johnson's attitude provided an even bigger stumbling block. For a while Wagner
(and the public) expected the NRA chief to testify on the bill—two
separate days were set aside for his convenience—but the General
never did take the opportunity to appear. Instead, in a statement that
he made public on April 10, Johnson declared that "the government
should not favor any particular form of [labor] organization." Employers should be allowed to initiate company unions, Johnson believed, although he felt that they should not "finance, foster, nor direct what the men do" once the company plan was put into effect.[21]

Aside from Perkins and Johnson, the general attitude of prominent New Deal officials toward the Wagner bill was one of stony
silence.

President Roosevelt's initial silence regarding Wagner's newest
measure naturally had an especially important bearing on its chances
for passage. Roosevelt had not been consulted at all in the drafting of
the bill. On March 2 he told newsmen he had not yet read it, and there
is little to indicate that he read it at any other time prior to the end of
the Congressional session. It does appear that during the automobile
strike Roosevelt and Johnson used Wagner's bill as a club in persuad-
ing the auto makers to accept the General's settlement of March 25,
but at no time during the Senate committee's hearings on the measure did the President comment on it one way or another.

By mid-April, however, as a series of violent strikes ripped one
city after another, while a strike in the vital steel industry loomed in
the offing, the President had become more amenable to putting something like the Wagner legislation on his "must" list for Congress.

[21] RFW to Hugh Johnson, March 17, April 6, 1934, RFW Papers; *New
York Times*, April 10, 1934; Bernstein, *The New Deal Collective Bargaining Pol-
icy*, p. 69; Frances Perkins, *The Roosevelt I Knew* (New York, 1946), pp. 239ff;
Leon H. Keyserling, interview.

Roosevelt still placed the emphasis on creating some kind of permanent and more effective *mediation* machinery; the auto strike had taken up too much of his time, he complained. Thus, like Johnson, F.D.R. viewed the problem essentially as one of keeping men at work rather than of ensuring the workers' right to free and unhampered self-organization. ("A tranquil relationship between employer and employee, while eminently desirable," Wagner was writing in *The New York Times* about this time, "is not a sole desideratum. It all depends upon the basis of tranquility. The slave system of the Old South was as tranquil as a summer's day, but that is no reason for perpetuating in modern industry any of the aspects of a master-servant relationship.")[22]

But Roosevelt's limited view of the bill's import made little difference to Bob Wagner; he felt confident that, once it was enacted with White House blessing, the measure would soon be serving the reform purposes that its author envisaged as well as the narrow aid-to-recovery functions that the President saw in it. And to secure that blessing the New York Senator now entered into the "compromising" phase of his lawmaking formula. On April 18 newspapers reported that Wagner was ready to accede to Johnson's suggestions by removing the ban against company *initiation* of employee organizations, although the Senator still pledged that the measure would be kept strong enough to guard against company-*dominated* unions. While some ardent organs of liberal opinion, like J. David Stern's Philadelphia *Record* and the Catholic magazine *America* insisted that "better than make this concession, Wagner should tear up his bill and throw it away," prominent figures in labor circles, such as W. Jett Lauck of the Miners' Union and Charlton Ogburn, a top-ranking A. F. of L. attorney, thought that the risk involved was worth taking in return for the expected presidential support. On April 20 a series of conferences, commissioned by the President and involving Wagner, Johnson, Richberg, Frances Perkins, and Harry Hopkins, got under way. During May the Senate Education and Labor Committee performed further surgery on the drafts presented to it by the White House conferees, and on the twenty-sixth Senator Walsh reported out its handiwork.[23]

[22] Transcripts of press conferences, March 2, 23, April 13, 1934, FDR Papers; Robert F. Wagner, "Company Unions: A Vast Industrial Issue," *New York Times Magazine*, March 11, 1934; Leon H. Keyserling, interview.

[23] Transcripts of press conferences, April 18, 20, 1934, FDR Papers; *New York Times*, April 18, 1934; RFW to Jacob Panken, March 30, 1934, RFW Papers; "Is the Wagner Bill Doomed?," *America*, April 28, 1934, p. 49; Philadelphia *Record*, March 31, 1934; also RFW Papers: W. Jett Lauck to RFW, March 27,

The "National Industrial Adjustment Act," as Wagner's S. 2926 was now called, bore deep scars as a result of the overhauling it had undergone. Particularly noticeable were those left by the scalpel of Frances Perkins, whose departmental solicitor, Charles E. Wyzanski, Jr., worked closely with Senator Walsh in drafting the revised bill. Not only was the proposed Labor Board to be placed under the Department of Labor but it would be unable to intervene in a labor quarrel unless directed to do so by the Secretary of Labor, and in no case could it intervene unless a strike or the threat of a strike existed. Moreover, not only had the ban against management's initiation of company unions been removed but the refusal of employers to recognize and bargain with their workers' certified representatives—one of the most prolific causes of recent labor unrest—had been stricken altogether from the list of unfair labor practices.

Despite these and other shortcomings, and despite the fear of some of his closest advisers that he was compromising too much this time, Wagner pronounced the Walsh version of his bill agreeable to him. The President told his press conference that he wanted the bill passed "very much," and, apparently on the basis of White House promises, Wagner told responsible journalists, such as Walter Lippmann, that its enactment "seems assured." But at the same time the New York Senator prepared a series of amendments designed to remedy the worst mutilations that had been performed on his measure. He evidently trusted that the skeleton of his creation might be fattened up a bit during the floor debate.[24]

In the end, however, that floor debate never came off in 1934. Since no one, including the bill's sponsor, seemed to be completely satisfied with the revised version, the President soon changed his mind about pressing it to enactment. Industry spokesmen asserted that the bill still embodied most of the objectionable features of the original, and powerful groups such as the NRA Code Authority of the Foundry Equipment Industry formally petitioned the President to oppose it. On the other hand, labor and liberal sentiment regarding its worth, unless it were strengthened by the Wagner amendments, was guarded and cool; the A. F. of L. made no public statement at all.

1934; Charlton Ogburn to RFW, April 13, 1934; files on "National Labor Relations Act, 1934"; also Leon H. Keyserling, interview; Bernstein, *The New Deal Collective Bargaining Policy*, pp. 71ff.
[24] Transcript of press conference, April 30, 1934, FDR Papers; also RFW Papers: Wagner speech file, May 31, 1934; RFW to S. L. Fuss, May 30, 1934; RFW to Walter Lippmann, May 26, 1934; files on "National Labor Relations Act, 1934."

Moreover, 1934 was an election year, and no doubt Roosevelt weighed the possible political effects that the Wagner bill might produce. Few politicians, including the President, had as yet formed much conception of the importance that the labor vote might possess; on the other hand, one conservative Democratic congressman from Ohio informed Roosevelt early in June that agitation over the controversial measure might cost half of the Buckeye State's Democrats their Congressional seats.

Anxious to have Congress adjourn, therefore, Roosevelt decided against staging the full-scale debate over labor policy that the pressing of Wagner's bill would precipitate. Instead, on June 13 he submitted to Congress a joint resolution, drafted by Richberg and Wyzanski, that empowered the President for a period of one year to establish a "Board or Boards authorized and directed to investigate issues, facts, practices or activities of employers or employees in any controversies arising under Section 7(a)." While the new presidential boards would thus have statutory status, the net result of the resolution was in effect merely to preserve the status quo by postponing the fundamental questions of national economic policy involved in the original Wagner bill.[25]

Certainly Bob Wagner faced a predicament when Senate Joint Resolution 143, having passed the House unanimously, was called up for debate in the Senate on the afternoon of June 16. The dilemma grew worse when Robert La Follette, Jr., Wagner's companion in many a battle for social reform, proposed the New York Senator's bill as reported by the Labor Committee, together with the corrective amendments that Wagner had intended to offer to it, as a substitute for the pending presidential measure. The Wisconsin senator did so with Wagner's foreknowledge, and apparently at first Bob had entertained thoughts of making the fight for his bill then and there. But just the night before he had decided to acquiesce in Roosevelt's wishes.

"This is really one of the most embarrassing moments of my whole political life," Wagner declared as he took the floor to explain his position. He still insisted that the principles of his original bill formed a necessary component to the success of the New Deal's recovery and reform program. "Again we are failing to maintain a bal-

[25] RFW Papers: Code Authority of the Foundry Equipment Industry to FDR, June 6, 1934; files on "Responses to the National Labor Relations Act, Pro and Con, 1934"; also A. P. Lamneck to FDR, June 5, 1934, FDR Papers; 78 *Congressional Record*, 11635ff; Bernstein, *The New Deal Collective Bargaining Policy*, pp. 76ff.

ance among production, profits, and wages," he warned. "In order that the strong may not take advantage of the weak, every group must be equally strong." Nevertheless, Wagner conceded, there might be some force in the argument that, in view of the great variety of sweeping changes enacted by Congress in the previous fifteen months, "it may be a good thing to allow these reforms to encounter an additional period of trial and error, so that the processes of education and understanding may catch up with the social program that has been inaugurated." That was the President's judgment with regard to the labor disputes bill, Wagner declared, "and I am prepared to go along with him. No one is in a better position than he to weigh the program in its entirety."

During the heated discussion that followed, Wagner allowed his emotions to sway his words more than at any other time during his long senatorial career. He reassured La Follette, Nye, and other supporters of his bill of his devotion to the cause of labor reform, "a devotion which has resulted in some sacrifice of my health." He accused Ernest Weir of Weirton Steel of making that company's quarrel with the NLB into a "personal matter." And when Senator Millard Tydings of Maryland recited the N.A.M.'s familiar story of labor-union dictation, coercion, and dynamiting, Wagner launched into a tirade that shocked colleagues who considered the New York member the most restrained and mild-mannered of gentlemen. "Who is this worker we are talking about?" Wagner retorted. "Is he some enemy of this country? Is there any reason why he, unlike other people, should be shackled in some way? He is a man of flesh and blood like you and me," Wagner fairly shouted across the desks at Tydings, "with hopes and aspirations, who wants to preserve America for himself and for his children. . . . That is the man for whom I am pleading. . . . I simply want to see him get an opportunity in life, because I love this country, which gave me my opportunity, and to which I owe everything I have." At that point Dave Walsh relieved the tension by stopping Wagner short with a technical question about labor board procedure. "I yield," Bob replied, regaining his composure. "I have already said too much."

In the end La Follette, too, regretfully gave up the fight for Wagner's bill. "He has some claim upon this piece of legislation," the Wisconsinite declared. "After all, it is the child of his brain." A few minutes later Roosevelt's joint resolution went through amid much hard feeling on the part of liberals toward the President's refusal to face a showdown on the vital issues presented by the Wagner bill. "The new deal is being strangled in the house of its friends," Senator

Bronson Cutting of New Mexico shouted angrily just before the question was put to a vote.

Still, the less impatient among the proponents of the Wagner bill could derive some encouragement from the determination that its author voiced on the Senate floor that afternoon. "We will fight for it next year," Wagner promised La Follette during the debate. "We are but commencing a new deal that will in proper time be pushed forward to its ultimate conclusions." [26]

When the Seventy-third Congress disbanded on June 18, 1934, Bob Wagner knew that he would have several fights on his hands in the next session. The second year of the Roosevelt Administration had brought frustration for Wagner and his allies not only in the fields of relief appropriations, public works, and labor legislation but also with respect to a number of other reform proposals close to their hearts. True enough, the 1934 session saw the enactment of several far-reaching measures: the Securities Exchange Act, for example, which tightened still further federal regulation of the stock markets; the Federal Communications Act; and a National Housing Act that created the Federal Housing Administration to insure loans made by private lending institutions for the construction and renovation of middle-income homes. But while some presidential advisers might feel, as Raymond Moley did in the spring of 1934, that "the New Deal is practically complete," others shared Wagner's conviction that "the only benefit of the depression, so far as I can see, is that it has brought into sharper relief the saliant evils of our political and economic system, and impelled us into a sweeping campaign for reform" —a campaign that had only half started.[27]

One item on the reform agenda of many liberals was the Costigan-Wagner Anti-Lynching bill, introduced early in January 1934. To make lynching a federal crime had long been the attempt of the National Association for the Advancement of Colored People—it was, in fact, the progenitor of the entire Negro civil rights movement of the twentieth century. A bill with that purpose had passed the House early in the 1920s, but a Senate filibuster proved to be an insuperable barrier then, as it would many times thereafter. Nevertheless, as Bob Wagner observed while testifying in behalf of the bill in 1934, "the 'times which try men's souls' often quicken their sense of justice and their aspiration for betterment." Encouraged by the reform impulse

[26] 78 *Congressional Record*, 12016ff; Leon H. Keyserling, interview.
[27] Leuchtenburg, *Franklin D. Roosevelt*, p. 93; Wagner speech file, Feb. 20, 1934, RFW Papers.

generated by the depression and the New Deal, the N.A.A.C.P. decided to try again.[28]

In December 1933 Senator Costigan announced that he would soon introduce the measure, and immediately, in a public statement, Wagner pledged to support it. The New York Senator was not an unknown figure to Walter White and the other leaders of the Negro-rights organization. In 1930 Wagner had been the only senator to mention Judge John J. Parker's alleged racial bias during the debate that resulted in rejection of Parker's nomination to the Supreme Court. In 1931 Wagner delivered the main address at the N.A.A.C.P.'s national convention in New York City; and in 1932 he had introduced a bill for a Senate investigation of working conditions among Negro laborers on the Mississippi River flood-control project. Undoubtedly Wagner's concern with the Negro's welfare was due in part to the increasing importance of the Negro vote in New York. But to allege, as Southern senators often did, that this was the only influence at work on a man whose interests in social betterment were so broad—and who knew himself what it meant to suffer discrimination on the basis of ethnic origin—would be not only uncharitable but shortsighted.

At any rate, by the time Costigan introduced the antilynching measure, Wagner, at White's invitation, had become not only a supporter of the bill but its cosponsor. "There is no greater evil than mob violence," he told the Senate Judiciary subcommittee at hearings in February, "and there is no reform for which I have pleaded with greater certainty of its wisdom than . . . this bill." [29]

Oddly enough, only three of the eighteen members of the Senate's powerful Judiciary Committee in 1934 were Southerners, and in April, after surprisingly little trouble, the committee reported the Costigan-Wagner bill favorably. According to White, enough members had agreed to support the measure to enact it; nevertheless the strength of the Southern Democrat contingent in the Senate, and its threat of a log-jamming filibuster, presented a knotty problem for

[28] 78 *Congressional Record*, 58; files on "Anti-Lynching Bill, 1934," and Wagner speech file, Feb. 20, 1934, RFW Papers; Robert L. Zangrando, "The Efforts of the National Association for the Advancement of Colored People to Secure Passage of a Federal Anti-Lynching Law, 1920–1940" (unpubl. doctoral dissertation, Univ. of Pennsylvania, 1963), *passim*; Walter White, *A Man Called White* (New York, 1948), *passim*.

[29] RFW to Walter White, Dec. 27, 1933, RFW Papers; 73 *Congressional Record*, 8336ff; also RFW Papers: files on "John J. Parker Nomination, 1930," and "Mississippi River Flood Control Project Investigation, 1932–1933"; Wagner speech file, Jan. 4, 1931, Dec. 27, 1933, and Feb. 20, 1934. Interviews with Simon H. Rifkind, Leon H. Keyserling, and Philip Levy.

the bill's proponents. During the remainder of the session Wagner, Costigan, and White worked to pursuade the President to put it on his "must" list—their only hope of success. They had a powerfully ally in Mrs. Eleanor Roosevelt, who helped arrange conferences for the N.A.A.C.P. official at the White House and who personally pestered her husband about the issue in his after-work hours. The President had condemned lynching in his State of the Union address and in other public pronouncements; yet when it came to the question of throwing his full weight behind the Costigan-Wagner bill, he held back. There were doubts about the bill's workability and its constitutionality, he told newsmen. But according to columnists, and later according to Mrs. Roosevelt herself, the President's fear of offending Southern congressmen was the main consideration that kept him from doing as much as he might have on behalf of the Costigan-Wagner bill and other civil rights measures that were proposed during his Administration.[30]

During the 1934 session, then, the antilynching bill remained something less than a stepchild as far as Roosevelt was concerned. His closest approach to adopting the orphan measure came on the evening of June 8 when Mrs. Roosevelt, in a conference with Walter White, directed the Negro leader to give Costigan and Wagner a message: "If the sponsors of the bill will go at once to Senator Robinson and say to him that, if, in a lull, the antilynching bill can be brought up for a vote, the President authorizes the sponsors to say that the President will be glad to see the bill pass and wishes it passed." The bill's authors immediately conveyed those words to the majority leader, but Robinson, himself a native of Little Rock, Arkansas, remained understandably unimpressed with such an indirect expression of presidential benediction for a controversial and far-reaching measure. When, during a lull on June 18, Senator Costigan sought unanimous consent to take up the civil rights bill, several Southerners objected, and Robinson made no effort to come to the rescue. A few hours later Congress adjourned.

"I am very disappointed that action was not taken on this measure," Wagner wrote White, "but I am very hopeful that favorable

---

[30] Walter White to Edward P. Costigan, April 20, May 8, 1934, Senator Edward P. Costigan Papers (Univ. of Colorado Library, Boulder, Colo.); also RFW Papers: White to Mrs. Eleanor Roosevelt, April 20, May 29, 1934; White to RFW, April 5, 21, 1934; files on "Anti-Lynching Bill, 1934"; also transcript of press conference, May 25, 1934, FDR Papers; Mrs. Eleanor Roosevelt, interview. I am indebted to Mr. Fred Greenbaum for providing me with photocopies of relevant material in the Costigan Papers.

consideration will be given it when Congress meets again in January." [31]

At the same time that he was consoling Walter White, Wagner sent similar letters of condolence to supporters of the Wagner-Lewis unemployment insurance bill—another casualty of the President's caution and indecision during the 1934 session.

As a result of the hearings conducted by the Senate's Select Committee on Unemployment Insurance in 1931, even the two Republican members who thwarted Wagner's hope to head that inquiry came around to support of federal encouragement for unemployment reserves; the New York Senator, wrote journalist William Hard, had succeeded in shocking Senators Hebert and Glenn "into at any rate a little recognition of reality." The report that the two Republicans signed in 1932 recommended that employers be allowed to deduct from their gross income for tax purposes a portion of contributions made to bona fide unemployment reserves—the exact idea involved in the bill Wagner had introduced two years earlier. By then, however, Wagner had moved beyond that device. In the individual views he submitted as the committee's minority member he suggested that employers be permitted to deduct thirty percent of such contributions, not from gross income but from their actual tax assessment. Despite the propaganda campaign waged by the American Association for Labor Legislation and allied organizations, Wagner's proposal, like that of Hebert and Glenn, got nowhere during the remainder of the Hoover Administration. During the First Hundred Days of the New Deal Congress in 1933 unemployment insurance was shunted aside in favor of more urgent matters. [32]

As the 1934 session got under way, however, proponents of social insurance brimmed with confidence. "The coming year is going to be critical in progress toward better conditions of work and living," Wagner told one newspaperman. "Unemployment insurance, old age pensions, health insurance, more leisure for the ordinary fellow—all these things are coming, and coming soon. They must come, not only because they are ethically right, but because the economic stability of our whole society depends on them." [33]

[31] Edward P. Costigan to Joseph T. Robinson, June 11, 1934, RFW Papers; 78 *Congressional Record*, 12421; RFW to Walter White, June 20, 1934, RFW Papers.

[32] U. S. Senate, 72nd Cong., 1st Sess., *Report of the Select Committee to Investigate Unemployment Insurance*, Senate Report 964 (Washington, D.C., Govt. Printing Office, 1932), *passim*; Jacob Billikopf to RFW, quoting Hard, Dec. 31, 1931, and files on "Unemployment Insurance, 1932–1933," RFW Papers; Irene Osgood Andrews, interview.

[33] Undated transcript of RFW press interview (Feb. 1934), RFW Papers.

Moreover, as far as unemployment insurance was concerned, a new and even more attractive device for bringing federal encouragement into play had come to Wagner's attention. Involved was a scheme, invented by Supreme Court Justice Louis D. Brandeis, for a federal payroll tax to be levied on employers, but with provision for a rebate to the extent that employers contributed to unemployment reserves established under state law. The plan was designed not only to encourage every state to create a reserve system (only one, Wisconsin, had done so thus far), but it would also leave each state free to experiment with the various types of reserve and insurance plans over whose merits the experts still quarreled. In any event, it would remove the fear of creating a competitive disadvantage for their businessmen that had hitherto prevented many states from acting on their own.[34]

The Brandeis proposal found a warm advocate in Frances Perkins. "It is probably our only chance in twenty-five years to get a bill like this," she told the President, "and I don't know of anything that will start unemployment insurance except this." Attorneys in her Department of Labor drew up a bill embodying the new formula, and Wagner together with Representative David J. Lewis of Maryland, who had begun work in a coal mine at the age of nine, introduced it in Congress early in February 1934.

During the House Ways and Means Committee's hearings on the measure President Roosevelt endorsed it in a letter to the committee's chairman, Representative Robert L. Doughton of North Carolina, which was made public on March 23. But thereafter certain of Roosevelt's remarks led to newspaper reports that he had changed his mind; the bill's proponents were kept busy reassuring the press that such impressions weren't true. "Do please telephone the Chief Performer on the Hill at once," Miss Perkins implored the President in the middle of April, "that this must come out of committee and pass." In response, a White House assistant a short time later, and at the President's direction, sent Doughton another copy of Roosevelt's endorsement letter of March 23, "which he understands you have misplaced"! It would seem, then, that neither the Chief Performer on the Hill nor the Chief Performer in the White House regarded unemployment insurance as an essential part of the "must" list of legislation at this time.[35]

The *coup de grace* came on June 8 when the President sent Con-

34 Schlesinger, *The Coming of the New Deal*, pp. 301ff. See also Paul H. Douglas, *Social Security in the United States*, 2nd ed. (New York, 1939), *passim*.
    35 78 *Congressional Record*, 1900–1902; also FDR Papers: Frances Perkins to FDR, April 17, 1934; FDR to Robert L. Doughton, March 23, 1934; Marvin McIntyre to Robert L. Doughton, May 9, 1934. Cf. Rexford G. Tugwell, "Reminiscences" (Oral History Research Office, 1950), pp. 52–53.

gress a message recommending that action be deferred until the following year, when, after further study, an even more extensive social security program involving old-age retirement as well as unemployment insurance might be enacted. Roosevelt was still uncertain about some of the details of the Wagner-Lewis bill and disturbed by the disputes that persisted between exponents of the "company reserve" (Wisconsin) plan of unemployment compensation and the "pooled reserve" (Ohio) plan of unemployment insurance.

Still, the leading proponents of *both* methods were united behind the Wagner-Lewis bill in 1934; they were willing to fight out their differences in the individual state legislatures, which would actually choose between the alternative plans. And they were united, too, in their regret over Roosevelt's decision to postpone federal encouragement of any kind. "There is of course no occasion for still another commission to 'study' this subject," wrote Dr. John B. Andrews of the American Association for Labor Legislation, which had long championed the Wisconsin scheme. Spokesmen for the American Association for Social Security, which advocated the "pooled reserve" system of unemployment insurance, were equally disappointed. "I cannot help feeling a certain amount of chagrin at the blocking of all our present legislation," the association's executive secretary, Abraham Epstein, complained to Wagner. "One cannot be too optimistic about the future promises of persons who are instrumental in blocking present progress." [36]

Wagner probably had better reason for confidence in Roosevelt's promises about social security legislation than did Epstein; he'd had frequent conferences with the President on that subject in the preceding weeks. At any rate, a few days after the White House message of June 8 the New York lawmaker confidently asserted on the floor of the Senate that "under the leadership of our socially-minded President" a comprehensive system of social security would be speedily devised. He delivered these remarks during debate on the Wagner-Hatfield bill, a measure that would establish a system of old-age retirement insurance for interstate railroad workers by means of a payroll tax levied on both employers and employees.[37]

Old-age pensions had long been part of Wagner's scheme of industrial reform, for if failure to create unemployment reserves constituted "an ethical eyesore," then failure to provide for "the worker who has worn himself out in harness" was even worse. "While unemployment may some day vanish," he reminded his colleagues, "we can

<hr>

[36] *New York Times*, June 9, 1934; John B. Andrews to RFW, March 3, 1934, and Abraham Epstein to RFW, May 18, 1934, RFW Papers.
[37] 78 *Congressional Record*, 11483.

never prevent the onslaught of old age." Of course such insurance would also fulfill the economically stabilizing function of sustaining purchasing power among a large and growing element of the population, Wagner pointed out. And he suggested still another economic purpose that retirement compensation might serve, in connection with unemployment relief. "Quite aside from the present depression," Wagner forecast with considerable prescience, "we face a technological situation in the foreseeable future when from four to six million people of youth and able bodies will be unemployed during so-called 'normal times.'" What better way to create places for the newcomers in the labor force, Wagner asked, than by making possible "the withdrawal of those who are older and less efficient, and who deserve and want a few years of rest?" [38]

While most discussions of old-age insurance viewed it as primarily a field for state operation, Wagner felt that establishment of such a system for the railroad industry, which seemed clearly subject to federal supervision, might provide "a laboratory for experiment" and "blaze the way for full treatment of the problem." In 1932 the New York Senator introduced a proposed railway retirement act that had the approval of the Railroad Labor Executives Association. But opposition from the carriers, and disputes among the workers' spokesmen themselves over the knotty actuarial problems involved, made for slow progress. Not until May of 1934 did the Senate's Interstate Commerce Committee report out a bill, cosponsored by Wagner and Republican Senator Henry D. Hatfield of West Virginia, that satisfactorily compromised the differences among the proponents of the measure. Once the matter reached the floor, however, success seemed assured despite the railroad operators' sustained opposition. Not even the *caveat* entered by the President's recently appointed Federal Coordinator of Transportation, Joseph B. Eastman, who feared that the proposed system might aggravate the railroad's financial difficulties, had any effect. In the closing days of the session both houses of Congress passed the Wagner-Hatfield bill unanimously. Apparently politicians entertained a much healthier respect for the highly organized railway labor vote than for the vague and amorphous "labor vote," of which they had yet to take much much notice.[39]

Following adjournment, when there were rumors that, at Eastman's urging, the President might veto the railroad pension bill, Wagner undertook to counter the coordinator's efforts in a direct appeal to the Chief Executive. He pointed out that the legislation re-

[38] *Ibid.*; Wagner speech file, March 21, Dec. 20, 1934, RFW Papers.
[39] 78 *Congressional Record*, 11483, 11486, 11489; files on "Railway Retirement Act, 1932–1934," RFW Papers.

quired the system's administrators to report to Congress after one year on any modifications needed; he stressed, too, that the measure "will afford the finest testing ground for the more comprehensive program of social security that I know is one of your fondest wishes." Nor did Wagner hesitate to remind the President of the bill's political significance. "I do not know of any other measure during the past few years that has tied to it so greatly the hopes and sympathies of the great masses of working people." To delay its enactment over the summer, Wagner concluded, "would be most unfortunate." [40]

A few days later Roosevelt signed the act, giving Bob Wagner his only clear-cut legislative victory of 1934.

If Wagner had some reason to be disappointed with the legislative output of Congress during its 1934 session, the same was true of the vacation trip he embarked on late in July at the end of his Washington labors. While en route by auto to a Canadian fishing camp with Congressman Anning Prall, Wagner found that his reputation as a daredevil driver had caught up with him. In the process of trying to pass another car Wagner's Cadillac went off the road, struck a ditch, and turned over several times. The accident happened near Lake Champlain in upstate New York, and the Senator spent the next six weeks at a cottage on the lake, nursing several broken ribs.

Although Wagner's bruises were painful, his confined "vacation" was not entirely wasted. The Westport Inn was nearby, and after he was up and about, Bob found its society quite conducive to recuperation. He formed a fast friendship with the local physician who attended him, and with other denizens, who must have found the presence of a United States senator at the resort an unexpected pleasure. "The guests here are very numerous," Wagner informed a friend, "and they always seem to be thirsty." His enforced inactivity also enabled Wagner to catch up on reading he had long postponed; Minna Ruppert and others who came up to Westport were asked to bring with them volumes that had piled up on the Senator's bookshelf. But the titles that he requested indicated that Wagner's mind was as active as ever in its accustomed groove despite his temporary physical disability. "The Senator wants Walter White's book on lynching and Epstein's book on old-age pensions," Miss Ruppert wired Leon Keyserling. "Also the hearings on the Labor Disputes Act." [41]

[40] Herman L. Ekern to RFW, June 22, 1934, and RFW to FDR, June 28, 1934, RFW Papers.
[41] Minna L. Ruppert to Leon H. Keyserling, Aug. 17, 1934, and RFW to Kurt Sell, Aug. 27, 1934, RFW Papers.

By mid-August Wagner and his assistants, assembled on the porch of his sun-bathed lakeside bungalow, were already preparing for the fall political campaign. "I am getting well rapidly and will be about within a day or two," the Senator had written in reply to a solicitous note from Franklin Roosevelt, "ready to enter the battle again for you and the New Deal." [42] Bob was as good as his word, and from Labor Day to election day he was on the campaign trail. He traveled not only throughout New York on behalf of Herbert Lehman's reelection as governor but also to out-of-state places like Indianapolis, and to Providence, Rhode Island, where he enjoyed the pleasure of helping defeat Senator Felix Hebert.

By the summer of 1934 most of the good will that conservatives had displayed toward the Roosevelt Administration at its inception had been exhausted. Mounting deficits, Roosevelt's approval of laws such as the Securities Exchange Act, and his leanings, however hesitant, toward the sort of measures sponsored by Bob Wagner in 1934, convinced many businessmen and conservatives in general that the New Deal was not only unsound but somehow un-American. By then Lewis Douglas had resigned as Director of the Budget; by then, too, the American Liberty League—financed by men of great wealth like the Du Ponts and graced by the presence of Al Smith's name on its roster—had risen to lead the crusade "to preserve our Constitution." [43]

In the fall campaign, therefore, Wagner, like other spokesmen for the Administration, directed considerable effort toward convincing the American people that "the philosophy of the New Deal was . . . not to subvert the American system, but to save it." Its objective, he told an audience at Glens Falls, was not to put government into business, "but to put business on its own feet." To those concerned over the new level of government spending for relief and for other purposes—a level that Wagner himself considered insufficient —the Senator pointed out that "The mere size of a budget or of bonded indebtedness is not the test of solvency. If it were, most large corporations would be less stable than small ones." The true test, he insisted, was whether the enlarged expenditures had produced a desirable national return; "and is not the increase in debt more than justified by the difference between the America of two years ago and the America of today?" Besides, Wagner continued, "If we bulk together the aid given to the farmers, the bankers, the industrialists, the home

[42] RFW to FDR, Aug. 16, 1934, FDR Papers.
[43] Schlesinger, *The Coming of the New Deal*, pp. 471ff; Leuchtenburg, *Franklin D. Roosevelt*, pp. 91–92.

owners, and the railroads, we find that for every dollar of relief being given to the unfortunates who have no jobs, ten dollars are being advanced or expended for the stimulation of normal private business on every front." "Let no one throw dust in your eyes," he declared in a speech at Buffalo. "The profit system is secure under the New Deal." [44]

But Wagner, like the President himself, was at his best not when trying to placate conservatives, but rather when expanding on what the future held in store. The Senator's keynote address at New York's Democratic state convention in September set the tone for this aspect of his campaign effort. "We pledge, not a reversal of policy," he told the cheering delegates at the outset, "but the perfecting of the New Deal." Much had been accomplished in the preceding two years, Wagner asserted, and America was to be congratulated that "under the democratic process, our people have had no need to resort to those radical theories which subordinate the individual to the State, emasculate personal liberties, and frustrate private initiative."

But much more remained to be done in the quest for "the true liberty which we seek." "The goal we have set before our eyes," Wagner told his audience, "is to create the conditions that make for a life worth living for all our people; to free them from the fear of unjustified want in this land of plenty; to give to each the unrestricted opportunity for the utmost spiritual development. These are the conditions of true freedom—freedom to live nobly in the present, and freedom to look serenely and securely to the future. That is what our patriots fought for," the Senator proclaimed in his peroration, "that is what the Constitution was framed for; that is what the New Deal stands for!"

All in all, Wagner's keynote speech in 1934 was a remarkable performance for one who had just recently been on the sick list; congratulatory notes flowed in from far and wide. And since, according to Wagner, "the President himself told me he thought it was one of the best expositions of the New Deal philosophy that he had ever read," Bob had reason to hope that—given favorable election returns—his batting average in the great legislative game at Washington might show decided improvement in 1935. [45]

[44] Wagner speech file, Sept. 26, Oct. 23, Nov. 4, 1934, RFW Papers.
[45] *Ibid.*, Sept. 26, 1934; RFW to Leo R. Sack, Nov. 9, 1934, RFW Papers.

CHAPTER 11

Nearer to Our Objective

WHEN AMERICANS WENT to the polls in the mid-term Congressional election of 1934 they not only upset the tradition that called for the party in power to lose seats in off years, they even made the "partisan" predictions of Jim Farley, who had forecast that the Democrats would "hold their own," look unduly conservative. Instead of winning the thirty-seven seats in the House that Vice-President John Nance Garner conceded them, the Republicans lost thirteen, while the nine places the G.O.P. lost in the Senate gave the Democrats there the greatest margin of superiority that either party had ever enjoyed. The result constituted "a vindication of the New Deal beyond the expectations of the most optimisic of the New Dealers . . . proving that the trend of the times is toward liberalism," Bob Wagner wrote joyfully to a friend. "I am sure," the New York Senator added, "that our efforts in the next two years will bring us nearer and nearer to our objective of economic security." "Boys—this is our hour," exulted Harry Hopkins elsewhere in Washington. "We've got to get everything we want—a works program, social security, wages and hours, everything—now or never."

But those who expected that endorsement by the voters would add an immediate and forceful thrust to the Administration's program were wrong, for the New Deal's captain, Franklin Roosevelt, still seemed indecisive. Despite the vindictiveness of businessmen's attacks during the campaign, Roosevelt continued to hope that he might woo their support; indeed, to some it appeared that he feared conservatives less than he did the spenders and "radicals" within the ranks of his own supporters. The knowledge that cases testing the constitutionality of earlier New Deal measures would soon be decided by the Supreme Court also exerted a cautionary influence on the Chief Executive's attitude. And most perplexing of all was the fact that, despite the assortment of remedies applied to the nation's ailing economy, or perhaps because of their bewildering variety, recovery had bogged down at the highly unsatisfactory level achieved the previous spring.

During the first five months of 1935, therefore, the President felt compelled to ride at anchor, while an unruly Congress and a restless electorate waited for commands. To some observers, friends and foes of Roosevelt alike, the New Deal appeared to be running out of ideas, or out of the will and momentum to press any one of them to a meaningful conclusion.[1]

The messages that the President dispatched to the overwhelmingly Democratic Congress that assembled in January 1935 were more remarkable for their moderation than for anything else; Roosevelt himself conceded privately that his budget message was "tory." [2] The President recommended a revamped work-relief program and an omnibus social security system, but that was about all. And even with respect to the details of these two measures, which had been in the offing long before the 1934 election in any case, the influence of the more conservative faction among the President's array of advisers was much in evidence.

Of course, Roosevelt's request for a $4.8–billion work-relief appropriation—the largest amount ever requested for a specific project in peacetime—staggered the remaining Republicans in Congress: Senator Arthur H. Vandenburg of Michigan pronounced it "the most astounding contemplation in the history of Anglo-Saxon institutions." Conversely, New Dealers like Bob Wagner hailed the plan, which was designed to employ 3,500,000 jobless men for a period of one year, as "the next step in our recovery program"; "no method of stimulating reemployment and industrial revival," Wagner reiterated, "contains greater national values." [3]

[1] RFW to Leo R. Sack, Nov. 9, 1934, RFW Papers; William E. Leuchtenburg, *Franklin D. Roosevelt and the New Deal: 1932–1940* (New York, 1963), pp. 116–117, 146–147; Arthur M. Schlesinger, Jr., *The Age of Roosevelt: The Coming of the New Deal* (Boston, 1959), pp. 506–507, and *The Politics of Upheaval* (Boston, 1960), pp. 1ff, 211ff.

[2] Schlesinger, *The Politics of Upheaval*, p. 267.

[3] 79 *Congressional Record*, 2187–88.

Yet the New York Senator and liberals of his stripe were soon disillusioned by the revelation that the Administration intended to pay workers under the new dispensation a monthly "security wage" that, while higher than relief dole payments, would be considerably below the "prevailing rate of wages" in private industry. Appalled by the abandonment of the National Recovery Act's wage philosophy, which aimed at raising, or at least maintaining wage levels, Wagner parted ways with the Chief Executive. "Congress does not need further experimentation to demonstrate that, if the employers of 3,500,-ooo men slash wage rates, others will be forced to follow suit," he declared. "It has been demonstrated a thousand times; its recognition is the mainspring of the whole recovery program."

During February, while the nation witnessed a prolonged and public split between the President and his liberal supporters in Congress, Wagner helped lead the fight for Senate adoption of an amendment to the relief bill that would compel payment of the prevailing wage to those employed under it. "If those on public works are treated on a relief basis," the New Yorker asserted in a floor speech on the nineteenth, "every objective of public works will be defeated. Morale will be lowered, not restored; wages will go down, not up; purchasing power will shrivel, not expand; business will be demoralized, not stabilized. The wage policy of the New Deal will be thrown into reverse, and the business machine will be driven back into the deepest trough of depression." Those were harsh words of criticism for a friend of the Administration to utter, yet in concluding his argument Wagner went even further. The New Deal had been at pains to preserve private interest rates, he pointed out, and no one seriously contemplated limiting the private profits that resulted from public spending. "Why then this disregard for the wage standards that have been built up by ceaseless years of unremitting toil?" Wagner demanded. "Is the worker an outcast in our society?"

The searching questions asked by Wagner and by colleagues like George Norris and Bob La Follette, coupled with pressure exerted by the A. F. of L. and other labor-liberal groups, produced an effect; on February 21 the Senate adopted the prevailing-wage amendment 44–43. The vote was a major rebuff to the President, and perhaps that fact, together with the urgings of budget-conscious elements in the executive circle, strengthened his determination to withstand the Senate's will. Threatening a veto, Roosevelt forced recommittal of the bill, and for weeks thereafter the Senate's Finance Committee sought to hammer out a compromise formula. Eventually the Administration agreed to an amendment that directed the President to fix work-relief wages at levels that would not adversely disturb prevailing wage standards in the communities affected. The A. F. of L. was unsatisfied, but Wagner, fearful that those who opposed the bill altogether were using the wage question as a means to block the whole program, accepted the olive branch. On March 15, displaying his independence of organized labor as effectively as he had shown his independence of the President a month before, Wagner led enough liberals in voting for the compromise amendment to put it across. A short time later the measure, which resulted in creation of Harry Hopkins' fabulous Works Progress Administration, passed.

Aside from its political ramifications, the fight over the prevailing-wage issue in 1935 possessed economic significance in that it separated those who viewed work relief as a "charity program," as Senator Marvel M. Logan of Kentucky described it, from those who, like Wagner, looked on it as a means of guaranteeing Americans their "right to work." For the time being it appeared that the former school of thought, enjoying the President's blessing, carried the day. Nevertheless, Wagner and his allies had won at least a partial victory for their point of view. Moreover, the New York Senator was vindicated completely when, in 1936, the WPA adopted a solution that Wagner himself had suggested during the debates a year earlier. Then Hopkins' agency began paying the hourly prevailing-wage rates to the workers on its rolls, keeping within its budget simply by limiting the number of hours that an individual might work each month.[4]

Had he chosen to do so, Wagner might have joined in another contest with the President, this time over the social security program that Roosevelt presented to Congress in January 1935—and the result might have been a better system than the one that actually emerged. The Administration bill, which Wagner introduced in the Senate and Representatives Lewis and Doughton cosponsored in the House, resulted from the deliberations of the Cabinet-level Committee on Economic Security created by Roosevelt in the summer of 1934. Chaired by Frances Perkins and assisted by a technical staff and an Advisory Council composed of a nongovernmental experts, the committee recommended a program that seemed comprehensive enough. It called for federal grants-in-aid to the states to further their assistance to dependent mothers and children, to the blind and physically handicapped, and to the needy aged over sixty-five no longer able to

---

[4] *Ibid.*, pp. 2189ff, 2395–96, 369ff, 3724; files on "Works Progress Administration, 1935–1936," RFW Papers; Edward Ainsworth Williams, *Federal Aid for Relief* (New York, 1939), p. 254.

hold jobs; establishment of a national old-age insurance system to which workers under sixty-five and their employers would contribute; and creation of a federal-state unemployment insurance system incorporating the device of taxes and rebates called for in the Wagner-Lewis bill of 1934.[5]

Nevertheless, bitter disagreements had marked the deliberations of those connected with formulating the details of the program, and the scars they left were slow in healing. With respect to unemployment insurance, for example, a majority of the independent experts on the Advisory Council voted at one time to discard the tax rebate method altogether in favor of a purely national system of unemployment compensation. The leaders of that faction insisted, at the very least, on the need for rigid federal standards to which the individual state systems must comply; the alternative, they contended, would be a chaotic hodge-podge of forty-eight agencies, many of which might be expected to fall short of providing adequately for the workers' needs.

When the Administration bill, which was drafted in the Secretary of Labor's office, failed to provide even the minimal standards prescribed by the Wagner-Lewis bill the year before, experts like Professor Paul H. Douglas felt that Miss Perkins had gone overboard in favoring the Brandeisian idea that the states should be afforded the utmost freedom to "experiment." Wagner shared the fear that much of the experimentation might be done at the workingman's expense. During February he received suggestions for augmenting federal control from Douglas, Abraham Epstein, and others who had served on the Advisory Council. At a meeting with the dissidents in his office he agreed to press, at least before the Finance Committee, for adoption of a series of strengthening amendments. It appeared that Wagner and Secretary Perkins, who had clashed the year before regarding the status of the Senator's proposed new national labor board, might be headed for another collision.[6]

At the same time Secretary of the Treasury Henry Morgenthau, Jr., testifying before the House Ways and Means Committee on February 5, announced a shift in Administration policy regarding financing of the proposed old-age insurance system that further astounded some of the nation's leading pioneers in the field of social insurance.

[5] 79 *Congressional Record*, 545ff; files on "Social Security Act, 1934–1935," RFW Papers; Paul H. Douglas, *Social Security in the United States*, 2nd ed. (New York, 1939), *passim*; Schlesinger, *The Coming of the New Deal*, pp. 304ff; interviews with Frances Perkins, Irene Osgood Andrews, and Leon H. Keyserling.

[6] RFW Papers: Paul Kellogg to RFW, Feb. 15, 17, 25, May 4, 1935; J. Douglas Brown to RFW, Feb. 22, 1935; files on "Social Security Act, 1935."

Faced with the fact that workers who retired in the early years of the system would not have paid enough taxes to cover the annuities they would draw, the Committee on Economic Security—including Secretary Morgenthau himself—had agreed that the "deficit" thus created in the insurance fund should be made up by federal contributions directly out of the government's general tax revenues. As originally planned, the government's contributions did not need to start until 1965; and it was this consideration that increasingly disturbed Morgenthau after the committee had submitted its report. Both he and the President came to feel that there was something immoral in "borrowing from the future" to pay the costs of the plan: "It is almost dishonest," Roosevelt concluded. They determined to put the system on a strictly self-supporting basis, even though that necessitated (1) making the annuities received by those who retired during the first thirty years of the plan smaller than originally proposed, and (2) doubling the initial tax rates on employers and employees, and increasing them at a more rapid pace than called for in the bill as introduced. That way a huge reserve fund capable of making the insurance system self-sustaining would soon accumulate, and the need for government contributions in the future would be eliminated.[7]

While the new formula salved the consciences of the Secretary of the Treasury and the President, it involved propositions that, according to some members of the Advisory Council, Morgenthau's own spokesmen had labeled "fantastic" during earlier deliberations on the bill. Marion B. Folsom of the Eastman Kodak Company pointed out in a letter to Wagner that the increased rates of taxation now proposed would unnecessarily drain consumers of purchasing power and thus produce deflationary tendencies harmful to the whole economy. Liberals like Abraham Epstein, who viewed the idea of government contributions to the retirement fund as a means of bringing about a desirable redistribution of income, denounced Morgenthau's scheme as one that would "actually relieve the wealthy from their traditional obligation under the ancient poor laws."

Wagner shared Epstein's objective of income redistribution, and he also shared Folsom's fears regarding the effect of the Morgenthau plan on the recovery drive. "I hope to make myself felt in connection with this matter when the bill is discussed on the Senate floor," he assured the Eastman Kodak official shortly after the House committee had agreed to accept the Treasury Secretary's proposal.[8]

---

[7] Schlesinger, *The Coming of the New Deal*, pp. 309–311; John Morton Blum, *From the Morgenthau Diaries: Years of Crisis, 1928–1938* (Boston, 1959), p. 300.

[8] RFW Papers: Barbara Nachtrieb Armstrong to RFW, Feb. 15, 1935;

In the end, however, despite the urgings of the Douglases, the Epsteins, and the Folsoms, Wagner decided not to make a fight on the social security bill; prudence and discretion were chosen as the better part of valor. For one thing, the Senator felt less certain about the details of the complicated measure than he would have liked; it had not been drafted in his office, nor was he even a member of the Senate committee that had it in charge. Even more important was the fact that by the time the bill reached the crucial stages of consideration in the Senate, Wagner was deeply involved in an almost singlehanded effort to get his National Labor Relations act passed. Since the President seemed committed to support of the Perkins-Morgenthau version of the social insurance bill, while his position on the New York Senator's key measure of the session was problematical at best, Wagner's political instincts convinced him that he had already gone far enough for the time being in risking the displeasure of the White House.

Moreover, the progress of even the admittedly inadequate Administration security bill through Congress was so painfully slow that agitation on behalf of liberalizing amendments might conceivably result in killing social insurance altogether. It took the House three months to pass the measure; in the Senate more weeks of dalliance ensued even while May gave way to June. As liberals grumbled about the President's failure to assume leadership in goading Congress into action, Wagner concluded that the main essential was to get a social security bill of some kind passed in 1935. "In a long-term program such as this," he counseled a correspondent, "we cannot afford to quarrel . . . at the expense of alienating . . . support that may be necessary to secure the passage of the bill. Legislation," he added in consolation, "never begins with perfection." [9]

If the Senate's dilatory handling of the social security measure exasperated Wagner and Administration officials in the spring of 1935, so too did the manner in which the lawmakers disposed of the fate of the National Recovery Act, which was due to expire in mid-June.

In September 1934 the President had ordered a major shake-up in the administrative personnel of the NRA; Hugh Johnson was eased

M. B. Folsom to RFW, Feb. 12, May 13, 1935; RFW to Folsom, Feb. 19, May 27, 1935; Abraham Epstein to RFW, May 8, May 29, 1935; files on "Social Security Act, 1935"; also 79 *Congressional Record*, 9424, 9647.

[9] RFW to Willystine Goodnell, Feb. 21, 1935, RFW Papers; Leon H. Keyserling, "The Wagner Act: Its Origin and Current Significance," *George Washington Law Review* (Dec. 1960), pp. 211–212; Leon H. Keyserling, interview.

out, and a committee dominated by Donald Richberg assumed direction of the Blue Eagle agency. But despite these and other changes,
criticism of the NRA continued unabated. Wagner was among those
who saw considerable substance in charges that the operation had become unwieldy and that monopolistic-minded elements had been permitted to take unfair advantage of small business, labor, and the consumers. During the winter he consulted with experts both within and
without the Administration in an effort to secure suggestions whereby
the legitimate advances made under the code-making device might be
retained while abuses were eliminated. He agreed with senators such
as Borah that "drastic changes" might have to be made in the system,
but he was anxious to preserve the salutary features of the act—"and
most of them have been salutary, I think," he told his colleagues,
"despite what has been said." [10]

In February the President asked for a two-year extension of the
National Recovery Act, but with a series of amendments designed to
clarify its purposes and standards of administration. In testimony
thereafter Richberg and other of Roosevelt's spokesmen indicated the
NRA's intention to concentrate in the future on the labor, working
conditions, and "fair competition" aspects of the industrial codes.
They also promised to eliminate price-fixing and production-limiting
arrangements, except in the mineral-resources industries and where
those devices were used to outlaw the loss-leader practice of selling
below cost. Another proposal would exempt small-scale enterprises
from the operation of the codes altogether.

The Administration-endorsed modifications coincided, in the
main, with Bob Wagner's own assessment of what was needed to
make the NRA work more effectively and equitably. To Tom Girdler
of Republic Steel, and to the many other businessmen, labor leaders,
and ordinary citizens who wrote him in support of the Administration's plan, Wagner pledged "vigorous support of the President's
efforts to extend the N.R.A. for another two years." [11]

Nevertheless, contrary-minded elements in the Senate held the
upper hand. In March they came within ten votes of attaching a rider
to the work-relief bill that would have repealed the entire industrial
code provision of the Recovery Act; and several members voted "nay"
only on the ground that the amendment wasn't germane to the legislation under consideration. Meanwhile the Senate Finance Commit-

[10] 79 *Congressional Record*, 4167, 4179; files on "National Industrial Recovery Act, 1934–1935," RFW Papers; Schlesinger, *The Coming of the New
Deal*, pp. 152ff, and *The Politics of Upheaval*, pp. 214ff.

[11] RFW Papers: RFW to Tom Girdler, May 1, 1935; RFW to William
Green, May 23, 1935; files on "National Industrial Recovery Act, 1935."

tee was conducting hearings on the NRA that covered seven long weeks. When its inquisition finally ended in the early part of May, the Committee scuttled the Administration's proposal in favor of a resolution that continued the life of the Recovery Act for a mere ten months, to April 1, 1936. In addition, the measure indiscriminately outlawed price-fixing agreements in all codes except those covering the mineral-resources industries.

Since the committee had acted by a vote of 16–4, any hope for working out the kind of careful revision of the NRA scheme that Wagner and the Administration desired seemed futile. While New York's Senator lamented the fate of small retailers who would once again face the loss-leader competition of the chain stores, and while he questioned whether the courts might not interpret even the setting of minimum wages as a form of illegal price-fixing, the Senate on May 14 pushed the committee's proposal through to enactment without the formality of a roll-call vote. The bill that was sent to the House that day left the future of the New Deal's most important recovery effort in a limbo of uncertainty that could not help but disturb economic conditions adversely—even if the NRA survived the Supreme Court test looming ahead.[12]

The President's seeming lack of either the will or ability to control the doings of the Seventy-fourth Congress sorely dismayed those of his supporters who supposed that he had substituted mastery for drift in 1933. "I find it more and more difficult to stand by you and your program," historian Arthur Schlesinger complained in a letter to Roosevelt, "because I know less and less about what is going on." Undoubtedly Bob Wagner shared that disappointment with respect to some matters; in March, for example, he agreed with Paul Kellogg that "some pressure is needed so as to revive public interest in the whole social security program." [13]

Yet, in one instance at least, the President's *laissez-faire* attitude toward Congress that spring proved helpful to the New York Senator's ambitions in the crucial matter of securing enactment of his all-important labor-relations bill. True enough, the White House still lent Wagner no affirmative support until the concluding stages of his campaign; the President, Frances Perkins has stated, "never lifted a

[12] 79 *Congressional Record*, 4166ff, 7470ff, 7478ff, 7483.
[13] Schlesinger, *The Politics of Upheaval*, p. 10; RFW to Paul Kellogg, March 28, 1935, RFW Papers. While emasculating the NRA and dragging its heels on the social security bill in the spring of 1935, Congress also passed a veterans' bonus bill that the President opposed, and defeated his proposal to have the United States join the World Court.

finger" for the labor relations act.[14] Nonetheless, contrary to 1934, when Roosevelt's intervention prevented Wagner's measure from coming to a vote on the Senate floor, the President adopted a neutral position in 1935. Rejecting the advice of some top Democratic leaders in Congress, the Chief Executive gave Wagner a green light in order to see how far he could get, on his own, with his pet bill. The outcome astonished the President perhaps as much as it did anyone else.

The National Labor Relations Board created by the President under authority of Public Resolution No. 44 in June 1934, and chaired in turn by Lloyd K. Garrison and Francis Biddle, had encountered the same frustrations that beset the original Labor Board headed by Bob Wagner. Increasing resistance from employers, challenges to its authority in the courts, and the failure of either the NRA or the Justice Department to cooperate wholeheartedly in enforcing its orders reduced the board to impotence. During the latter part of 1934 a series of strikes, many of them based on employers' alleged denial of the "right" of collective bargaining guaranteed workers under the Recovery Act, shook the nation from coast to coast. Violence flared in San Francisco, Butte, Milwaukee, Indianapolis, New York, and scores of other places; in Toledo and elsewhere newsmen reported that a state of virtual civil war existed. By Labor Day, when textile workers north and south began the largest single strike ever undertaken in the country, Wagner was more determined than ever to renew his drive for the legislation that had been sidetracked several months before. During the fall and winter Leon Keyserling, assisted by NLRB lawyers, redrafted the labor disputes measure. Once again the work proceeded independently of White House sanction; nor, this time, was Madame Perkins' Department of Labor consulted.[15]

The labor bill that Wagner introduced on February 21, 1935, differed in several important respects from the original 1934 version. The three-member Labor Board that it proposed to create would consist exclusively of "public" members; the idea of a tripartite body

[14] Frances Perkins, interview; Leuchtenburg, *Franklin D. Roosevelt*, pp. 150–151. *Cf.* Frances Perkins, *The Roosevelt I Knew* (New York, 1946), p. 239.

[15] RFW to Paul Blanshard, Nov. 19, 1934, and files on "National Labor Relations Act, 1934–1935," RFW Papers; Leon H. Keyserling Papers; interviews with Leon H. Keyserling, Philip Levy, Milton Handler, Frances Perkins; William H. Davis, "Reminiscences" (Oral History Research Office, Columbia Univ., 1958), pp. 164–165; Irving Bernstein, *The New Deal Collective Bargaining Policy* (Berkeley and Los Angeles, 1950), pp. 84ff; Lewis L. Lorwin and Arthur Wubnig, *Labor Relations Boards* (Washington, 1935), pp. 291ff; Leuchtenburg, *Franklin D. Roosevelt*, pp. 111ff; Schlesinger, *The Coming of the New Deal*, pp. 385ff.

representative of labor, industry, and the public was abandoned. Gone, too, was the board's authorization to engage in mediation and conciliation work. The changes were made in order to emphasize the board's position as a "Supreme Court" of labor relations, the main burden of whose work would center on the enforcement of labor's rights rather than on the settlement of labor disputes. Thus the new measure made clearer than ever the difference between Wagner's approach to labor relations and the "get them back to work at any price" approach shared by people like Hugh Johnson and, to some extent, by the President himself. Other changes based on the experience of the Garrison-Biddle board were also incorporated in the new draft. But the rights that this "Supreme Court" was to enforce, and the list of "unfair practices" that the bill would deny employers, were the same as those that Wagner's bill of the previous year had made familiar.

Familiar, too, was the response that greeted the newest Wagner bill. For while the A. F. of L. and other labor-liberal groups labeled S. 1958 the one measure pending before Congress of "transcending importance," the National Association of Manufacturers and its allies undertook a campaign of denunciation called by one newspaper "the greatest ever conducted by industry regarding any Congressional measure." [16]

The hearings before the Senate Labor Committee in March and April commanded nationwide attention and front-page coverage in the newspapers, but they produced few arguments by either the bill's supporters or its opponents that had not been heard the year before. Senator Wagner, supported by such labor leaders as William Green and John L. Lewis and labor relations experts such as William E. Leiserson of Antioch College, carried the burden of testimony in favor of the measure. Once again James Emery of the N.A.M., Henry I. Harriman of the U.S. Chamber of Commerce, and spokesmen for similar groups mounted the assault. The leaders of American business were joined by the leaders of the American Communist party, who also opposed the Wagner bill, but for very different reasons; the Senator found it amusing—and also deemed it a tactical advantage—when he was able to arrange that the Reds should testify during the same week that the committee heard the industrialists!

Both Lloyd K. Garrison and Francis Biddle spoke in favor of Wagner's measure, but aside from them and other employees of the

---

[16] 79 *Congressional Record*, 2368ff; Bernstein, *The New Deal Collective Bargaining Policy*, pp. 110–111; files on "Responses to the National Labor Relations Act, Pro and Con, 1935," RFW Papers; Leon H. Keyserling Papers.

existing NLRB, the only Administration official who appeared at the hearings was Frances Perkins. Again the Labor Secretary's remarks were lukewarm and ambivalent, and again her main interest lay in securing an amendment that would house the board in her department. But the Labor Committee's favorable report on the bill, presented May 2, disappointed Miss Perkins, along with everyone else who had crossed swords with Wagner during the hearings. Not only did the committee sustain the board's status as an independent regulatory agency, but it failed to recommend a single amendment that had not received the approval of the New York Senator.[17]

As a matter of fact, at the behest of Chairman David I. Walsh, the Labor Committee's report was actually written by Senator Wagner and his assistant, Leon Keyserling. In it they stressed, as did the declaration of policy that made up the first section of the bill itself, the two main objectives of the legislation: first, to remove a primary cause of strikes by making more secure the workers' right to organize; and second, to ameliorate the business cycle by restoring better equilibrium between production and consumption through an increase in wages, which only effective collective bargaining could bring about. Since both strikes and depressions obstructed interstate commerce, the authors of the report maintained, legislation designed to limit their incidence was clearly within the purview of Congressional power. The labor relations bill, they insisted, would therefore stand up successfully to the challenges in the courts that were bound to come if Congress passed the measure.

In Wagner's efforts to promote support for his bill through speech-making and articles in the press—efforts to which he devoted every ounce of his energy in the spring of 1935—emphasis fell again and again on the same arguments that underlay the Senate Labor Committee's report. "Men versed in the tenets of freedom become restive when not allowed to be free," the Senator had warned in 1934, and he predicted then that "increasing unrest is inevitable if the hopes inspired by the Recovery Act are frustrated." Events later that year bore him out, he believed, and so he portrayed his 1935 bill as one that was responsive "to the serious industrial disturbances of last summer, when blood ran freely in the streets and martial law was in the offing."

[17] U. S. Senate, 74th Cong., 1st Sess., Committee on Education and Labor, *Hearings on S. 1958: National Labor Relations Board* (Washington, D.C., Govt. Printing Office, 1935), *passim*, and *National Labor Relations Board*, Senate Report 573, *passim*; Frances Perkins to FDR, May 18, 1935, FDR Papers; Bernstein, *The New Deal Collective Bargaining Policy*, pp. 100ff; Leon H. Keyserling, interview.

Contrary to those who charged that his bill would foment class warfare, Wagner insisted over and over that it was designed to promote industrial peace, the kind of equitable peace that "rests upon freedom, not restraint; upon equality, not subservience; upon cooperation, not domination." For, to Wagner's way of thinking, the isolated worker, "caught in the labyrinth of modern industrialism and dwarfed by the size of corporate enterprise," became a mere "plaything of fate" unless allowed to attain equality and dignity by uniting with his fellows. The labor relations bill, which would facilitate that process, might thus be viewed as "the next step in the logical unfolding of man's eternal quest for freedom." Far from constituting a radical departure from America's past traditions, Wagner contended that the bill should appeal "to the conscience and intelligence of all those who know the history of our country and are imbued with its high ideals." And far from being considered class legislation, it should appeal to all elements, for "in applying the healing balm of an upright, impartial, and peaceful forum to industry and labor," the New York Senator maintained, "it will benefit employers, workers, and the country at large." [18]

The philosophy that underlay Wagner's whole approach to questions of economic stability and prosperity had undergone considerable refinement by 1935, and his arguments in behalf of the labor relations bill now presented that philosophy in its almost full-blown version. Drawing heavily on recently completed studies by the Brookings Institution, the Twentieth Century Fund, the NRA's own research division, and such independent scholars as Adolph A. Berle, Jr., and Gardiner C. Means, Wagner helped familiarize the public with what has become the classic interpretation of what went wrong with the economy in the 1920s. "Technological changes doubled the productive capacity of the average worker between 1919 and 1933," he told his Senate colleagues in one address. "They opened up new vistas of comfort and security to the average man"; but instead of capitalizing on those opportunities, the nation allowed the wage earners' share in the product created by manufacturing to decline steadily at the same time that "we suffered from the prevalence of poverty in a land of plenty." Profits, dividends, and corporate surpluses rose and sought outlet through investment in plant facilities: "contrasted with the 10 percent rise in wages between 1922 and 1929, the production of machinery increased 91 percent and of capital equipment 70 percent." As a result, "production mounted beyond any possibilities of market

[18] Wagner speech file, March 18, 1934, May 26, 1935, RFW Papers; 79 *Congressional Record*, 7565ff.

absorption," for the workers' low level of income "prevented the vast majority of consumers from draining the market of its flood of goods."

"For a short while," the Tammany Senator's lecture in economics continued, "we staved off inevitable disaster by the pipe dream of installment selling and by lending Europe money with which to buy our own products. But when the domestic market finally closed to further investment . . . the crash came." The Hoover Administration, which "clung to the same policies which had brought the calamity and which were prolonging its ravages," went down to defeat. In its place had come the New Deal program of recovery and reform, "designed not merely to set the forces of revival in motion, but, above all, to eradicate permanently the evils that had done so much harm in the past."

Thus far Wagner's analysis represented orthodox Democratic dogma. But in spite of his close identification with the Roosevelt Administration, the New York Senator did not shrink from subjecting the record of its first two years to the same rigorous analysis that he applied to that of the Republicans. Far from offering an apologia for the New Deal, Wagner told his senatorial colleagues in the spring of 1935 that the breakdown of Section 7(a) of the Recovery Act had "driven a dagger close to the heart of the Recovery program." Only in a few industries where labor was well organized—as in the coal, needle, and building trades—had workers enjoyed a proper voice in the writing of NRA codes, Wagner maintained, and only in such industries were standards of wages and hours showing anything near the improvement that was essential to his conception of the New Deal's program. "Unemployment is as great as it was a year ago," he pointed out. "Average weekly hours of work, which stood at 37¼ when the codes were established in the fall of 1933, stand at 37½ today. The real income of the individual worker employed full time is less than in March, 1933. The average worker's income in 1934 was $1,099, or $813 less than the amount required to maintain a family of five in health and decency."

In substantiation of his pessimistic appraisal, Wagner reeled off statistic after statistic in a way that must have delighted the ears of the New Deal's opponents, although that was not his purpose. "In December 1934, pay rolls registered only 60 percent of the 1926 level, while dividend and interest payments were fixed at 150 percent of that level. Total wages have risen only 28 percent in the past 2 years, while 840 large corporations have increased their profits from $471,-000,000 in 1933 to $673,000,000 in 1934, a gain of 42 percent. Net profits of 1,435 manufacturing and trading companies increased from $64,000,000 in 1933 to $1,071,000,000 in 1934, or 64 percent, while their annual rate of return rose from 2.7 percent to 4.5 percent." In light of such figures, Wagner felt compelled to confess that "the re-alignment of profits and wages, which we contemplated so confidently in the spring of 1933, has not taken place."

The short history of the New Deal's two years in office, Wagner contended, should make it clear again "that failure to maintain a sane balance between wages and industrial returns will be attended by the same fatal consequences as in the past." Already the nation had experienced several recovery "booms" in 1933 and 1934, only to see them end in stagnation. To Wagner the reason for the failure of recovery was clear: "no adequate purchasing power had been built up to sustain it." And "if the more recent quickening of business activity is not supported by rises in wages," he declared in a statement for *The New York Times* in the spring of 1935, "either we shall have to sustain the market indefinitely by huge and continuous public spending, or we shall meet the certainty of another collapse." For that reason, he maintained, his National Labor Relations bill constituted "the only key to the problem of economic stability if we intend to rely upon democratic self-help by industry and labor, instead of courting the pitfalls of an arbitrary or totalitarian state." "With the evil and the remedy in such clear relief," the Senator told the Senate on May 15, the day debate opened on S. 1958, "Congress cannot hesitate to atone the error of allowing section 7(a) to languish." [19]

The Senate Labor Committee's action in voting to report the Wagner bill to the floor sorely disappointed the opponents of the measure. "If it comes to a vote," James Emery of the N.A.M. confided privately a few days later, "it will undoubtedly pass." Their only hope lay in the possibility that the President might again intervene or, failing that, in getting the Senate to so amend the bill that Wagner and his allies would themselves abandon it.

In their desire for White House interference against Wagner's bill, business conservatives were joined by Senators Joseph T. Robinson, Pat Harrison, and other leading Democrats who wanted again to defer action on the controversial measure for at least another year. That question was thrashed out at a White House conference during which Bob Wagner mustered every argument he could think of to deter the President from endorsing the conservatives' course.

[19] 79 *Congressional Record*, 7565ff; Wagner speech file, May 26, 1935, and files on "National Labor Relations Act, 1935," RFW Papers.

When the meeting ended, Roosevelt still refused to give the bill his blessing, but the New York Senator had won the President's consent to let it be voted on by the upper chamber. That was all Wagner wanted, for, like Emery, he felt certain about what the outcome would be.[20]

The Senate's debate on S. 1958, which lasted only two days, proved rather spiritless. Wagner's bill had been discussed for more than a year in Congress, in the nation's press, and over the radio; when senators arrived at the Capitol on the morning of May 16, they had long ago made up their minds how they would vote on the measure. A few of them had worked almost as long and hard as its sponsor to bring about its enactment; a larger number, more recent converts, had been won over by Wagner's relentless criticism of the New Deal's shortcomings and by a feeling that throughout the country there was a growing demand that *something* more be done. Some senators were influenced by the propaganda campaign waged by the A. F. of L. and other liberal-labor groups that spring; perhaps a few in this category felt that while currying support from labor, they might rely on the Supreme Court to nullify the law in the end.

In any event, so strongly did the current seem to be running in Wagner's favor that toward the end the opposition virtually collapsed. Senator Daniel O. Hastings of Delaware, who had prepared a lengthy speech against his New York colleague's proposal, decided that it was useless to prolong the debate and therefore merely inserted his address in the *Congressional Record*. On the afternoon of the sixteenth the crippling amendments prepared by the N.A.M. were turned down uniformly—the major one, introduced by Maryland's Millard Tydings, received a 50–21 drubbing on the roll call. An hour later, by an overwhelming majority of 63–12, the Senate voted to pass what historians have called "one of the most drastic legislative innovations of the decade." [21]

"We who believed in the Act," one of Wagner's supporters later recorded, "were dizzy with watching a 200-to-1 shot come up from the outside." How had it happened? Certainly the "temper of the times" —the force of the reform spirit, the prevalence of labor strife, and the seeming stalemate arrived at in the nation's recovery drive—had a lot

[20] Bernstein, *The New Deal Collective Bargaining Policy*, pp. 114–115; Keyserling, "The Wagner Act," p. 202; interviews with Leon H. Keyserling and Philip Levy.
[21] 79 *Congressional Record*, 7565ff, 7648ff, 7675ff, 7681; interviews with Leon H. Keyserling, Hugo Black, Henry Ashurst, Burton K. Wheeler, and Harry S Truman; Bernstein, *The New Deal Collective Bargaining Policy*, pp. 115–117; Leuchtenburg, *Franklin D. Roosevelt*, p. 151.

to do with it; Leon Keyserling has written that perhaps the act could have been passed in no other year than 1935. The support accorded by labor and liberal groups was essential too, and so was the President's "hands-off" attitude, which enabled the bill's sponsor to bring it to a vote.

But, as Keyserling has also written: "There would never have been a Wagner Act or anything like it at any time if the Senator had not spent himself in this cause to a degree which almost defies description." He was its legislative instigator and tactician, and before Congress, the President, and the public he was its most ardent champion. Contemporaries, friend and foe alike, paid tribute to the skill with which the New Yorker waged his fight. "I was astonished really at the time," an official of the Biddle labor board has said, "because it seemed to be almost as if Senator Wagner were getting this bill . . . through by himself."

And, in another connection, just a short time before the vote on the labor bill took place, Virginia's conservative Senator Carter Glass had given his interpretation of the passage of another controversial "Wagner bill," the NIRA, back in 1933. "We enacted that legislation under the persuasive influence of the Senator from New York," Glass told the Senate. "He is entitled to all of the credit, and—well, I will not say anything more." Perhaps Glass, who detested equally both of the Wagner-sponsored measures, muttered similar sentiments to himself as he left the Senate chamber on May 16, 1935.[22]

The day before, in answer to newsmen's questions about his attitude toward the Wagner labor bill, Franklin Roosevelt had informed his press conference that he had not "given it any thought one way or the other." [23] But the Senate's action forced the President to make up his mind, especially since it appeared that the House was inclined to follow the example of the upper chamber. For here was a display of Congressional independence far more impressive than any of the others that had preceded it earlier in the session.

Moreover, since the particular piece of legislation involved was the one that businessmen regarded as anathema above all others, its impending passage threatened to alienate from the Administration once and for all whatever was left of its support in conservative circles. Roosevelt had already become incensed when, at its national convention early in May, the U. S. Chamber of Commerce had denounced

---

[22] Malcolm Ross, *Death of a Yale Man* (New York, 1939), p. 170; Keyserling, "The Wagner Act," p. 201; Thomas I. Emerson, "Reminiscences" (Oral History Research Office, 1953), p. 320; 79 *Congressional Record*, 4181.

[23] Transcript of press conference, May 15, 1935, FDR Papers.

the New Deal in stinging terms; since then he had paid increasing attention to such advisers as Felix Frankfurter and Justice Brandeis, who urged him to abandon the apparently fruitless effort to coddle his enemies. It would appear that in the days following the Senate's approval of the Wagner bill the President decided to embrace it as a means for asserting a new burst of leadership along more progressive, reform-centered lines.

When House leaders approached Roosevelt on May 19, therefore, they found him privately agreeable to consideration of the Wagner bill on the floor of the lower chamber; the next day the House Labor Committee reported S. 1958 favorably. On the twenty-fourth the President went a step further and announced publicly his support for the principles of Wagner's measure. Three days later, when, in the Schechter Case, the Supreme Court nullified the entire NRA structure, the Wagner bill assumed even greater importance in Roosevelt's eyes not only as an economic measure to help fill in the newly created vacuum in the New Deal's recovery program but also as a political weapon to offset the blow the Administration had just suffered. Chastising the court's narrow interpretation of interstate commerce as a return to "the horse-and-buggy-days"—and disregarding the added doubts that the Schechter decision cast about the constitutionality of Wagner's bill—Roosevelt finally put it on his "must" list of legislation for enactment before Congress adjourned that summer.[24]

Later, in June, the House of Representatives passed the bill without even a roll-call vote; on July 5 the President signed it into law. The National Labor Relations Act, as it is officially known, has been cited as one of the first and most important products of Franklin Roosevelt's Second Hundred Days. But it has been cited too, and even more properly, as evidence of the fact that "under our system of government, and wisely so, strength and courage and public spirit in the Congress . . . are needed no less than in the vicinity of the White House." [25]

[24] Transcript of press conference, May 24, June 4, 1935, FDR Papers; *New York Times*, May 25, 1935; Bernstein, *The New Deal Collective Bargaining Policy*, pp. 117ff; Leuchtenburg, *Franklin D. Roosevelt*, pp. 145ff; Schlesinger, *The Politics of Upheaval*, pp. 284ff.

[25] Keyserling, "The Wagner Act," p. 227.

CHAPTER 12

Additional Legislation

Endorsement of the Wagner Labor Relations Act was only one move that Franklin Roosevelt made in reasserting executive leadership after months of quiescence in 1935. In the days following the Schechter decision the President presented Congressional leaders, who had imagined they were on the verge of adjournment, with a long list of measures that he insisted must be passed before they could escape the sweltering heat of Washington. Enjoying high priority was the Wagner-Lewis-Doughton social security bill, and on June 19, the same day that the House of Representatives passed his National Labor Relations Act, Wagner had the pleasure of watching the Senate finally give its approval to another measure with which he was identified. When the President signed the Social Security Act later in the summer the New York Senator was on hand and added another White House pen to his growing collection. A few days later Professor Paul H. Douglas wrote Wagner asking permission to dedicate his latest book to three "Pioneers in the Movement for Genuine Social Insurance." Two of the men he had in mind were the eminent sociologists, Abraham Epstein and I. M. Rubinow. But "I would esteem it a privilege," the Chicago professor informed the Tammany-bred Senator, "if I might put your name at the top of the three." [1]

By the time the first session of the Seventy-fourth Congress adjourned late in August it had enacted a series of other Administration approved measures of far-reaching importance. Among them were the

[1] Paul H. Douglas to RFW, Aug. 12, 1935, RFW Papers.

Guffey-Snyder Act and the Connally Act, which were designed to preserve for the coal and oil industries certain features of the defunct
NRA codes; the much-controverted Public Utilities Holding Company Act, which sought to unravel the pyramids of monopolistic corporate control that had become a feature of the electric utilities industry; a new, more stringent Banking Act; and a tax measure that
Roosevelt's opponents quickly labeled a "soak the rich" scheme.

None could deny that the Second Hundred Days produced a
dazzling array of legislative innovations, but what their net effect was
on the direction of the New Deal puzzled observers at the time and
has remained an enigma to historians since then. Focusing their attention on the holding company and tax measures, some have contended that Roosevelt's "new" program reflected a conscious decision
to abandon the idea of government economic "planning" in conjunction with business and to return to a regime of more intense, govern-
ment-policed competition in the economic order. It has been said
that, surveying the wreckage of the NRA experiment, and convinced
that businessmen had been guilty of ingratitude, the President
brought the day of the "planners" to an end; the day of the "atomists," particularly the protégés of Brandeis and Felix Frankfurter, had
arrived. Roosevelt turned his back on the New Nationalist philosophy
of his cousin Teddy and moved closer to the New Freedom doctrines
of Woodrow Wilson.

Some who have claimed to perceive this pattern of drastic change
present it as a turn in a more radical direction. "The messiahs," columnist Thomas Stokes has written, "gradually shoved President Roosevelt toward the left." Others view the same pattern as a reversion
toward conservatism, since it rejected the attempt to reconstruct the
country's economic institutions and rested on the more traditional
and "naïve" assumption "that the classical model of the market was
somehow recoverable." But regardless of their differing interpretations
of the direction in which Roosevelt was moving, the writers in this
school agree in seeing in the events of mid-1935 nothing less than the
launching of a Second New Deal.[2]

[2] Thomas Stokes, *Chip Off My Shoulder* (Princeton, 1940), p. 420; Arthur
M. Schlesinger, Jr., *The Age of Roosevelt: The Politics of Upheaval* (Boston,
1960), pp. 391–392. The concept of "two New Deals" is to be found in most
writings on the Roosevelt era; Schlesinger discusses the subject in considerable detail in *The Politics of Upheaval*, pp. 385ff. But William E. Leuchtenburg ex-
presses reservations about the validity of the thesis in his *Franklin D. Roosevelt
and the New Deal: 1932–1940* (New York, 1963), pp. 162ff. And see especially
Leon H. Keyserling's incisive *caveat*, which Schlesinger quotes at length in *The
Politics of Upheaval*, pp. 690–692. The present writer derived much benefit from
conversations about this interpretational matter with Mr. Keyserling, whose views
confirmed the author's own impressions concerning the nature of the New Deal.

On closer scrutiny, however, it appears that the attempt to define a Second New Deal may be as misleading as the attempt to depict the so-called First New Deal of 1933 in terms of a coherent, prearranged plan of action imposed from the top by the President and a single-minded group of brain trusters. It might be closer to the truth to view Roosevelt's actions in the summer of 1935 as essentially pragmatic responses to a political situation—bred by economic stalemate, adverse court decisions, and a clamor for leadership among the people—that threatened to work to the Administration's disadvantage unless *something* was done. Surely the President was rather indiscriminate, as between "planners" and "atomists," in choosing the legislative weapons with which to break the deadlock. For if the Public Utility Holding Company Act was dear to the hearts of those who believed in a more competitive economy, the Wagner Act was deeply rooted in the more intregrated, over-all approach to economic problems that had led the Senator to interest himself in things like the National Recovery Act in the first place. So, too, of course, were the Guffey and Connally Acts that Roosevelt sanctioned at the same time.

It would appear, then, that the Brandeis-Frankfurter faction failed to win a clear-cut victory during the Second Hundred Days. Nor would it do so in the months that followed; in fact, three years later the President was still toying with the idea of somehow reviving a semblance of the NRA scheme.[3] In 1935, as in 1933, Franklin Roosevelt characteristically played the tune "by ear." And the course of his Administration, in the future as in the past, would continue to emerge out of the bewildering pattern of conflicts that enveloped the advisers who sought the President's confidence.

One of those advisers was Bob Wagner, who remained as determined as ever to make his influence felt in the battles raging on the Potomac.

Wagner was disappointed with the outcome of the Schechter Case, of course, but he accepted the decision with good grace as might be expected of a former judge. He even thanked the court for the "service" it had performed in teaching Congress to be more careful in framing its enactments!

At the same time, however, Wagner scorned those "designing people" who read the court's decision as if it had foreclosed for all time federal attempts to grapple with nationwide economic and social problems. He held to the hope that the majority on the bench might yet adopt broader and more liberal interpretations of the Constitution's crucial clauses. Or, if need be, the amending process might be

[3] Leuchtenburg, *Franklin D. Roosevelt*, p. 163.

resorted to. Either way, Wagner told his Senate colleagues, the constitutional barrier could and would be hurdled, for "the United States
was founded upon the proposition that where there is a conflict between a specific provision of the Constitution and the welfare of the
people, it is the provision and not the people that must yield. The
spirit of law is the spirit of growth."

And since to Wagner's mind it was "unthinkable that . . . we
should return to the destructive planlessness which existed two and a
half years ago," neither the Administration nor the people should surrender their will to move ahead. "Let us bear in mind," Wagner told
a nationwide radio audience as the 1935 Congress neared the end
of its action-packed session, "that additional legislation there must
be." [4]

In charting his own course through the turbulent waters stirred
up in the wake of the Schechter decision, the New York Senator devi-
ated little, if at all, from the underlying principles that had guided his
actions since the beginning of the depression. He voted for the Holding Company Act and the other measures that Roosevelt espoused
during the early summer of 1935, but if they did mark the launching
of a Second New Deal radically different from the first, Wagner
seemed unaware of it, as his rejection of any "return to . . . destructive planlessness" clearly indicates. To the end of his days he remained convinced that the NRA had not been a useless experiment.
Indeed, "under its inspiration," he told the Senate in August 1935,
"there have been accomplished the greatest social advances in so short
a period within our memories." "The principles of N.R.A. will not be
abandoned," he added, "so long as sensible men believe that cooperation is superior to strife. They will not be forsaken so long as we hold
that light is better than ignorance in respect to the practices whereby
business is run. They will not be surrendered so long as we believe in
the stabilization of wages and hours, not only as a humane dictate of
conscience but also as the basic requirement for steady and profitable
business operations." Neither industry nor labor nor the consumer
liked everything that the NRA did, the New York Senator readily
conceded. "But neither industry nor labor nor the consumer will ever
be willing to return to the exploitation and deception that we witnessed in the past." [5]

For the time being, nevertheless, Wagner felt compelled to ad-

[4] 79 *Congressional Record*, 9418, 14232; Wagner speech file, June 13, 1935,
RFW Papers.
[5] 79 *Congressional Record*, 14230. See also Robert F. Wagner, "The Ideal
Industrial State," *New York Times Magazine*, May 9, 1937.

mit that the NRA scheme had been too grandiose, and he remained aloof from those in the Administration who sought ways to revive it, or something like it, on a similar grand scale. "In some respects the Recovery Act was ahead of the country," he wrote one correspondent. "In other respects it was hampered by administrative mistakes." While confident that "time will cure both of these defects," Wagner in 1935 and the years immediately thereafter thought it best that the New Deal limit its efforts to salvaging those parts of the NRA system that had proved their worth in promoting industrial stability. "This involves first of all the encouragement of rational cooperation among business men," he declared, "in order that they may produce and sell goods with an adequate knowledge of market conditions, and with full protection against unfair and degrading competition." It was on this premise that Wagner supported the Guffey-Snyder and Connally Acts of 1935, the 1936 Robinson-Patman Act forbidding manufacturers to give discriminatory discounts to chain stores and other large buyers, and the 1937 Miller-Tydings Act that lent federal support to state-sanctioned "fair trade" laws.[6]

Even more important to the cause of stability, in Wagner's mind, remained the problem of coordinating production and wages in such a way as to maintain a steady market for factory output, "instead of provoking repeated depressions by the collapse of purchasing power." To this end Wagner began urging, soon after the Schechter decision, enactment of permanent federal legislation regulating minimum wages and maximum hours. A partial victory was gained in 1936 when Congress passed the Walsh-Healey Act requiring federal government contractors to live up to minimum labor standards. Thereafter Wagner and others who were determined that "Neither the sweat shop's day nor the pauper's pay can be countenanced again" kept up their campaign until, in 1938, the Fair Labor Standards Act applied to all industries in interstate trade the kind of wage and hour provisions that had first come on the national scene under Wagner's Recovery Act of 1933.[7]

But the fixing of minimum wages and maximum hours by government fiat constituted "merely the foundation upon which can be

[6] RFW Papers: RFW to Mordecai Ezekiel, Feb. 28, 1936; RFW to Gilbert H. Montague, June 17, 1936; files on "Business Conditions and Practices, 1935–1937"; Wagner speech file, June 28, 1935. For a description of some alternative plans to the NRA following the Schechter decision, and particularly Mordecai Ezekiel's plan, see Schlesinger, *The Politics of Upheaval*, pp. 215ff, 287–289.

[7] 79 *Congressional Record*, 9418, 14232; also RFW Papers: Wagner speech file, June 13, 28, 1935, and May 6, 1936; files on "Walsh-Healey Act, 1935–1936" and "Fair Labor Standards Act, 1935–1938."

built the mutual efforts of a revived industry and a rehabilitated labor," Wagner maintained. To expect the government to do more would be to run the risk of erecting a "despotic state." The working out of most arrangements in the American industrial complex must be left in the field of private management-labor relations, and they must be worked out on the basis of true equality of representation. "That is why the cultivation of collective bargaining is not merely an abstract matter of freedom for the worker," Wagner insisted, "but rather a concrete foundation for the general welfare." While a great many employees, encouraged by the American Liberty League's 1935 pronouncement that the National Labor Relations Act was clearly unconstitutional, openly flouted the new law durings its first two years of existence, Wagner pleaded that it be observed in its true light—as a measure designed to "clear the way for free and full cooperation between industry and labor." [8]

While he was confident that the steps he proposed would lead to greater stability in the American economy, Wagner disclaimed any affiliation with those "Utopian philosophers" who believed that the elimination of unemployment was already in sight. "Industry can not run with the mechanical perfection of a gyroscope," he warned, "and out of simple caution we must continue to devise methods of dealing with those who may be severed from their normal work despite our best efforts." The new Social Security Act marked the beginning of that quest, Wagner told a nationwide radio audience shortly after the bill's passage, but, he admonished, it should be regarded "not as the last but as the first step in affording economic security to the American people." "These beginnings are modest," he stated a few days later. "The prospects that they open up," he added in a way that must have chilled conservatives who thought the new act radical enough in itself, "are illimitable." And before long the New York Senator's office was serving as the legislative clearinghouse for people, both within the Administration and outside it, who were determined to make the social security system still more comprehensive. [9]

Such were the major outlines of the program for future action shaped up by Bob Wagner in the aftermath of the Second Hundred Days. But in formulating plans for consolidating and expanding his version of the New Deal, Wagner was conscious most of all of "the

[8] 78 *Congressional Record*, 12196–97, and 80 *C. R.*, 3300–3301; Wagner speech file, June 28, 1935, and Feb. 29, 1936, RFW Papers; National Lawyers' Committee of the American Liberty League, *Report on the Constitutionality of the National Labor Relations Act* (Sept. 5, 1935), Leon H. Keyserling Papers.

[9] Wagner speech file, June 20, 28, Aug. 15, 24, 1935, and files on "Social Security Act Amendments, 1935–1949," RFW Papers.

ground not yet won." "A dark and terrible uncertainty envelopes millions of our fellow countrymen" the New York Senator told his colleagues three days before the 1935 Congress ended its labors. "Recipients of relief, they have not yet been granted the right to work." The government's first and most immediate task, he declared, "is the restoration of that right."

With the subsidence of the Blue Eagle's screeches, Wagner turned once again, and with renewed vigor, to his long campaign for large-scale public works to serve as a job-creating and pump-priming device "until private business takes up the slack." Nor was he content merely to rely on exhortations that existing New Deal construction agencies, such as the PWA, step up their pace. For already, in March 1935, Wagner had introduced a measure that he hoped might inject new energy into the government's sluggish public works program. Its title read: "A bill to promote the public health, safety, and welfare by providing for the elimination of insanitary and dangerous housing conditions, to relieve congested areas, to aid in the construction and supervision of low-rental dwelling accommodations, and to further national industrial recovery through the employment of labor and materials." [10]

Thus, months before the so-called Second New Deal made its debut, the trial balloon that indicated the direction of Bob Wagner's next major legislative effort had already appeared, and the wise ones in the press gallery were wagering that sooner or later it would become law. "The Wagner housing bill" as reporters soon dubbed it, was a recovery measure to be sure, as its title indicated. But that it was something more too—another step in Wagner's lifelong effort to orient American liberalism toward the problems of the nation's urban-industrial population—was also clear. "Nothing quickens the imagination and fires the intellect more," Wagner told the Senate in August 1935, "than the thought of bringing space and sanitation into the dreary lives of those who now inhabit the slums." [11]

As with many other reform movements that came to fruition in the New Deal years, the housing crusade had its roots in the Progressive Era. True, the progressives' efforts had centered mainly on achieving merely public *regulation* of the conditions under which private realtors built and operated, but a few of them had begun campaigning for public *construction* of adequate housing for the under-

[10] 79 *Congressional Record*, 4419, 14233; Wagner speech file, March 25, 1935, RFW Papers.
[11] 79 *Congressional Record*, 14233.

privileged by the time that earlier era of reform subsided after the First World War.[12]

The coming of the Great Depression reactivated and fortified the strength of the "housers," and in 1931 social workers Edith Elmer Wood, Mary Kingsbury Simkhovitch of Greenwich House, and Helen Alfred became the moving spirits in forming a National Public Housing Conference. Spokesmen for this group saw to it that Senator Wagner, in formulating the Relief and Construction Act of 1932, included a provision for RFC loans to limited-dividend housing corporations regulated by state law. (At the time only New York State, under the aegis of Governor Al Smith, had made provision for chartering such semipublic housing agencies.) The following year Miss Simkhovitch and Father John O'Grady of the National Conference of Catholic Charities, representing the N.P.H.C., called again at Wagner's office. As a result of their missionary activity the National Recovery Act that Wagner introduced in May 1933 clearly specified slum clearance and low-cost housing projects as part of the Administration's public works program.

Between 1933 and 1937 Harold Ickes' Public Works Administration built or aided in the building of about fifty public housing projects. Nevertheless, PWA's Housing Division found its efforts hobbled by adverse court decisions that denied the federal government any power of eminent domain for slum-clearance operations, and also by President Roosevelt's penchant for shifting PWA funds to more expeditious work-relief projects of the type that Harry Hopkins' WPA specialized in. By 1935, therefore, the "housers" had already decided that a new approach was needed, and in Bob Wagner the National Public Housing Conference found a willing sponsor for the desired legislation.[13]

The 1935 version of Wagner's housing bill was designed to make the promotion of public, low-cost housing a long-range function of the federal government rather than a mere emergency expedient. To circumvent constitutional obstacles thrown up by the courts, the measure contemplated leaving actual construction and administration of the projects to local housing authorities established under state law; the contribution of the federal government would consist in the financial arrangements of the operation. To this end the Wagner bill

[12] For background to the public housing movement of the New Deal period see Roy Lubove, *The Progressives and the Slums* (Pittsburgh, 1962), *passim*; Timothy L. McDonnell, S.J., *The Wagner Housing Act* (Chicago, 1957), chap. i.

[13] Files on "Relief and Construction Act, 1932," "National Industrial Recovery Act, 1933," and "Slum Clearance and Housing, 1929–1934," RFW Papers; McDonnell, *The Wagner Housing Act*, pp. 29ff.

Wagner as President pro tem of the New York State Legislature

During an investigation of strike conditions at the Pricedale mines in 1928, Wagner and other senators appear with the children of the strikers. Left to right, Senator W. B. Pine of Oklahoma, Senator Frank R. Gooding of Idaho, Senator Burton K. Wheeler of Montana and Senator Wagner

President Roosevelt and Senator Wagner at the Madison Square Garden rally on the final Saturday night of the presidential campaign in 1936

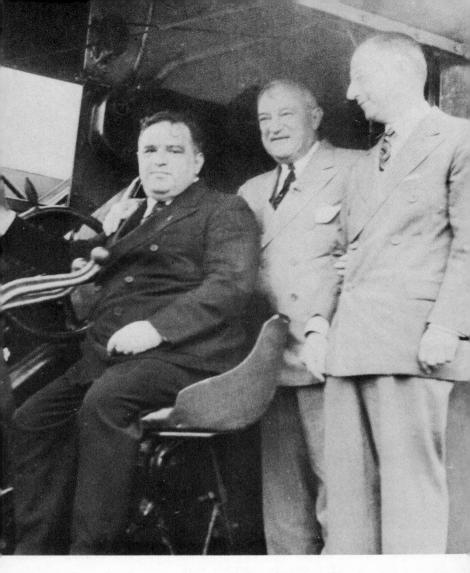

Fiorello La Guardia, Senator Wagner and Nathan Straus, U.S. Housing Administrator at ceremonies for a housing project in Brooklyn in 1938

proposed to create a permanent Housing Division in the Interior Department, whose duty it would be to dispense outright capital grants (up to 30 percent of the cost of a project) and to make loans at favorable rates of interest to local public bodies submitting feasible slum-clearance and low-cost housing plans.[14]

Although Senator David I. Walsh's Education and Labor Committee held three days of hearings on the Wagner housing bill in the spring of 1935, it was understood that the New York Senator did not expect the measure to pass at that session. The Labor Relations bill monopolized most of his legislative efforts that year ("He never scatters his fire"), and, after the Schechter decision, Congress was kept busy enough coping with the President's own Second Hundred Days program.

Moreover, Wagner himself wanted more time to study another housing bill, which had been introduced simultaneously by Congressman Henry Ellenbogen of Pennsylvania. Representing the ideas of the Labor Housing Conference—an agency created by the Pennsylvania Federation of Labor in 1934—the Ellenbogen bill seemed in several of its features to be more liberal and workable than the measure that bore Wagner's name. During the fall and winter the two lawmakers and their consultants held frequent conferences, and a short time after the Second Session of the Seventy-fourth Congress convened in 1936 a composite bill was ready for introduction.

The new Wagner-Ellenbogen bill vested administration of the proposed housing program in an independent government corporation, the United States Housing Authority; members of the Labor Housing Conference and others were critical of the efficiency of Ickes' Housing Division under PWA. The Housing Authority was authorized to float $550,000,000 worth of bonds during the next four years and to use the proceeds to extend loans to local public housing agencies. Moreover, the Housing Authority might also provide grants out of the federal treasury totaling up to 45 percent of the cost of a project, by means of either a one-shot, lump-sum capital grant made at the launching of an enterprise, or in the form of proportional yearly annuity payments that could extend over a period as long as sixty years—the anticipated life span of a housing project.

Proponents of the yearly annuity form of subsidy claimed for it at least three advantages over the capital-grant method: it would enable

[14] U. S. Senate, 74th Cong., 1st Sess., Committee on Education and Labor, *Hearings on S. 2392: Slum and Low-Rent Public Housing* (Washington, D.C., Govt. Printing Office, 1935), *passim;* files on "Public Housing Act, 1935," RFW Papers.

local housing authorities to keep rents at a lower level, and thus make them capable of catering to the lowest economic strata of slum dwellers; it would give the USHA more effective and continuing control over the practices of the local authorities; and, most important of all, it would permit the USHA to get more housing started immediately with a lower initial appropriation from Congress than would be required under the capital-grant system. Thus the 1936 version of the bill authorized a mere $51,000,000 appropriation to cover the first year's grants, in contrast to the $800,000,000 called for in Wagner's 1935 measure. However, it would, of course, commit the government to possibly a sixty-year annual outlay for housing grants—a feature that Wagner regarded as an additional asset of the bill, but one that the opponents of a government housing program were soon assailing.[15]

By the beginning of 1936, then, the housing bill enjoyed top priority on Wagner's list of legislative objectives. In speech after speech, in the Senate and before every public gathering that would listen, he depicted it as a challenging social reform that should find a natural place in the New Deal's program. Wagner made liberal use of the reams of studies provided him by the professional "housers," who sought to relate inadequate housing to inordinately high rates of infant mortality, disease, crime and delinquency, and to frustrated hopes and ambitions. But the Senator did not have to rely solely on dry statistics collected by social workers. For, as he sometimes reminded his audience when his mind wandered back over the years, "I know what the slums are like."

Implicit in Wagner's plea was a repudiation of the pessimistic assertion that people lived in slums because they liked to or because they were inherently incapable of living by better standards, and often he made that repudiation explicit. "It must be emphasized frankly and at once," he told a nationwide radio audience in April 1936, "that the slum problem is not a problem of low individual standards of morals or of taste. It cannot be solved by education, nor by propaganda, nor by preachments about better living." Rather, in Wagner's view, it was a problem created by the fact that "millions of decent and respectable people . . . have not sufficient incomes to live decently," by the fact that "at the present time eighteen million families in America have earnings of less than $1,000 a year." Those figures indicated, Wagner contended, that "fundamentally the slum is a product of economic maladjustment," the same maladjustment in the distri-

[15] Files on "Public Housing Act, 1935–1936," RFW Papers; interviews with Leon H. Keyserling and Boris Shishkin; McDonnell, *The Wagner Housing Act*, pp. 97ff, 144ff.

bution of purchasing power that lay at the root of the Great Depression itself. Consequently the tax burden that his bill would impose on the public at large would be justified, for "it embodies recognition on the part of a socially awakened people that the distribution of our national income has not been entirely equitable, and that partially-subsidized housing, like free schools, free roads, and free parks, is the next step that we must take to forge a better order."

Wagner was not so naïve, then, as to believe that the provision of shiny new apartments in place of rickety old tenements would of itself automatically end all of the social problems associated with a substandard environment. He recognized clearly that "the slum is primarily a by-product of poverty," and that "the attack on poverty must be an attack on unemployment." "If we house everyone comfortably today, and allow millions of men to remain unemployed or underpaid," he warned one assemblage of social workers, "we shall have done a praiseworthy but entirely inadequate job. But if we can also provide full-time employment and decent incomes," he continued, "the major manifestations of poverty will gradually diminish." To Wagner's mind the twin purposes, social and economic, of the housing program he was seeking to promote constituted its special allure, for "while providing better living conditions at once," he asserted, "it also offers the most fertile field for the large-scale cultivation of reemployment." [16]

By early 1936, the failure of employment figures to keep pace with the encouraging signs of recovery in production and profits presented a cause for alarm among many New Dealers; in Wagner's estimation it was "the central problem confronting the American nation." The index of industrial production had reached 90 percent of its predepression level, but as yet fully two-thirds of those unemployed at the depth of the depression had failed to find jobs in private industry. By now it had become clear to some observers that the discrepancy was not attributable to overly long hours alone, but rather, as Wagner phrased it, to the fact that "in our search for new employment opportunities, we are constantly running a race against the technological displacement of men by machines."

Careful studies indicated that during the depression the productivity of the average workman had increased about 5 percent each year; therefore, Wagner insisted, the pursuit of a self-sustaining prosperity must involve not only the restoration of men to their old jobs but the creation of new ones for workers displaced by automation.

[16] Wagner speech file, Dec. 3, 1935, Jan. 24, April 21, 27, 1936, and Aug. 2, 1937, RFW Papers; 80 *Congressional Record*, 4889–90, 6259.

"No one desires to rob civilization of the wealth that flows from the development of new machine processes," the Senator declared in January 1936, for " in the long run, machinery contributes to the progress of the race. But to satisfy the immediate needs of millions who are still unemployed," he urged, "and to face the immediate threat to business and to additional thousands of workers that is implicit in these technological improvements, new enterprises must be developed on the broadest possible base."

A mammoth housing program, designed to provide at least ten million new family units during the next ten years, offered "a unique opportunity" for absorbing "both the unemployment in the durable goods industries and the overflow of the technologically unemployed from other fields," Wagner asserted. Most of that construction could and should be carried on by private enterprise, encouraged by even more liberal federal assistance of the FHA type. But in order to stimulate the kind of building for the lowest-income groups that private builders could not be expected to undertake, he maintained, the Wagner-Ellenbogen bill was essential.

Thus the public housing campaign possessed the kind of multipurpose objective that was particularly attractive to the Senator from New York. "The argument [for it] may be stated to the banker or industrialist or tradesman in economic terms because many of us are engaged in these various pursuits," he told the U. S. Conference of Mayors late in 1935. "But it can be stated to the whole population in humanitarian terms, because all of us are human beings . . . who want the children of America to live and work and play in healthy surroundings, rather than in an atmosphere oppressively heavy with disease and crime." During 1936 and 1937 he stated those arguments time and again; to the end of his career in the Senate he remained convinced that the housing problem represented not only one of America's greatest challenges but one of its greatest opportunities as well.[17]

Wagner's hope that the public housing bill would appeal to the economic sense and humanitarian sensitivities of businessmen fell short of complete fulfillment. Powerful groups that maintained strong lobbies in Washington actively opposed the measure; among them were the U. S. Chamber of Commerce, the National Association of Real Estate Boards, the United States Building and Loan League,

[17] Robert F. Wagner, "Problem of Problems: Work," *New York Times Magazine*, Feb. 16, 1936; Wagner speech file, Nov. 19, 1935, Jan. 30, April 20, 27, 30, 1936, and April 5, Aug. 2, 1937, RFW Papers; 80 *Congressional Record*, 4889, 6259.

and the National Retail Lumber Dealers' Association, whose members feared that government-subsidized apartment developments would be built of steel and concrete. The opposition's arguments ran the gamut of charges ranging from unconstitutionality to socialism, and from the assertion that relief of unsatisfactory housing conditions was a job for private philanthropy to the claim that federal subsidization would further unbalance the budget and thus impede recovery. Its cause drew sustenance from the fact that important figures within the Roosevelt Administration, and particularly in the Treasury Department, agreed with one or more of these objections to the bill. Significantly, Secretary Morgenthau's special adviser on housing matters during 1935 and part of 1936 was Peter Grimm, a former president of the Real Estate Board of New York.[18]

On the other hand, important elements in the business world— building contractors, architectural firms, and producers of most types of building materials, for example—did support the public housing measure. In fact, not since the introduction of the National Recovery Act in 1933 had a Wagner bill commanded so much enthusiasm in conservative circles.

As usual, nonetheless, the major drive behind Wagner's proposal was provided by the liberal and labor organizations that the New York Senator had come to rely on in his numerous battles for social reform. In the spring of 1936 he inserted a list of the bill's endorsers in the *Congressional Record*, and it covered four pages of that oversized volume. Scores of local housing authorities, formed since the PWA had started its building program, were on it; so were groups representative of the major religious faiths. Organizations such as the Consumers' League lent the measure their support, and the N.A.A.C.P. did also. The American Federation of Labor called for a public housing program at its 1935 convention, and in 1936 President William Green declared that the Wagner-Ellenbogen bill occupied first place on his union's list of "must" legislation.

Several organizations worked virtually full time promoting Wagner's measure and contributed the key individuals who, under Leon Keyserling's supervision, actually helped draft the successive versions of the bill. Forceful personalities were involved—among them Edith Elmer Wood, Mary Kingsbury Simkhovitch, and Helen Alfred of the National Public Housing Conference; Catherine Bauer and Boris Shishkin of the Labor Housing Conference; Langdon Post of the New York City Housing Authority; Coleman Woodbury, Ernest J.

[18] Files on "Public Housing Act, 1935–1937," RFW Papers; McDonnell, *The Wagner Housing Act*, pp. 138ff; John Morton Blum, *From the Morgenthau Diaries: Years of Crisis, 1928–1938* (Boston, 1959), pp. 285–286.

Bohn, and Warren Jay Vinton of the National Association of Housing Officials—and peace and harmony did not always pervade their
ranks. But Senator Wagner managed to keep them united behind the
major objectives of the housing venture, and among them they helped
stir up public interest in the housing issue.[19]

So important and so complex had the New Deal's involvement
with housing matters become that in the summer of 1935 President
Roosevelt established a Central Housing Committee composed of
representatives from the growing number of government agencies
that had an interest in the subject. During the first three months of
1936 Wagner and Congressman Ellenbogen refrained from introducing their own bill while, in numerous meetings with members of the
committee, they sought to hammer out a comprehensive Administration measure that would reinvigorate both the public and private sectors of the construction industry. They received encouragement for
their public housing proposal from some of the committee's personnel, notably Harold Ickes. But the group as a whole was dominated by
men from agencies such as the Home Owners' Loan Corporation and
the Federal Housing Administration, who thought primarily in terms
of encouraging the building industry by expanding already existing
programs of government loans and mortgage insurance for private enterprise. Wagner was in agreement with their suggestions, of course—
he had already sponsored several bills augmenting the funds and functions of the HOLC and the FHA—but they failed to reciprocate and
showed little enthusiasm for the public, low-cost housing scheme.

At length Wagner despaired of arranging a compromise, and on
April 3 he submitted his bill to the Senate. Some reporters, caught
unawares, expressed surprise at the introduction of the "Administration" housing measure at this time; current information indicated
that the White House's program was still "in abeyance." Capitol correspondents cleared up the mistake the next day: not only was
Wagner's bill *not* an official Administration proposal, *The New York
Times* reported, but spokesmen for the HOLC and the FHA actually
regarded it as "a challenge." Newsmen became aware then that, as on
other occasions, it was the Senator from New York and not the Chief
Executive who was attempting to move the Congress in new directions.[20]

    [19] Files on "Public Housing Act, 1935–1937," RFW Papers; 80 *Congres-
sional Record*, 7893–97; McDonnell, *The Wagner Housing Act*, pp. 116ff; interviews with Leon H. Keyserling and Boris Shishkin.
    [20] RFW Papers: files on "Public Housing Act, 1936," "Home Owners' Loan
Corporation, 1933–1936," and "Federal Housing Administration, 1934–1936";
Wagner speech file, June 19, 1934, and Jan. 30, 1936; also 80 *Congressional Rec-*

Certainly Franklin Roosevelt sympathized with the plight of slum dwellers in both urban and rural areas; the efforts of the New Deal to improve the lot of tenant farmers, for example, testified to this. During the early months of 1936 newspapers reported that he was anxious that "something be worked out" to launch a low-cost housing program at the current session of Congress. And at his press conference on May 5, a few days after the Senate Labor Committee had concluded extensive hearings on Wagner's bill, Roosevelt declared that he was in "substantial agreement" with the principles and objectives of the measure.[21]

Nonetheless, several circumstances dampened the President's enthusiasm for the Wagner-Ellenbogen bill's approach. Roosevelt did not really like the idea of large, multiunit housing projects in the first place. He believed that families should have individual homes of their own, however modest, and he kept hoping that some form of government mortgage insurance might yet be devised that would enable private enterprise to fulfill his ideal for even the lowest-income groups. Moreover, the President's attitude was governed considerably at this juncture by the advice of his budget-conscious Secretary of the Treasury, who considered the financial provisions of the Wagner bill "terrible." And in addition, Roosevelt had already promised some of his more conservative friends that the year 1936 would be a "breathing spell" free of novel and possibly inflammatory New Deal programs— at least until after the election.

So it was that in his May 5 statement to the reporters Roosevelt cautioned them against labeling the Wagner-Ellenbogen proposal an Administration measure: "There is lots of desirable legislation I will give my blessing to, but don't call it a 'must' bill." Nor was the New York Senator's pet project included in the list when, on May 15, Senator Joseph T. Robinson outlined the legislative program that the Democratic leadership hoped to complete before Congress adjourned in June for the national political conventions.[22]

Undeterred, Wagner and his allies only accelerated their campaign to get Congressional action on the measure before the conven-

---

ord, 4889ff; interviews with Leon H. Keyserling and Boris Shishkin; McDonnell, *The Wagner Housing Act*, pp. 122ff, 144ff, 170; Blum, *Morgenthau Diaries: Years of Crisis*, pp. 283ff.

[21] Unidentified newspaper clipping, March 27, 1936, RFW Papers; transcript of press conference, May 5, 1936, FDR Papers.

[22] Interviews with Leon H. Keyserling and Boris Shishkin; Leuchtenburg, *Franklin D. Roosevelt*, pp. 134–136, 170; Blum, *Morgenthau Diaries: Years of Crisis*, pp. 287–288; transcript of press conference, May 5, 1936, FDR Papers; 80 *Congressional Record*, 7385.

tion season started. Within the next two weeks Wagner made three major radio addresses on behalf of the housing bill. Favorable newspapers ridiculed the Administration's alleged plan to make up for its inaction by including a strong housing plank in the Democratic platform. "Why pledge a housing act in the future," the St. Louis *Star-Times* editorialized, "when one can be provided at once?" Individuals and organizations interested in the bill bombarded congressmen with mail, and they bombarded the White House too.

Most effective of all, however, were the frequent visits that Bob Wager himself made to the executive mansion in an effort to counteract the "go slow" advice that seemed to prevail there. Finally, at a meeting of determined Senate liberals with the President on May 29, Wagner won Roosevelt's consent to bring the bill to a vote before Congress adjourned.[23]

Nevertheless, the Senator had to make concessions to win his point—the bill as reported to the upper house on June 3 reduced the first year's appropriation for grants from $51,000,000 to a mere $10,-000,000—but Wagner was used to that. "We have to begin on a rather small scale," he told his colleagues on June 15, the day the Senate took up the measure, and thus he gave fair warning that this was just the beginning of the spending he envisioned for the housing program. Conservatives, of course, were already fully aware of the Wagner tactic of "getting a foot in the door," and so they sought to frustrate the New Yorker's hope of rushing his "modest proposal" through in one day by asking what Wagner frankly described as "embarrassing" questions. Was there a figure available indicating the sum total of the low-cost housing need, Senator Arthur Vandenburg of Michigan wanted to know. "Yes there is," Wagner responded, "but I would not dare mention it." Had the Treasury Department approved of the scheme, Vandenburg asked at another point. Whereupon Wagner, in a masterful display of political circumlocution, replied that the department had not submitted a report on the particular bill under consideration, "although I have consulted the Treasury Department with reference to the proposed legislation"![24]

A coalition of conservative Democrats and Republicans managed

---

[23] Files on "Public Housing Act, 1936," RFW Papers; also FDR Papers: Catherine Bauer, Coleman Woodbury, and Helen Alfred to FDR, April 24, 1936; Langdon Post to FDR, June 4, 1936; also St. Louis *Star-Times*, June 9, 1936; Leon H. Keyserling interview; McDonnell, *The Wagner Housing Act*, pp. 185ff, 189–190.

[24] 80 *Congressional Record*, 9153ff, 9348ff; McDonnell, *The Wagner Housing Act*, pp. 190ff.

to postpone the Senate's decision on the Wagner-Ellenbogen bill for one day, affording Senator Walter F. George of Georgia time to prepare a speech urging Congress to "turn back before we have gone into a state of Socialism." But his call went unheeded. A few minutes after the conservative Democrat concluded his address—and while conservative Republican Vandenburg complained that no one in the Senate chamber except Wagner and David I. Walsh could pass "even a kindergarten examination upon the bill" and its implications for the future—the upper house approved the measure 42–24.[25]

Any celebration on the part of the "housers" was well tempered, however, by the knowledge that at the other end of the Capitol their measure was encountering a less kind fate. In the House the Wagner-Ellenbogen bill had come under the jurisdiction of the Banking and Currency Committee, whose chairman, Henry B. Steagall of Alabama, was inclined to view it in much the same light as did his Southern colleague, Walter George. Throughout the session Ellenbogen failed to move Steagall even to the point of holding hearings on the bill.

More amazing still was the fact that even a message from the President himself on June 5—"Tell Steagall for heaven's sake to have these hearings held . . . I want the thing all ready to shoot"—apparently produced no effect. After the bill came over from the Senate on June 16 an attempt by a liberal minority of Steagall's committee to report it to the floor of the House proved unavailing. When Congress adjourned on the twentieth, therefore, the housing bill still reposed in one of the Alabama congressman's pigeonholes.[26]

"I did all I could," Roosevelt assured Mary Kingsbury Simkhovitch a few days later, leaving the housing reformers two possible conclusions to draw. Either the President's "all" had not sufficed to move a recalcitrant committee chairman of his own party—which many found hard to believe—or else Roosevelt's support of the measure throughout had been something less than wholehearted—which some *did* believe and complained of in print. Consolation might be taken from the last sentence of the President's letter to Miss Simkhovitch: "Next winter, I am confident, we will get a good housing bill." But for the time being the reform forces had to be satisfied with the prospect of nailing a strong housing plank into the platform about to be constructed at the Democrats' national convention.[27]

[25] 80 *Congressional Record*, 9557ff, 9564–66.
[26] FDR to Marvin McIntyre, June 5, 1936, FDR Papers; McDonnell, *The Wagner Housing Act*, pp. 210ff.
[27] FDR to Mary Kingsbury Simkhovitch, June 24, 1936, FDR Papers; Edith

That they would get at least that much seemed assured, for at the head of the party's platform committee was the Senate sponsor of the Wagner-Ellenbogen bill.

Elmer Wood, "The Hands of Esau," *Survey Graphic* (Oct. 1936), pp. 556ff; McDonnell, *The Wagner Housing Act,* pp. 214–215.

CHAPTER 13

From Friends in Need

Bob Wagner's contribution to Franklin Roosevelt's campaign for reelection in 1936 began early in the year with a series of Sunday afternoon broadcasts that stretched from March until the first week in June. In the course of the series, during which the Senator shared the air with a succession of Republican spokesmen, he extolled the accomplishments of virtually every one of the New Deal's myriad agencies and enactments. By the time he accepted the job of supervising the writing of his party's platform, therefore, it appears that Wagner had tired of retrospectively "looking at the record." Despite the many hands that had something to do with preparing the official campaign document—congressmen, agency heads, White House personages, and finally the Philadelphia convention's Resolutions Committee itself—the end product fairly well resembled the kind of pronouncement that Wagner had determined to make it: "a coherent, inspiring expression of general social-economic philosophy . . . that will serve as a call to arms." [1]

The preamble to the platform, couched in the phraseology of the Declaration of Independence, set forth a series of twentieth-century "self-evident truths" proclaiming that "government in a modern civilization has certain inescapable obligations to its citizens, among which are: (1) Protection of the family and the home, (2) Establishment of a democracy of opportunity for all the people, and

[1] RFW Papers: Wagner speech file, March–June, 1936; files on "Democratic Party Platform, 1936"; Felix Frankfurter to RFW, June 13, 1936.

(3) Aid to those overtaken by disaster." Sprinkled liberally through-out the statement were other phrases that bore a characteristically Wagnerian ring: a social security plank, for example, pledging "that this benefit shall keep step with the ever-increasing capacity of America to provide a high standard of living for all its citizens"; a plank on unemployment relief that promised "work at prevailing wages"; and, of course, a plank that pledged the government to "steadily extend its housing program toward the goal of adequate housing for those forced through economic necessity to live in unhealthy and slum conditions."

The platform as a whole was unusually short, and back-patting for past accomplishments was kept to a minimum. Harry Hopkins thought it "certain to be regarded as one of America's greatest political documents." The President was so impressed with Wagner's reading of it before the packed convention hall audience that he put through a long distance call to express personally his congratulations. Wagner himself was so proud of the job that he had a copy of the platform's text engraved and framed to hang in his Washington office.[2]

During the ensuing campaign Wagner was especially active in helping cement into the Roosevelt coalition elements of the population that had been initiated in a new degree of political awareness by measures particularly associated with his name. The Good Neighbor League, an organization created early in the year to recruit independent voters behind the Roosevelt banner, had been assigned also the job of weaning Negroes away from their traditional Republicanism. The league's director, Stanley High, sought Wagner's advice on how to proceed, and, among other things, Wagner was instrumental in putting him in touch with Walter White, the N.A.A.C.P. official, who had become somewhat disaffected by Roosevelt's indecisiveness on civil rights legislation. In the end the N.A.A.C.P.'s official publication, *The Crisis*, all but endorsed Roosevelt openly, and on election day the bulk of the Negro vote swung decisively into the Democratic camp. The fact that the antilynching bill bore the name of two distinguished Democrats, Wagner and Costigan, played at least a minor role in bringing about that result.[3]

[2] Harry Hopkins to RFW, June 26, 1936, RFW Papers; transcript of press conference, June 26, 1936, FDR Papers; Minna L. Ruppert, interview. The text of the platform is printed in full in *The New York Times*, June 26, 1936.

[3] Stanley High to RFW, Sept. 10, 1936, and files on "1936 Campaign," RFW Papers; Arthur M. Schlesinger, Jr., *The Age of Roosevelt: The Politics of Upheaval* (Boston, 1960), pp. 425–438, 598–600; William E. Leuchtenburg, *Franklin D. Roosevelt and the New Deal: 1932–1940* (New York, 1963), pp. 185–187.

By this time the importance of the labor vote, too, had become obvious to many Democratic politicians, and in the party's appeals to the workingmen no name figured more prominently than that of the author of the National Labor Relations Act. Organized labor, as such, participated in the 1936 campaign more directly and effectively than ever before. In New York State, for example, union leaders were instrumental in launching the American Labor Party, which became the vehicle for attracting hundreds of thousands of independents and Socialists to the Roosevelt-Lehman ticket. Directing the new party's first campaign was Elinore Morehouse Herrick, a social worker who became something of a Wagner protégée when, in 1933, the Senator asked her to head the New York Regional Labor Board. Protesting at first that she "knew nothing about politics," Mrs. Herrick asked for and received a good deal of political education during the fall of 1936 from her Tammany mentor. On election day the ALP contributed 300,000 votes to Roosevelt's sweeping victory in New York.

The ALP itself was an offshoot of Labor's Non-Partisan League. Formed early in 1936 by John L. Lewis, Sidney Hillman, and other leaders whose secession from the A. F. of L. the previous fall had led to the creation of the rival Committee for Industrial Organization, the league nonetheless won the adherence of some A. F. of L. unions in its determination to help reelect Roosevelt. Unions affiliated with the league contributed vast amounts to the President's campaign fund, besides carrying on intensive propaganda efforts of their own in key states. And when on Labor Day the league inaugurated a series of nationwide radio broadcasts in Roosevelt's behalf, it seemed natural that its first speaker should be Senator Bob Wagner.[4]

During his own extensive campaign tour in September and October Wagner hammered away particularly at Alf Landon's ambiguous position on the Labor Relations Act and other social measures that formed such a prominent part of the New Deal's record. His speeches analyzing the Republican candidate's vagueness concerning the Social Security Act seemed particularly effective, and one of them, reprinted in pamphlet form, was circulated as a campaign document by the Democratic National Committee. On election eve an exceptional amount of time was allotted to the New York Senator during the Democrats' nationwide "wind-up" broadcast in an attempt to combat a last-minute smear campaign that certain businessmen and Republican leaders had launched against the Social Security Act. Denouncing

[4] RFW Papers: Elinore Morehouse Herrick to RFW, undated letter (1936); Herrick to the author, Jan. 20, 1962; Wagner speech file, Sept. 2, 1936; also John L. Lewis, interview; files on "1936 Campaign," RFW Papers; Schlesinger, *The Politics of Upheaval*, pp. 592–595; Leuchtenburg, *Franklin D. Roosevelt*, pp. 188–189.

the opposition's "brazen falsehoods" and the "deceitful little notices" that had found their way into employees' pay envelopes—some of them intimated that workers would be fingerprinted and issued numbered dog tags under the Act—Wagner urged his listeners to make their endorsement of President Roosevelt "so tremendous that no one will ever dare again to raise the ugly head of reaction to threaten your progress." [5]

Despite the panic that "the Social Security scare" created among some Democratic strategists, Wagner was supremely confident of the election's outcome at the end of the campaign. As was his habit, he bet on the results with many of his friends, including Samuel S. Koenig and other high-ranking leaders of New York's Republican organization. At a convivial gathering in New York's Biltmore Hotel on election night Wagner predicted that the President would carry the city by 1,200,000 votes, a figure that even the most ardent Rooseveltians in the jovial crowd thought "a little optimistic." The next day one of them penned the Senator a note: "We are ready to award you the palm, for one who can prognosticate within one per cent is good. The *Literary Digest* should be interested in your future predictions."

"What a triumph! What a vote of confidence! Democracy is secure!" Wagner wired Roosevelt as the lopsided returns poured in. Two weeks later he was at the White House offering his personal congratulations—and urging the President to make low-cost public housing the first matter of business in his new term of office.[6]

The rhetoric of Franklin Roosevelt's 1936 campaign instilled new hope in the hearts of the more reform-minded among his followers. So, too, did the President's second inaugural address of January 20, 1937, when he called attention to "the one-third of a nation ill-housed, ill-clad, ill-nourished." To Wagner the President's "stirring remarks" constituted "the harbinger of determined and comprehensive action at this session of Congress toward eradicating the slums and putting America in the vanguard of the better-housing nations." So obvious did it seem now that a public housing bill would soon be enacted that officials of the United States Building and Loan League sent Wagner what they described as "helpful . . . suggestions" designed to make his 1936 bill more palatable to its opponents. Even Congressman Henry Steagall wanted to climb on the bandwagon, and

[5] Wagner speech file, Sept.–Oct. 1936, and Oct. 3, Nov. 2, 1936, RFW Papers; Schlesinger, *The Politics of Upheaval*, pp. 613–614, 635ff.

[6] Samuel S. Koenig to RFW, Bob W. Austin to RFW, RFW to FDR, Nov. 5, 1936, RFW Papers; Timothy L. McDonnell, S.J., *The Wagner Housing Act* (Chicago, 1957), p. 236.

early in January he preempted Representative Ellenbogen's place as cosponsor of the Wagner housing bill! [7]

Nevertheless, Roosevelt's first specific recommendation to the new and overwhelmingly Democratic Seventy-fifth Congress had nothing directly to do with housing, clothing, or feeding the country's underprivileged third. Instead, on February 5 he called for reform of the Supreme Court by means of legislation that would empower him to enlarge its membership in the hope of overcoming the conservative majority that had undone so much New Deal legislation.

The "court-packing bill," as it soon became known, took the country by surprise. Few, if any, of the leading Democrats in Congress had received advance notice of the President's intent. In fact, just three days earlier Bob Wagner had inserted in the *Congressional Record* resolutions recently passed by the National Consumers' League that advocated broadening the power of the federal government in the field of social legislation by means of a constitutional amendment—the method the Democratic platform of 1936 had also endorsed. The Chief Executive's drastic proposal nearly monopolized the deliberations of Congress during 1937, and, more importantly, it stirred up opposition even in the ranks of usually staunch New Dealers.[8]

Coming when and as it did, and in view of its decimating effect on the Democratic majority in Congress, Roosevelt's court proposal proved especially embarrassing to Wagner. The New York Senator was primarily interested in getting his housing bill enacted in 1937, and hence anxious to avoid entanglement in any distracting controversy that might alienate support for that measure. But because of his intimacy with the President, many observers erroneously assumed that Wagner favored the court-packing plan; indeed, some newspapers even reported that Roosevelt had promised him the first appointment to the bench that would become available if the reform plan were enacted.

Wagner scotched that rumor, and all others concerning his position on the issue, by maintaining strict silence throughout the many months that the battle raged. "I have enough troubles of my own to

[7] 81 *Congressional Record*, 316–317; Wagner speech file, Jan. 21, 1937, and Morton Bodfish to RFW, Dec. 2, 1936, RFW Papers; McDonnell, *The Wagner Housing Act*, pp. 236–250.

[8] 81 *Congressional Record*, 877–881, Appendix, 116ff; files on "Democratic Party Platform, 1936," and "Proposals Affecting the Supreme Court, 1935–1937," RFW Papers; interviews with Henry Ashurst and Burton K. Wheeler. On the 1937 battle over Roosevelt's Supreme Court bill see Leuchtenburg, *Franklin D. Roosevelt*, pp. 231–238.

keep me busy," Wagner told Henry Ashurst, who, as chairman of the Senate Judiciary Committee, was Roosevelt's chief lieutenant in trying to round up support for the Administration's bill. (According to the Arizona senator, neither he nor the President sought in any way to pressure the New York lawmaker during the long period that the court issue was pending. He was exempt from the kind of tactics that the Administration employed as a matter of course in dealing with other lawmakers.) Neither Ashurst nor Wagner's closest associates—such men as Leon Keyserling and Simon Rifkind—ever succeeded in getting him to state his attitude on the matter, even privately.

Possibly there were other reasons, too, for Wagner's reticence about the court-reform bill. For one thing, at the very time that Roosevelt threw his bombshell in the direction of the country's highest tribunal, cases involving the constitutionality of two of Wagner's most important legislative achievements, the National Labor Relations Act and the Social Security Act, were pending before it. The Senator kept in close touch with the government lawyers in charge of the litigation, and to him, if not to the President, discretion may have dictated a policy of refraining from outright attacks on the very men in whose hands rested the fate of those crucial New Deal measures. It appears likely, moreover, that Wagner, who had been a judge himself, harbored strong sentiments in favor of judicial independence. While he might, and frequently did, urge occupants of the bench to liberalize their interpretation of the Constitution in tune with twentieth-century realities, he could not generate any great enthusiasm for Roosevelt's oblique approach to the issue.[9]

So it was that while Roosevelt launched and lost his court fight between February and August 1937, a prominent senator from the President's own state remained silent—strangely so, it seemed to many. On July 20 Governor Herbert Lehman, one of the ardent Rooseveltians who nevertheless parted ways with their chief on the court issue, chose the medium of an open letter to Wagner as the means for making public his own opposition to the court plan. Furious that Lehman's letter was released to the press before he had received a copy of it, Wagner interpreted the missive as being in part an attempt to "smoke him out." He issued a reply that, in the words of one

[9] McDonnell, *The Wagner Housing Act*, p. 270; interviews with Henry Ashurst, Leon H. Keyserling, Simon H. Rifkind, and Philip Levy; RFW to Homer Cummings, Cummings to FDR, Jan. 12, 1937, FDR Papers; also RFW Papers: RFW to Charles Fahy, Feb. 27, 1936; Stanley Reed to RFW, Jan. 15, 1937; RFW to Reed, Jan. 18, 1937; also Leon H. Keyserling, "The Wagner Act: Its Origin and Current Significance," *George Washington Law Review* (Dec. 1960), pp. 210–211.

admirer, firmly but politely told the governor "to go to hell." "We who are in such complete agreement as to our social objectives," Wagner intimated, "should not permit these essentially secondary disagreements to draw us apart or divide our forces. . . . It is an obligation toward the leader of whom we are both so justly proud." His own position on the court bill, the Senator advised Lehman, would be formulated if and when the matter came to a vote in the Senate, according to "the dictates of my conscience, and the counsel of my own experience." [10]

In the end it proved unnecessary for Wagner to commit himself on the merits of the controversial measure one way or the other. On July 22, the day Wagner's reply to Lehman was published in *The New York Times*, Roosevelt and the Administration forces were compelled to acquiesce as the Senate voted to return the court bill to the Judiciary Committee, from which it never returned. Several circumstances had forced the President to retreat: the unexpected strength of the opposition, as such prominent Senate Democrats as Burton Wheeler, Joseph O'Mahoney, and Tom Connally openly joined Republicans in denouncing the proposal; the sudden demise in mid-July of the loyal Senate majority leader, Joseph T. Robinson; and an eloquent public statement by Chief Justice Charles Evans Hughes that seemed to completely refute Roosevelt's allegation that the court, undermanned by overage justices, had fallen behind in its work.

Most devastating of all to the fate of Roosevelt's scheme, however, was the Supreme Court's own about-face during the spring of 1937. On March 29, in a 5–4 decision, it upheld a Washington minimum-wage law similar to a New York statute it had overturned just a year before. During the next two months the tribunal also ruled favorably on two prime pieces of New Deal legislation, Wagner's Labor Relations Act, and the Wagner-sponsored Social Security Act. "The switch in time that saved nine," as some have called it, marked a historical turning point in the nation's constitutional development, but it also served to deflate Roosevelt's charge that the Supreme Court was an insuperable obstacle to progress.[11]

After the President backed down on the court issue in the summer of 1937 he subsequently contended that although he had lost the

[10] Herbert H. Lehman to RFW, July 19, 1937, and RFW to Lehman, July 21, 1937, RFW Papers; *New York Times*, July 20, 22, 1937; Evelyn Wagner to RFW, undated letter (July 1937), relaying comment by former Mayor James A. Walker of New York, RFW Papers. Evelyn Wagner, the Senator's niece, was Mayor Walker's personal secretary.

[11] Henry Ashurst, interview; Leuchtenburg, *Franklin D. Roosevelt*, pp. 236–238.

battle, he had won the war—a claim that has been subject to dispute in view of the drastic brake that the court fight applied to the New Deal's legislative momentum. Bob Wagner, who had declined to join the Roosevelt forces in their dubious legislative onslaught, was nonetheless equally elated that at last the long contest between judicial conservatism and judicial realism had been won. "The court has thrust aside its more recent stereotyped and narrow generalities concerning federal power," he declared on the day of the Labor Act decision, "and has adopted a broader concept fitting the organic interdependence of our nationwide social and economic system." In a newsreel interview that showed him haggard and in need of a shave— he had not slept the night before the court rendered its verdict— Wagner hailed the decision as a vindication of all those "in public life and elsewhere who for so long have pleaded for a system of constitutional law responsive to our modern way of life." [12]

In the meantime Wagner dedicated his energies to the renewed fight to enact public housing legislation that now, ironically enough, became known as the Wagner-Steagall bill. So convinced had Wagner become of the merits of the annual subsidy form of federal assistance, as compared to the capital grant method, that the 1937 version of the measure specified that type of aid alone for local housing projects. The bill envisaged a billion-dollar program of federal loans for construction to be contracted by an independent United States Housing Authority over the following four years. The loans would be amortized over a sixty-year span, and a system of annual grants from the federal treasury would enable local housing authorities to at least meet the yearly interest due on their debts to the government corporation.

Wagner's bill was ready for introduction in February, and he confidently sent a copy of it to the White House. But to his dismay Roosevelt again suggested another round of conferences with Treasury, PWA, FHA, and HOLC officials to iron out differences; and it became evident that the President read the meaning of the 1936 election returns differently from the Senator.

Disappointed with Roosevelt's dilatory approach, Wagner disregarded the President's suggestion, and on February 24 he introduced his bill in the Senate without prior consultation with any Administration officials. Nevertheless the White House had its way, and during March, April, May, and June, Wagner and his spokesman, Leon Key-

[12] Wagner speech file, April 12, 1937, RFW Papers; Leon H. Keyserling, interview; Leuchtenburg, *Franklin D. Roosevelt*, pp. 238–239.

serling, engaged in a seemingly interminable series of conferences. Once again the financial aspects of the public housing proposal were the nub of the dispute, and again the Treasury Department was the seat of the strongest opposition to Wagner's annual subsidy proposal.[13]

Henry Morgenthau, whose youthful experience as a worker at New York City's Henry Street Settlement had familiarized him with slum conditions, favored a public housing program. But Morgenthau's abhorrence of anything that resembled "borrowing against the future" to launch a desirable social reform—an aversion that had governed his attitude toward the Social Security bill in 1935—set him against Wagner's plan. It even made him susceptible to the argument put forth by some of his Treasury subordinates that, under the Wagner formula, the government would pay out two billion dollars for one billion dollars' worth of housing—a fallacious charge that confused the loan and subsidy phases of the bill and ignored the fact that the principal of the loans would be repaid to the government by the local housing authorities it aided.

Neither Wagner's facts and mathematics, nor his cajolery—"Henry, forget about your money for a moment," the Senator interjected at one tense session, "and try to understand the provisions of my bill"—could move the keeper of the Treasury, however. Instead, Morgenthau formulated an alternative bill that would extend one-shot capital grants to local housing agencies of up to 85 percent of their projects' costs, as a charge against the government's current budget. To him that approach seemed "terrific from the standpoint of finance," but to Wagner the amount of housing that could realistically be launched under the costly plan would be but "a drop in the bucket." "I don't want to get a housing bill," he told the Treasury official, "that just looks like a housing bill, and nothing happens."

Late in May, and with the President's approval, Morgenthau explained his scheme to a group of labor and public housing spokesmen he had assembled in Washington. When they turned thumbs down on it, and repledged their allegiance to the Wagner bill, the Secretary of the Treasury began to retreat from the field.[14]

[13] Files on "Public Housing Act, 1937," RFW Papers; FDR to James Roosevelt, Feb. 19, 1937, FDR Papers; Drew Pearson and Robert S. Allen, "Washington Merry-Go-Round," June 22, 1937, clipping in RFW Papers; 81 *Congressional Record*, 152ff; McDonnell, *The Wagner Housing Act*, pp. 251–273.

[14] RFW Papers: Leon H. Keyserling to Henry Morgenthau, Jr., March 3, 1937; American Federation of Housing Authorities, press release, March 3, 1937; RFW to Nathan Straus, March 6, 1937; files on "Public Housing Act, 1937"; also "Statement by William Green, June 23, 1937," in 81 *Congressional Record*,

Wagner's battle was still not won, however, for as late as June 8 President Roosevelt told his press conference that he hoped to "reconcile" the two conflicting approaches. "I don't think," he added in reply to a further question about his personal preference, "we ought to obligate this government or any other government for a sixty-year period ahead." The Morgenthau plan, he asserted, was "more on the 'pay-as-you-go' principle"—a principle that, it appears, was still quite sacred to the Chief Executive.

In the middle of June Wagner agreed to soothe Morgenthau by adding the capital grant form of assistance to his bill as an alternative to the annual contribution system (the alternative has never been used, incidentally), and it appeared that he was making progress in attaining firm Administration support for his measure. Nevertheless, delay and procrastination continued for still another month. Exasperated, Wagner, on July 12, issued an angry public statement: "Despite the almost unanimous agreement of every group which has studied the housing problem for years . . . that the Wagner-Steagall Bill embodies the one practical method of clearing slums and putting the slum-dweller in a decent home, the press still carries reports of new committees being formed to 'explore' the problem afresh and to determine how private enterprise alone may be stimulated to build for the very low income groups. The impossibility of reaching the slum-dweller without public housing and public subsidy has long been proved. The time for 'study' is over. The time is ripe for action now."

Whether prompted by the Senator's outburst or by the long campaign of pressure exerted by labor and public housing groups that Wagner's statement capstoned, Roosevelt at length made his decision to commit the Administration to the New Yorker's bill. The very next day the President directed his son, James Roosevelt, to speak to Congressman Steagall about conducting House hearings on the measure (a process that had been completed in the Senate two months earlier). On July 23, the Senate Labor Committee reported the housing bill favorably, and on August 2, the day Senate debate on the measure began, Steagall finally opened his committee hearings.[15]

Appendix, 1568–69; John Morton Blum, *From the Morgenthau Diaries: Years of Crisis, 1928–1938* (Boston, 1959), pp. 287–290; New Jersey State Housing Authority to RFW, June 5, 1937, RFW Papers; McDonnell, *The Wagner Housing Act*, pp. 274ff; interviews with Leon H. Keyserling and Boris Shishkin.

[15] Transcript of press conference, June 8, 1937, FDR Papers; Wagner speech file, July 12, 1937, RFW Papers; FDR to James Roosevelt, July 13, 1937, FDR Papers; U. S. Senate, 75th Cong., 1st Sess., Committee on Education and Labor, *Creating a United States Housing Authority*, Senate Report 933 (Washington, D.C., Govt. Printing Office, 1937), *passim.*

Debate on the housing bill in the two branches of Congress during August (after Roosevelt's court fight had ended) brought into bold relief both the growing strength of conservative opposition to New Dealism and the deepening cleavages within the New Deal coalition itself upon which that opposition fed. Legislative jealousy of the inflation of executive power that had taken place under Roosevelt, for example, was reflected in the approval of an amendment that required all presidential appointees to jobs paying $4,000 or more under the United States Housing Act to receive senatorial confirmation.

Even more directly detrimental to the prospects of Wagner's housing program was the charge made by representatives from rural areas, Republicans and Democrats alike, that the entire undertaking was designed to benefit New York City and a few other metropolises of the Northeast alone. "Upon what recognized theory of Government [did] it ever become the business of the national government . . . to tax all the American people to clear up slums in certain specified parts of the country," Virginia's venerable Senator Carter Glass demanded to know. His anxiety was seconded by other farm-area spokesmen, who insisted that public housing funds be apportioned among the states on the basis of population.

Wagner and his allies maintained that the provisions of the bill as it stood were equally applicable to rural slum clearance projects and to urban ones, and they pointed out also that, in any case, Congress had never required that drought relief and other forms of agricultural aid be shared proportionately with the industrial states. In the end the rural coalition won a substantial victory, however, and the bill as passed required that no more than 10 percent of the funds of the USHA be spent in any one state. (Ironically enough, during the next two decades a higher proportion of federally aided housing projects and units were constructed in the South than in any other section of the country, including the Northeast.) In the House rural spokesmen added another amendment to the bill, barring aliens from occupying federally supported housing accommodations, but in the conference committee that restrictive provision, which "former alien" Bob Wagner found particularly obnoxious, was stricken out.

Moreover, the appropriations authorized by the Wagner-Steagall bill represented an acknowledged departure from the Administration's announced intention of balancing the budget in the near future, an objective toward which the President devoted much attention during 1937. Roosevelt, under Wagner's prodding, had at length agreed to make housing an exception to his retrenchment program, but conservative Republicans and Democrats wedded to the economy drive fought a longer and partially successful battle against the "profligates." The result was Congressional approval, despite the New York Senator's best efforts, of several amendments that considerably circumscribed the housing bill's financial provisions. The total amount of public housing loans authorized was cut in half, from a billion dollars to $500,000,000; loans advanced by the USHA to local housing agencies might amount to only 90 percent, rather than 100 percent, of the projects' cost; and states or cities were required to supply 20 percent of the annual contribution or capital grant approved by the federal housing agency.[16]

Despite these curtailments, the housing measure—now on the Administration's "must" list—finally emerged from the legislative mill. The Senate passed it on August 6 by a vote of 64–16, and on August 18 the House turned back a death-dealing motion to recommit by a vote of 140–221. Two weeks later the President set his signature to still another "Wagner bill." "While it is not all that I expected," the Senator informed an admirer, "it nevertheless cannot be minimized because it is a tremendous step forward." Once again the camel had gotten its nose under the tent.[17]

Particularly galling to Wagner as he savored the mixed fruits of victory was an amendment that Congress had added to the housing measure placing the new United States Housing Authority in Harold Ickes' Interior Department. Ickes had rendered valuable support to the principles of Wagner's bill, but at the same time he was determined to retain administrative control over any permanent agency that might supplant his PWA's Housing Division. Critics of the Housing Division and of its head, Howard Gray, insisted, on the other hand, that the USHA be given status as an independent agency, and, with Wagner, they felt that the housing program was too important to risk subordination among the many other activities of the Interior Department. During 1937 both Ickes and Wagner carried their fight to the White House, and at first it appeared that Wagner had triumphed. He secured Roosevelt's word that the Chief Executive didn't care where the agency was put, and the bill as reported by the Senate Labor Committee conformed to the Senator's views.[18]

[16] 81 *Congressional Record*, 7967ff, 7972, 7992, 8194, 8199, 8256, 8262, 8266, 8282, 8372–73, 9261, 9289, 9580ff; Robert Moore Fisher, *20 Years of Public Housing* (New York, 1959), p. 13; McDonnell, *The Wagner Housing Act*, pp. 323ff.
[17] 81 *Congressional Record*, 8373, 9293–94; RFW to Rev. Edward Roberts Moore, Aug. 23, 1937, RFW Papers.
[18] American Federation of Housing Authorities to RFW, Aug. 4, 1937, RFW Papers; also FDR Papers: Harold Ickes to FDR, May 17, June 8, 1937;

The Old Curmudgeon didn't give up easily, however, and on the next to last day of the Senate's debate on the measure Senator Marvel M. Logan of Kentucky introduced an amendment transferring the USHA to Ickes' department. Wagner called the proposal a surprise move, which "frankly I do not think . . . is fair to me," and he managed to stave off an immediate vote on the matter. But as one reporter related, that evening "the Ickes lobbying squad, which is one of the most efficiently organized of the departmental divisions of legislative influence, went into action." It was said that Ickes personally telephoned thirty senators before the night was out; at any rate, when the roll call came the following afternoon, the Logan amendment prevailed by the narrow margin of 40–37.[19]

Now the Wagner-Ickes feud shifted to the question of who was to head the new Housing Authority. Ickes assumed that the post would go to Howard Gray, but Wagner, still bristling for battle, urged Roosevelt to appoint another candidate. The Senator's nominee was Nathan Straus, a New York businessman and philanthropist, who, as Wagner's political protégé, had entered the state legislature during the 1920s and thereafter had served on New York City's Public Housing Authority.

The struggle over the Housing Authority appointment, which according to Washington columnist Joseph Alsop approached "the proportions of a bureaucratic Armageddon," raged all during September and into October as both Wagner and Ickes brought every persuasive tactic at their command to bear on the beleaguered President. Finally on October 13, following a Columbus Day trip to Hyde Park by Wagner, Roosevelt announced the selection of Straus to head the new agency. "Ickes takes it mighty hard," a friendly newspaperman warned Wagner a few days later. "He's doing considerable growling among his own, so watch out for reprisals." But there were none. Instead, Ickes virtually washed his hands of the housing program thereafter, and, while the United States Housing Authority remained lodged in the Interior Department until 1941, for all practical purposes it functioned as an independent agency.[20]

The New York Senator—that "nice gentlemanly person who

Nathan Straus to FDR, Aug. 3, 1937; memorandum of telephone conversation between RFW and Marvin McIntyre, Aug. 4, 1937; also New York *Herald Tribune*, Sept. 21, 1937; interviews with Leon H. Keyserling and Nathan Straus; McDonnell, *The Wagner Housing Act*, pp. 288ff.

[19] 81 *Congressional Record*, 8282ff, 8288–89, 8352ff, 8357; New York *Herald Tribune*, Sept. 21, 1937.

[20] New York *Herald Tribune*, Sept. 21, 1937; Raymond G. Carroll to RFW, Oct. 22, 1937, RFW Papers; McDonnell, *The Wagner Housing Act*, pp. 305–306; interviews with Leon H. Keyserling and Nathan Straus.

didn't like to offend anybody," and who rarely engaged in the capital's unending patronage squabbles—could still demonstrate that he had been weaned by the Tammany tiger when, rightly or wrongly, he felt that he had been "crossed"!

A few nights after Congress passed the public housing law Wagner, as a special guest of Hollywood producer Samuel Goldwyn, attended the world premiere of *Dead End*—a motion picture that more than one critic described as "excellent propaganda for better housing." In mid-November he was feted at a testimonial victory dinner sponsored by the National Public Housing Conference. Five hundred persons assembled at the Hotel Astor to pay tribute to the legislative pilot of the New Deal's latest reform program. Two children, spokesmen for the Lower East Side Public Housing Conference, presented to the Senator a silver loving cup engraved with the words:

> From Friends in Need,
> To a Friend in Deed.

When the time came for the Senator to respond, he was introduced by Assemblyman Robert F. Wagner, Jr., who just a week before had won his first election to the legislature from the same Yorkville district that had chosen his father a third of a century earlier. "My closest friend, my severest critic, my idol, my Dad" were the words the young assemblyman used in calling on the main speaker of the evening. Seconds seemed to stretch into minutes while the two Wagners exchanged places at the microphone, and toastmaster Herbert Bayard Swope interjected a few words: "I can understand," he said, "the tears in Bob Wagner's eyes." [21]

[21] Samuel Goldwyn to RFW, Aug. 20, 1937, RFW Papers; New York *Post*, Nov. 13, 1937.

CHAPTER 14

Treading Water

I f the year 1937 marked a break-through of sorts for New Dealers in their relations with the Supreme Court, in retrospect it can be seen also as the year that marked the beginning of a sharp decline in the ability of the Roosevelt forces to control the lawmaking branch of the government. "The new Court might be willing to uphold new laws," historian William E. Leuchtenburg has written, "but an angry and divided Congress would pass few of them for the justices to consider." [1] Aside from Bob Wagner's public housing law, Congress enacted only one other noteworthy piece of reform legislation in 1937— a measure designed to aid sharecroppers and tenant farmers. In the two years remaining before the outbreak of war in Europe, the New Deal's momentum slackened even more noticeably. Heartened by their success, Congressional conservatives from both parties sharpened their knives in preparation for the operation that they hoped would excise many of the progressive measures put through earlier during the heyday of Roosevelt's popularity.

Among the developments of 1937 that played into the hands of the New Deal's opponents several stand out: the fight over the President's "court-packing" proposal; an upsurge of industrial strife early in the year, distinguished particularly by labor's resort to the sitdown strike; and a disastrous business recession that began in the fall and threatened to wipe out all the progress toward recovery made in previ-

[1] William E. Leuchtenburg, *Franklin D. Roosevelt and the New Deal: 1932– 1940* (New York, 1963), p. 239.

ous years. Roosevelt's court reorganization bill brought conservative Republicans and Democrats into closer coalition than ever before; the coalition's success in defeating the bill demonstrated its strength impressively and destroyed both Congressional and popular belief in the President's political infallibility.

Victory in that encounter also served to whet the conservatives' appetite for revenge against "that man in the White House," who allegedly was bent on establishing a personal dynasty built on patronage and the subversion of the legislature's and court's prerogatives. In senatorial debate they frequently vented their spite in cranky charges that too large a proportion of federal appointments and relief funds was going to citizens of Bob Wagner's Empire State, which was also Roosevelt's state. The upshot was a serious and somewhat successful drive to handcuff the Chief Executive by limiting his discretion in the allocation and spending of WPA money, and by prescribing that appointments to even relatively minor posts receive senatorial sanction.[2] All in all, the charge that the Roosevelt Administration represented a power-crazed conspiracy hell-bent for dictatorship drew considerable nurture from the acrid debates over the court-reform bill. It put the President's supporters on the defensive, and for that reason some observers have called it Roosevelt's greatest political mistake.

Equally sinister in the eyes of conservatives were the rising power and aggressiveness of organized labor as, during the winter of 1936–37, John L. Lewis' Congress of Industrial Organizations pushed its drive to unionize the mass-production industries. With the C.I.O.'s resort to the sitdown strike, a new note of hysteria accompanied the charges that, under the New Deal, American business was being subjected to domination by a radical and subversive labor union monopoly. Inevitably conservatives identified the sitdown as a Communist-inspired tactic; inevitably, too, they charged that it had been fostered by the New Deal's Wagner Labor Relations Act. To them the solution of the nation's unprecedented outbreak of labor strife seemed simple in the early months of 1937: outlaw the sitdown strike by federal legislation (conservative congressmen made several attempts to do so during March and April), and trust the Supreme Court to soon render the Wagner Act unconstitutional.[3]

On March 31 the author of the National Labor Relations Act took the floor of the Senate to offer an explanation of labor's unrest

[2] 81 *Congressional Record*, 760ff, 5718–19, 5814–15, 5882ff, 7956, and 83 C. R., 2627.

[3] 83 *Congressional Record*, 3085ff, 3121ff; Leuchtenburg, *Franklin D. Roosevelt*, pp. 239ff.

that differed markedly from that of the New Deal-haters. Seventy percent of the workers involved in recent labor disputes, Wagner pointed out, were agitating *not* on behalf of wage demands pushed by a grasping union monopoly, but rather for the very rights to union recognition and collective bargaining that Congress had granted them by law many months earlier. While Wagner refused to sanction the sitdown tactic in those situations where it was illegal under local statute, he did insist that this "uprising of the common people has come, as always, only because of a breakdown in the ability of the law and our economic system to protect their rights." "The sitdown has been provoked by the long-standing and ruthless tactics of a few great corporations," Wagner contended, "who have hamstrung the National Labor Relations Board by invoking court actions, which they have a perfect legal right to do; who have openly banded together to defy this law of Congress quite independently of any court action, which they have neither the legal nor the moral right to do; and who have systematically used spies and discharges and violence and terrorism to shatter the workers' liberties as defined by Congress, which they have neither the legal nor the moral right to do. The organized and calculated and cold-blooded sitdown against Federal law has come . . . not from the common people, but from a few great vested interests." Pleading that his colleagues recognize which evil was the underlying cause and which was merely the effect, Wagner urged that the government have the power and the determination to enforce the Labor Relations Act on a national scale; then, he assured his listeners, "the nationwide conflict will subside." "Make men free, and they will be able to negotiate without fighting."

When, two weeks later, the Supreme Court upheld the Wagner Act to the consternation of its opponents, the sitdown tactic had already been repudiated by most labor leaders, and the wave of strikes had begun to subside amidst a series of victories for the workers. Thereafter strike statistics indicated that there was much substance to Wagner's analysis of the violence, tear gas, and killings that had marred the industrial scene in the winter of 1937. During 1938—the first full year after the Labor Act was validated by the Supreme Court—there were only half as many strikes, one-third as many workers involved, and less than one-third as much working time lost compared to 1937. Indeed, fewer workers went on strike in 1938 than in any year since 1932.[4]

[4] 81 *Congressional Record*, 2939ff; Leon H. Keyserling, "Why the Wagner Act?," in Louis G. Silverberg, ed., *The Wagner Act: After Ten Years* (Washington, 1945), pp. 17–18.

Nonetheless, the Supreme Court's benediction failed to sway conservatives from their determination to dilute the principles of the New Deal's labor legislation. Unable any longer to count on the courts for total invalidation of the Wagner Act, its opponents now switched to demands for amendments to make its workings "fairer" to management and to correct its alleged prolabor "one-sidedness." The fact that the Act placed restrictions on employers alone, and not on the workers or their unions, was invoked repeatedly to justify the assertion that it represented "class legislation" foreign to traditional American standards of fair play. After April 1937 such Republicans as Arthur Vandenburg of Michigan and anti-New Deal Democrats as Edward R. Burke of Nebraska vied with one another in proposing amendments to the Act and in calling for investigation of the operations of the NLRB. For a while they took comfort in the attitude of some A. F. of L. leaders who, asserting that the board's personnel was prejudiced in favor of the C.I.O., launched a campaign for revision of the Administration, but not the substance, of the Act.[5]

Wagner and his allies countered by arguing that the labor measure had not yet been given sufficient chance to prove itself, since, during its first two years in existence, it was openly flaunted by many employers who were convinced of its unconstitutionality. As for its alleged one-sidedness, the New York Senator conceded that "if an uninitiated person examined the Act in a vacuum or on the planet Mars, he would be fairly overwhelmed by the obvious justice of these criticisms." But when viewed properly within the total context of American law and the actual conduct of industrial relations, Wagner contended, the restrictions placed on workers and their unions, economic, social, and legal, became so clear as to render criticisms of the Wagner Act's bias "absolutely meaningless." "No one would assail the traffic laws," the Senator pointed out to a Yale Law School audience in the spring of 1937, "because they regulate the speed at which automobiles travel, and not the speed at which pedestrians walk." [6]

As for the A. F. of L.'s complaints, Wagner admitted that the split in the labor movement had introduced complications that were

[5] Files on "Proposed Amendments to the National Labor Relations Act, 1937–1940," RFW Papers; 81 *Congressional Record*, 7725ff, and 83 *C. R.*, Appendix, 534–535; Edward R. Burke, "The Labor Board Is WRONG," *Factory Management and Maintenance* (March 1938), pp. 56ff; William Green to Royal S. Copeland, Jan. 24, 1938, in 83 *Congressional Record*, 2368; Harry A. Millis and Emily Clark Brown, *From the Wagner Act to Taft-Hartley* (Chicago, 1950), *passim*.

[6] Wagner speech file, April 16, 1937, RFW Papers; RFW letter to the editor of *The New York Times*, April 25, 1937; Robert F. Wagner, "Wagner Challenges Critics of His Act," *New York Times Magazine*, July 25, 1937.

unanticipated at the time he drafted the law. But efforts at healing the breach in labor's ranks, he felt, would prove more rewarding to the A. F. of L. in the long run than a course of action that played into the hands of labor's bitterest foes. Wagner's suspicion that the campaign to make the Labor Board's personnel and procedures "fairer" was really a device for opening a Pandora's Box of changes that would strike at the very roots of the Act's principles depended for support not alone upon the advice of sympathizers like the renowned labor economist William L. Leiserson. "The labor board is the ostensible target of employer attack just now," wrote the conservative columnist David Lawrence early in 1938, "but the aim is to break down the Wagner Act." For despite the Supreme Court's ruling, Lawrence observed, "the fight against collective bargaining itself is kept going with undiminished intensity." [7]

During 1937, and for a good while thereafter, Wagner and his New Deal allies managed to stave off the clamor for amending the Labor Act. Nevertheless, further proposals for strengthening the Act's effectiveness, such as the Wagner-sponsored measure of 1937 that would deny government contracts to firms that violated the labor law's provisions, failed to secure the approval of a stalemated Congress.[8] As with the court reform proposal, so, too, in the field of labor legislation New Dealers found themselves on the defensive by 1938. Forward momentum seemed to have ended.

Contributing further to the Administration's embarrassment was the economic recession that got under way in August 1937 and that by the end of the year threatened to wipe out all the advances made toward recovery during the previous five years. Interpretations of the cause and of the potential cure for the setback ranged over a bewildering spectrum and, in particular, brought the debate over government fiscal policy into greater prominence than ever before. Conservative Administration officials, like Treasury Secretary Morgenthau, emphasized businessmen's hesitancy to expand their operations in the face of continued government spending and mounting deficits; a policy of federal retrenchment would overcome those fears and encourage a re-

[7] RFW Papers: RFW to Daniel J. Tobin, Nov. 13, Dec. 20, 1935; William L. Leiserson to RFW, April 29, 1937; David Lawrence, "Today in Washington," clipping from the Schenectady *Gazette*, Feb. 2, 1938; also Thomas I. Emerson, "Reminiscences" (Oral History Research Office, Columbia Univ., 1953), pp. 653–654; Charles Fahy, "Reminiscences" (Oral History Research Office, n.d.), pp. 184ff; interviews with Leon H. Keyserling, Simon H. Rifkind, and Philip Levy; Keyserling, "Why the Wagner Act?," pp. 25–33.

[8] Files on "Wagner Amendment to the Walsh-Healey Act, 1937–1938," and Wagner speech file, March 21, 1938, RFW Papers; 83 *Congressional Record*, 1488–89.

vival of job-producing investment in the private sector of the economy. Contesting that advice were New Dealers like Harry Hopkins
and Secretary Ickes, who attributed the debacle to the fact that Roosevelt was already too much under the influence of the Morgenthau
school. For in June of 1937 the President, convinced by the Treasury
official's argument that the private economy was ready to stand on its
own feet, had ordered a drastic cut in WPA rolls and virtually ended
PWA operations as the first steps in a concerted drive to make good
his often-repeated promise of bringing the budget into balance. But
the abandonment of the government's pump-priming functions had
come too soon, the spenders maintained, as the economic indices
plummeted in the closing months of the year; only a revival of those
functions, they argued, could make up for the President's mistake.[9]

The side that Wagner would take in the fiscal debate touched off
by the recession was not difficult to prophesy. "When the federal
government abruptly cut down its contributions to purchasing power
by $250,000,000 a month last year . . . there promptly began the
sharp decline of business," Wagner told a radio audience in the spring
of 1938. "Let us remember," he admonished, "that it is the way of
folly to cut down public activity faster than private industry can assume the load."

Nor was it only with the advantage of hindsight that the New
York Senator sought again to inculcate that lesson. For during the
previous June's debate on the relief appropriation, while senators like
Millard Tydings sought to cut the amount even lower than the reduced figure asked for by the President—"We are not now in a depression," the Maryland lawmaker offered in explanation, "we are out
of it"—Wagner remained one of a small band of skeptics who expressed doubt about the wisdom of the budget-balancing drive. "Does
the Senator think a country that still has eight or nine million people
unemployed is out of the depression completely?" he asked his opto-
mistic colleague. And since the statistics that he had continued to
marshal still failed to indicate that improvements in profits and production were being matched proportionately by increases in employment, wages, and consumer purchasing power, Wagner was convinced
that business' current semblance of prosperity was due primarily "to
the farsighted vision of the government, in creating work and purchasing power and markets for goods through the use of the public credit.

[9] Leuchtenburg, *Franklin D. Roosevelt*, pp. 243ff; John Morton Blum, *From
the Morgenthau Diaries: Years of Crisis, 1928–1938* (Boston, 1959), pp. 380ff.
For a succinct statement of the "budget balancers' " view, see editorial in *The
New York Times*, May 10, 1938; for the "spenders' " position see editorial in the
New York *Post*, Feb. 1, 1937.

To remove this public prop from our business structure more rapidly than private industry is prepared to substitute its own support," the Senator warned, "would send us tumbling backward into the depths of depression." When, in the second half of the year, that prediction seemed to come true, Wagner might have felt vindicated. Since then most economists and historians have joined in corroborating his view of the nature of the "Roosevelt depression." [10]

Still, when Congress assembled for a special session in mid-November 1937, the President had not yet chosen to heed the advice of the spenders in his New Deal family. Roosevelt did recommend enactment of minimum-wage legislation and a new price-support program for farmers as means of maintaining purchasing power for large numbers of consumers. But for the major attack against the "marked recession" that admittedly had set in, he seemed content to rely on the policy of increasing "the use of private capital to create employment." He endorsed particularly a liberalization of FHA requirements, so as "to encourage private capital to enter the field of new housing on a large scale." The President did hint that "if private enterprise does not respond, government must take up the slack." But in order to encourage that response he held out once again the favorite lure of his more conservative advisers; the budget to be submitted shortly after the New Year would be one "which I expect can be brought within a definite balance." [11]

The special session lasted five weeks, and it gave Roosevelt nothing that he had asked for—neither minimum-wage nor farm legislation, nor a reorganization act empowering him to rearrange executive agencies, nor a regional planning act authorizing creation of "seven little TVA's." The FHA bill came closest to approval; Bob Wagner had been working on liberalizing amendments since early in the year, and both houses passed the bill without much dispute. Nevertheless, minor differences in the House and Senate versions necessitated appointment of a conference committee. By the time Wagner and the other Senate conferees were ready to get down to business on December 21 most of their House counterparts, unwilling any longer to cut into the Christmas holidays, had packed up and gone home. The special session, which Roosevelt originally envisioned as an opportunity to regain some of the political splendor that had become so tarnished during the course of the year, ended up a dismal failure.[12]

[10] Wagner speech file, May 22, 1938, RFW Papers; 81 *Congressional Record*, 5871ff, 5879.
[11] 82 *Congressional Record*, 5-7.
[12] Files on "Federal Housing Administration, 1937," and "Home Owners' Loan Corporation, 1937," RFW Papers; 82 *Congressional Record*, 418–420, 1987ff, 2021; Leuchtenburg, *Franklin D. Roosevelt*, p. 251.

When Congress reassembled in January 1938 the same ill-tempered, perplexed mood continued to pervade its deliberations. The more conservative members, disturbed by the new emphasis that the President had placed on executive reorganization in his State of the Union message, thought they detected a bid for power similar to the assault on the judiciary of the previous year, and they became more suspicious of Roosevelt's motives than ever. Even the Administration's friends, worried by the continuing downward spiral of the economy, were disturbed by the President's indecision in the face of the crisis. Nor was the temper of the Senate sweetened by the knowledge that, thanks to the parliamentary adroitness displayed by Bob Wagner a few months earlier, the first order of business facing it was the highly inflammatory Wagner-Van Nuys-Gavagan antilynching bill.

The cause of making lynching a federal crime, which Wagner first embraced in partnership with Senator Edward P. Costigan during 1934, made little progress in the ensuing two years. But in April 1937 Congressman Joseph A. Gavagan of New York, who had become House sponsor of the N.A.A.C.P. measure, succeeded in pushing through a discharge petition that freed the bill from the tentacles of the Rules Committee. On the very day that House debate reached its zenith the press reported the lynching of two Negroes at Duck Hill, Mississippi. Shocked by the ghastliness of the crime—the lynch mob had put its victims to death with blowtorches—the House approved Gavagan's bill by a 2-to-1 majority. By the end of June Senator Frederick Van Nuys of Indiana, who succeeded Costigan as Wagner's cosponsor in the upper house, had maneuvered the bill through the Judiciary Committee and won a favorable report for it. But the controversial measure lay at the bottom of the Senate's calendar, and since the President persisted in his refusal to make it "must" legislation, Southerners rested comfortably in the belief that it had been buried permanently.[13]

As it happened, however, a new majority leader, Alben W. Barkley of Kentucky, headed the Senate's Democrats after death claimed Joseph T. Robinson at the height of the court-packing fight. In August, as the battle-scarred session neared its close, Barkley did his best to see that none but Administration-blessed measures reached the floor of the chamber. But the inexperience of the new leader was demonstrated by events that transpired on August 11. To be sure, he had arranged that when the pending bill was disposed of, Senator King of Utah should rise and move to make the innocuous District of Colum-

[13] Files on "Anti-Lynching Bill, 1935–1937," RFW Papers; *Time*, April 26, 1937, pp. 16–17; 81 *Congressional Record*, 6113, 7741.

bia airport bill the next order of business. But when that moment arrived neither King nor Barkley were in their places. Only one senator, Bob Wagner of New York, was on his feet demanding recognition, and the presiding officer had no alternative but to grant him the floor. As murmurs grew into a chorus of moans, Wagner moved that the Senate take up the antilynching bill. By now Barkley was sputtering and fuming, but it was too late; the Democratic leader's plans for bringing the session to a quick and orderly end went up in smoke.

During the rest of the day, and most of the next, Barkley tried to get Wagner to withdraw his motion, while Southerners hotly declared their intention to debate it until Christmas, if need be, in order to prevent it from coming to a vote. But the New Yorker held his ground; he, too, seemed ready for a showdown. In the end Barkley was forced to offer a resolution making the antilynch bill the special order of business at the next regular session of the Congress. Wagner and the N.A.A.C.P. leadership acquiesced (better to face a filibuster at the beginning of a session than at the end); weary senators, anxious to escape Washington's heat, voted their approval.[14]

Thus had the stage been set for the filibuster that, from January 6 through February 21, 1938, tied up the Senate's and the nation's legislative work. At the outset the bill's supporters seemed confident that they would eventually prevail. The long months of preparation afforded them by Barkley's resolution enabled the staff of the N.A.A.C.P. to assemble a veritable arsenal of historical and constitutional arguments for use by the measure's legislative exponents, of whom Wagner was the leader. (Wagner also received help from a colored waiter employed in the Senate restaurant, who deposited in his office a compendious, hand-written list of presidential pronouncements against lynching and mob violence from the time of Benjamin Harrison down.) Fourteen of the Senate's sixteen Republicans, as well as a large majority of the Democrats, were on record as favoring the bill. Most encouraging of all were the widespread rumors that Southern delegates intended to stage merely a peremptory filibuster against the measure "for home consumption," after which they would protestingly acquiesce in its passage by their Northern colleagues. During the fall of 1937 several Southern congressmen had been quoted in the press as stating publicly that sentiment for the bill had become so overwhelming as to be irresistible.[15]

[14] 81 *Congressional Record*, 8694–97, 8737ff, 8758–59; also RFW Papers: RFW to Walter White, Aug. 13, 1937; White to RFW, Aug. 13, 1937; National Association for the Advancement of Colored People, press release, Aug. 13, 1937; also *Time*, Jan. 24, 1938, p. 8.

[15] RFW Papers: files on "Anti-Lynching Bill, 1937–1938"; Samuel N. Clark to RFW, Feb. 8, 1938; Walter White to RFW, Oct. 20, 1937; clipping from an

Nevertheless, prospects for the bill's passage began to change within a short time after debate on it got under way. The high-level discussion of constitutional issues that prevailed at the outset soon lapsed into long-winded speeches of a purely obstructionist nature, such as North Carolina Senator Robert Reynolds' marathon travelogue that afforded his colleagues a two-day description of the wonders of Europe, the Orient, the British Isles, South America, Africa, and the Malay States. Senators like Mississippi's Theodore Bilbo specialized in garish depictions of the horrors that would befall America if racial "amalgamation," toward which the "Communist-inspired" antilynching bill was the first step, came about. Southern members who, according to newsmen, had long but secretly envied Wagner's position and influence in the Senate "club," now turned their barbs against him openly, as they questioned his motives and sincerity in sponsoring the lynch bill, and tried to drag him down to their own level of debate. ("I learned long ago that when one has a just cause," Wagner responded to one series of jibes, "he does not have to resort to personal attacks. Besides," he added with excessive humility, "I would not know how to, anyway.") Swayed perhaps by the shrillness and volume of their own oratory, and rallied by Louisiana Senator Allen J. Ellender's call to "at all cost preserve the white supremacy of America," the Dixie contingent seemed to gain strength and determination as the "peremptory" filibuster developed into the real thing. By the end of January crusty old Tom Connally of Texas, the captain of the Southern defensive, was telling reporters once again that he and his band were ready to carry on until Christmas.[16]

Encouraging to the Southerners, and disappointing to the lynch bill's supporters, was the outcome of the first attempt to impose cloture, which was made on January 27. While much more than a majority of the Senate had pledged to vote for the bill itself, far less than the necessary two-thirds were willing to cut off debate, and the cloture motion went down to defeat with only 37 "ayes" to 51 "noes." The common reason for their action given by the large number of non-Southerners who voted in the negative was stated by the minority leader, Charles McNary, whose lead was followed by all but one of his Republican colleagues. "I am not willing to give up the right of free speech," the Oregonian proclaimed. "That right is the last palladium . . . it may be the last barrier to tyranny." And while his reasoning

unidentified magazine, Michael Frost, "Borah the Lynch Bill-Buster," April 7, 1938, pp. 88ff.
    [16] 83 *Congressional Record*, 154ff, 1339, 2205; *Time*, Jan. 28, 1938, pp. 8–10; Frost, "Borah the Lynch Bill-Buster," p. 90.

perhaps seemed noble enough to believers in the abstract principle of untrammeled debate, it only evoked smiles among those in the press galleries who knew that McNary and most of his Republican followers had voted *for* cloture on many previous occasions—*nine*, to be exact, in McNary's case. Many of the correspondents therefore chose to believe that the Republicans' tactics were dictated by political expediency rather than devotion to high principles, and that they were out to cut short the Democratic party's growing allure to Negro voters by blaming the overwhelmingly Democratic Seventy-fifth Congress with failure to enact antilynching legislation.

Yet there was truth enough in McNary's charge that the Senate's eighty Democrats must bear the major burden of the cloture motion's defeat, and in his contention, too, that the Democratic President had raised not a finger in its behalf. For, by the time the Senate voted on Wagner's second cloture petition on February 16, the bill's proponents, still bereft of White House support, had managed to round up only five additional votes. Despite Theodore Bilbo's announcement that he was preparing a speech that would take a month to deliver, cloture again went down to defeat 42–46.[17]

Working in the Southerners' favor, too, was a mounting impatience with the Senate for "wasting its time" in the midst of an economic crisis as days stretched into weeks of debate, an impatience reflected in the scores of editorials from Northern newspapers that Georgia's Senator Richard B. Russell gleefully spread over eighteen pages of the *Congressional Record* late in January. Recognizing that time had begun to work against them rather than against their opponents, Wagner and his followers offered to lay aside the antilynching bill temporarily at any time in order to consider other essential legislation; but the Southerners were shrewd enough to block any such move. Thus, ironic as it was, the impression grew that the bill's proponents, rather than the Southern bloc, bore the responsibility for prolonging the filibuster. Since only seven lynchings had taken place during 1937, some newspapers reasoned, the problem was on the way toward "solving itself." "Passage of an anti-lynching bill from even the standpoint of its advocates," declared the Hartford *Times*, "is not immediately imperative." "Why . . . should the Senate waste precious days discussing an anti-lynching bill," asked the Providence *Journal*, "at a time when the recession-ridden country expects solid think-

[17] 83 *Congressional Record*, 1165–66, 1339ff, 2005–2007, 2204–2205, 2207–2208; National Association for the Advancement of Colored People, press release, Dec. 6, 1938, RFW Papers; *Time*, Jan. 24, 1938, p. 10; Frost, "Borah the Lynch Bill-Buster," pp. 88ff; transcripts of press conferences, Jan. 14, March 22, 1938, FDR Papers.

ing and swift action from Congress?" "It is much like the fiddling that went on while Rome burned," opined a Montana journal. One of the most crushing blows of all came when the veteran progressive Republican Senator George W. Norris of Nebraska added his voice to the chorus and urged that the bill be abandoned. "Perhaps this is not the time," the Nebraskan added in justification, "to open wounds that may not heal." [18]

During the five days following defeat of the second cloture motion Alben Barkley, armed with a relief appropriation bill that the White House had labeled "urgent," persuaded Bob Wagner that the fight was hopeless, and on February 21 the majority leader moved to take up the Administration measure. The New York Senator made one last attempt to amend Barkley's motion so that consideration of the lynching bill might resume on March 28, but Southerners threatened to filibuster against Wagner's amendment as long as they had against the bill itself, and he was forced to back down.[19]

Thus the Senate's first major civil rights debate of the New Deal era ended in defeat for the proponents of racial justice, and the scene would be repeated many times in the years to come. Nevertheless, the fight did redound to the benefit of several people, and among them was Wagner himself. For if Wagner had sought to reap political benefit from his championing of the cause, as Southerners repeatedly charged, certainly the N.A.A.C.P.'s statement regarding the "bitter dose" of February 21 brought him his reward. "We wish to express our deep appreciation to Senator Wagner and other senators," declared Walter White, "who loyally, and in the face of bitter abuse and personal attacks, stood firm." (In marked contrast was the private letter that White addressed that same day to the deservedly revered father of TVA. "But what, my dear Senator Norris," the colored official poignantly asked, "is the worth to a man of an electrically lighted home if he can be taken from that home as easily as from a cabin lighted by candles, and burned to death by a howling mob?")

Another beneficiary of the civil rights debate of 1938 was an obscure young Negro mill hand in Greensboro, Alabama, named Lee Jones. On the verge of being strung up by a hysterical crowd, Jones had been saved only on the plea of a local official that lawless violence might embarrass the Southern representatives in Washington who were resisting the Wagner-Van Nuys-Gavagan bill. Indeed, according to Walter White, several other murders were averted under similar circumstances while the bill was pending. Following the removal of its

[18] 83 *Congressional Record*, 2265–83; *Time*, Jan. 24, 1938, p. 10.
[19] 83 *Congressional Record*, 2201ff, 2210.

deterrent power after February 21, however, five more unfortunate Americans met death at the hands of lynch mobs before the year was out.[20]

The Administration relief bill that displaced the antilynching bill was a purely stopgap measure. The small $250,000,000 appropriation that it carried was hardly designed to launch new, large-scale pump-priming operations; on the contrary, the money would suffice merely to keep the WPA going at its current rate of activity until the end of the fiscal year in June. Since it was well known that thousands of those thrown out of work by the recession were not even being provided for by Hopkins' agency, a band of Senate liberals, among whom Bob Wagner was one, sought to increase the appropriation to $400,-000,000. But their arguments proved futile against the fact that the lesser figure was all the President had asked for, and their amendment went down to defeat. Roosevelt still refused to concede that a major governmental effort was called for; by March, enactment of the Wagner-sponsored FHA liberalization bill stood as the Administration's only overt response to the economic downswing. "As I see it," a pleased Henry Morgenthau remarked to the President in the middle of the month, "what you are doing now is just treading water . . . to see what happens this spring." "Absolutely," his chief replied.[21]

The first weeks of spring brought little improvement in the country's economic health. But they did bring another political setback for the Administration at the hands of a restive Congress that nearly equaled the blow dealt by defeat of the court-reform measure a year earlier. This time the rebuff to Roosevelt's leadership consisted in the rough handling given his executive reorganization bill. The proposal, which would allow the President to shift departments and bureaus around virtually at will, had by this time generated considerable opposition. Not only were conservatives and professional Roosevelt-haters against it, the A. F. of L. and some social workers, concerned that such power might enable a future Chief Executive to abolish or deci-

[20] National Association for the Advancement of Colored People, press release, Feb. 21, 1938, and Walter White to George W. Norris, Feb. 24, 1938, RFW Papers; Montgomery *Advertiser*, Jan. 12, 1938; *Time*, Jan. 24, 1938, p. 8; Wagner speech file, Nov. 3, 1938, RFW Papers. In a letter to George R. Van Namee (Wagner's 1938 campaign manager) on Nov. 1, 1938, White declared that the Senator's "unceasing campaign for the Anti-Lynching Bill . . . stands out as one of the most heroic battles ever fought for equal justice under the law" (RFW Papers).
[21] 83 *Congressional Record*, 1338, 2235ff, 2284, Appendix, 578–579; files on "Federal Housing Administration, 1938," RFW Papers; Blum, *Morgenthau Diaries: Years of Crisis*, p. 415.

mate agencies deemed essential to labor's welfare, had also come out against the President's bill. So, too, had many Catholic spokesmen who feared that the measure was the prelude to creation of a federal Department of Education that in some way might interfere with the integrity and independence of the parochial school system.[22]

Such pressures were of the sort that a New York Senator might naturally be expected to heed. And it has sometimes been held that their influence motivated Bob Wagner's decision to take his stand with the President's opponents—a stand that provided one of the more sensational developments of the whole reorganization episode.

Yet there may well have been, as Leon Keyserling thought, more profound reasons behind the Senator's latest display of legislative independence. "He believed," Wagner's administrative assistant has written, "that basic decisions as to the administrative structure could not be separated from those fundamental questions of substantive policy and program which should remain subject to initial control by the Congress." Wagner was aware, for example, that the effectiveness of the Federal Employment Stabilization Board, created by one of his original Three Bills during the Hoover Administration, had been reduced to the vanishing point as a result of an earlier reorganization carried out in the early days of the New Deal. Of even more recent memory were his battles with prominent Cabinet officers regarding the status of the agencies created by his Labor Relations and Public Housing acts. Having lost the housing fight to Ickes, Wagner appeared more anxious than ever to preserve the independent status of the National Labor Relations Board against the continuing wiles of Madame Perkins. In April 1937, long before Roosevelt's reorganization bill had attracted much attention, Wagner informed a constituent of his determination to keep the NLRB from becoming merely a departmental agency. "I regard the treatment of the independent regulatory commissions in the reorganization report," he added significantly, "as falling very short of a penetrating discussion of the real issues involved." [23]

Such misgivings, rather than the thousands of unread telegrams

[22] RFW Papers: files on "Executive Reorganization Bill, 1937–1938"; William Green to RFW, March 21, 1938; George Meany (president of the New York State Federation of Labor) to RFW, March 21, 1938; George M. Harrison (chairman of the Railway Labor Executives Association) to RFW, March 24, 1938; Charles I. Stengle (president of the American Federation of Government Employees) to RFW, April 26, 1938.
[23] New York *Daily News*, March 30, 1938; Leon H. Keyserling, "The Wagner Act: Its Origin and Current Significance," *George Washington Law Review* (Dec. 1960), p. 210; RFW to Lewis Douglas, Dec. 30, 1933, and RFW to Abraham M. Kobrick, April 28, 1937, RFW Papers.

piling up in his office, probably prompted Wagner's hard decision to cast his vote with the New Deal's opponents on March 28, 1938. Roosevelt's bill managed to survive the Senate roll call by a scant margin, but a few days later, on April 8, the House turned it down 204–196. More than a hundred Democratic representatives bolted their leader at the crucial moment; it appeared that, just as Roosevelt had lost control of the Senate during the court fight a year earlier, so, too, the lower house had now gotten away from him. Like Washington's political observers, the President himself was stunned. "I can't understand it," he lamented to Jim Farley. "There wasn't a chance for anyone to become a dictator under that bill." [24]

Prompted by the failure of business to respond to "private enterprise" nostrums, and perhaps by the blow to his political prestige that the close Senate vote on his reorganization bill presaged, Roosevelt decided on the second day of April 1938 to abandon the passive role the Administration had assumed toward the economy in the months since the recession had gotten under way. At lunch with Harry Hopkins he divulged his inclination to resume government spending; in a message to Congress on April 14 he outlined the details of his program. While calling for reinvigoration of the WPA, the CCC, and other New Deal relief agencies, Roosevelt also endorsed augmented appropriations for the PWA and the government's other pump-priming heavy construction agencies, including the United States Housing Authority. "He was completely stampeded," mourned Henry Morgenthau in acknowledgment of the spenders' latest triumph. For the other side, Bob Wagner was among those who hailed the President's move. "If we learned anything in the bitter years between 1929 and 1933," he told a nationwide radio audience in defense of the President's new program, "it was the danger of sitting idly by and allowing the downward spiral to go unchecked." [25]

In the ensuing weeks Wagner and other New Deal stalwarts struggled to preserve the President's program against Congressional conservatives bent on undermining it. In addition to their general desire to reduce the size of virtually all the appropriations recommended by the Administration, economy-minded lawmakers sought particularly to require the states to match the WPA relief funds allocated to them. ("Any proposal to transform a great national duty into

[24] 83 *Congressional Record*, 4204; Leuchtenburg, *Franklin D. Roosevelt*, pp. 277–280.
[25] 83 *Congressional Record*, 5381–84; Wagner speech file, May 22, 1938, RFW Papers; Leuchtenburg, *Franklin D. Roosevelt*, pp. 256–257; Blum, *From the Morgenthau Diaries: Years of Crisis*, pp. 417ff, 421.

the separate responsibility of 48 states," Senator Wagner retorted, "would . . . return us to the devastating combination of 'do-nothingism' on the one hand, and the bread line, the soup kitchen, and the dole on the other." Senators such as Virginia's Harry F. Byrd were equally determined to strike out the moneys requested for the PWA and other major construction agencies, on the ground that four years' experience had proved the ineffectiveness of the public works "cure" for depressions. (Wagner maintained, on the contrary, that the remedy had hardly been tried, even under the New Deal. "The trouble with us," he insisted at one point during the floor debate, "is that we wait until it is too late," and then reduce the expenditures "too soon.") On the whole the Administration forces were able to rebuff most of the conservatives' attacks; they were aided by the fact that it was an election year, and many congressmen hesitated to vote against relief and recovery spending under the circumstances. But although the measure passed in June authorized $3.75 billion in new expenditures, the liberals had been forced to compromise on some points. The amount finally made available to the Housing Authority for new public housing loans, for example, fell $200 million short of the $500 million sought in the bill that Wagner had introduced earlier in the year.[26]

Before adjourning in the middle of June Congress approved two other bills requested by the President. One created a Temporary National Economic Committee, composed of congressmen and executive department officials, to probe the extent and effects of monopolistic tendencies in the business system. Wagner, long concerned over the tendency of prices and profits to outrun wages and purchasing power during periods of recovery, vigorously supported the investigation proposal. "That is a problem which Congress must face," he told his colleagues, adding his fear that "the beneficial effects of the new spending program will be diminished through our failure heretofore to deal effectively with the monopoly problem." [27]

The second measure, the Fair Labor Standards Act setting minimum wages and maximum hours for industries involved in interstate commerce, had become so riddled with exemptions in the course of passage that its final form disappointed many of its keenest propo-

[26] 83 *Congressional Record*, 6717–18, 7919ff, 7922, 7926, 7956–57, 8059–66, 9573–74; Wagner speech file, May 22, 1938, and files on "Public Housing Act, 1938," RFW Papers.
[27] 81 *Congressional Record*, 9221–22; 82 C. R., Appendix, 572; 83 C. R., 7248, 7475, 7922; Leuchtenburg, *Franklin D. Roosevelt*, pp. 246ff, 257ff. For the rationale of Wagner's and the Administration's concern that excessive monopolistic profits sapped the effectiveness of the government's recovery expenditures, see Drew Pearson and Robert S. Allen, "The Washington Merry-Go-Round," clipping from the Binghamton *Press*, April 20, 1938, RFW Papers.

nents. Still, by reinstituting one of the most worthwhile features of the doomed NRA experiment, the act promised to curb in some degree the return to sweatshop conditions that occurred in many industries following the Supreme Court decision of 1935. That was the estimate placed on the measure by Wagner, who for three years had worked for its enactment as hard as anyone else. In fact, so often had Wagner spoken in its favor, and so in tune was it with his well-known views about the relationship of wages to prosperity, that many people erroneously identified him as the bill's sponsor when it finally became law in the spring of 1938.[28]

When the Seventy-fifth Congress ended in the middle of June, then, Wagner could feel reasonably satisfied with the result of the session's labors. True, Roosevelt had refused to extend White House aid in the fight to enact the antilynching bill, while Wagner caused a stir by voting with the opposition on the issue of executive reorganization. But on the matter of economic policy—and that remained the country's most vital concern—they were working in tandem again. The liberal faction felt they had regained the upper hand in the President's councils, at least for the time being. Despite the rocky road constructed of external opposition and internal dissension, Wagner and those like him cherished the hope that the New Deal had rediscovered its appointed path.

The Congressional session of 1938 had been a grueling one, nonetheless, wearing on the nerves of all those involved ("That's that," sighed the President as he finished signing the last batch of bills on June 25), and especially wearing on Bob Wagner's overtaxed health. In 1937 Wagner had already lost ground in a bout with pneumonia, followed by a slight stroke, which had sent him to the recuperative climate of Florida for several weeks even while his public housing bill was entering the crucial stages of consideration. Early in 1938 a recurrence of the respiratory ailment kept him from the floor of the Senate for days while the lynch-bill filibuster raged; Southern orators made caustic references to his absence despite the doctor's orders that necessitated it.[29]

Yet even adjournment brought no respite to the Senator prior to

[28] 83 *Congressional Record*, 9173, 9178; Wagner speech file, May 6, 1936, and files on "Fair Labor Standards Act, 1935–1938," RFW Papers; Leuchtenburg, *Franklin D. Roosevelt*, pp. 261–263. During the summer of 1935 Anna M. Rosenberg, New York Regional Director of the NRA, forwarded to Wagner copies of reports indicating rapid and widespread resumption of sweatshop conditions in the New York metropolitan area following the Schechter decision. See files on "Business Conditions and Practices, 1935," RFW Papers.

[29] Leuchtenburg, *Franklin D. Roosevelt*, p. 262.

the opening of the fall campaign in which he was expected to seek another endorsement by the voters of his state. July and August found Wagner once again back at Albany, in the same Assembly chamber where he had begun his career many years before, serving as vice-president and minority leader of the convention charged with re-vamping the Empire State's constitution. He had agreed to stand for election as a delegate-at-large the previous November, envisioning the convention as an opportunity for expanding and solidifying the re-form programs that the Smith-Roosevelt-Lehman administrations had initiated in New York. Despite overwhelming approval of Wag-ner's candidacy by the voters, however, his party managed to elect only seventy-five delegates compared to the Republicans' ninety-three. And despite the fact that a band of New York City Republicans stood ready to second the Wagner-Lehman brand of liberalism that had proven so popular with the state's urban population, the addition of their strength was offset by the defection of disillusioned Democrats, led by Wagner's old pal Al Smith, who were determined to "take a whack at the New Deal." [30]

Thus the final result of the convention's long deliberations (they began in April, making it necessary for Wagner to commute from Washington until Congress adjourned in June) represented some-thing less than the triumphant ensconcement of a "little New Deal" that the Senator had anticipated. True, the delegates approved a pro-posed "Bill of Rights" for labor, guaranteeing among other things the right to organize and bargain collectively. Another article specifically legalized social security expenditures, and authorized the state to in-augurate and contribute to a system of compulsory health insurance. But that measure had been defeated on the first roll call, and it won a narrow majority of votes two weeks later only after Wagner, reverting to the role he had played in his younger days, managed by herculean efforts to assure that there would be a full house of Democratic and liberal Republican delegates on hand for reconsideration. The hous-ing article, authorizing a state system of public housing subsidies pat-terned after Wagner's federal act, was so loaded with restrictive amendments in its final form as to be barely palatable to the Senator. And the civil rights declaration introduced by Wagner, which would have gone to the then-novel length of outlawing discrimination in all establishments soliciting the patronage of the general public, was so watered down in its final form as to represent, in its sponsor's own words, an "innocuous" restatement of guarantees already contained in the Constitution.

[30] "Delegates to Constitutional Convention of 1938," RFW Papers; War-ren Moscow, interview.

Moreover, a whole series of liberal proposals, such as the article declaring the inalienability of the state's water power resources, failed even to emerge from conservative-dominated committees. Most disturbing of all to the liberals was a provision in the judiciary article, pushed through by the coalition of conservative Democrats and Republicans, that would subject the orders of the state's independent regulatory agencies (including the Labor Relations Board created by New York's "little Wagner Act") to incessant judicial review.[31]

The progressives succeeded in getting the convention to submit its handiwork to the voters in nine separate articles rather than as a single piece, however, and in the time remaining before the November election Wagner and his allies strove to educate the public regarding the merits and demerits of the various proposals. The results on election day rewarded their efforts. Every one of the measures approved by the liberals was ratified by the electorate; every one that they opposed was defeated. The social insurance article won the biggest majority of all; the reactionary judiciary article went down to the worst defeat![32]

Those returns indicated that the majority of New York's voters, at least, were still in a "New Dealish" mood. And so, too, did the results in the election of state officials, which brought victory to the entire Democratic slate. Particularly gratifying to New Dealers was the fact that Bob Wagner, who by now had become a focal point of attack for conservatives and reactionaries, led all the rest of his ticketmates.

Those who made the mistake of ascribing authorship of the Fair Labor Standards Act of 1938 to Senator Wagner might perhaps be forgiven. For, as Franklin Roosevelt declared in a speech during the fall of that year endorsing the New York Senator's reelection: "So often since 1933 has new legislation been described as 'The Wagner Act' that the phrase has become confusing, because there have been so many Wagner Acts." [33] On that record of legislative achievement— characterized, the President added, by "courageous and intelligent leadership, constructive statecraft and steadfast devotion to the common man and the cause of civil liberties"—Wagner staked his hopes of serving still another term in the Senate.

[31] FDR Papers: files on "New York State Constitutional Convention, 1938"; "Summary of Principle Proposals of Constitutional Convention (Confidential Statement for President Roosevelt), Aug. 31, 1938"; also *New York Times*, Aug. 19, 1938.
[32] Wagner speech file, Sept. 12, 1938, RFW Papers; *New York Times*, Nov. 9, 1938.
[33] White House press release, Nov. 4, 1938, RFW Papers.

"Standing on the record" was not, of course, a novel campaign tactic for an incumbent to use; Wagner himself had employed it in his first bid for reelection six years earlier. Nevertheless, in 1938 it was expected to be a more difficult thing for him to do successfully. His record was lengthier now, more controversial, and therefore more vulnerable in some respects. The Senator's long period of service in public life inevitably led to hints that he had grown old and tired. At the same time his prominence as a supporter of the New Deal evoked charges that he had become a "yes man" to the White House; he was guilty, his Republican opponent asserted, of "blindly following President Roosevelt." Columnists like David Lawrence, overlooking the many occasions on which Wagner had parted ways with or been far in advance of the President, wrote that the New York contest afforded a chance to strike a blow at "one-man rule with rubber-stamp legislators." *The New York Times* viewed it as an opportunity to curb "the whole dangerous trend toward centralization of authority" by electing to the Senate a man possessing "a greater degree of independence of the Executive." The *Daily Mirror* used earthier terms when, at the end of a distorted presentation of Wagner's record, it phrased its indictment in the form of a question: "Is Senator Wagner a statesman or a stooge?" (That particular editorial literally caused the Senator to "hit the ceiling," a companion recalled. When he had finished reading it, Wagner jumped from his seat, muttering curses. Unfortunately he had forgotten that he was riding in a car, en route to a campaign meeting, and his head struck the roof with a force that nearly knocked him unconscious!) [34]

While some of those opposed to Wagner's reelection emphasized his alleged subservience to the White House, others, somewhat paradoxically, pressed the charge that his chief fault lay in being one of the extremist leaders along the New Deal's more radical fringes. In this respect Wagner's championing of the National Labor Relations Act served as the focal point of attack. Throughout the campaign Wagner reiterated his willingness to support such amendments to the Act as adequate experience might dictate, but he steadfastly refused to endorse any of the specific changes then being pressed by interested parties, even though enticed by an offer of support from the publisher of an important New York newspaper chain if he would do so. To some people Wagner's refusal to be "stampeded during a political campaign," as he put it, represented excessive pride of authorship in

---

[34] *New York Times*, Nov. 1, 1938; David Lawrence, "Today in Washington," unidentified newspaper clipping, and undated clipping from the New York *Daily Mirror*, RFW Papers; Theodore Granik, interview.

his handiwork, or downright bullheadedness. To others it represented something even more sinister. Under the heading "Wagner's Defeat Declared Vital If Radicalism Is To Be Checked," the nationally syndicated columnist Mark Sullivan wrote: "It seems to be a fact that four related conditions—Senator Wagner's labor act, the attitude of the Labor Board, the sit-down strike, and the C.I.O.—compose a mechanism which can be used to carry America into a Communist form of society." Sullivan did add charitably that Wagner was part of the chain leading toward communism "perhaps unwittingly"—which was more than some of those who employed the Red-smear tactic against the Senator were kind enough to do.[35]

The Communist issue played a part in the campaign against New Deal candidates in several states during 1938—since the summer conservatives had reveled in the grossly exaggerated tales of Red infiltration of the Administration "unearthed" by the new House Committee on Un-American Activities chaired by Congressman Martin Dies. But the issue achieved special prominence in New York when in the middle of October the Communist party, going through the "popular front" phase of its shifting tactics, endorsed Wagner, Lehman, and several others on the Democratic ticket. The candidates quickly repudiated that unwanted backing. "Since I am unalterably opposed to what the Communists stand for," Wagner declared, "I cannot accept their support." Despite that, and despite Wagner's frequent reiteration that his Labor Act was designed to chart a "middle way" between the extremes of Fascist and Communist totalitarianism, the misconception that the Wagner Act had somehow been spawned by a Red conspiracy took firm root in some people's minds. It was one of the things that caused sleepless nights for the managers of the Senator's campaign in 1938.[36]

Another factor that Wagner and his supporters had to contend with that year was the superior quality of the man the Republicans ran against him, compared to the unknown quantity who had been his opponent in 1932. John Lord O'Brian of Buffalo was a prominent attorney who had seen public service in the federal government under four presidents, including Democrats Woodrow Wilson and Franklin D. Roosevelt himself. In fact, at the very time he was nominated to oppose Wagner, O'Brian was representing the government before the Supreme Court in important litigation seeking to establish the

---

[35] Wagner speech file, Sept. 29, Nov. 1, 3, 1938, RFW Papers; Keyserling, "The Wagner Act," p. 205; New York *Herald Tribune*, Nov. 3, 1938.

[36] *New York Times*, Oct. 16, 1938; Wagner speech file, Sept. 29, 1938, RFW Papers; Jeremiah T. Mahoney, interview.

constitutionality of the TVA. In order to accommodate the government's special counsel, the court put aside arguments in the case for the duration of the campaign. ("History shows," quipped a pundit in *The New Yorker*, "that running against Bob Wagner is not a job that can be done in your spare time.")[37]

At the outset O'Brian was depicted as a progressive Republican, as was his gubernatorial runningmate, Thomas E. Dewey. Consequently the voters of New York State were treated for a while to the kind of "me-too, but I can do it better" campaign with which the whole nation was soon to become familiar. The Republican senatorial candidate, hoping to split Wagner's labor support, endorsed most of the procedural changes in the NLRA then being advocated by the American Federation of Labor; but he was careful to avow his agreement with "the basic aims of the law." At the same time he indicated his support of many other aspects of the New Deal, taking it to task only on those issues that seemed to have raised considerable public antagonism in the previous two years: Roosevelt's attempt to "pack" the Supreme Court; the alleged one-sidedness and pro-C.I.O. bias in the administration of the Wagner Act; and the Administration's obvious failure to cure the depression and provide "real jobs," which, according to O'Brian, constituted "the most crucial moral and economic issue present in this campaign."

Nevertheless, in 1938 New York's Republicans had not yet become as adept at "me-tooism" as they would later. Before long O'Brian, perhaps in an attempt to perk up his campaign among the G.O.P.'s conservative upstate supporters, was voicing sentiments akin to those that had become the favorite complaints of the New Deal's most ardent opponents in Washington. He began taking the Administration to task on another count that apparently bore spiritual overtones: deficit spending, which, as O'Brian put it, "has now become so habitual and so menacing as to present a moral issue." Like the conservatives already in Congress, he advocated returning the administration of relief funds to the states. In addition, the Republican candidate suggested that the Social Security Act be revised so as to base old-age benefit payments on the individual's needs rather than on his earning power in the past—a proposal that, according to most of the proponents of the act, would abandon the old-age insurance system "as a matter of right" and substitute for it "the discredited methods of the poorhouse." All this seemed to lend substance to Bob Wag-

[37] Harold Brubaker, "Of All Things," *The New Yorker*, undated clipping in RFW Papers; New York *World-Telegram*, Oct. 24, 1938; files on "1938 Campaign—O'Brian Campaign Literature," RFW Papers.

ner's warning to the electorate: "In this campaign you have to contend with something more dangerous than open enemies," he told
audience after audience. "You have to beware of false friends—the
leaders of the Republican Party coming before you with a mask of
liberalism on their faces, and the dagger of reaction held behind their
backs." [38]

In the meantime Wagner's forces made headway in combating
the other strikes that, according to some observers, had already
counted him "out." His ambitious campaign itinerary belied the
claim that long service had dampened the Senator's vitality, and so
did the vigor he displayed in his many public appearances. Following
a speech dedicating the Red Hook public housing project, for example, Wagner clambered atop a woodpile in full view of the audience
and there, together with Mayor La Guardia and Housing Administrator Nathan Straus, worked out details for the launching of a second
project, which was announced on the spot. And to the dismay of
those advisers who worried about conserving his health, Wagner still
insisted, as in the old days, on appearing personally, as one of them
expressed it, "at every dinky club-house, rally, and gathering" in the
city of New York.[39]

Moreover, despite overwhelming newspaper support of his opponent (in contrast to 1932), the few journals that remained faithful to
Wagner did their best to refute the "rubber-stamp" charge. "No Senator now extant," editorialized the *Daily News*, "has a higher standing than Senator Wagner." "If you could take a big eraser (it would
have to be big) and wipe off the statute books the legislation written
by Senator Wagner," the New York *Post* pointed out, "the sturdiest
portions of the New Deal would be gone." The incumbent had been,
the *Post* added, "not a follower of the New Deal but a leader of it, its
truest, clearest voice in the Senate." "New York would inflict a grave
loss on the whole nation if it didn't re-elect him," wrote columnist
Ernest K. Lindley, who believed that Wagner, like George Norris and
Robert La Follette, had become "one of the five or six truly national
Senators . . . whose influence, standing above party, rests upon character and well-thought-out argument." [40]

Useful in combating the assertion that Wagner was the dupe of a

[38] Files on "1938 Campaign—O'Brian Speeches," RFW Papers; *New York
Times*, Oct. 22, 31, 1938; Wagner speech file, Oct. 29, 1938, RFW Papers; New
York *Journal-American*, Nov. 4, 1938.
[39] Files on "1938 Campaign—Itinerary," RFW Papers; New York *World-
Telegram*, Nov. 3, 1938; Jeremiah T. Mahoney, interview.
[40] New York *Daily News*, Nov. 3, 1938; New York *Post*, Nov. 5, 1938;
Brooklyn *Eagle*, Nov. 2, 1938.

Communist conspiracy, on the other hand, were the endorsements he received from Henry I. Harriman, Peter Grimm, and other prominent New York businessmen. Also welcome in the Wagner camp was an article in the October issue of *Fortune* magazine, the recognized organ of "enlightened" business opinion, that exonerated the Labor Act and the Labor Board of virtually every one of the charges leveled against them by their opponents. Perhaps most effective of all, however, was a statement given out by Franklin Roosevelt during the course of the campaign. Recalling their service together in the New York legislature years before, Roosevelt reminded reporters that "Senator Wagner and I were called Communists and Socialists because we worked for a fifty-four hour week law for women and children in industry; for a full crew law for railroad trains; for factory inspection and workmen's compensation. Today," the President added in driving his lesson home, "we are proud of that record." [41]

Throughout the fall Wagner kept his pleas for defense and expansion of the New Deal at the center of his campaign, unlike some of his more timorous partners on the Democratic ticket. (Not until a few days before the election, for example, did Governor Herbert Lehman make his allegiance to the Administration explicit enough to earn him the unqualified endorsement of the avidly New Dealish Mayor Fiorello La Guardia.) True, his campaign literature sought to placate businessmen by pointing out that "Senator Wagner's program has put a halt to growing social unrest threatening the destruction of our democratic institutions." But it also hailed him unabashedly as "The Architect of Social Justice in America." "What has been done must be defended," the Senator told virtually every audience he addressed. "What is unfinished must be completed. With your help," he added with an increasing air of confidence as the campaign wore on, "it will be." [42]

On election day Wagner's stubbornness, or his devotion to principle—depending on how one viewed his unswerving allegiance to his version of the New Deal—paid off. Bob received nearly 60,000 votes more than his nearest companion on the Democratic state-wide ticket, and he outran Governor Lehman by 106,000. True enough, Wagner's margin of 438,000 votes over O'Brian was considerably re-

[41] *New York Times,* Oct. 25, 1938; "The G—— D—— Labor Board," *Fortune* (Oct. 1938), 52ff; Brooklyn *Eagle,* Oct. 9, 1938; New York *Post,* Nov. 4, 1938.

[42] Files on "1938 Campaign—Campaign Literature," RFW Papers; New York *World-Telegram,* Oct. 28, 1938; New York *Post,* Oct. 26, 1938; New York *Journal-American,* Oct. 22, Nov. 4, 1938; New York *Daily News,* Nov. 5, 1938; Wagner speech file, Oct. 3, 1938, RFW Papers.

duced below the 781,000 plurality he had rolled up in 1932. But, significantly, nearly all of the decline was accounted for in the rural, upstate counties. "New Deal sentiment may not be as blazingly high as it was in the past," commented the New York *Post* on the election's outcome. "But liberalism still dominates the political life of **our** State," its editorial exulted. "That is the good word today." [43]

[43] *New York Times*, Nov. 9, 1938; New York *Post*, Nov. 9, 1938.

CHAPTER 15

For the Duration

THE POPULARITY of the country's "most urban Senator" remained virtually intact in the metropolitan areas of the Empire State on election day, 1938, and the returns from New York brought good word for liberals across the nation. But in most other places the election day portents were bad for New Dealers. Earlier in the year Bob Wagner had lamented the trend toward conservative resurgence: "As the goals of Democracy draw nearer the ancient shibboleths are heard once again . . . the rights of States . . . the danger of regimentation . . . the cry of dictatorship." [1] At the polls in the fall the shibboleths worked their magic; the Republicans won a net increase of eighty seats in the House and seven in the Senate. If New Deal programs had encountered increasing resistance at the hands of an unruly Congress during the previous two years, it seemed apparent that still more could be anticipated from a new Congress in which the strength of the bipartisan conservative coalition was further enhanced.

Not only were the forces of that coalition more numerous in 1939 and better led—Robert A. Taft of Ohio made his impressive debut in the Senate that year—but circumstances dictated from abroad played into their hands. From the time of Munich onward the attention of Americans fastened more and more on foreign affairs as the world tumbled toward a Second World War; domestic problems were relegated to secondary consideration. The New Deal's leader, Franklin Roosevelt, became wary of pressing too hard for controver-

[1] Wagner speech file, April 23, 1938, RFW Papers.

sial domestic programs that might alienate Southern Democrats and
other conservatives whose support he deemed necessary for the accomplishment of his foreign policies. The defense build-up that lay at
the center of those policies, and that entailed the expenditure of unparalleled federal sums, induced a degree of economic recovery that
first matched and then surpassed the "good times" levels of the 1920s.
The political effect of such affluence, however, was to widen still further the gaps between the disparate interests and population groups
who had huddled together to form the Roosevelt coalition during the
grim days of the Great Depression.

Even as he noted the closing of the New Deal's domestic phase,
however, Bob Wagner remained nonetheless optimistic. "A great nation will not return to the day when the solution for unemployment
was the bread-line, when the answer to the distressed home-owner was
foreclosure, when finance was the product of blue sky, when the wonders of electricity were denied to the bulk of our agricultural population, when the slums were no man's responsibility, when old age was
not a blessing but a curse. The frontiers of social responsibility," the
Senator prophesied, "have been enlarged in a manner that will endure." [2] His prediction was to prove accurate. But as the nation assumed a defensive posture militarily in the late 1930s, domestic liberalism, too, entered once again on a defensive phase.

President Roosevelt's opening message to the Seventy-sixth Congress in January 1939 signaled the Chief Executive's acquiescence in
the country's conservative mood. Asking only that deficit spending be
continued until full recovery from the previous year's recession had
occurred, he recommended no new legislation that might disturb conservatives and declared: "We have now passed the period of internal
conflict in the launching of our program of social reform. Our full
energies may now be released to invigorate the processes of recovery in
order to preserve our reforms." [3] During the ensuing months there
was little indication that Roosevelt extended wholehearted support to
liberal advances proposed by New Dealers like Wagner—proposals
that might "rock the boat" in a way detrimental to the formation of
the new consensus the President hoped to build.

But if Roosevelt was in a compromising mood, his conservative
enemies in Congress were not, and during the summer of 1939 they
won a stunning victory over Administration forces supporting the
President's remaining recovery plans. As chairman of the Banking and

[2] *Ibid.*
[3] 84 *Congressional Record,* 76.

Currency Committee, Wagner helped guide through the Senate the
two bills that formed the core of the pump-priming continuation program. One, drafted by economists in the Treasury Department, contemplated a three-billion-dollar program of federal public works and
federally underwritten loans to public bodies and to private businesses
for the stimulation of self-liquidating enterprises. The measure bore
many resemblances to the Relief and Construction Act of 1932 that
Wagner had piloted through Congress in Hoover's time. He was on
familiar ground, therefore, as in July of 1939 he helped Majority
Leader Alben Barkley persuade the Senate to pass the "spend-lend"
bill by the comfortable vote of 52–28. Even earlier, and by a larger
margin, the Senate had approved the second part of the Administration's recovery package: a Wagner-sponsored bill that would double
the existing $800,000,000 program of public housing.

But in the House of Representatives, where Republican gains
had been larger and where the more conservative-minded rural areas
of the country were overrepresented, the Administration met its
downfall. On August 1, by a vote of 193–167, the lower house refused
even to take up the "spend-lend" bill for floor debate. Two days later
it dealt out similar treatment to the public housing measure.[4]

Though less dramatic than the earlier Congressional rebuffs the
President had met in his plans to reorganize the judiciary and the
executive departments, these new setbacks were equally significant.
They provided the culminating evidence that, as far as domestic legislation was concerned, Roosevelt had met his match. He retired from
the field, and no further effort was made to press for the "spend-lend"
bill during the remaining tenure of the Seventy-sixth Congress. Nor
did the President display much will to fight thereafter as Congress
proceeded to cripple, or disband altogether, various New Deal relief
agencies that had become prime targets of conservative vengeance.

Fortunately, in a sense, the defense build-up and the federal outlays it entailed lessened the need for domestic pump-priming and relief programs as months of international tension gave way to outright
war in Europe in September 1939. But now government expenditures
went into the fashioning of instruments of destruction rather than
peace-serving social improvements; moreover, they were expenditures
that liberals and conservatives alike hoped would be only temporary.
But the zeal with which conservatives moved to obliterate recovery
and relief agencies gave clear indication that they wanted no vestiges
of these New Deal creations to survive the period of emergency and
rising employment.

[4] *Ibid.*, pp. 6842, 10512, 10717, 10957; John Morton Blum, *From the Morgenthau Diaries: Years of Urgency, 1938–1941* (Boston, 1965), pp. 36ff.

In contrast, Wagner and a dwindling band of liberals in Congress fought to continue and preserve the New Deal's peacetime functions, even while they supported the Administration's defense program. Generally, however, their fight on specific issues and appropriations was a losing battle, as one by one agencies such as the WPA, the CCC, and the National Youth Administration were stripped of funds, and finally passed into oblivion. In January 1940 Wagner's allies in the House succeeded in getting another vote on consideration of his public housing measure, but again their cause went down to defeat. Later that year Congress did pass a Defense Housing Act to provide accommodations for workers in congested defense plant areas. But at the insistence of the House of Representatives, the measure decreed that no government-built defense housing could be converted to public housing use after the emergency without specific Congressional authorization. Conservatives seemed determined that in the postemergency world the defense build-up should in no wise contribute to domestic reform programs that had been launched by New Deal legislation.[5]

Another target of the newly reinforced conservative coalition following 1938 was the Wagner Labor Relations Act. While, on one hand, charging the NLRB with inefficiency in carrying out its duties, conservatives sought periodically to reduce the agency's appropriation below the figures recommended by the Budget Bureau as the minimum required if the board was to get its job done. In 1940, for example, the House eliminated altogether the money requested for the NLRB's Division of Economic Research, largely on the basis of unsubstantiated charges of radicalism leveled by right-wing elements at the division's director, David Saposs. (Actually Saposs, a widely renowned labor economist, was an inveterate foe of Communist influence in the unions; the Reds considered him one of their wiliest opponents.) Indeed, the House even went so far as to forbid the board to indulge at all in the kind of basic research that Saposs' division had carried on. When the bill reached the Senate, Wagner was able to lift the ban on research as a function of the NLRB, but he was unable to save the Division of Economic Research itself—or Saposs' job.[6]

At the same time a consistent attack against the very principles of the Wagner Act emanated from a special committee, chaired by conservative Democrat Howard Smith of Virginia, which the House es-

[5] William E. Leuchtenburg, *Franklin D. Roosevelt and the New Deal: 1932–1940* (New York, 1963), pp. 272–274; files on "Housing Legislation, 1940," RFW Papers; interviews with Leon H. Keyserling and Nathan Straus.
[6] Files on "National Labor Relations Act, 1939–1941," RFW Papers; 86 *Congressional Record*, 13090ff; Eugene Lyons, *The Red Decade: The Stalinist Penetration of America* (New York, 1941), pp. 303–304.

tablished in July 1939 for the purpose of investigating the Labor Act's operation. After several months of public hearings, in which much of the testimony bordered on the purely sensational, the committee's two Republicans joined its chairman in introducing a series of proposed amendments that, in Senator Wagner's words, "would more than repeal the Labor Act." [7] In a Senate speech in March 1940 Wagner hammered away with statistics that gave the lie to the Smith bill's preamble declaration that "There has been an alarming increase in strikes and labor disputes generally." Wagner demonstrated that, on the contrary, the labor scene had grown more peaceful continually since the Supreme Court's validation of the Labor Act in 1937. "His cool statistical analysis," *Time* magazine commented, "was more devastating than any amount of emotional argument."

Nevertheless, emotional arguments prevailed as on June 8, 1940, the House approved the Smith bill by a vote of 259–129. Its passage was aided by a bargain in which A. F. of L. President William Green, who had denounced Smith's measure in vehement terms earlier, withdrew his opposition in return for Smith's adding to the bill a number of A. F. of L.-sponsored amendments designed to curb the Labor Board's alleged C.I.O. bias. In an interview following the vote Green announced that he was relying on the Senate to eliminate the antilabor provisions of Smith's bill, while keeping the A. F. of L. amendments intact.[8]

Green was playing a dangerous game, one that Bob Wagner declined to engage in. By now the New York Senator was seriously intent on devising methods to correct those defects in the working of his law that time and experience had confirmed. Wagner conceded that the Smith Committee had turned up evidence of administrative shortcomings and "misdirected zeal" on the part of some NLRB personnel; he therefore favored enlarging the board's membership from three to five members as the Smith bill proposed. At the same time he was involved also in attempts to arrive at some formula that would help guide the NLRB through the thickets of representation by craft

[7] Among other things, the Smith bill would redefine collective bargaining to make it have less significance than under the Wagner Act; specify that employers were not required to make counterproposals; "equalize" the Act by proscribing "unfair" labor practices of unions; severely limit the time within which complaints against employer violations of the Act could be filed; permit employers to "counsel and advise" their workers in matters of organization; create separate bodies to carry out the prosecuting and judicial functions of the existing board; and greatly augment the courts' power to exercise judicial review over the board's findings of fact.

[8] 86 *Congressional Record*, 2774ff, 7805; *Time*, March 25, 1940, pp. 21–22; Harry A. Millis and Emily Clark Brown, *From the Wagner Act to Taft-Hartley* (Chicago, 1950), pp. 346ff.

versus industrial unions, the issue that lay at the base of A. F. of L.–C.I.O. friction as far as their relations with the Labor Board were concerned.

But, political realist that he was, Wagner was not so sanguine as to believe that moderate and constructive amendments, guided by the Labor Act's friends, stood much chance of emerging unscathed from the Seventy-sixth Congress. Given the temper of the times, and particularly the temper of the House of Representatives, he hesitated to sponsor limited revision of his Act for fear of providing conservatives with a vehicle for its emasculation; he preferred to wait until the Senate and House were once more securely controlled by liberal forces. Unfortunately for the Senator, that condition was not to come about during his remaining years in Congress, and consequently some were led to believe mistakenly that Wagner was implacably opposed to *any* change in the labor legislation that bore his name. The truth was that he chose to live with the Wagner Act's principles intact, even though sullied by minor defects, rather than run the risk of living without them at all.[9]

In 1940 a liberal majority that still dominated the Senate Education and Labor Committee agreed with Wagner's tactics. When the Smith bill reached the Senate, Administration forces kept it pigeonholed until the legislative session ended. Meanwhile President Roosevelt attempted to placate the A. F. of L. and other moderate critics of the existing Labor Board by changing its personnel through his appointive power. Nevertheless, pressure for basic amendment of the Wagner Act continued to persist throughout 1941, and on December 3 the House again approved Congressman Smith's bill by a large majority. Whether or not the liberal element in the Senate could avoid a showdown this time seemed problematical; but the problem became a moot point four days after the House acted.[10]

With Pearl Harbor, and the labor movement's announcement of a voluntary "no strike" pledge a short time later, the voices of the antilabor contingent in Congress subsided somewhat "for the duration." But men like Bob Wagner knew that those voices were not stilled permanently, and that if Postwar II turned out to be anything like Postwar I, they would constitute an even more powerful chorus when the war against the Axis ended.

[9] Files on "National Labor Relations Act, 1939–1941," RFW Papers; interviews with Leon H. Keyserling, Philip Levy, and Robert F. Wagner, Jr.; Thomas I. Emerson, "Reminiscences" (Oral History Research Office, Columbia Univ., 1953), pp. 653–654.
[10] *New York Times,* Dec. 4, 1941; Emerson, "Reminiscences," pp. 654ff, 697; Millis and Brown, *From the Wagner Act to Taft-Hartley,* p. 353.

With basic New Deal measures under counterattack during the years 1939–41, it was unlikely that liberals could achieve much further progress; they tried, but the results were almost uniformly disappointing. In 1940 the Senate did pass a vastly watered-down version of a La Follette-sponsored bill, based on years of study by a special investigating committee, which sought to outlaw "oppressive labor practices" utilized by employers in breaking strikes and unions. But the House refused to act on the measure. On three other occasions during those years the Senate incorporated into defense appropriation bills provisions that would deny government contracts to firms that violated the National Labor Relations Act. The principle had the endorsement of the National Defense Advisory Commission and other defense production agencies, but each time the House, in conference committee, forced removal of the prolabor stipulations. In 1940 Senator Wagner introduced a bill that sought to relieve labor strife still further by improving the Department of Labor's mediation services; that measure failed even to make it out of Senate committee.[11]

Some progress was made in the field of social security legislation, for in 1939 Congress did adopt a series of liberalizing amendments to the old-age provisions of the Social Security Act that had been recommended by a bipartisan commission of experts. As passed by the Senate, the measure also contained an amendment, sponsored by Wagner, that would have created similar commissions to study the Act's unemployment-compensation features and the feasibility of adding disability benefits to the Social Security program. At the insistence of House spokesmen in the conference committee, however, Wagner's amendment was stricken out. The following year the New York Senator introduced bills that would bring fifteen million more persons under the Social Security system, and add payments for permanent disability to its coverage; both measures died in committee. At the same time Wagner announced his intention of sponsoring legislation that would authorize the federal government, through its post offices, to sell low-cost annuities at rates less than those charged by private insurance companies. That proposition had been eliminated from the Social Security Act in 1935, and now it again aroused such an outcry from the insurance industry, and from conservatives in general, that the Senator regretfully abandoned the project. The bill never was introduced.[12]

[11] 86 *Congressional Record*, 1847ff, 6904ff; Jerold S. Auerbach, "The La Follette Committee: Labor and Civil Liberties in the New Deal," *Journal of American History* (Dec. 1964), pp. 435–459; files on "National Labor Relations Act, 1939–1941," and "Mediation Bill, 1940," RFW Papers.

[12] Files on "Social Security Act, 1939–1940," RFW Papers.

But the most ambitious of all among Bob Wagner's legislative enterprises in these inauspicious years—and one to which he would devote much effort during his remaining tenure in Washington—was embodied in the National Health bill that made its appearance under his name in 1939. For many years reformers had been concerned with the devastating burdens that the inadequacies and high cost of medical care inflicted on the health and security of Americans, and particularly on the less affluent elements of the population. As early as 1915 the American Association for Labor Legislation had devised a model bill for state-sponsored health insurance; during the 1930s the American Association for Social Security secured introduction of a similar bill in several state legislatures. In 1932 a compendious report issued by a nonpartisan Committee on the Costs of Medical Care, headed by President Hoover's Secretary of the Interior, Dr. Ray Lyman Wilbur, focused renewed attention on the problem. Some framers of the 1935 Social Security Act favored including health insurance among its provisions; deeming the proposal too controversial, President Roosevelt established instead a study commission, the Interdepartmental Committee to Coordinate Health and Welfare Activities. Under the direction of Chairman Josephine Roche, the Interdepartmental Committee's Technical Committee on Medical Care, comprising representatives of the Social Security Board, the Children's Bureau, and the Public Health Service, worked out plans for a national health program during the next three years. At a National Health Conference held in Washington during July 1938 the committee unveiled its proposals and solicited the support of the more than two hundred doctors, social workers, government officials, and leaders of business and labor who attended.[13]

The National Health Conference thus marked the formal beginning of what was to prove a long, drawn-out fight to bring the federal government's direct assistance into the field of providing medical care for the American population. It was a cause ready-made for Bob Wagner, and in him its exponents found their first and foremost legislative champion. Wagner had been invited to address the National Health Conference as a matter of course; his duties at the New York State Constitutional Convention that summer prevented him from attending. But ever since passage of the Social Security Act in 1935 the New York Senator had referred repeatedly to the beckoning necessity of moving on to "the inviting field of health insurance" in

---

[13] Files on "National Health Bill, 1939," RFW Papers; Emerson, "Reminiscences," pp. 511–512; James G. Burrow, *AMA: The Voice of American Medicine* (Baltimore, 1963), *passim*; Irene Osgood Andrews, interview.

order to combat "perhaps the single greatest cause of economic inse-
curity." In April 1938 he sponsored, unsuccessfully, a bill to create a
select Senate committee to study the adequacy, cost, and means of
improving medical care. (Concurrently Assemblyman Bob Wagner,
Jr., introduced a similar measure that did result in the creation of
such a committee by the New York State legislature.) As Josephine
Roche and her Administration cohorts prepared to shift operations to
the legislative arena, therefore, they already knew who their Congressional pilot would be.

During the fall and winter of 1938–39 Senator Wagner and his
new legislative assistant, Philip Levy,[14] worked out the details of the
National Health bill with members of the Technical Committee on
Medical Care. In January 1939 President Roosevelt transmitted the
committee's proposals to Capitol Hill, recommending them "for careful study by the Congress" without specifically adding his endorsement. On February 28 Bob Wagner introduced the measure that was
designed, in his words, "to conquer this last remaining frontier of
social security in America." [15]

The newest Wagner bill still adhered to the method of extending
federal grants-in-aid to the states that, for political and constitutional
reasons, had been employed in earlier phases of government intervention in the field of social welfare during the 1930s. It proposed to
make available on a matching basis, variable according to the per-
capita wealth of the states, grants of money to assist state programs
that met minimal federal standards in five areas: (1) child and mater-
nal health care, (2) state public health services, (3) state systems of
temporary disability insurance, (4) construction of hospitals and
health centers, and (5) state-sponsored "general programs of medical
care." Since the last-mentioned category could include state-administered programs of health insurance, it quickly became the center of
controversy, even though, as Wagner repeatedly stressed, his bill envisioned no direct federal program of compulsory health insurance.
Moreover, since the measure authorized an appropriation of 80 million dollars out of the federal treasury the first year—an amount that

[14] Leon Keyserling left his position with Senator Wagner late in 1937 to become General Counsel of the newly created United States Housing Administration. His successor was an NLRB lawyer whose talents had come to Wagner's attention during the time the Senator headed the original labor board under the
NRA.

[15] RFW Papers: files on "National Health Bill, 1939"; RFW to Josephine
Roche, July 7, 19, 1938; Wagner speech file, May 6, 1936, May 25, 1937, and
Oct. 3, 18, 1938; also *American Federationist* (May 1938), pp. 470–471; 83
Congressional Record, 5189, and 84 *C. R.*, 630, 1976ff; interviews with Philip
Levy and Robert F. Wagner, Jr.

would rise to at least 275 million in the third year, and to unspecified levels thereafter—observers predicted that the Wagner health bill would provoke "the battle royal of the session" during the Seventy-sixth Congress.

The line-up on both sides, as that battle got under way before the Senate's Committee on Education and Labor in April 1939, was familiar enough. On one side were most of the liberal-labor spokesmen and organizations that had supported earlier Wagner bills. A group of doctors and medical educators—the Committee of Physicians for the Improvement of Medical Care—who had declared their "independence" of the American Medical Association in 1937, lent general support to the health bill's principles, and offered to help in perfecting its complex details.

Far different was the attitude of the American Medical Association, however, whose leaders undoubtedly spoke for a large majority of the nation's doctors. The A.M.A. had previously opposed, at least at the outset, virtually every suggested innovation in American medical service, including group practice and *private* prepaid medical and hospitalization insurance. Its position on the National Health Program materialized as expected; in May 1939 all 174 delegates to the association's national convention concurred in condemning the Wagner bill, listing twenty-two reasons for their action. When the chairman of the organization's Board of Trustees, Dr. Arthur W. Booth, testified at Senate hearings on the measure he admitted that he had not read it; nevertheless he was certain that it represented an unwise and dangerous intrusion into an area where the government should fear to tread. "A little sickness," commented Dr. Morris Fishbein, the editor of the association's *Journal*, "is not too great a price to pay for maintaining democracy in times like these." [16]

With that the A.M.A., whose members exercised a peculiarly intimate influence over the opinions of millions of Americans, assumed a position of leadership among the conservative and anti-New Deal forces determined to withstand further expansion of the welfare state. During the ensuing months state and local medical societies passed numerous resolutions denouncing the Wagner bill; some levied special assessments on their members to help finance an expensive educational campaign against it. Pharmaceutical firms and drug chains also contributed to the doctors' war chest. Thousands of physicians and

[16] Files on "National Health Bill, 1939," RFW Papers; *Survey Midmonthly* (Jan. 1939), p. 15; John F. Peters to RFW, May 10, 1939, RFW Papers; *New York Times*, May 18, Nov. 9, 1939; T. Swann Harding, "Who Fought the Wagner Bill?", *Dynamic America* (March 1940), pp. 9ff; Burrow, AMA, pp. 221ff.

drugstores distributed tons of literature prepared by such groups as the
Physicians' Committee for Free Enterprise in Medicine, and by publisher Frank Gannett's National Committee to Uphold Constitutional Government—the organization that had succeeded the Liberty
League as the chief exponent of general anti-New Dealism.

The burden of the propaganda barrage centered on the "excessive cost" of the National Health Program and on its alleged "socialistic" and "dictatorial" overtones. In addition, some of its opponents
recalled that the 1915 state health insurance bill sponsored by the
Association for Labor Legislation had been defeated in part by pin-
ning a "Made in Germany" label on it; opponents of the 1939 Wagner bill did not neglect, therefore, to point out that it was "sired by a
Senator not born in this country." Given the interrelation between
foreign affairs and domestic issues in 1939, the opposition's frequent
harping on Bob Wagner's German origins may well have exerted
some influence on popular attitudes toward his health proposal.[17]

Nevertheless, the strength of the conservative attack failed to
sway the liberal majority of the Senate's Education and Labor Committee, and when the Congressional session ended in August 1939
Chairman James E. Murray of Montana issued a preliminary report
indicating that favorable action would probably be forthcoming the
following year. That was enough to satisfy Wagner who, as usual, had
not expected instant passage of his far-reaching legislation. In November he was at the White House seeking presidential encouragement to press the fight when Congress reassembled, and according to
newspaper reports, he received it.

Yet, just a month later President Roosevelt applied the *coup de
grace* to the hopes of the health bill's proponents. In a public statement a few days before Christmas the President indicated that in
1940 he would settle for a limited experiment in only one of the several phases of the National Health Program: he called for federal construction of fifty hospitals in parts of the nation where they were
acutely needed. Subsequently the facilities would be turned over to
the states for support and operation.

Roosevelt's announcement surprised and disappointed supporters of the Wagner bill. A short time later Josephine Roche resigned as
chairman of the Interdepartmental Committee to Coordinate Health
and Welfare Activities, while Dr. John B. Andrews of the Association

[17] Files on "National Health Bill, 1939," RFW Papers; undated (1939)
clipping from the *Weekly Roster* (Official Bulletin of Medical Organizations in
the Metropolitan Philadelphia Area), RFW Papers; Irene Osgood Andrews, interview; Burrow, *AMA*, p. 208.

for Labor Legislation publicly berated the project for "fifty little . . . hospitals" as a tremendous letdown. There was much speculation about whether A.M.A. opposition, the cost of the health program in the midst of rising defense expenditures, or Roosevelt's current penchant for wooing conservatives constituted the basic motive for his retreat. It's probable that all three considerations affected the Chief Executive's decision; possibly Bob Wagner gave the best summary when early in 1940 he ruefully admitted to reporters that "This is supposed to be a conservative year." The year 1940 was, after all, a presidential election year.[18]

While liberals lamented Roosevelt's shelving of the ambitious National Health Program, Senator Wagner perforce found himself a sponsor of the bill designed to carry out the President's hospital construction proposal. In the spring of 1940 the Senate approved the measure; the endorsement given it by Senator Taft, whose conservatism was broad enough to concede at least a minimal role for federal participation in welfare activities, helped pave the way for passage. But in the House of Representatives the hospital bill languished, and it remained unacted on when the Seventy-sixth Congress ended. As far as the more conservative branch of the national legislature was concerned, even the very modest advance of the domestic New Deal represented by Roosevelt's hospital project had to be shelved—"for the duration," if not forever.[19]

"For the duration." During the defense build-up of 1939–41, even before the United States entered the Second World War as a belligerent, those words proved increasingly potent in stalling the hopes of domestic New Dealers. Preoccupation with the international situation distracted not only the President's attention and the public's but also that of the Congress and its key figures. As a member of the Senate Foreign Relations Committee and chairman of the Banking and Currency Committee, even Bob Wagner found himself compelled to devote a large part of his time to the political and financial aspects of the country's growing involvement in international complications.

Wagner started out his career in the Senate as an "internationalist" of the sort, common in the 1920s, who hoped through treaties and

[18] 84 *Congressional Record*, 10983; clippings from the Philadelphia *Record*, Nov. 22, 1939, and Washington *Post*, Dec. 24, 1939, RFW Papers; transcript of press conference, Dec. 22, 1939, FDR Papers; John B. Andrews, "While Millions Suffer," *American Labor Legislation Review* (March 1940), p. 3; John L. Lewis, interview.

[19] 86 *Congressional Record*, 881ff, 7158ff.

the strengthening of the rule of law to reduce armaments and the causes of international conflict. One of his earliest speeches in the Senate was made in behalf of ratification of the Kellogg-Briand Pact, that "international kiss" of 1928 in which most nations of the world agreed to "outlaw" aggressive war. He also supported the arms-limitation agreements negotiated at subsequent international conferences, and in 1935 he backed Franklin Roosevelt's ill-fated proposal that the United States join the World Court. Deep in his heart Wagner remained skeptical regarding the practical efficacy of these well-meaning but impotent agreements. "I am in accord with you," he wrote in a letter to a close friend, "that pious declarations of themselves don't do much more than mobilize a public opinion which, though articulate, seems to be ineffective." Nevertheless, in public he supported them as symbolic "crystallizations of the human will to peace." Later, like many other Americans, he would smile at his naïveté in having placed any trust whatsoever in such gestures.[20]

Following Hitler's rise to power in Germany, and while militarists elsewhere in the world emulated him in tearing to shreds the "scraps of paper" on which civilization had rested its hope for an end to war, Wagner lost little time in denouncing the disturbers of the peace. At a Madison Square Garden rally in March 1933, the immigrant Senator from Yorkville roundly denounced the new German regime, and thereafter he was among the most sought-after speakers at anti-Nazi demonstrations. Wagner was especially vehement in condemning Hitler's persecution of the Jews. He was one of the first members of Congress to join the American Palestine Committee organized in 1932 to mobilize Christian support for the maintenance of a Jewish homeland in Palestine under the terms of the mandate awarded Great Britain in 1918. Critics fastened on the importance of "the Jewish vote" in New York as the explanation for the Senator's position. But condemnation of anti-Semitism in Germany and in America was fully in line with the views of the sponsor of the antilynching bill; in this case, moreover, it's probable that his own origins made Wagner particularly sensitive to the barbarities perpetrated by those who had assumed power in the land of his birth.[21]

Through most of the 1930s, however, Wagner's—and America's —moral support of the victims of persecution and aggression re-

[20] RFW Papers: files on "International Affairs, 1927–1939"; Wagner speech file, Jan. 8, 1929, and July 21, 1930; RFW to Dorothy Straus, Dec. 18, 1933; transcript of RFW interview with Dorothy Dunbar Bromley, 1939.

[21] RFW Papers: Wagner speech file, March 27, 1933; files on "International Affairs, 1933–1939" and "Palestine, 1932–1939"; also interviews with Simon H. Rifkind, Leon H. Keyserling, and Philip Levy.

mained just that: *moral*, and verbal, and ineffective. While he vigorously supported the defensive rearmament drive that the Roosevelt Administration gradually launched as the decade moved on, and while he favored letting the dictators know that our "sympathies" would be against them in the event of war, the New York Senator repeatedly voiced his opposition to American *involvement* in the hostilities that seemed to loom on the horizon. In 1935, 1936, and 1937, for example, Wagner voted for the series of Neutrality Acts whereby an isolationist-dominated Congress attempted to insulate the United States against foreign troubles. And during his 1938 campaign for reelection Wagner, in company with just about every other candidate on either ticket in New York State that year, answered "Yes" to the *Daily News'* demand for a pledge "never to vote to send troops to Europe to fight in any foreign war." [22]

Early in 1939, however, Wagner did move slightly ahead of public opinion—and the Administration's—in an effort to give some more practical effect to America's humanitarian sympathies for the victims of Nazi oppression. Acting on behalf of a national Non-Sectarian Committee for the Relief of German Refugee Children, the Senator and Republican Representative Edith Nourse Rogers of Massachusetts introduced a bill that would lift America's restrictive immigration bars high enough to admit 20,000 young German refugees to the United States outside of quota limitations. The measure immediately ran into strong criticism from ardent isolationists and nativists. Perhaps for this reason the State Department refused to endorse it, and the bill never came up for a floor vote in either chamber. Even in the summer of 1940 isolationist sentiment remained strong enough in the Democratic national convention's Platform Committee, over which the New York Senator personally presided, to prevent insertion of a platform plank endorsing the admission of additional refugee immigrants.[23]

By that time, however, the outbreak of hostilities in Europe (in the fall of 1939) had projected the debate over American foreign policy into a new phase. Isolationism, voiced by groups like the America First Committee and by a powerful bipartisan bloc in Congress, still maintained that Hitler posed no threat to an America secure behind a two-ocean moat. At the opposite pole stood a much smaller group of

[22] RFW Papers: files on "International Affairs, 1933–1939"; transcript of RFW interview with Dorothy Dunbar Bromley, 1939; clipping from the New York *Daily News*, Oct. 11, 1938.

[23] 84 *Congressional Record*, 1278; files on "Wagner-Rogers Bill, 1939–1940," and "Democratic Party Platform, 1940," RFW Papers; Philip Levy, interview.

outright interventionists, who were convinced that the Fascist forces overrunning the Continent presented a direct menace to America, and who therefore favored immediate participation in the war at the side of England and her dwindling number of effective allies. Somewhere in between, and constituting the majority element in the Great Debate, were those who agreed with the interventionists' interpretation of the Nazi threat, but who nonetheless hoped that America's responsibility might be limited to providing an "arsenal of democracy" from which the Allies might draw the material aid needed to turn back the Axis. Leading this camp of "limited interventionists" was the Roosevelt Administration, and enrolled in its following was a majority of Congress, including Senator Wagner.

Step by step, from late 1939 until December 7, 1941, the President recommended and Congress approved increasingly warlike measures whereby the United States, while arming itself, also undertook to provide more direct and effective aid to the beleagured Allies. Invariably the President depicted his policies as means to keep America *out* of war, and frequently he repeated the pledge not to send American boys to fight in foreign wars. Administration spokesmen reiterated these views. In one of the culminating speeches of the Senate's debate on Roosevelt's proposal to repeal the arms embargo provision of the Neutrality Acts in October 1939, for example, Wagner asserted that "the deep yearning of all America for uninterrupted peace will be fully realized through the enactment of the joint resolution under consideration." A year and a half later, in lending support to Roosevelt's Lend-Lease Act, which relieved the British of the necessity for paying cash for American arms, Wagner described the measure as "our one chance to avoid war." And during the 1940 presidential campaign the New York Senator was only one among the many Democratic orators urging voters to "keep America out of war by uniting behind Franklin Roosevelt—who is strong enough to keep aggression away from our shores, experienced enough to keep us out of foreign embroilment, and humane enough to care more for peace than for anything else in the world." [24]

If the President was less than candid in preparing the American people for the ultimate eventuality of war that his pro-Allied policies might entail, there is no evidence to suggest that Bob Wagner was a party to any "plot" to deceive the electorate or that he knew one existed. The New York Senator's hope of defeating the Axis without

[24] 85 *Congressional Record*, 243; also RFW Papers: Wagner speech file, Oct. 29, 1940, and March 4, 1941; undated (1941) clipping from the Miami *Herald*.

shedding American blood might be naïve and unrealistic, but it was sincere; at times it even led him to deviate from Administration positions. During debate on the Selective Service Act in August of 1940, for example, Wagner voted in favor of an Administration-opposed amendment that would have postponed the draft pending an attempt to raise a sufficient army by voluntary enlistment.[25]

Nevertheless, on the basic question of all-out material aid to the Allies, Wagner was in agreement with the Administration's announced position. In December 1940 he told a nationwide radio audience that Hitler had "shattered forever the lingering hope in some quarters that somehow, by some form of agreement or appeasement, the Nazi system and the democratic system could thrive side by side in peace and security." Early in 1941, when isolationists like Burton K. Wheeler urged the President to press for a negotiated peace between England and Germany, Wagner took the lead as an Administration spokesman in denouncing such proposals for a "super-Munich." On the whole, then, the New York Senator was prepared to follow where Roosevelt led in the foreign policy field, even as that path edged closer to war.[26]

Wagner's seat on the Senate Foreign Relations Committee had come to him in the early 1930s primarily as a status symbol, rather than as an indication of where his legislative interests lay. Nevertheless, after 1939 his occupancy of it—which isolationists like Wheeler envied and resented—helped assure Administration control of the vital decisions that that committee was now called on to make.

But it was through Wagner's other major committee assignment, the chairmanship of the powerful Banking and Currency Committee, that he brought his influence particularly to bear on behalf of the Administration's defense and foreign policies. During the domestic phase of the New Deal it had become customary for Wagner's committee to handle legislation dealing with such matters as the Reconstruction Finance Corporation, the Export-Import Bank, the Treasury's monetary Stabilization Fund, and the President's power to alter the weight of the dollar. In 1939 these agencies and devices assumed a new importance as they were transformed into instruments for defense mobilization and for a type of international economic warfare that was designed to curb the totalitarian powers and lend support to their victims. The legislative job of strengthening those instruments,

[25] 86 *Congressional Record*, 11137.
[26] Wagner speech file, Dec. 23, 1940, and clipping from the Washington *Daily News*, Jan. 11, 1941, RFW Papers.

and of preventing their being dulled by isolationists who feared that "meddlesome" interventionists might use them to trip the country into war, therefore fell on Wagner's shoulders.

At midnight on June 30, 1939, for example, the executive department's discretionary monetary and stabilization powers actually lapsed as Senate filibusterers successfully blocked a vote on the bill renewing them; it took several more days of strenuous effort on the part of Wagner, Majority Leader Barkley, and other Administration stalwarts to round up the support necessary to pass a new act. In late 1939 and early 1940 isolationists who opposed American aid to Finland—a victim of Russian aggression—tried to defeat enlargement of the lending authority of the Export-Import Bank because it might be used to extend credits to the invaded Scandanavian country; after a two months' fight, Administration forces, marshaled by Wagner, managed to win approval of bills that made the loan possible. Loans made by the Administration out of Export-Import and Stabilization Fund resources to China and to various Latin American nations, in an effort to bolster their economies against Axis assaults, also encountered constant criticism from isolationist sources. In 1940 Senator Taft waged a powerful fight for an amendment that would foreclose extension of such credits for any purpose except the stockpiling of critical materials necessary for America's own defense. But after considerable debate, in which Wagner played a leading part, Taft's proposal was beaten back.[27]

As Hitler's armies overwhelmed Europe, Wagner also found himself charged with responsibility for highly technical legislation dealing with such matters as the disposition of occupied countries' accounts and properties in the United States, so that those assets might not fall into Nazi hands. And as the American defense build-up gained momentum—accompanied inevitably by a certain amount of hysteria—other matters pressed for his attention. In October 1940, for instance, at the request of the War Department, the New York Senator secured "emergency passage" of a bill establishing federal criminal penalties for the mistreatment of homing pigeons, which someone in the department obviously regarded as a critical component in the building of an efficient modern army. President Roosevelt returned the measure along with a veto message suggesting that "this is carrying national defense a little too far." The Homing Pigeon bill was the

[27] Burton K. Wheeler, interview; files on "Reconstruction Finance Corporation, 1939–1941," "Stabilization Fund, 1939," "Export-Import Bank, 1939–1941," and "Finland, 1939–1940," RFW Papers; 84 *Congressional Record*, 7404ff; 85 C. R., 916ff; 86 C. R., 360ff, 9555ff; Blum, *Morgenthau Diaries: Years of Urgency, passim.*

first and only "Wagner bill" that F.D.R. ever "shot down"—at least *after* it had secured Congressional approval![28]

The pigeon situation was not the only one affected by the "emergency" psychology that developed as the nation's defense build-up moved ahead. Motivated in part by a sincere desire to maximize war-material production, and in part by a residual antagonism to the reform measures of the 1930s, conservatives in the prewar years pressed for amendment or discard of "many of the New Deal laws which have been hampering industry at every step." After Nazi Panzer divisions rolled across the Maginot Line in the spring of 1940, for example, some business spokesmen publicized a new slogan that added a note of impending disaster to their long-standing opposition to New Deal labor legislation: "The 40 Hour Week Defeated France!" (The French legislation referred to, which during the 1930s forbade *factories* to operate more than 40 hours a week, was actually far removed from American laws that merely required payment of time-and-a-half to *workers* employed more than 40 hours.) As Senator Taft expressed it in mid-1940: "We can't have all the frills that have looked so tempting over the past few years." Among the measures the Ohio senator included in that category were the Walsh-Healey Act regulating work on government contracts, the Fair Labor Standards Act, and the National Labor Relations Act itself.[29]

Staunchly opposed to such sentiments were the New Deal liberals who insisted, with Bob Wagner, that "the social gains we have made in the past few years are neither luxuries nor frills—they are the measure of a democracy's concern for human welfare." To abandon them now, the Senator added, "would be to lay ourselves open to the propaganda of the enemy. . . . We cannot hope to succeed by adopting Hitler's methods."

In defending their position, the liberals also recalled the experience of World War I, when "our wartime agencies actually improvised a mass of 'social legislation'—defense housing, minimum wages, maximum hour standards, healthful working conditions, collective bargaining through freely chosen representatives, employment exchanges, machinery for mediation and adjustment of labor disputes" —all for the purpose of stimulating production by maintaining worker morale at a high level. Now, Wagner observed, "these very

[28] 86 *Congressional Record*, 5006ff, 9772ff, 13388, 13587.
[29] RFW Papers: "The American Forum: Does National Defense Require Modification of Existing Labor Laws? Yes! Says Taft. No! Says Wagner," clipping from the Washington *Daily News*, June 22, 1940; Wagner speech file, Aug. 24, 1940.

measures . . . placed on a permanent basis, are ready at hand in our present defense drive." Referring to those aspects of the New Deal that bore his particular imprint, the Senator went on to declare that "no satisfaction that I received when these instruments were in the making exceeded that of today, when I see them playing their central part in making America strong—when I see a housing program planned in 1937 now sheltering defense workers and thus speeding up defense industries; collective bargaining machinery established in 1935 now functioning to prevent the causes of strikes in vital industries; the employment service . . . now guiding millions of unemployed workers to jobs in defense industries; public works projects now entering the belt-line of defense production; and a revived industry, a rehabilitated labor, and a restored agriculture now rising to their respective tasks in molding the security of the whole nation." To weaken or discard such measures, the New York Senator insisted, "would be to weaken ourselves. This step the Congress will never take." [30]

Owing in part to the vigilance of lawmakers like Wagner, Congress did not discard such measures nor even weaken them substantially, despite the exigencies of the defense emergency. Time and again, as appropriation bills were rushed through the Senate, Wagner and other liberals were on their feet securing approval of amendments insuring that time-and-a-half would be paid for overtime work on defense contracts or that the Walsh-Healey Act would apply to negotiated "cost-plus" contracts as well as to advertised bid contracts. When Congress passed an act authorizing government conscription of essential war plants, a Wagner amendment provided that all federal and state labor laws applicable to such installations should remain in full force. When the Selective Service Act of 1940 passed, it authorized courts to order the reinstatement of draftees to their former jobs; a Wagner-sponsored proviso also empowered the courts to direct payment of back wages lost during the course of litigation.[31]

Indeed, in at least one area of growing liberal concern—Negro rights—the defense drive of the prewar years actually spurred a degree of advance that had proved unattainable even during the height of the domestic New Deal. In the rush to pass the Draft Act in the summer of 1940, as an example, Southern senators opposed, but did not dare filibuster against, a Wagner amendment that forbade racial discrimination as far as voluntary enlistment in the armed forces was

[30] RFW Papers: Wagner speech file, Aug. 24, Dec. 23, 1940; clipping from the Washington *Daily News*, June 22, 1940.
[31] 86 *Congressional Record*, 7924, 8824ff, 10925ff, 11090ff.

concerned. Although this provision did not end segregation in the services, it did open up to Negroes the Air Corps and various branches of the Army and Navy that previously had been closed altogether to colored enlistees.

As the demand for war material created large-scale employment opportunities, moreover, Negro leaders moved to strike against existing racial barriers that often blocked colored workers from jobs in defense industries. At Walter White's suggestion in January 1941, Senator Wagner dispatched a public letter to Office of Production Management Director William Knudsen requesting an investigation of employment discrimination against Negroes in aircraft plants. A month later Wagner's name headed the list of four sponsors of Senate Resolution 75, which would create a special committee to investigate the utilization of Negro manpower in the defense effort. In the spring that proposal remained unacted on, but by then White, A. Philip Randolph of the Brotherhood of Sleeping Car Porters, and other Negro spokesmen were formulating plans for a mammoth "March on Washington" in support of the Wagner-Barbour-Capper-Brown resolution. Partially in response to that threat, President Roosevelt on June 25 circumvented the possibility of a showdown on Senate Resolution 75 by issuing Executive Order Number 8802, creating a Fair Employment Practices Commission to hear and adjust complaints of job discrimination.[32]

Thus, at the very end of the domestic New Deal, as a result of defense emergency pressures, the American Negro secured the most substantial official recognition of his burgeoning aspirations that was to come during all of the Roosevelt years.

One final—but premonitory—matter occupied Bob Wagner's attention during the prewar years as government defense expenditures blotted out the unemployment problem that had remained unsolved despite all of the New Deal's ministrations. And that was the question: What will happen when the defense emergency comes to an end? When the government ceased spending billions of dollars for arms, the New York Senator asked, "will we be faced with the twin evils of an expanded but largely unused industrial capacity and many millions of unemployed?" The alternative that he offered was "the way to a brighter future," for "in producing for defense, virtual mira-

[32] *Ibid.*, pp. 10789ff, and 87 *C. R.*, 1150f; also RFW Papers: RFW to William S. Knudsen, Jan. 13, 1941; Knudsen to RFW, Jan. 31, 1941; RFW–Walter White correspondence, 1940–41; files on "Draft Bill, 1940" and "Fair Employment Practices Commission, 1941."

cles have been wrought, and armament schedules surpassed. With the same urgency and sacrifice," he declared, "we can win the battle of production for peace," *provided* that "we begin thinking and planning now for that goal."

In order to initiate that thinking and planning Wagner joined Representative Jerry Voorhis of California early in January 1941 in introducing a Congressional resolution to establish a Post-Emergency Economic Advisory Commission. Composed of three senators, three members of the House, and six public representatives chosen by the President, the commission would be directed "to study the economic problems likely to confront the Nation upon the termination of the present defense emergency, and to formulate a comprehensive program for the full utilization of America's resources of men and machines in maintaining and improving the economic well-being of all the people." [33]

That resolution never was acted on by either house of Congress. But it did serve to stimulate postemergency planning efforts during an emergency that was to last much longer than the bill's sponsors, or anyone else, imagined.

As it turned out, the Wagner-Voorhis resolution marked the last measure that the Senator was on hand to personally introduce during the eventful months of 1941 that led up to the attack on Pearl Harbor. On January 20, in high spirits and in the company of a festive crowd of invited friends from New York, Wagner attended Franklin Roosevelt's third inauguration. The next day he came down with a cold that rapidly developed into influenza and then culminated in pneumonia; all of which left Wagner's heart in still more weakened condition. When he was well enough to leave Washington he went to Florida to recuperate; in the spring he returned to New York, and he summered along the Long Island shore. On physicians' advice he stayed away from the Senate most of the year.[34]

Thus the Congressional scene was deprived of a familiar figure during one of its most critical periods. But despite his protracted illness and convalescence, Wagner continued by means of articles, interviews, and public statements to support causes that commanded his allegiance. At the end of March, for example, it was announced that the Senator had agreed to assume the chairmanship of a revivified

[33] Robert F. Wagner, "Plan for Millions of Post-War Jobs Vital to Cushion End of Arms Boom," *American Laborite*, Aug. 15, 1941, pp. 7ff; files on "Full Employment, 1941," and Wagner speech file, Jan. 11, 1941, RFW Papers.

[34] Files on "RFW, Personal Correspondence, 1941," RFW Papers; interviews with Robert F. Wagner, Jr., Minna L. Ruppert, and Philip Levy.

American Palestine Committee devoted to securing removal of immigration restrictions that the British had recently imposed in Palestine, restrictions that threatened to deprive many of Europe's persecuted Jews of a refuge. And during the Senate's crucial debate on the Lend-Lease bill, Wagner told reporters who interviewed him at his New York apartment that if his vote were needed to pass the measure, he would board the train to Washington "doctors or no doctors." [35]

"Relaxing" for such an extended time was about the hardest work Bob Wagner could imagine ("No use telling you to take it easy," Marguerite Cummins wrote from her summer vacation retreat, "unless I want to get my head knocked off"), and he strained to get back into action. By the fall of the year he was well enough to take a hand in the Administration's efforts to resolve a coal mine strike, called by John L. Lewis, which threatened to disrupt the country's supply of a crucial commodity. The miners finally returned to work on November 22; the next evening, over a nationwide radio network, the father of the nation's basic Labor Act offered his analysis of the critical situation that had come about. While he felt that on the merits of the dispute management had been unreasonable in refusing the miners' terms, Wagner nonetheless warned labor that public opinion would not tolerate an "all or nothing" attitude on its part. But at the same time he cautioned against hysterical adoption of drastic antiunion curbs. What was needed, the Senator asserted, was more effective government machinery for mediation and voluntary arbitration of industrial disputes, along lines embodied in the bill he had unsuccessfully sponsored the year before. When Congress reconvened in January 1942, Wagner promised, he would be back in Washington working for just such measures.[36]

Neither Congress nor Bob Wagner was allowed to wait until January to return to Washington, however. On December 8, 1941, when Franklin Roosevelt asked for a declaration of war, and as the United States and the world embarked on a new phase of history, New York's senior senator was in his seat.

[35] Wagner speech file, March 28, 1941, and clipping from the New York *Post*, May 17, 1941, RFW Papers.
[36] Marguerite Cummins to RFW, Aug. 8, 1941, and Wagner speech file, Nov. 23, 1941, RFW Papers.

PART III

The Second World War
& the
Postwar World

CHAPTER 16

A Prologue as Well as
an Epilogue

BETWEEN 1941 AND 1945 Americans did more than successfully repulse the strongest military attack their country had ever sustained. Equally important was the fact that they did so with only a minimal curtailment of traditional liberties and without any permanent damage to the structure of social reform so recently advanced by the New Deal. Indeed, during the war years foresighted Americans laid the groundwork for even further domestic progress that would unfold, sometimes haltingly but seemingly ineluctably, in the postwar years. They also took the steps that committed the nation to acquiescence in the position of world leadership that was thrust upon it at war's end. In short, they sought to prepare America for the role she would be called on to play in the postwar world: a model of liberal society to which emergent peoples the world over could look for assistance, and from which they might borrow in fashioning their own ways of life, as an alternative to totalitarian patterns.

Toward the achievement of all these ends, few men in government worked harder than Robert F. Wagner. Despite advancing age and recurring illness, Wagner labored incessantly to insure that Postwar II would not witness a repetition of either the domestic or international attitudes that had marred Postwar I. True enough, at the time in 1947 when poor health forced the Senator to retire, the outcome seemed in doubt. But as an influential member of the national legislature, Wagner had done more than his bit to fortify against future trials the modern American liberalism he had helped mold in the past.

Following his return to the Senate in December 1941 Bob Wagner readily admitted that his long bout with sickness had made him slow down considerably. "I am feeling improved," he told a correspondent early in 1942, "but have not gotten back that old zest for working and living that I used to have." His blood pressure now posed a persistent problem; during the winters, moreover, colds and viruses continued to plague the Senator, and periodically he sought relief in the Florida sunshine. Capitol Hill associates, too, did what they could for him. Henry Wallace kept Wagner supplied with a brand of vitamin tablets that the Vice-President found to be especially potent, while Senator John Overton of Louisiana recommended a homier prescription: "I hope . . . that you are taking two or three teaspoonsful of honey every morning."

Poor health had a particularly blighting effect on Wagner's social life after 1940. "I have had to decline all evening engagements," he informed Francis Biddle in response to a dinner invitation from the Attorney General in mid-1942. And seldom thereafter did the senior senator from New York grace the drawing rooms of Washington. In part that inhibition may have been self-imposed, however, for according to some who knew him well Wagner gradually wearied of humoring conservative matrons whose conversation invariably started out: "But Senator, you can't *really* believe in all those radical bills you've sponsored!"

During the summer of 1943, while Wagner vacationed in the Adirondacks, a companion informed Minna Ruppert that the Senator had frequented the casino "and danced several times," but apparently even that form of socializing was rare enough now to merit special notice. And perhaps a nostalgic note might be detected in the letter Wagner wrote to his son relating that a mutual friend of theirs had dropped off several pairs of hard-to-get nylon stockings at his Senate office that morning. "I suppose," the Senator commented, "that poor John must think that an old codger like me still has an eye for the ladies." [1]

Wagner's loneliness was intensified in these years by the fact that, like fathers across the country, he experienced the absence of a

[1] Files on "RFW, Personal Correspondence, 1941–1945," RFW Papers; RFW to FDR, Feb. 26, 1942, FDR Papers; also RFW Papers: RFW to Harry Angelo, April 11, 1942; John H. Overton to RFW, Nov. 9, 1944; RFW to Francis Biddle, May 20, 1942; Leo Lowenthal to Minna L. Ruppert, Aug. 17, 1943; RFW to Robert F. Wagner, Jr., Aug. 4, 1943; M. H. Lewis to Henry A. Wallace, March 15, 1944; RFW to Edward R. Finch, Nov. 28, 1943; also interviews with Robert F. Wagner, Jr., Minna L. Ruppert, Marguerite Cummins Hayes, Leon H. Keyserling, Philip Levy, and David Delman.

son away in the service. Soon after Pearl Harbor the younger Bob Wagner became one of the first members of the New York legislature to volunteer for duty. During 1942 he received Air Corps training; in 1943 he was in Europe, not to return until after hostilities had ended. For a father and son so unusually close—the two had continued to share the same apartment in Yorkville all along—the separation was especially painful.

Circumstances forced Senator Wagner to assume more the role of a "home body," then, as he passed the accustomed retirement age of sixty-five in 1942. Fortunately, however, he now had more of a family than he had known since his wife's death many years earlier. Shortly after he entered the service Bob, Junior, had married a Greenwich, Connecticut, girl he had known since college days. Early in 1944 another Robert Ferdinand Wagner was born, and the Senator found himself a grandfather. Like many brides at the time, Susan Wagner continued to live with her parents during her husband's absence, but her newly acquired father-in-law became a frequent visitor to Greenwich. The Senator reported to friends that "the baby-talk tonic" was the best health restorative he had yet found.

In New York City Wagner frequently was looked after now by his niece Evelyn—Gus's daughter—and her husband, business executive Kenneth Steinreich. The couple escorted the Senator as he made his accustomed rounds visiting old friends and mending political fences, and they saw that he got to ball games, the theater, and his favorite restaurants often enough. One Saturday's activities received detailed description in a letter Steinreich wrote to Major Bob Wagner the following week. After an afternoon Broadway matinee and dinner at the New York Athletic Club (where Wagner once worked as a bellhop, he reminded his companions for the hundredth time), the party ended up—at the Senator's insistence—at the Copacabana night club. The old gentleman enjoyed himself immensely, Steinreich related, and the chorus girls seemed to attract his particular attention. It must have had a tonic effect, Wagner's nephew-in-law added, for "we heard not another word about your father's 'aches and pains' during the remainder of his stay in the city!" [2]

If Wagner continued to enjoy more of "an eye for the ladies" than he credited himself with, the record indicates that he also possessed more of that "old zest for working" than he realized. Of course, those aches and pains about which he frequently complained did cur-

[2] RFW to Simon H. Rifkind, Jan. 21, 1944, and Kenneth Steinreich to Robert F. Wagner, Jr., May 11, 1944, RFW Papers; interviews with Robert F. Wagner, Jr., and Kenneth Steinreich.

tail his political activities to some extent. Public appearances and speeches became fewer; younger members of Congress' liberal contingent had to assume more of those chores now on behalf of the bills that the New York Senator introduced.

Moreover, Wagner was under strict orders to avoid involvement in Senate debate; when he spoke there now he frequently asked not to be interrupted until he had finished his presentation. But in the more important context of personal contact with his colleagues and in the calmer deliberations of the committee room Wagner retained much of his old charm and effectiveness. After the Senator piloted the Bretton Woods monetary agreements to enactment in 1945, Simon Rifkind sent him a congratulatory note concluding: "Apparently you continue to possess the magic touch which guides legislation through Congress." Two years after the event the Treasury Department official who had been especially responsible for those agreements reaffirmed in a letter to Wagner that "much of the credit for their realization belongs to you." "I like to recall," he added, "how splendidly you handled the Banking and Currency Committee." [3]

Witnesses who opposed Wagner's views continued to acknowledge the fair and courteous treatment he accorded them. And "friendly" witnesses, in particular, could always count on him to help them out of any jam into which they worked themselves. One such individual was William H. Davis, the head of the National War Labor Board, who in his memoirs recalled how during an exasperating day of testimony before the Banking and Currency Committee, Senator Taft bombarded him with statistics that seemed to contradict the point that Davis was trying to make. Taft, in his somewhat imperious manner, then started to move on to another line of questioning. "Well, Wagner gently but firmly backed me up," Davis recounted. "He said enough so that I was permitted to go ahead and discuss . . . that discrepancy." After several more minutes it appeared to everyone's satisfaction, and to Taft's great surprise, that the Ohio Republican had been referring to completely irrelevant figures in his grilling of Davis. Even so, Taft made no move to apologize to the witness for his error. "Now, Wagner would never do that," Davis concluded. "He never had that besetting sin of thinking he was always right." [4]

Capitol Hill correspondents, who voted Wagner "the hardest-working Democrat in the Senate" in a poll that *Life* magazine con-

[3] Philip Levy, interview; Simon H. Rifkind to RFW, July 23, 1945, and Harry D. White to RFW, April 2, 1947, RFW Papers.
[4] William H. Davis, "Reminiscences" (Oral History Research Office, Columbia Univ., 1958), pp. 55ff, 171.

ducted in 1939, continued to remark on his industriousness in the
1940s.[5] Nor did they note any diminution in his devotion to the objectives he had already set for himself during the prewar defense build-
up of 1939–41—the preservation of gains already made and the planning of still further advances along the path of modern liberalism. It
was to these causes that Wagner devoted his main strength during the
1940s, even while contributing his part to the home-front war effort
against the Axis, and to the assumption by the United States of a new
set of postwar international responsibilities.

Behind the front lines the most crucial battle of the Second
World War was the battle for production. The United States won
that contest, for enlisted wholeheartedly in it were virtually all the
farmers, businessmen, and workers who constituted the vital parts of
America's remarkably effective economic machine. Although equally
devoted to the cause of providing enough food and material to roll
back the enemy, however, spokesmen for each of those elements entertained different notions as to how output could best be encouraged, and that involved in turn the question of how the mounting
prosperity derived from the nation's war-stimulated economy should
be distributed. From this situation, combined with the shortage of
civilian consumption goods, arose the threat of a runaway inflation
that would be detrimental to the interest groups themselves, to consumers in general, and to a government that had now become the
country's largest customer of all. To the task of curbing that threat,
which Bob Wagner called "the basic domestic problem of a nation at
war," the Roosevelt Administration devoted much of its executive
energy after 1941. It also proved to be the single most demanding
subject on which Wagner expended his legislative energy during the
war years.

Just two days after Pearl Harbor, Wagner convened the Senate's
Banking and Currency Committee for hearings on an anti-inflation
bill. Congress passed the measure in January 1942, and under its
provisions the President established the Office of Price Administration. (At the same time a National War Labor Board was created
with authority to regulate wages and resolve labor disputes.) The
OPA's powers were further expanded in the fall of the year by a bill
that Wagner cosponsored with Senator Prentiss Brown of Michigan.
Thereafter all legislation pertaining to price control passed through
the Banking and Currency Committee. On the shoulders of its chair-

[5] "Washington Correspondents Name Ablest Congressmen in *Life* Poll,"
Life, March 20, 1939, pp. 13ff.

man—who had had firsthand experience with World War I inflation in his capacities as a New York State legislator and judge—fell the burden of sustaining against vigorous attack the policies and programs that the OPA deemed necessary to the accomplishment of its task.

The basic drive of the Administration's war against inflation centered on an attempt to stabilize wages and prices at the levels they had attained by mid-September 1942, a point at which the cost of living had already increased 20 percent over the 1939 level. This was the approach applied to wages by the War Labor Board in its "Little Steel" formula, and it was the approach of the OPA as reiterated by the President in his "hold the line" order of April 1943. The objective itself proved irksome to farmers, businessmen, and workers, and so did many of the specific devices that the government employed in efforts to accomplish its aim. Consequently wartime controls, and particularly the OPA, became a prolific source of political bitterness and legislative maneuver.[6]

From Wagner's viewpoint, the severest threats to effective price control emanated from two main sources: the farmers and business. In an important sense the fight over the OPA quickly assumed the form of a rural-urban conflict. Farmers wanted to receive high prices for the crops they grew; urban consumers and workers, on the other hand, wanted low food bills. Farm bloc spokesmen in Congress therefore took a dim view of OPA price controllers, and their hostility adopted many forms. From the outset they insisted that control legislation pertaining to food prices should be referred to the Senate's Agriculture Committee, a creature of their own, rather than to a Banking and Currency Committee whose urban orientation was personified in its chairman. Repeatedly, too, the rural lawmakers tried to take control of food prices out of the hands of the OPA—an outfit run by "Harvard economists" who assuredly knew nothing about farming—and to vest it instead in the Agriculture Department's War Food Administration. In 1943, when the OPA rolled back the price of meat and butter by several cents, while compensating producers and processors with subsidies paid out of the general treasury, the farm bloc once more rebelled. The better policy, its spokesmen insisted, would

[6] Files on "O.P.A. and Price Controls, 1941–1945," RFW Papers; 88 *Congressional Record*, 7042ff, 7202ff; *New York Times*, April 9, 1943; Lester V. Chandler, *Inflation in the United States: 1940–1948* (New York, 1951), *passim*. For general accounts of the waging of World War II see Eliot Janeway, *The Struggle for Survival: A Chronicle of Economic Mobilization in World War II* (New Haven, 1951); A. R. Buchanan, *The United States and World War II*, 2 vols. (New York, 1964); Kenneth S. Davis, *Experience of War* (Garden City, N. Y., 1965).

be to let food prices take their "natural" course, as a stimulant to greater production and as a matter of justice to the farmers. By various methods the farm group also sought to alter, in the farmers' favor, the method of calculating the parity standards that by law the OPA had to observe in setting food prices.

The attack on the OPA from business quarters was equally vigorous. As voiced by Senator Taft and other conservative-bloc spokesmen in Congress, the general tenor of their complaint was that the OPA's rigorous price controls, by allowing insufficient profit margins, tended to stifle production. Small businessmen in particular were being driven to the wall, Taft contended, because of their inability to operate under prices established on the basis of costs characteristic of larger, more efficient firms. ("I sometimes think the Senator from Ohio must maintain in his office a hospital for sick business," Alben Barkley quipped during one of the Senate's OPA debates.) Moreover, as the tide of victory turned decisively in the Allies' favor during 1944, conservatives found a new and even more menacing threat in the plans of those "left-wingers" who seemed intent on continuing the OPA into the postwar era. Only prompt abandonment of controls and the restoration of the profit motive, the business spokesmen declared, could unleash the productive capacity necessary to avoid postwar chaos. The OPA—an outfit run by "Harvard economists" who assuredly knew nothing about business—must quickly disappear with the coming of peace.[7]

Wagner did his best to appreciate the farmers' and businessmen's points of view. He acquiesced, for example, in the 1943 measure guaranteeing farmers that high parity levels would prevail for at least two years after the war. Along with many other liberals in these years, moreover, Wagner also shared Senator Taft's concern about the adverse effects that wartime conditions—not just price controls, but the government's contract and priority procedures as well—might have on small business. "I have never been an old-fashioned trust buster, because I believe that big business serves a useful purpose," Wagner declared on one occasion. But, he insisted, "We must prevent monopolies from getting a stranglehold on the resources of our country." Fearful that big business' strategic advantage in a period of emergency war effort might entrench it more strongly than ever in private control

---

[7] Files on "O.P.A. and Price Controls, 1941–1945," RFW Papers. The annual battle over price controls during the war years may be followed in the *Congressional Record*, Vols. 88–91. The Barkley quote is from Vol. 91, p. 5865. With respect to Congress' skeptical attitude toward the OPA's "academic" economists see also Thomas I. Emerson, "Reminiscences" (Oral History Research Office, 1953), pp. 801–802.

of vital sectors of the nation's economy, Wagner, in 1942, led his Banking and Currency Committee in securing Congressional approval of legislation creating a Smaller War Plants Corporation that was supposed to look after the interests of small business in the conduct of the war effort. In 1945 he supported extension of the life of this agency into the peacetime reconversion period.[8]

But on the really vital issues involving inflation and price control that aligned farm and business elements as opponents of the OPA, it was to be expected that Wagner would incline toward the urban consumer-worker viewpoint. Seconded by labor and liberal elements who shared that viewpoint, Wagner stood by the OPA in the press, on the radio, and in the halls of Congress as that beleaguered agency fought its public battles. In private, closeted with successive OPA directors Leon Henderson, Prentiss Brown, and Chester Bowles, the New York Senator proved a valued counsel in planning political and legislative strategy. "As I leave Washington," Bowles informed Wagner in the summer of 1946, "I want you to know how much I appreciate all you've done to support the stabilization program and me personally during the three rather tough years I have been down here. A great part of the satisfaction that I've gotten out of what we have been able to accomplish," Bowles added, "comes from the knowledge that a few people like you have gone down the line so consistently for us." [9]

Within the confines of his Banking and Currency Committee, Wagner's influence on the OPA's behalf was decisive, and during the war years price-control bills were invariably reported out from it in the form the Administration desired. On the floor of the Senate and in the House of Representatives, however, the combined strength of the rural and conservative blocs made for a different situation. In 1943 both houses of Congress seemed so intent on emasculating a bill extending the OPA's powers that, for the first and only time in his career, Wagner resigned membership on the conference committee after three days of frustrated attempts to salvage something of the Administration's original program. Only after the President had vetoed the bill Congress sent him was a satisfactory compromise worked out, and only the pending threat of additional vetoes enabled Wagner to secure barely acceptable Congressional action on price controls in 1944 and early 1945.

[8] 88 *Congressional Record*, 4877ff; also RFW Papers: files on "Smaller War Plants Corporation, 1942–1945"; Wagner speech file, April 17, 1942, Nov. 4, 1944, and Dec. 6, 1945; also Bruce Catton, *The War Lords of Washington* (New York, 1948), *passim*.

[9] Files on "O.P.A. and Price Controls, 1942–1945," and Chester Bowles to RFW, July 10, 1946, RFW Papers.

When the first phase of victory in the war came with Germany's surrender in May 1945, Wagner warned that "The history of the last war shows that the cost of living in America rose most rapidly after the Armistice was signed." The Senator's history was correct. But in view of the demonstrated power of the farmer-conservative blocs in Congress, it appeared that liberals faced a real fight if they hoped to preserve for very long in peacetime the kinds of controls they thought necessary for orderly and equitable reconversion.[10]

Moreover, while Wagner and other urban liberals regarded the demands of farmers and businessmen as the greatest threat to war-time and postwar economic stability, many other Americans identified a different element—organized labor—as the chief culprit. By the middle of 1943 industrial workers were chafing under the wage controls and other restrictions that the War Labor Board imposed on them—controls that enjoyed Wagner's wholehearted blessing—and the number of work stoppages increased. But most of these strikes were brief, involved few workers, and had no significant effect on war production; they therefore attracted relatively little public attention.

In May of 1943, however, in direct defiance of the War Labor Board, John L. Lewis again took his followers out of the coal mines. Prominent union leaders joined Senator Wagner in publicly denouncing Lewis' blatant violation of labor's "no strike" pledge in a vital industry, while pointing out how atypical the mine chieftain's conduct was in view of labor's general wartime record.[11] President Roosevelt ordered seizure of the mines, and the nation's supply of coal was assured. But, predictably, Lewis' action rekindled the antilabor fires that had been banked since the war's outbreak. The result was the Smith-Connally Act, which Congress passed in June.

At the outset Senator Tom Connally's bill did nothing more than reaffirm and define more precisely the presidential war powers under which Roosevelt had taken over the coal mines, and in that form it enjoyed Wagner's support. Before it emerged from the legislative mill, however, the bill carried such irrelevant, and obviously political, provisions as one banning union contributions in federal political campaigns. Its most important feature virtually repealed labor's "no strike" pledge by authorizing strikes to take place after workers had been secretly polled on the question by the NLRB, following a thirty-

[10] 89 *Congressional Record*, 6321ff, 6691ff, 6818ff, 7051ff; Wagner speech file, May 8, 1945, RFW Papers.

[11] Wagner speech file, June 3, 1943, RFW Papers; Harry A. Millis and Emily Clark Brown, *From the Wagner Act to Taft-Hartley* (Chicago, 1950), pp. 274ff.

day "cooling off" period. *The New York Times* called the bill "one of the stupidest pieces of legislation ever passed by Congress," and predicted that it would actually foment even more work stoppages. Senator Wagner concurred and voted against it; President Roosevelt concurred and vetoed it. But the conservative-dominated Congress easily overrode the White House. Among other things, the whole process confirmed Wagner's conviction regarding the unkind fate that even well-intentioned labor legislation would inevitably suffer at the hands of an antilabor Congress.[12]

Thereafter even the most conscientious of labor leaders found it increasingly difficult to abide by their "no strike" pledge; pressure to "keep up with the Lewises" in demanding modifications of the "Little Steel" formula often proved too strong, and union heads were compelled to request an NLRB poll. In January 1945 a group of harried C.I.O executives asked Wagner to intercede with the President for a general revision of the wage formula, in hopes of thwarting Lewis' organizing incursions into their own domains. The Senator—whom some described as a "tool" of labor—spoke to the C.I.O. leaders about their problems, urged them to reaffirm the "no strike" pledge, but declined to convey their plea to the White House. Wagner's devotion to averting inflation was, it would appear, even-handed.[13]

Nevertheless, strikes continued to make bigger headlines than farm bloc proposals to recalculate parity, or businessmen's proposals for revising OPA pricing formulas. By the time of Victory-in-Europe Day a good many men in Congress were busy devising bills that would amend the Wagner Act and impose new restrictions on union activity. A short time after Hitler surrendered, the combined handiwork of three of them, Senators Ball of Minnesota, Burton of Ohio, and Hatch of New Mexico, made its appearance in the legislative hopper. The B_2H bill, as the press quickly dubbed it, went the whole length by proposing that compulsory arbitration be introduced in industries deemed essential to the national welfare.

As conservatives took up the cry to make the B_2H bill, or something like it, a permanent feature of America's postwar economy, Chairman Harry A. Millis of the National Labor Relations Board ended his term of office. In doing so, the distinguished University of Chicago labor relations expert issued an appraisal that described the Wagner Act as "without precedent in scope or promise in the history of our nation. . . . the product of experience, a fertile mind, and

---

[12] Files on "Smith-Connally Act, 1943," RFW Papers; 89 *Congressional Record*, 3811ff, 3993, 5719ff, 6487ff; *New York Times*, March 14, 1945; Millis and Brown, *From the Wagner Act to Taft-Hartley*, pp. 298ff.

[13] Clifford McAvoy to RFW, Feb. 24, 1945, RFW Papers.

social vision." The act's sponsor savored that tribute—he inserted it in the *Congressional Record*—but it's not likely that he lingered over it very long. For Wagner and his dwindling band of Congressional allies were already girding to withstand the rash of attacks on the Labor Act that would be pressed, the New York Senator accurately predicted, "the minute the war is over." If the vote on the Smith-Connally Act was any indication, they faced another stiff battle.[14]

Liberals had their own broad plans for averting labor strife and other forms of social unrest in the postwar era, but they moved in an opposite direction from imposing novel restraints on traditional American liberties such as the right to strike. What they envisioned instead was a resumption and extension of the New Deal reform program in ways that would obviate the causes of social discontent on which radicals of the left and right thrived, take up the economic slack that the government's reduction of military expenditures was expected to entail, and strengthen America for the demands that overseas needs for help and reconstruction would place on her.

During the early years of the war considerable planning along those lines was carried on in the executive branch of the government by the National Resources Planning Board. When President Roosevelt gingerly transmitted the board's reports to Congress in the spring of 1943, however, the legislators responded by cutting off funds for continuation of the agency's activities. Conservatives wanted no part of what they derisively called the American version of Britain's socialistic "Beveridge Plan," which would guarantee citizens "cradle to grave" security.

Nor did Congress respond sympathetically when Roosevelt spoke of formulating a postwar "economic bill of rights" in his State of the Union message early in 1944. Indeed, the special committee on postwar planning that the Senate had created in 1943, under the chairmanship of ultraconservative Walter F. George of Georgia, seemed intent mainly on cutting short the kinds of programs in which New Dealers were interested. So did its counterpart in the House of Representatives. Absorbed by international questions, President Roosevelt made little effort during the last year of his life to prod a reluctant Congress into concretely preparing for the kind of postwar America that his new "bill of rights" envisioned.[15]

As the war drew to a close, then, American liberals rallied behind

[14] Files on "Labor Legislation, 1945," RFW Papers; 91 *Congressional Record*, 7045–46; Wagner speech file, Nov. 3, 1944, RFW Papers; Millis and Brown, *From the Wagner Act to Taft-Hartley*, pp. 286–287, 358ff.

[15] 89 *Congressional Record*, 4965ff, Appendix, 712, and 90 C. R., 78.

postwar projects that had been devised by progressive organizations and by individual lawmakers acting rather independently of either presidential or Congressional direction. It came as no surprise that many of those proposals were associated with the name of Robert F. Wagner. "Let us make the impending victory a prologue as well as an epilogue," the New York Senator declared in 1944, "—a prologue to the ample satisfaction of the material needs of man, so that he may have more time and more capacity to contemplate and to enjoy the higher spiritual values." [16] Those words merely restated the veteran New Dealer's old objectives, but now he had ready at hand a new set of far-reaching programs designed to advance them.

The most ambitious of the New York Senator's measures, and indeed the single most comprehensive among all the legislative measures proposed for postwar America during the war years, was the bill that Wagner introduced in June 1943 in collaboration with Senator James E. Murray of Montana and Representative John Dingell of Michigan. It was a voluminous bill comprising nearly two hundred pages, and it touched on many phases of the emerging welfare state. In briefest summary, its provisions called for: nationalizing the United States Employment Service; nationalizing and extending the unemployment insurance system; expanding both the coverage and benefits provided by old-age insurance; instituting new national systems of both temporary and permanent disability payments; national compulsory health insurance; paid-up benefit rights to veterans for time spent in the service under all social security programs; special unemployment compensation benefits to veterans during their period of readjustment to civilian life; and a revamping of all federal programs of grants-in-aid to the states for public assistance.

The Wagner-Murray-Dingell bill had been assembled in Wagner's office by Philip Levy and the Senator's other legislative assistants, who drew upon numerous sources in concocting its specific provisions. Spokesmen for the A. F. of L. and the C.I.O were particularly instrumental in fashioning its social security features, and many organizations such as the Committee of Physicians for the Improvement of Medical Care and the American Association for the Blind also contributed their assistance. The bill's draftsmen utilized the reports and recommendations of the ill-fated National Resources Planning Board, while some of its technical features were worked out by experts associated with government agencies, such as the Social Security Board, the Public Health Service, the Children's Bureau of the Department of Labor, and the United States Employment Service.

[16] Wagner speech file, Sept. 10, 1944, RFW Papers.

But, as usual, nothing of importance found lodgment in the measure without Senator Wagner's personal approval.[17]

After the complex measure was drafted, Wagner sent a copy of it to Franklin Roosevelt; the President wished him "good luck with it," but that was about the extent of direct White House involvement in the bill that quickly became the focal point of New Dealers' hopes for the postwar future. Nor did Wagner entertain any delusions about the measure's immediate prospects when he first introduced it in 1943. During the next two years it lay dormant as far as Congressional action was concerned. In the meantime, however, liberal newspapers and journals like the *Nation* and the *New Republic* took up the cause of the W-M-D bill. At Senator Wagner's invitation, moreover, an Informal Conference Committee, composed of representatives of labor and liberal organizations, assembled periodically in Washington —sometimes in the Banking and Currency Committee room—to plan strategy for mobilizing public support behind the measure, and to consider suggestions for its improvement. In 1945, when a new Congress assembled, the bill's sponsors introduced a perfected version as victory in the war approached.[18]

Aside from its broadening of existing social security programs and the extension of social security principles into new and controversial fields like health insurance, the most striking feature of the Wagner-Murray-Dingell bill was its propensity to *nationalize* programs that, earlier, had been conceived in terms of federal encouragement to *state* initiative. In this category fell the proposals to nationalize the employment service, the unemployment insurance system, and the projected health insurance system. In part this centralizing tendency stemmed from the wider scope for federal government activity afforded by the trend of Supreme Court decisions after 1937. It was stimulated further by the growing conviction among liberals that wartime experience—which involved *temporary* nationalizing of the United States Employment Service, for example—proved conclusively the greater efficiency and comprehensiveness of federal, as compared to state, direction of welfare services. "We could not win this war with forty-eight separate armies under forty-eight state commanders," Bob Wagner observed in 1944. "We cannot win the peace with forty-

[17] 89 *Congressional Record*, 5257ff; files on "Wagner-Murray-Dingell Bill, 1943," RFW Papers; interviews with Philip Levy and Boris Shishkin.

[18] FDR Papers: RFW to FDR, June 13, 1943; FDR to RFW, June 16, 1943; FDR to William A. Green, Oct. 6, 1943; FDR to Philip Murray, Oct. 19, 1943; also files on "Wagner-Murray-Dingell Bill, 1943–1945," RFW Papers; interviews with Philip Levy and David Delman.

eight separate economic programs, for our whole economic system is one and indivisible." [19]

As they contemplated the future development of the welfare state in postwar America, therefore, liberals in the 1940s embarked on that preference for federal action that has marked their attitude from that time onward.

At the same time conservatives viewed with abhorrence the impetus toward centralization that the war had induced. They endured it, in matters such as the employment service, as a temporary wartime necessity; but they were resolved that at the war's end those functions that Washington had assumed should revert to state responsibility and control. And even as a growing number of conservatives tended in the 1940s to accept the types of federal programs of grants-in-aid to state welfare services that the New Deal had initiated in the 1930s —programs that the conservatives of *that* decade had bitterly opposed —they prepared to battle against the new liberal trend that sought to augment the federal government's direct intervention in those fields.[20]

During the war years, therefore, the conflict between liberals and conservatives moved to new ground; but it still went on. And in the immediate postwar period much of it would center, as in the past, around the newest Wagner bill, the Wagner-Murray-Dingell bill.

As reintroduced in 1945, the Wagner-Murray-Dingell bill lacked the provisions pertaining to veterans that the original version had included. In 1944 Congress passed legislation, popularly known as the G.I. Bill of Rights, that afforded veterans numerous forms of government assistance ranging from mustering-out pay to federal aid in acquiring college education, vocational training, homes, farms, or a start in business. Although the G.I. Bill came under the jurisdiction of Senator George's Finance Committee, of which Wagner was not a member, the New York Senator nonetheless was placed in charge of formulating the measure's social insurance provisions. As finally enacted, the G.I. Bill included provisions that were lifted practically bodily out of the W-M-D bill; it credited veterans' Social Security accounts with the time spent in service, and entitled them to twenty dollars a week of federal unemployment compensation for a period of readjustment that could range up to a year. Conservatives denounced the latter provision as "an invitation to idleness," and in the House a

[19] Wagner speech file, Aug. 10, 1944, RFW Papers.
[20] On May 9, 1945, Senators Taft and Millard E. Tydings of Maryland sent Wagner a copy of the recently published book *Decentralize for Liberty*, by Tom Hewes, which together with Friedrich Hayek's *The Road to Serfdom* served as something of a Bible for the new school of conservatism. (Letter from Taft and Tydings in RFW Papers).

concerted effort was made to reduce the Bill's liberality in several other respects. A firm stand by the Senate's conferees turned back the attack, however, and the end result was a measure that satisfied liberal standards as to what the nation owed its defenders. According to a study conducted by Bernard Baruch, under the G.I. Bill America's veterans would enjoy more generous treatment than those of any of the Allies. As far as veterans were concerned, at least, the United States was to take unprecedented steps in the direction of the welfare state in the immediate postwar era.[21]

But if Congress proved exceptionally liberal in its treatment of veterans, such was not the case with respect to the provision it made for easing the readjustment problems of civilian war plant workers on the home front. After 1939 thousands of Americans entered the labor force for the first time, or crossed state lines to take jobs in defense industries. At war's end many of them would face layoffs, during which, under the country's state-administered unemployment insurance system, benefits would vary from area to area, often be inadequate in size and duration, or even totally lacking because of an individual's failure to have built up sufficient credits to qualify for coverage. Pointing out that Congress had already made generous promises of government aid to businessmen in reconverting their plants to peacetime production, Senate liberals joined in the summer of 1944 in support of a measure known as the Murray-Truman-Kilgore bill, which would establish for two years a supplementary system of federal unemployment compensation designed to provide civilian war workers roughly the same readjustment benefits accorded G.I.s under their Bill of Rights. But the liberals were unable to overcome conservative forces mobilized by Senator Taft and Senator George, and their cause went down to defeat by a vote of 49–25.

After V-E Day, Administration officials in charge of the reconversion program confirmed fears regarding the inadequacy of the existing unemployment insurance system for the task that lay ahead, and on May 28, 1945, Harry S Truman, who had now become President of the United States, again recommended establishment of temporary federal benefits. A short time later Bob Wagner joined five other Senate liberals in sponsoring the measure Truman requested, as during the summer the postwar era neared reality.[22]

[21] Files on "G.I. Bill of Rights, 1944," RFW Papers; 90 *Congressional Record*, 1637ff, 2490–91, 4839ff, 5752ff, 5760; Samuel I. Rosenman to FDR, Oct. 6, 1943, and FDR to Rosenman, Oct. 29, 1943, FDR Papers; also RFW Papers; undated (1944) clipping from *The New York Times*; Bernard M. Baruch to Edward C. Johnson, Nov. 21, 1945.
[22] Files on "Reconversion Legislation, 1944–1945," RFW Papers; 90 *Con-*

Liberal-conservative dispute about the treatment of veterans and war workers fell into the realm of immediate problems of temporary postwar concern. But by the summer of 1945 another issue had emerged that, like the Wagner-Murray-Dingell bill itself, involved a profound confrontation regarding the direction that American society would take in the long-range postwar era. At stake was the familiar but newly pressing question of national economic planning, and the role of the federal government therein. To liberals the defense build-up and wartime experience afforded new evidence of the beneficial effect that the government and its policies could exert as "a balance-wheel in the economy." On the theoretical level, moreover, interest in the subject was enhanced by wider dissemination of the "compensatory spending" ideas of the British economist John Maynard Keynes.

In his 1944 State of the Union message President Roosevelt mentioned "the right to a useful and remunerative job" as an aspect of his postwar economic Bill of Rights; the Democratic platform that year also spoke of ensuring "full employment" in the postwar world. Early versions of what evolved into the Murray-Truman-Kilgore bill provided for establishment of new federal planning agencies to be charged with achieving that objective. Particularly appealing to Senator Murray was a proposal submitted to him in the summer of 1944 by James G. Patton of the liberal National Farmers Union calling on the federal government to ensure an annual volume of total investment sufficient to guarantee full utilization of the nation's manpower and resources. On August 8, 1944, Murray inserted Patton's plan in the *Congressional Record*; a short time later he had one of his legislative assistants, Bertram Gross, draft a bill that used Patton's suggestion as its point of departure. By the end of the year Gross had ready for introduction what would soon become known as the Full Employment bill of 1945. Among the Washington figures whom Gross consulted in its preparation was Leon H. Keyserling.[23]

"The right to work," "a balance-wheel in the economy," "national economic planning," "Leon Keyserling"—the words themselves suggest that Robert F. Wagner was not far offstage as the "full employment" concept once again marched toward legislative embodiment during late 1944. Indeed, in September Wagner informed James Patton that he was "deeply interested" in the Farmers Union

---

gressional Record, 6764ff, 6785ff, 6827ff, 6904ff, 6917ff, 7897ff, 8015ff, and 91 C. R., 5171f, 7589ff.
[23] Files on "Full Employment, 1944–1945," RFW Papers; interviews with Leon H. Keyserling and David Delman; Stephen Kemp Bailey, *Congress Makes a Law: The Story Behind the Employment Act of 1946* (New York, 1950), *passim*.

proposal: "It is receiving careful consideration and study by me and, I believe, by other Senators with the thought of obtaining early action on this important matter when Congress reconvenes." And on January 22, 1945, when Senator Murray introduced S. 380, he listed Wagner as one of its cosponsors along with Elbert Thomas of Utah and Joseph C. O'Mahoney of Wyoming. Logically the bill might have been referred to any one of a half-dozen Senate committees, but its sponsors made sure that it went to Banking and Currency. For there it was certain to receive expert and considerate handling by the man who, way back in 1931, had secured passage of the Federal Employment Stabilization Act, the acknowledged earliest forerunner of the new Full Employment bill.[24]

As introduced early in 1945, S. 380 stated the purpose of the federal government to so direct its economic policies as to stimulate "the highest feasible levels of employment opportunities through private . . . investment and expenditure"; to the extent that such policies failed to afford Americans their "right to work," the government would "provide such volume of federal investment and expenditure as may be needed to assure continuing full employment." It directed the President, with the assistance of his Cabinet, to prepare and submit to Congress an annual National Production and Employment Budget, along with such legislative proposals as he deemed necessary to fulfill the bill's policy declaration. A newly created Congressional Joint Committee on the National Budget was charged with studying the President's recommendations and supplementing them with its own. Within limits to be prescribed by Congress, the President would be empowered also to vary the rate of federal expenditure during the course of the budget year, in order to maintain a full employment economy.

In the months following the bill's introduction Senators Wagner and Murray assumed chief responsibility in preparing for the legislative battle that loomed ahead. Leon Keyserling devoted as much time as he could spare from his official duties to counseling his old mentor, but the bulk of the staff work fell to Bertram Gross, who now assumed a position with Wagner's Banking and Currency Committee. In a basement room of the Senate Office Building Gross and his associates drew up detailed studies for use in propagation and defense of the Full Employment bill. Letters bearing Senator Wagner's signature solicited comments and opinions from more than fifteen hundred leaders in American business, labor, and civic life, in a way that

[24] RFW to James G. Patton, Sept. 22, 1944, RFW Papers; 91 *Congressional Record*, 377ff; Bailey, *Congress Makes a Law*, pp. 100–102.

was reminiscent of the technique used by Simon Rifkind during the campaign for Wagner's original Three Bills many years earlier. A committee of noted economists lent its support. So did the battery of liberal and labor groups with whom Wagner had worked in the past; the Union for Democratic Action (forerunner of Americans for Democratic Action] assembled a Full Employment Kit, which was made available to opinion-formers throughout the country. To coordinate the activities of these organizations an informal Continuations Group held weekly meetings, at which Senator Wagner sometimes presided; indeed, its membership and the organizations represented overlapped very considerably with the strategy board that had been formed sometime earlier to work on behalf of the Wagner-Murray-Dingell bill.[25]

In order to stimulate public concern with the Full Employment bill and its ramifications, Wagner's Banking and Currency Committee held two days of public hearings, on July 30 and 31, 1945, just a short time before Congress began an anticipated two months' post V-E Day vacation. Only the bill's sponsors and three other congressmen who favored it were heard at that time. As the lead-off man in propounding the bill's virtues, Bob Wagner called it "as important a proposal as any before Congress within our memory." Admitting that the New Deal had failed to solve the unemployment problem satisfactorily, Wagner depicted the tremendous task that the United States would be confronted by when its enlarged work force and productive capacity encountered the drop in government demand for goods and services that would come with the war's end. "Even to contemplate failure in this task is unthinkable," he observed, "for there will be no such thing in the postwar world as the possibility of continuing freedom *plus* continuing mass *un*employment. Either we must conquer unemployment, or unemployment will destroy our freedom."

Yet, "under the pressure of war we have achieved full employment," the Senator pointed out, "because we marshaled all our resources and organized them systematically according to plan." And while he conceded that no one would suggest retaining, in the postwar period, the degree of centralization and control that had been necessary during the war, Wagner insisted that "the war has taught us what the indispensable *minimum* requirements are for maintaining full production and full employment." Only "these indispensable *minimum* requirements," he asserted, "are incorporated in the Full

[25] Files on "Full Employment, 1945," RFW Papers; interviews with Leon H. Keyserling and David Delman; Bailey, *Congress Makes a Law,* pp. 61ff.

Employment Bill."

When the two days of favorable testimony ended, Wagner issued an assurance that the bill's opponents would be afforded a full hearing when Congress reassembled in the fall. Since Senator Taft had already described the measure's underlying philosophy as one "completely at variance with my whole idea of the American system," it appeared certain that conservatives intended to subject the Full Employment bill to careful scrutiny after Congress ended its recess.[26]

As Wagner pointed out in his testimony, the Full Employment bill created only a framework within which the government might develop specific employment stabilization programs. As the war neared its end the Administration and Congressional liberals unlimbered a number of concrete proposals whereby the government might contribute its part in taking up the economic slack that the postwar situation was expected to induce. One example was the Saint Lawrence Seaway project that had lain dormant since the 1930s. Senator Wagner had opposed the project then—one of the few instances in which the parochial viewpoint of his own New York City overcame what one would assume to be his natural inclination. But in 1944 the New York Senator voted for an unsuccessful authorization measure; in 1945, after President Roosevelt hinted that Bob's name on the bill might enhance its chances of passage in the new Congress, Wagner joined Senator Barkley and others as one of its cosponsors.[27]

Much more prominent than seaway plans in Wagner's mind, however, were the potentialities of further government programs in housing, a field that to Wagner still presented unmet social needs as well as a broad area for the exercise of government efforts to stimulate and stabilize the general economy. In 1943 the legislator who had pioneered the federal public housing program introduced, for purposes of study and discussion, an even more comprehensive "urban redevelopment" scheme in which the Urban Land Institute, a private research group, had interested him. During that same year Senator Taft, whose conservative conscience nonetheless had permitted him to support at least a moderate public housing program ever since his debut as a lawmaker, introduced a resolution on behalf of himself, Wagner, and Senator Allen J. Ellender of Louisiana, calling for crea-

[26] U. S. Senate, 79th Cong., 1st Sess., *Hearings Before a Subcommittee of the Senate Committee on Banking and Currency, on S.* 380 (Washington, Govt. Printing Office, 1945), *passim;* Wagner speech file, July 30, 1945, RFW Papers; 91 *Congressional Record,* 383.

[27] Files on "Saint Lawrence Seaway," RFW Papers; FDR to RFW, March 3, 14, 1944, and Jan. 22, 1945, FDR Papers.

tion of a special Senate committee to study the postwar housing problem. That resolution was not acted on, but a short time later Senator
George's postwar planning committee did establish a Subcommittee
on Housing and Urban Redevelopment composed of the measure's
three sponsors. Perhaps because he had introduced the separate resolution, or because of the generally conservative bent of George's committee, Taft was designated chairman of the subgroup.[28]

Wagner played relatively little part in the intensive investigations
and hearings that "the Taft committee" conducted during the next
year and a half in preparation for compiling its report; he was entirely
familiar with the issues and conflicting answers that emerged from the
reams of material that Taft collected. Indeed, early in 1945 the veteran New Dealer showed some impatience with his Ohio colleague.
"I don't think housing needs more investigation," Wagner declared
in a public statement. "I think it needs action."

By that time, moreover, the New York Senator already had his
staff—now headed temporarily by David Delman, following Philip
Levy's induction into the army—hard at work on a comprehensive
housing bill. The National Public Housing Conference, the Urban
Land Institute, the A. F. of L., and the C.I.O. helped particularly in
working out the details of its public housing and urban redevelopment features, while experts from other private groups and from the
government's National Housing Agency concentrated on devising
methods whereby FHA- and HOLC-type aids to private building operations might be made even more effective in meeting the housing
needs of middle- and upper-income groups. In April 1945, newspapers
reported that Wagner's Democratic colleague Senator Ellender was
ready to join him in cosponsoring a five-billion-dollar omnibus housing bill. From the Mediterranean Theater of Operations Phil Levy
sent his boss a note of congratulations: "I knew all along that you
would not stand by and let a certain gentleman from Ohio 'walk
away with the ball game.'"[29]

But Wagner knew better than to go too far and possibly alienate
the valuable support that Taft might bring to the public housing
cause. During May and June he purposely refrained from introducing
his own measure in the hope that Taft's committee might in the
meantime submit its report to Congress; moreover, to accommodate

[28] 89 *Congressional Record*, 1378, 5357; Richard O. Davies, " 'Mr. Republican' Turns 'Socialist': Robert A. Taft and Public Housing," *Ohio History* (Summer 1944), pp. 135ff.
[29] RFW Papers: files on "Housing Legislation, 1943–1945"; Wagner speech
file, Jan. 15, 1945; Philip Levy to RFW, April 24, 1945; also interviews with Leon
H. Keyserling, David Delman, and Boris Shishkin.

the Ohio senator's more moderate views, Wagner restricted the *pub-lic* housing aspect of his bill to a smaller scale than that he personally thought necessary. Nevertheless Wagner was anxious to have his measure publicized and discussed during the two months' recess that Congress had scheduled to begin on the second day of August. "In deference to your wishes, I have waited to give Senator Taft's com-mittee an opportunity to make its report," he wrote National Hous-ing Administrator John B. Blandford late in July. "However, the in-terest in this legislation is too great for me to run the risk of not getting it in before the Senate adjourns." On August 1, therefore, the New York Senator introduced the Wagner-Ellender Housing Bill of 1945.[30]

That same day Taft finally submitted the results of his study to the Senate. His recommendations regarding the augmentation of fed-eral encouragements to *private* housing closely paralleled the provi-sions of the Wagner-Ellender bill; in any event, no one anticipated that much opposition would develop around that phase of the prob-lem. But on the critical and controversial issue of federal aid to *public* housing, Taft's report disappointed his ultraconservative admirers by continuing to lend support to at least a moderate expansion of the New Deal program launched in 1937. "I do not think the most op-timistic American or the most optimistic admirer of private enter-prise could wander through the city of Washington . . . and see the kind of shacks in which people live," Taft explained, "and feel that we . . . are particularly advanced in the subject of housing." Follow-ing the presentation of his report to the Senate, Taft promised that he would study Wagner's bill during the Congressional recess; like Wag-ner, he hoped that the ironing out of minor differences might enable him to add his name as a sponsor of the measure by the time Con-gress reassembled.[31]

Naturally Senator Wagner welcomed the Republican leader's support. But to those who supposed that Taft's blessing would assure an early victory for comprehensive housing legislation, Wagner ad-dressed a warning. "Practically every interest group in the country which opposed public housing in the past," he declared at the mid-summer convention of the National Public Housing Conference, "is opposing it even more vigorously today." Wagner suspected that many of Taft's usual allies on the conservative side would desert him on the public housing issue—as many of them did—and he pointed

---

[30] RFW Papers: Wagner speech file, June 19, 1945; RFW to John B. Bland-ford, July 24, 1945; also 91 *Congressional Record*, 8235ff.

[31] 91 *Congressional Record*, 8248ff, and 92 C. R., 3510.

out that the Ohio Republican "will have to work hard to change the record of his party in Congress on public housing, just as I will have to work hard to change the record of a . . . minority of my own party." But "progress results only from struggle," the veteran legislator reminded his audience of reformers, and "it is brought about only by those who are willing to fight, and to risk themselves in combat. . . . Total unity means that a matter has ceased to be a vital public issue," he observed. "Where that has happened, my efforts are no longer needed."

That Wagner's efforts were still needed in the public housing fight seemed apparent to him as he spoke, however, for from the New York Senator's point of view that matter stood near the very center of the "burning issues" that Americans would confront in the postwar world:

> We face the issue of whether public funds shall be used to help guarantee full employment—and public housing raises this issue.
>
> We face the issue of whether subsidy shall be used to share our wealth more equitably among the people of this country—and public housing raises this issue.
>
> We face the issue of whether we shall solidify or break down the ghettos of segregation in our cities—and public housing is confronted with this issue in every step it takes. . . .
>
> We face the dramatic challenge of rebuilding America —the greatest challenge ever issued to our inventive genius, plant capacity, and physical and mental resources. Without public housing, no such rebuilding program can even commence to get started.
>
> We will be faced with a postwar challenge from overseas—from the other nations that will be building or rebuilding their cities.
>
> If we want to lead the world, the people of America cannot be left living in slums.[32]

"If we want to lead the world, the people of America cannot be left living in slums." "Full employment in America . . . is the most vital single requirement for lasting peace among all the peoples of the earth." "America cannot exert its rightful influence on world morality if our own hands are dirty with . . . signs of racial discrimination." "I firmly believe that human welfare and social security will play a far

[32] Wagner speech file, June 19, 1945, RFW Papers.

greater role in the world of the future than any mere political combination or military alignment." [33]

In phrases such as these Bob Wagner reflected the new and broader context within which American liberals conceived their domestic programs as the war years unfolded and the outlines of America's postwar responsibilities of world leadership emerged more clearly.

Pearl Harbor quickly transformed Wagner, along with most liberals and most Americans, into a confirmed believer in international collective security; soon after he returned to the Senate in December 1941 he joined in the campaign for "a new and more effective league of nations to promote and defend the security of mankind." In the months that followed he vigorously supported the steps whereby the United States took the lead in formulating plans for a permanent United Nations Organization. By the time the U.N. charter was agreed to at San Francisco in April 1945, American membership in the world organization had become a bipartisan objective. In July the Senate ratified the treaty agreement by an overwhelming vote of 89–2.[34]

Unlike some Americans and some of his Congressional colleagues, however, Wagner understood that defeat of the Axis and creation of the United Nations meant just the beginning, and not the end, of a costly, demanding, and continuing American involvement in world affairs. "America must help war-wrecked and devastated nations to get on their feet economically," the Senator declared in 1944. "We must help them get started with tools and machinery. We must help them to train skilled personnel. We must provide credit where necessary." And if civilization was ever to begin approaching a kind of world order based on the Atlantic Charter and the Four Freedoms, he warned, the United States must be willing to help promote a world economy "which seeks progressively to narrow, rather than broaden, the gap between the advanced and the retarded nations." "You won't stop the spread of Fascist and Communist ideas," Wagner predicted in 1943, "by drawing a line on the map or licking one set of dictators." [35]

In wartime pronouncements such as these Wagner realistically summarized many of the hard foreign policy lessons that Americans

[33] *Ibid.*, Oct. 10, 1944, June 19, July 30, 1945, April 12, 1946; Robert F. Wagner, "Post-War Security for All the People," *The Progressive*, Sept. 27, 1943, pp. 1ff.
[34] Wagner speech file, June 17, 1942, and files on "Foreign Affairs, 1942–1945," RFW Papers.
[35] Wagner speech file, May 25, 1942, Oct. 25, 1943, and Sept. 10, Nov. 4, 1944, RFW Papers.

would be compelled to learn as the postwar era unfolded; and some had failed to learn them long after Wagner's labors ceased. But the New York Senator contributed more than mere prescience and preachment to the processes whereby at least a beginning was made in that national learning experience. For, as chairman of the Senate's Banking and Currency Committee, he carried a vital responsibility in the handling of legislation that was designed to carry out the social aspects of America's role in postwar global politics.

In June of 1945, for example, Wagner served as legislative pilot for the Administration bill that vastly increased the capital of the Export-Import Bank, the agency that had been pressed into foreign service again as a dispenser of rehabilitation loans to the war-ravaged countries of Europe. Senator Taft's grudging approval of the measure helped ensure its passage in July, although the Republican lawmaker expressed doubt "whether we should ever again provide for continuing this policy. . . . I hope we shall not have to continue emergency relief beyond . . . twelve months." [36] Certainly the Ohio senator, and others who entertained similarly limited views of the future's demands, were in for a series of shocks!

Even more ambitious as a long-term expression of economic internationalism was the bill that Wagner cosponsored with Senator Charles Tobey in February 1945 affirming America's participation in the International Monetary Fund and World Bank for Reconstruction and Development that had been proposed at a multinational conference in Bretton Woods, New Hampshire, the previous summer. The Bretton Woods Agreements envisaged a cooperative effort toward economic rehabilitation, development, and stabilization, in the hope of reducing the kinds of economic friction that had contributed to the causes of war in previous eras. Not unexpectedly, the agreements called on the United States, the world's richest nation and the combatant least scarred by the war, to shoulder the major part of the venture's costs. But the Administration, whose Treasury Department had formulated the plan, stood steadfastly behind it. So did 90 percent of those members of the American Economics Association who responded to a poll conducted by the Economists' Committee on the Bretton Woods Program. So did Bob Wagner, who had been a delegate to the New Hampshire conference and who regarded the arrangements worked out there as a formula that would "give all the peoples of the world a chance to improve their standards of living." And so did Senator Tobey of New Hampshire, the ranking Republi-

[36] Files on "Export-Import Bank, 1945," RFW Papers; 91 *Congressional Record*, 7839, 7841.

can member of the Banking and Currency Committee, whose recent conversion from conservative isolationism to liberal internationalism was commonly credited in large part to the immense admiration and affection he held for that committee's chairman.[37]

To remaining isolationists and to economic conservatives, on the other hand, the Bretton Woods program represented an unprecedented and dangerous international experiment. The American Bankers Association described it as a plan that was "contrary to accepted credit practices," and called for its reformulation along lines that were less "unsound." Some charged that the conference had been dominated by Russia, while others found Lord Keynes's presence as one of its moving spirits particularly disturbing. The Monetary Fund and World Bank schemes, according to one conservative critic, "were merely instruments to siphon off American resources." [38]

In July 1945, after Wagner's Banking and Currency Committee concluded hearings on the controversial bill, Senator Taft indicated that he would move to postpone its consideration until the fall, so that another international conference might be summoned to revise the plan in the interim. But at the same time President Truman, preparing for his first personal encounter with the leaders of Britain and Russia at Potsdam, informed Majority Leader Barkley that "it would strengthen my hand very much in the Big Three Conference if the Bretton Woods legislation were to be enacted before the Conference were concluded." Barkley huddled with Wagner, and by the time Congress recessed on August 2 they had maneuvered the House-approved measure through the Senate, Senator Taft's objections notwithstanding. "How fitting it is," Ambassador John G. Winant wrote Wagner in a congratulatory note from London, "that you should be assisting in achieving world-wide security as a supplement to your national program of social security, in these times which have brought close to all of us the 'one world' concept." [39]

Wagner's concern for the betterment of oppressed peoples in the postwar era embraced with particular urgency the plight of the

[37] Files on "Bretton Woods Agreements, 1944–1945," RFW Papers; 91 *Congressional Record*, 987ff, 1114ff, Appendix, 741–742; Seymour E. Harris to RFW, May 3, 1945, and Wagner speech file, Aug. 10, 1944, RFW Papers; interviews with Leon H. Keyserling and David Delman.
[38] Files on "Bretton Woods Agreements, 1944–1945," RFW Papers; Robert F. Wagner, "Money's Role in Peace," *Free World* (April 1945), pp. 53–56; Samuel Crowther, "What Happened at Bretton Woods," *Economic Council Papers* (July 1945), pp. 1ff, RFW Papers.
[39] 91 *Congressional Record*, 7556ff, 7669ff, 7757ff, 7780; Harry S Truman to Alben W. Barkley, July 5, 1945, and John G. Winant to RFW, July 20, 1945, RFW Papers.

world's most oppressed minority of all, the remnant of European Jews who had managed to escape Hitler's extermination machine. In 1942 the leaders of American Zionism launched a campaign not only to lift the restrictions that Britain had imposed on Jewish immigration into Palestine but also to bring about the establishment of a free and independent Jewish commonwealth there. Convinced that homeless Jews could find a permanent refuge in no other part of the world, Wagner thereafter devoted a great deal of effort to promoting the Zionists' twin objectives. His name and voice lent prestige and effectiveness to the American Palestine Committee's drive to mobilize Christian support behind the Jews' aspirations for nationhood, while in 1944 he was instrumental in incorporating a pro-Zionist plank into the Democratic national platform. During the ensuing election campaign, moreover, Wagner's personal intercession with Franklin Roosevelt elicited from the President not only an expression of "satisfaction" with the party's platform position but an even firmer commitment on his part that "if re-elected, I shall help to bring about its realization." [40]

Pending in the Senate since early in 1944, meanwhile, was a resolution that sought to put Congress on record on the Palestine issue. Cosponsored by Wagner and Senator Taft, the measure proposed that "the United States shall use its good offices and take appropriate measures to the end that the doors of Palestine shall be opened for free entry of Jews into that country, and that there shall be free opportunity for colonization, so that the Jewish people may ultimately reconstitute Palestine as a free and democratic Jewish Commonwealth." Taft had been particularly pleased to join Wagner in cosponsoring the Palestine resolution, the Ohio Republican told an audience on one occasion, "because he and I, while we are the closest of friends, have had some difficulty in agreeing on a good many domestic policies." The two giants of the Senate were at loggerheads on many issues, but they were one in their humanitarian concern for the fate of Hitler's chief victims.[41]

Obviously the Zionist cause enjoyed a good deal of bipartisan support in America, but it also encountered serious resistance both from abroad and from sources at home. Throughout the war years

[40] Files on "Palestine, 1942–1945," RFW Papers; FDR to RFW, Oct. 13, 1944, and RFW to FDR, Oct. 14, 1944, FDR Papers. See Richard P. Stevens, *American Zionism and U. S. Foreign Policy: 1942–1947* (New York, 1962), *passim*; Samuel Halperin, *The Political World of American Zionism* (Detroit, 1961), *passim*.

[41] 90 *Congressional Record*, 963ff; also RFW Papers: files on "Palestine, 1944"; "Address by Honorable Robert A. Taft . . . March 9, 1944" (mimeographed copy).

Great Britain, fearful that Arab unrest might result in the cutting of her vital life line to the oil-rich Middle East, adhered steadfastly to the restrictive immigration policies whose end result would keep the Jews a minority in Palestine, and thus frustrate their hopes of creating a state of their own. And despite President Roosevelt's frequent public statements of sympathy with the program of the Jews, the policies followed by his Administration in practice reflected the same misgivings that motivated the British. In the spring of 1944, for example, when it appeared that Congress was ready to endorse the Wagner-Taft resolution overwhelmingly, Secretary of War Henry Stimson and Army Chief of Staff George C. Marshall urged Congressional leaders to postpone action until the military situation in the Middle East cleared. In December Stimson informed Wagner and Taft, who were anxious to move again, that military considerations should no longer control the measure's fate; nevertheless this time Secretary of State Edward R. Stettinius intervened. Once again the Senate Foreign Relations Committee deferred to executive department judgment, but with a great deal of reluctance.[42]

In a private talk with Roosevelt on the eve of his departure for Yalta, early in 1945, Wagner again urged on the President the importance of a prompt settlement of the Palestine issue. A few days later the Senator committed his thoughts to paper in a confidential letter to the Chief Executive. "If the proposal for the establishment of a Jewish State were carried through with determination and speed," Wagner suggested, "the Arabs would in the end . . . accept the accomplished fact of the existence of such a state," especially if, at the war's end, the United States in collaboration with Britain should make provision "on broad and generous lines for the political and economic future of the Arab countries." But, the Senator warned, "A long transition period would be disastrous." "You once said in speaking of the postwar world," Wagner admonished his chief in closing, "that we are now getting a second bite at the cherry. That bite must put an end once and for all to the homelessness of the Jewish people."

In July, as another President, newly installed, prepared for his first meeting as a representative of the Big Three, Wagner offered Harry Truman the same counsel regarding the festering Middle East. But the "transition period" was getting longer, and it was proving disastrous, especially for the thousands of displaced Jews released from Hitler's concentration camps, who had no place to go.[43]

[42] 91 *Congressional Record*, 12140ff; Henry L. Stimson to Robert A. Taft, Oct. 10, 1944, and RFW to FDR, Dec. 2, 1944, RFW Papers.
[43] RFW to FDR, Jan. 15, 1945, and RFW to Harry S Truman, July 3, 1945, RFW Papers.

As the war in Europe ended, then, and as the war in the Pacific was pushed to a conclusion during the summer of 1945, Bob Wagner found himself enmeshed in a wide variety of issues, partisan and bi-partisan, touching on the fundamentals of America's postwar posture both at home and abroad. The OPA, labor, and social security; full employment, the Saint Lawrence Seaway, and housing; international politics, economic assistance, and Palestine—these were only the *major* legislative matters that competed for his attention. Altogether it represented an ambitious program for an aging lawmaker who, in 1944, had seriously entertained thoughts of retiring as his current term of office neared expiration.

During the spring of that election year Wagner convinced many of his intimates that the time had come for him to step aside; on the basis of information supplied from home, Bob Wagner, Jr., believed that his father was ready to "take it easy" for a change. Following a confidential chat with President Roosevelt in June, however, the vet-eran Senator announced his availability for another term. Over an army field radio in England the younger Wagner first learned of his father's surprise decision.[44]

By now Wagner had endeared himself to the nation's liberals even more than before. Writing in the *Nation*, I. F. Stone declared that the reelection of "the United States Senate's foremost progres-sive . . . is second in importance only to the re-election of the Presi-den." In October the N.A.A.C.P. broke a thirty-five-year precedent by allowing Executive Secretary Walter White to make an avowedly political speech in Wagner's behalf. Asked whom he was supporting in the senatorial campaign, peppery Mayor Fiorello H. La Guardia gave a quick and concise reply: "Curran was a good Alderman; Wag-ner is a great United States Senator. Draw your conclusion from that." [45]

As indicated, the diminutive stature of Thomas J. Curran, Wag-ner's opponent in the 1944 contest, constituted one of the Senator's major campaign assets. A Westchester newspaper that endorsed Dewey for President nonetheless sized up the Republican senatorial candidate as "one who is personally as colorless as dishwater, and whose political record of achievement matches that dubious distinc-tion." *The New York Times*, which had deserted Wagner in 1938, returned to his support in 1944.

Curran was notable mainly because although he was an Irish

[44] RFW Papers: RFW to James A. Foley, March 4, 1944; Meyer Jacobstein to RFW, Nov. 9, 1944; Frank Bowen to RFW, Nov. 24, 1944; also interviews with Robert F. Wagner, Jr., Leon H. Keyserling, and David Delman.
[45] I. F. Stone, "Robert F. Wagner," *Nation*, Oct. 28, 1944, p. 507; Walter White to RFW, Oct. 3, 1944, RFW Papers; Warren Moscow, interview.

Catholic, he was a Republican. Having risen through the ranks of G.O.P. organization politics, he had served two terms as a member of New York City's Board of Aldermen; at the time he was nominated for the Senate he held office as Governor Thomas E. Dewey's Secretary of State. During the 1944 contest Curran emphasized the incumbent senator's alleged radicalism. "It does seem to me that two months is a long time to speak of nothing but the dangers of Communism," Wagner wrote Bob, Junior, midway through the campaign. An effort was made also to stir up Irish and Catholic sentiment on Curran's behalf. "The methods of the Ku Klux Klan were again used in this campaign," a Catholic constituent complained to Wagner when it was all over, "only this time they were used by some of the members of the Church to which I belong." In addition, Curran and his supporters tried hard to depict the Senator as "a stooge of the New Deal," who "has outlived his usefulness." [46]

For his own part, Bob Wagner found the campaign an introduction to some modern innovations in the art of political canvassing; "swoon-crooner" Frank Sinatra made records in Italian on his behalf, for example, and Wagner delivered several speeches via the experimental medium of closed-circuit television. As in days of old, Jere Mahoney managed the campaign; having acquired something of a reputation for closeness with the dollar, Mahoney made a special effort to end up with a campaign treasury surplus, and he succeeded. (At an early meeting of the campaign strategy board Jere informed the assembled Wagner intimates that he was "one of the few Democrats who ever ran for Mayor of New York without losing money." "You're also one of the few Democrats who ever lost," rejoined Minna Ruppert.) And although Mahoney's strict accounting methods irked some campaign workers, his prediction of the election's outcome proved accurate. Wagner's victory margin over Curran almost equaled his 1938 showing; moreover, the Senator's plurality amounted to nearly 80,000 votes more than Roosevelt's plurality over Thomas E. Dewey in the presidential contest in the Empire State.[47]

Contrary to the fears of his family and close associates, the re-

[46] Undated editorial (1944) from an unidentified Westchester County newspaper, RFW Papers; *New York Times*, Oct. 31, 1944; also RFW Papers: RFW to Robert F. Wagner, Jr., Sept. 6, 1944; Thomas H. Dowd to RFW, Nov. 9, 1944; Jeremiah T. Mahoney to John S. Young, Nov. 2, 1944; Samuel Cohen to RFW, Nov. 3, 1944; clippings from the New York *Herald Tribune*, Oct. 19, 20, 1944, and New York *World-Telegram*, Oct. 24, 28, 1944; files on "1944 Campaign."

[47] Lillie Shultz to William Rosenblatt, Oct. 31, 1944, and files on "1944 Campaign," RFW Papers; interviews with Leon H. Keyserling, Minna L. Ruppert, David Delman, Theodore Granik, and Jeremiah T. Mahoney; *New York Times*, Oct. 3, Nov. 8, 1944.

election ordeal actually invigorated the Senator. "I think I surprised all my friends and myself in this campaign," Wagner informed his physician a short time after the election. And in a congratulatory note written a few days later the vice-chairman of the Democratic National Committee, who had campaigned in upstate New York with the Senator during the latter part of October, commented that "It was certainly good to see your reaction to the crowds, and how it buoyed you up." [48]

Wagner's political rejuvenation exorcized his "aches and pains," at least temporarily, and, as we have seen, during the first half of 1945 he was engaged in a legislative program that would have taxed the energies of a man thirty years his junior. Nonetheless, by August he was looking forward eagerly to the two months' rest that the impending Congressional recess was supposed to bring, for as he told a friend late in July, "we are a tired bunch." "Sometimes I believe that I am being asked to do more than should be expected of a fellow of my age," Wagner complained to James A. Foley at about the same time. "But it is hard to slow down," he added characteristically, "when there is so much to be done." [49]

[48] RFW to Dr. Harry M. Kaufman, Nov. 10, 1944, and Oscar R. Ewing to RFW, Nov. 16, 1944, RFW Papers.
[49] RFW to John F. Carew, July 20, 1945, and RFW to James A. Foley, Sept. 7, 1945, RFW Papers.

CHAPTER 17

The Trend and the Tide
Were Against Us

ON AUGUST 6 AND August 9, 1945, American planes dropped atomic bombs on the Japanese cities of Hiroshima and Nagasaki; on August 14 Japan surrendered. The Second World War was over—much sooner than anyone expected.

During the week in which victory became imminent President Harry S Truman requested that committees of Congress working on basic reconversion legislation return to Washington as quickly as possible to prepare their recommendations for submission to the full Congress when it reconvened in September. The two months' vacation that Bob Wagner had anticipated in July was abruptly cut short. On August 21 his Banking and Currency Committee reassembled—the first to respond to the President's request, Wagner boasted—and resumed hearings on what the Senator called "the Number One legislative proposal before the United States Congress," the Full Employment bill. "No longer can we use the term 'postwar' with reference to the future," Wagner declared in his opening statement. "For this is it: the beginning of the postwar era."

Wagner embarked on that era full of ambition and confidence: "We must carry forward between 1946 and 1950 a . . . program which is as bold and advanced, for these times, as Roosevelt's . . . program between 1933 and 1937 was for his time." "Anyone who guesses that the people have turned reactionary," he added, "or that they are less liberal than they were ten years ago, is in for a big surprise." With all the energy at his command Wagner threw himself into the renewed fight for the Full Employment bill, health and social security legislation, housing, civil rights, and measures designed to meet the new political and economic responsibilities that the postwar situation thrust on the United States. "Now we can commence in earnest to build the America of the future," the Senator exulted "—an America that will be first in peace as we have been first in war—an America of ever-increasing social and economic progress—an America of universal tolerance and good will toward every race, creed, and color and toward all our fellow men." [1]

In the year and a half that followed, America did meet successfully the challenges posed by her new importance in the international arena, even when the emergence of a cold war with totalitarian communism inflated those challenges beyond anything that had been imagined when the hot war against fascism ended.

But in the realm of domestic affairs the record of accomplishment of the Seventy-ninth Congress fell far short of what such liberals as Wagner had aimed for. Impatient with wartime restrictions, and eager to lavish on individual wants the pent-up purchasing power that wartime prosperity had amassed, the general public was apathetic to calls for bold new programs of social action. Bereft of Franklin Roosevelt's leadership, moreover, liberals seemed enveloped by an air of defeatism that even Wagner was gradually, though regretfully, compelled to acknowledge. The real inclinations of Roosevelt's successor in the White House remained something of an enigma during his first year in office, and even when Truman aligned himself with his party's progressive wing, he seemed unable to generate the enthusiasm or display the political effectiveness that fact and legend attributed to F.D.R.

The result, then, was a condition of legislative stalemate as far as domestic programs were concerned during late 1945 and throughout the following year. And when in the fall of 1946 the electorate resolved the stalemate at the polls, it did so in a way that severely disappointed the hopes of the nation's decimated liberals. "The whole country will breathe more easily if over the Republican caucus room were inscribed the words: 'Don't Turn Back the Clock,'" Senator Wagner declared when the election returns gave the G.O.P. control of the national legislature for the first time in a generation.[2]

By then the veteran New Dealer was too old and too ill to put up much of a fight as, during 1947, the Eightieth Congress did attempt

---

[1] Wagner speech file, Feb. 17, Aug. 21, 1945, and April 12, 1946, RFW Papers.
[2] *Ibid.*, Dec. 30, 1946.

to turn back the clock, at least a little bit. But as the forces of modern liberalism lost the services of one of their pioneers, he left with them a message of hope and encouragement whose wisdom would be borne out in the years ahead. "From the depths of my experience of more than forty years of public service," Wagner wrote David Dubinsky in the summer of 1947, "I have learned that the path of progress is not unbroken, that setbacks are only that, and that they must be used as stepping stones for further advances. The fight for freedom is never won and never lost," the Senator added. "But history is on our side." [3]

In the field of postwar foreign policy Bob Wagner generally continued to follow where the President led, as between 1945 and 1947 the Truman Administration gradually evolved the far-reaching and often novel international policies that constituted the more successful side of its early record. In December of 1945, for example, Wagner's vote helped beat back the drive led by Burton K. Wheeler and other neo-isolationists that would have required the President to seek specific Congressional authorization before committing American troops to the implementation of United Nations directives—a requirement that might have had dire consequences when, in 1950, the Korean War broke out. Nor did Wagner pay any heed to those constituents of his who, disturbed by reports that the U.N. was to be housed in the United States, insisted that the world organization was "doomed to failure," compared it to the "Trojan Horse," or demanded that its headquarters should be located "on some island in the middle of the ocean." Instead, in 1947, with his Republican colleague Irving Ives, Wagner cosponsored the Congressional resolution that effectuated the location of the United Nations in New York City. [4]

As chairman of the Senate Banking and Currency Committee, moreover, Wagner continued to help guide through Congress legislation whereby the Administration sought to keep up with the requests for loans and assistance that streamed in from war-devastated countries abroad. As the cost of foreign aid mounted, fiscal conservatives stepped up their attack on Harry Truman's "international W.P.A." A seemingly gigantic loan of nearly three billion dollars to Great Britain provided an especially important test in the spring of 1946. After Wagner's committee reported the bill favorably, Administration

[3] RFW to David Dubinsky, June 26, 1947, RFW Papers.
[4] 91 *Congressional Record*, 11586, and 93 *C. R.*, 8205–8206; also RFW Papers: files on "United Nations Organization, 1945–1947"; Thomas H. Williams to RFW, Feb. 12, 1946.

forces had to repulse a series of crippling amendments proposed by Senators Taft, Knowland, Capehart and others, which would have reduced the size of the loan considerably, restricted its use to purchases of American-made goods, or killed the project altogether. In the end, with the assistance of Republican internationalists such as Senators Arthur Vandenburg of Michigan and Charles Tobey, the measure went through. "American welfare can rest only upon appreciating the problems of other nations, and helping them to surmount their immediate difficulties," Wagner insisted throughout the course of such debates. "Those who are strong can best afford to be generous." [5]

It was not unusual that the New York Senator should defend postwar collective security arrangements and liberal rehabilitation expenditures against the attacks of isolationists and conservatives: while Franklin Roosevelt lived, Wagner had already indicated his full concurrence in the steps whereby the wartime President pointed American policy in those directions. But surprising in some circles was the loyalty to presidential leadership that Wagner continued to demonstrate as, during 1946, Truman's early suspicions of Russia's postwar motives materialized into a decidedly "tough" stance against Communist encroachments in Europe and elsewhere. What surprise existed was based on misapprehension, however, for despite Wagner's advanced liberalism, and despite the charges of "radicalism" leveled against him by opponents at election time, the Senator had never succumbed to the "common front" blandishments of the Communists during the war against the Axis. "The story of Bob Wagner . . . is the story of a man who has done more to protect our country from communism than any other member of Congress," a speaker on Wagner's behalf declared during his 1944 campaign for reelection, and the Senator would readily agree that thwarting the totalitarianism of the left, as well as that of the right, *was* one objective of his liberal reform efforts. "Where liberty is banished, social justice cannot abide," he declared on one occasion. "No, my friends, we cannot choose between them, for human liberty and social justice are one and inseparable." [6]

As postwar developments unfolded, Wagner became convinced that Communist expansionism had replaced Fascist ambition as the

---

[5] 92 *Congressional Record*, 4697ff, 4785ff, 4814ff, 4839ff, 4898ff; Wagner speech file, April 12, 1946, RFW Papers.

[6] RFW Papers: "Address by Samuel J. Foley . . . November 4, 1944" (mimeographed copy); Wagner speech file, April 17, 1947. On the development of postwar foreign policy see John Spanier, *American Foreign Policy Since World War II* (New York, 1965), *passim*; Harry S Truman, *Memoirs*, 2 vols. (Garden City, New York, 1955, 1956), *passim*.

great menace to both liberty and justice in the world; with the lessons of the 1930s in mind, he was prepared to support the vigorous and expensive moves whereby the Truman Administration sought to stem the new totalitarian tide. During 1946 it became evident, for example, that the foreign-aid bills Wagner helped steer through Congress were aimed not only at liquidating the effects of the war against the Axis but also at shoring up weakened economies and social systems abroad against Communist subversion. "There are those overseas who have lost faith in the democratic system, who believe that some form of totalitarian regime is necessary to solve the problems of the twentieth century," the Senator told a New York City audience in May 1946. He conceded that any nation had the right to choose its own form of government. "But at the same time," Wagner continued, "I believe that these totalitarian systems set up a competition in the world of ideas"—a competition of ideologies that might conceivably eventuate in a competition of arms. "There is one defense, and only one, against the atomic bomb," he admonished, "and that is a contented world. America has the responsibility to lead in achieving that contentment." [7]

By March 1947 Wagner was ready to support military as well as economic aid to Greece and Turkey on the ground that, as President Truman expressed it, "it must be the policy of the United States to support peoples who are resisting attempted subjugation by armed minorities or by outside pressures." Later in the summer this "Truman Doctrine" was followed up by the even more ambitious and expensive Marshall Plan of large-scale rehabilitation aid to all the countries of Europe. To anti-Communist but fiscally conservative constituents who complained about the cost of the Administration's newest "containment" proposal, Wagner returned a standard reply. "During the war we spent about two billion dollars a week to destroy people," he observed, "and it seems to me that we certainly can afford to spend five billion to ten billion dollars a year in rehabilitating people and thus help them to fight against the very danger with which you, yourself, are so concerned." [8]

With critics on the left, who were prone to blame Truman rather than the Communists for starting the cold war, Wagner was equally firm, even though many among them had been his allies in the fight for domestic reform. In 1947 Henry A. Wallace announced his inten-

[7] Wagner speech file, April 12, May 17, 1946, RFW Papers.
[8] 93 *Congressional Record*, 1980; also RFW Papers: Wagner speech file, March 12, 1947; files on "International Affairs, 1946–1947"; RFW to William B. Tanner, Nov. 5, 1947.

tion of forming a new Progressive party that would allegedly restore the Rooseveltian spirit of international friendship and good will to the nation's foreign policy. While some New Dealers rallied to the former Vice-President's cause, while many others wavered in doubt, a quick and decisive reaction was voiced by the man who had been the New Deal's chief legislative pilot. "Henry Wallace's silence on the Soviets' aggressions, their vetoes, their falsehoods, and their repression of even minimal civil rights is deafening," Wagner declared in a public statement. Resenting his erstwhile comrade's invocation of Franklin Roosevelt's name on behalf of the disruptive third-party movement, the New York Senator concluded by adding: "Yes, the angels are weeping and there is a great man and a good friend of Henry Wallace who, I am sure, weeps with them." [9]

"Across the seas has arisen a challenge to all the values that we treasure most—the challenge of opportunists who rose from the chaos of governments which did *too little,* and in their despotism established governments which do far *too much.* We in the twentieth century here in America can avoid the onslaught of governments which do *too much* only by developing a government which does *enough.*"

Wagner spoke those words in 1940 while analyzing the causes of democratic failure in Europe that had made way for the Hitlers and Mussolinis. But in the context of the new totalitarian threat that the United States faced in the postwar era, he remained thoroughly wedded to that principle. For while he willingly supported measures that afforded military and economic assistance "to help those in need of help to resist aggression," he repeated again and again that such steps were not enough. "We in America can make ourselves safe . . . only by making the American system work better than any other system on the face of the earth." Only by making herself a model of the sufficiency of democratic methods in affording employment opportunity, social progress, and racial justice at home, the Senator insisted, could the United States successfully weather the competition of totalitarian orders in the world at large. For, given the new polarization of power between America and Russia that the Second World War had brought about, now more than ever before, Wagner warned, "The eyes of the world are upon us." [10]

In the realm of strengthening the American democratic welfare state at home, however, Bob Wagner and his fellow liberals seemed to meet only defeat and stalemate in the immediate postwar years.

[9] Wagner speech file, Dec. 29, 1947, RFW Papers.
[10] *Ibid.,* Oct. 23, 1940, May 17, 1946, July 27, 1947.

True enough, within six months of Wagner's resummoning his Banking and Currency Committee after V-J Day the Seventy-ninth Congress did provide the framework for Executive-Congressional planning of the kind of vigorous peacetime mobilization that liberals envisioned: in February it passed the Employment Act of 1946. During the course of its enactment, however, more than just the title of what had originated as the *Full* Employment bill of 1945 underwent revision. By the time the Senate voted on the measure early in October 1945 enough of its key words had been qualified and modified so that even Senator Taft could say "aye" when his name was called; it passed 71–10. In the House, moreover, virtually an entire new bill was substituted for the Senate version. The House measure spoke rather innocuously of maintaining "a high level of employment"; it was lavishly studded, too, with expressions of devotion to "the American system of free competitive enterprise," to "sound fiscal policies," and to "avoiding competition of government with private business enterprise." [11]

Soon after conference committee sessions on the divergent versions began, illness forced Wagner to absent himself from the Senate again. Alben Barkley took over as head of the more liberally inclined conferees, although in a hospital room in New York City Wagner affixed his signature to the conference report that finally resulted. In the compromise measure that the President signed into law the federal government undertook to *promote maximum* employment, rather than to *assure full* employment, as the original bill proposed. Consequently terms suggestive of a "right to work"—which had involved Wagner and Taft in seemingly endless semantic difficulties on the floor of the Senate earlier— no longer appeared in the bill. Nor did there remain any mention of "federal investment" as a means for achieving the government's goal; instead, reference was made to the devotion of its "functions and resources . . . consistent with . . . other essential considerations of national policy" to the pursuit of its now modified objective.

There were changes, too, in the planning procedures envisioned in the original bill. Gone was the concept of a presidentially constructed National Production and Employment Budget; instead, the Chief Executive was called on merely to submit an annual economic report to Congress. A notably constructive change was the creation of

[11] 91 *Congressional Record*, 8916ff, 8954ff, 12094ff, and 92 *C. R.*, 975ff, 1134ff; file on "Full Employment, 1945–1946," RFW Papers; Stephen Kemp Bailey, *Congress Makes a Law: The Story Behind the Employment Act of 1946* (New York, 1950), pp. 99ff.

a three-member Council of Economic Advisers who, in place of the Cabinet, were to be specially charged with keeping the President informed on the state of the nation's economy. About the only mechanism of the original bill that survived intact in the final Act was the establishment of a special Congressional Joint Committee on the Economic Report.

A few die-hard conservatives in Congress still viewed the watered-down Employment Act of 1946 as the entering wedge of socialism or worse; a few idealistic liberals denounced the compromise bill as a "fraud." But Senator Taft, speaking for most conservatives, was satisfied that the measure's most "dangerous" features and its "Keynesian" overtones had been removed. Barkley, Wagner, and other realistic liberals, on the other hand, interpreting the Act's hair-splitting verbiage quite differently, accepted it as an adequate if abbreviated official endorsement of progressive principles.[12]

In retrospect the Employment Act passed by the Seventy-ninth Congress has come to be looked on as a significant milestone in the assumption of economic planning and stabilization responsibilities by the federal government; so it would appear that Wagner and the liberals who portrayed the measure as a triumph in 1946 gave a more accurate evaluation of it than did their conservative contemporaries. Moreover, the fight for the Act represented one of the few causes around which the nation's liberal and labor forces rallied in the postwar years with some semblance of early New Deal enthusiasm; it was also one of the few instances that afforded them the savor of at least partial victory. In achieving it, their spokesmen again acknowledged the value of Wagner's leadership. "It seems natural for you to be heading the fight for full employment now," the veteran social reformer Helen Hull wrote in a letter to the New York Senator shortly after the battle began, "as you did for unemployment relief, employment services, and public works fifteen years ago when so few were awake to the need." And although the employment bill eventually acquired eight senatorial sponsors, the endorsement of President Truman, and the support of an imposing phalanx of labor and liberal organizations, Paul Sifton, director of the Union for Democratic Action's extensive propaganda campaign on behalf of the measure, still maintained that Wagner's work for S. 380 constituted the most important single factor in pushing it through the Senate.[13]

---

[12] 92 *Congressional Record*, 975ff, 1134ff; interviews with Leon H. Keyserling and David Delman.

[13] Helen Hall to RFW, Aug. 1, 1945, RFW Papers; Bailey, *Congress Makes a Law*, p. 101.

In any event, whether the Employment Act represented a substantial victory for liberal objectives or a compromise of them, and whether or not Bob Wagner deserved the accolade bestowed on him by the field commander of the U.D.A., the measure was the last important one bearing the New York Senator's name that attained the status of law during the remainder of his public career. Wagner would be the first to admit that the Employment Act represented "a minimum rather than a maximum program for our postwar well-being." [14] Yet the skeleton was all that the Seventy-ninth Congress was willing to provide. The high-riding coalition of conservative Republicans and Democrats proved able to throttle just about every other substantive domestic proposal sponsored by Wagner, or, for that matter, any other liberal member of Congress.

In September of 1945, for example, the Senate took up the bill recommended by President Truman and sponsored by Wagner and five other liberals that would have created a temporary system of supplementary federal unemployment compensation benefits for displaced war-plant workers. But Senator George and his conservative colleagues on the Finance Committee reported it out in such an emasculated form that Wagner accused them of following the principle of "billions for defense, but only a few cents for tribute to those who made victory possible." A Barkley amendment aimed at salvaging parts of the original bill was beaten decisively by a 51–29 vote, and other liberalizing amendments went down to defeat. Senator Wagner became so disgusted with the proceedings that he declined even to call up for consideration the amendments he had prepared in consultation with Administration officials.

As finally passed by the Senate, the George substitute bill did at least create a federal revolving fund designed to enable the states to continue paying benefits to jobless Americans for a longer period of time than most state laws provided. But when it reached the House of Representatives the Administration's "emergency" measure received no consideration whatever, and it died in committee. The United States had won the war under a unified command centralized in Washington, but its civilian workers were compelled to readjust to peacetime conditions under forty-eight varying systems of unemployment insurance.[15]

Since Congress refused to sanction even a two-year *temporary* fed-

[14] Robert F. Wagner, "The Meaning of 'The Right to Work,' " *New York Times Magazine*, Sept. 23, 1945, p. 8.

[15] 91 *Congressional Record*, 8668ff, 8729ff, 8735ff, 8804ff, 9114; files on "Reconversion Legislation, 1945," RFW Papers.

eralizing of unemployment benefits, it most assuredly was in no mood
to approve *permanent* federalizing of unemployment insurance, or of
the United States Employment Service, as proposed in the omnibus
Wagner-Murray-Dingell bills of 1943 and May 1945. Separate bills
designed to accomplish these purposes, introduced by Wagner and
other Congressional liberals, remained buried in committee pigeonholes during the whole of the period under consideration. Distinct
measures embodying other parts of the W-M-D bill's comprehensive
overhauling of the Social Security system—affecting coverage, amount
of benefits, and the introduction of temporary and permanent disability benefits, for example—met a similar fate. Nor did the measure that emerged in November of 1945 as *the* Wagner-Murray-Dingell bill of the postwar era—a newly introduced proposal embodying
only the health provisions of the earlier versions—fare much better.[16]

In White House conversations during September 1945 Senators
Wagner and Murray secured President Truman's specific endorsement of the health aspects of their original comprehensive program.
On November 19 the President recommended enactment of their
plan in a special message to Congress; later in the day the two liberal
lawmakers introduced a new bill embracing compulsory national
health insurance under the Social Security system, additional federal
grants-in-aid to state public health and child-care programs, and augmented federal subsidization of medical research and education. Con-
spicuously lacking in the bill were any provisions for financing the
additional outlays it called for, either by increased payroll levies or
general taxes. That omission was purposely contrived, however, in
order to circumvent the Senate Finance Committee, where, under
Senator George's skeptical eye, the previous two W-M-D bills had
lain dormant since 1943. This time the authors secured referral to the
Senate's Education and Labor Committee, where Senator Murray
himself presided as chairman.[17]

During 1946, therefore, the Wagner-Murray-Dingell Health bill
at least attained the dignity of being afforded public hearings. Again
representatives of labor and liberal groups, organized now into a
Committee for the Nation's Health, and doctors who had declared
independence of the American Medical Association, organized into a
Physicians' Forum, testified on the measure's behalf. Nevertheless,
they were unable to overcome the powerful defensive fight waged by

[16] Files on "Social Security Legislation, 1945–1946" and "United States Employment Service, 1945–1946," RFW Papers.
[17] RFW Papers: Files on "Wagner-Murray-Dingell Bill, 1945"; David Delman to Will Maslow, Sept. 4, 1945; also 91 *Congressional Record*, 10789ff,
10817ff; David Delman, interview.

the A.M.A. and conservatives in general. The A.M.A. *Journal* portrayed the W-M-D bill as "the attempt to enslave medicine as first among the professions, industries, and trades to be socialized," and it described the Physicians' Forum as an organization of doctors "mostly inclined toward communism." Local medical societies again levied special assessments on doctors for support of a costly propaganda campaign, as full-page newspaper advertisements (in French, in Lowell, Massachusetts) urged citizens to sign petitions against the health bill "at your nearest drugstore." A Surgical-Medical Supply Committee composed of representatives of pharmaceutical and drug-chain companies helped pay the printing bill for the petitions and for the tons of other literature that was circulated against the dangerous and "socialistic" measure sponsored by an "alien" lawmaker who, it was falsely alleged, "didn't even speak English until he was more than 12." [18]

The campaign of obstruction proved too much for even Senator Murray's liberal-oriented Committee on Education and Labor to cope with; this time, unlike in 1939, Murray was unable to issue even a *preliminary* favorable report on the national health bill by the time the Seventy-ninth Congress expired in mid-1946. Yet even so, the agitation created by Senator Wagner's health proposals since the late 1930s produced indirect effects conducive to wider distribution of better health care to the American people. In 1946, for example, Congress passed the Hill-Burton Act extending federal grants-in-aid to state-administered hospital construction programs—a measure that traced its origin back to the Wagner Health bill of 1939. Senator Taft actively supported the 1946 version, and while it matched neither the size nor degree of federal supervision that senators like Wagner and Murray desired—providing another reflection of the new grounds of conservative-liberal difference in the postwar era—they voted for it since they foresaw no hope of securing a more satisfactory program. [19]

During 1946, moreover, Senator Taft introduced a health bill of his own as an alternative to the Wagner-Murray-Dingell health insurance proposal; under its terms federal grants-in-aid would be extended to the states so that they might provide free medical care to indigent citizens who could demonstrate no other means of securing it. Senator

[18] Files on "Wagner-Murray-Dingell Bill, 1945–1946," RFW Papers; 91 *Congressional Record*, 10828; also RFW Papers: RFW to Dr. Morris Fishbein, June 16, 1945; clippings from *L'Etoile* (Lowell, Mass.), Jan. 31, 1946, and the Charlotte (S.C.) *Observer*, May 26, 1946; also James G. Burrow, *AMA: Voice of American Medicine* (Baltimore, 1963), pp. 294ff.

[19] 91 *Congressional Record*, 10569–70, 11710ff, 11734ff, 11779ff, and 92 C. R., 10482ff, 10522–23.

Wagner considered Taft's proposition a degrading form of "government handout" at variance with social insurance principles. Nevertheless, Taft's measure constituted the forerunner of the Kerr-Mills bill enacted more than a decade later during the Eisenhower Administration.

Finally, it might be noted that since 1939, and at least partly in response to the federal programs advocated by Bob Wagner, the A.M.A. itself had become a proponent of private group medical care and hospitalization plans, which enjoyed rapid growth during the war and postwar years. Indeed, by 1946 the physicians' lobby was portraying Blue Cross- and Blue Shield-type programs as adequate paths toward ensuring sufficient health care for the whole population. All of which prompted Wagner to recall that in 1932, when President Hoover's Committee on the Costs of Medical Care recommended expansion of such *voluntary* health insurance plans, the A.M.A. *Journal* had shrilly condemned the committee's report as "socialism and communism—inciting to revolution." [20]

The Hill-Burton Hospital Act, the moderate enlightenment of Senator Taft and the A.M.A., all this seemed to the good as Wagner contemplated his decade-long interest in national health programs in 1946. But as for the comprehensive approach embodied in the Wagner-Murray-Dingell bill, that would have to wait. "I am rather pessimistic about our chances . . . during this session of Congress," Wagner confessed to a constituent and to himself in the summer of 1946. He assessed the situation correctly, for the public, and therefore the Congress, were not ready for social security health insurance yet.[21]

In one other field, at least—housing—Wagner had reason to believe that the American people *were* ready for action. For while the general aura of inflated postwar prosperity might distract popular attention from the troubles of displaced war workers whose unemployment benefits ran out, and from long-range programs of social security improvement and health insurance, there seemed to be plenty of evidence of popular agitation over the housing shortage, which wartime and postwar conditions made only more acute for people in all income brackets. Moreover, following lengthy negotiations with Senator Taft during the fall of 1945, Wagner won the Ohio Republican's agreement to cosponsor what had been introduced in August as the Wagner-

[20] 92 *Congressional Record*, 4389ff, 9705; William S. White, *The Taft Story* (New York, 1954), pp. 48ff; manuscript of article by Robert F. Wagner, "Health Insurance for the American People" (1946), RFW Papers; Burrow, *AMA*, pp. 228ff; RFW to Dr. Morris Fishbein, June 16, 1945, RFW Papers.
[21] RFW to John J. Connery, July 1, 1946, RFW Papers.

Ellender Housing bill. During the winter a Housing Legislation Information Service that Wagner initiated mobilized the propaganda efforts of the labor, liberal, and veterans' groups who endorsed the measure while, under Senator Barkley's direction during Wagner's illness, the Senate Banking and Currency Committee concluded public hearings on it. On April 11, 1946, Wagner, back in harness, opened Senate debate on the housing bill. Four days later the upper chamber voiced its overwhelming approval of the "bipartisan" Wagner-Ellender-Taft bill without even the formality of a roll call. All seemed to be going well.[22]

In the House of Representatives, however, the groups opposed to the measure—the Home Building Industry Committee, the National Association of Real Estate Boards, the National Association of Home Builders, and the United States Chamber of Commerce among others —had many more friends. All these organizations approved the numerous aids to the *private* housing industry that the W-E-T bill included, but they were even willing to forego them in order to kill the moderate *public* housing feature of the bill. Not even Robert Taft's explanation of the need for such a program for the lowest-income groups produced much effect in ultraconservative circles. Instead, in one issue of its newsletter the National Association of Real Estate Boards came to the startling conclusion that Taft "does not any longer believe in the American private enterprise system. He is at heart a socialist"! Bob Wagner's warning to overoptimistic liberals in 1945 proved accurate.[23]

Nor was Wagner entirely satisfied, apparently, with the support afforded the W-E-T bill by his own Democratic Administration. In a September 1945 message to Congress President Truman endorsed the principles embodied in Wagner's comprehensive bill, but soon thereafter he awarded top priority to a far more modest measure known as the Veterans' Emergency Housing bill. After a protracted fight Congress finally passed the emergency measure in May 1946: its main features liberalized FHA terms for veterans, sought to stimulate production of building materials and prefabricated houses through various systems of government subsidy, and empowered a Federal Housing Expeditor to control and allocate the nation's scarce supply of construction materials. All programs and powers authorized in the

[22] Files on "Housing Legislation, 1945–1946," RFW Papers; 91 *Congressional Record*, 10642ff, and 92 *C. R.*, 3488ff, 3685ff; Richard O. Davies, *Housing Reform During the Truman Administration* (Columbia, Mo., 1966), *passim*.

[23] Files on "Housing Legislation, 1945–1946," RFW Papers; Richard O. Davies, "'Mr. Republican' Turns 'Socialist,'" *Ohio History* (Summer 1964), p. 140.

Act were due to expire automatically at the end of 1947.[24]

Wagner supported the Veterans' Housing Act willingly enough, but at the same time the preference assigned it by the Administration held up action on his own bill. Moreover, after the Administration's emergency measure passed, conservatives cited *it* as an additional reason why the W-E-T bill was not needed. In extempore remarks at a liberal rally in the middle of June 1946 the New York Senator frankly aired his belief that it had been "a profound mistake" to "sidetrack" the W-E-T bill in favor of the other measure. "I insist that, from any broad vision, America's main housing problem is not to get lumber or nails," the Senator declared, "but whether we shall get good houses that the mass of our people can afford—whether we recognize the national obligation in housing—this is the *real problem*." "It is a problem to which some extend only lip service," he went on. "Some people in high places have regarded the Wagner-Ellender-Taft Bill as something to be given a polite nod of approval." But because the W-E-T bill faced forthrightly the central issues of the postwar era—full employment, economic planning, social and racial justice—"it is up against a fight that cannot be won by soft speaking or by oblique approaches," Wagner maintained. "This fight can only be won by frontal attack: I call upon the President to put this bill on his must list." [25]

How much of the Senator's wrath was aimed directly at Truman, and how much was reserved for National Housing Agency officials drawn from private industry who instinctively subordinated public housing to private housing programs, is problematical. But in any event, never before, despite similar provocations during the New Deal years, had Wagner publicly and so vehemently criticized the leaders of his own party's Administration. Apparently the sense of personal loyalty that bound him so closely to Franklin Roosevelt, and muted his frustration with the New Deal's leader, was not duplicated in his relations with Roosevelt's successor.

At the time Wagner unburdened himself the House of Representatives was finally moving toward consideration of the Wagner-Ellender-Taft bill. On June 28, 1946, as congressmen strained to leave Washington and head home for the elections that loomed in November, the conservative-dominated House Banking and Currency Committee belatedly opened its hearings on the controversial bill, and a remarkable scene ensued. Wagner was the first to testify, and the

---

[24] 92 *Congressional Record*, 2508ff, 4750ff, 4912ff, 4934ff; Davies, *Housing Reform During the Truman Administration, passim.*

[25] Wagner speech file, March 15, April 29, June 17, 1946, RFW Papers.

congressmen listened respectfully enough to "the dean of Senate liberals." But a few minutes after Senator Taft replaced Wagner in the witness chair, a Republican member of the committee raised the point of order that the hearings could not proceed because the House was in session. Supporters of the W-E-T bill protested invocation of that antiquated and seldom-used rule, but the Republican-Southern Democrat majority of the committee insisted that it be upheld. Taft fumed, and later in private he upbraided House Minority Leader Joseph Martin for the humiliation he'd been subjected to, but to no avail. The following day the hearings were disrupted again when conservatives persisted in raising other outdated points of order. It soon became evident that, through such dilatory tactics, they were determined to drag out the hearings interminably.[26]

More was damaged in the process than Senator Taft's ego, however, for the opponents of the Wagner-Ellender-Taft bill succeeded in waging what amounted to a filibuster against committee consideration of the measure. The Seventy-ninth Congress ended about a month later, and with that, at least temporarily, the housing bill was dead.

If the House of Representatives proved more often than not to be the graveyard of progressive social and economic legislation in the postwar years, the Senate served as the final resting place of another liberal cause. "If we in America cannot solve our minority problems by uniting all our people into one harmonious commonweal," Bob Wagner declared in 1944, "what hope or prospect is there for the future of the world—a whole world of minorities?" [27] With that added imperative stimulating their efforts, Wagner and his allies sought during the war and postwar period to further the campaign for racial justice that they had launched in the New Deal era. Three times, in 1942, 1944, and 1946, they succeeded in getting an antipoll-tax bill through the House. But each time the measure reached the Senate, Southerners filibustered against it; each time, when liberals tried to force a vote by invoking cloture, they failed.

Another focal point of civil rights strife was the Fair Employment Practices Commission that had been established in 1941 by executive order. In 1945, when fiscal conservatives started putting the ax to all sorts of wartime emergency agencies, the Southern bloc capital-

---

[26] *Ibid.*, June 28, 1946; Lowell Mellett, "On the Other Hand," column clipped from an undated, unidentified newspaper (June 1946), RFW Papers; National Public Housing Conference, Inc., *Public Housing* (Aug. 1946), pp. 1ff; Davies, *Housing Reform During the Truman Administration*, pp. 47–49.

[27] Wagner speech file, May 3, 1944, RFW Papers.

ized on its opportunity to get rid of the racial-justice commission. By the terms of the appropriation bill passed that year, the FEPC was directed to close its doors at the end of fiscal 1945.

In the meantime Senator Wagner had added his name to that of other liberals as cosponsor of a bill that would put the FEPC on a statutory basis and make it permanent; together with Senator Arthur Capper of Kansas, moreover, Wagner also served as Honorary Co-Chairman of the National Council for a Permanent FEPC formed by A. Philip Randolph and other Negro leaders to push the civil rights cause. In January 1946, through the alertness of Senator Denis Chavez of New Mexico, the FEPC bill was called up for floor consideration in a parliamentary maneuver that caught Southern watchdogs offguard. Nevertheless, they recovered quickly, and during the ensuing month the Senate's business was disrupted by another filibuster. In his hospital bed in New York City Bob Wagner signed the cloture petition brought up to him from Washington; but when the vote to end debate was taken in February, the liberals again went down to defeat.[28]

On June 30, 1946, therefore, the FEPC went out of business. This time Congressional conservatives not only blocked further liberal advance but they also forced reversal of one of the few forward steps that progressives had managed to take during the years since the New Deal had been interred.

Reaction scored victories in fields other than civil rights during the Seventy-ninth Congress; for example, it thoroughly dashed the hopes of those who wished that semblances of wartime economic controls might be continued long enough to permit an orderly reconversion to a peacetime basis without unleashing devastating inflationary pressures. With V-J Day, popular demands for a release from wartime restrictions set the stage for the success of those conservative lawmakers who were determined to foil the "economic planners" and to restore the "free economy" at the earliest possible moment.

In May 1946, after months of haggling, the House of Representatives finally passed an OPA extension bill that in Senator Wagner's words amounted "virtually to repeal of price control." But when the bill reached the Senate this time Wagner was unable to control even his own Banking and Currency Committee. On June 7 he submitted a *minority* report for himself and three other committee members calling for a simple one-year extension of the OPA beyond its current expiration date of June 30; the gradual removal of controls and price regulations was left up to the OPA's discretion.

[28] Files on "Fair Employment Practices Commission, 1945–1946," RFW Papers; 92 *Congressional Record*, 81ff, 1219–20; David Delman, interview.

The committee's majority report, presented by Alben Barkley, preserved more of the OPA's powers than the House bill allowed, yet it made many concessions to the demands of Senator Taft and other conservatives: livestock, poultry, and milk products were singled out for specific decontrol on June 30, 1946, for example, and power over remaining food prices thereafter would be lodged in the Secretary of Agriculture. The majority's bill "writes the death sentence for effective . . . stabilization in the United States," Wagner complained. Nevertheless, during the course of floor debate the Senate adopted additional amendments offered by Senators Taft, Kenneth Wherry of Nebraska, and others that weakened the OPA still further. "The lobbyists seem to be in full command," price administrator Chester Bowles lamented in a note to Wagner as the Senate approved the crippling measure 53–11.[29]

On June 29 President Truman backed up Bowles and his handful of liberal allies by vetoing the bill Congress sent him. At midnight the next day price controls lapsed altogether, and the cost of living, which the OPA had managed to limit to a 3 percent increase since V-J Day, leaped ahead at a dizzying rate. During July Congress formulated a new recontrol measure, which was, if anything, even weaker than the one the President had vetoed. Facing up to the realities of the situation, Truman signed the bill. Price regulations were reimposed on some items, but irreparable damage had been done. In the face of continuing hoarding, shortages, black-market operations, and complaints from every direction, in November the President ended all price controls except those on rents, rice, and sugar. By the end of the year the cost-of-living index had risen to unparalleled heights. But the American people had had restored to them the "free economy" for which, in their conservative mood, they seemed to yearn.[30]

At the end of 1945 President Truman precipitately abolished the War Labor Board and its wage-control apparatus. His action did more than provide conservatives with another argument against continuation of OPA price controls. It also gave impetus to the strike wave that had already gotten under way with the expiration of labor's "no strike" pledge on V-J Day. During the winter of 1945–46 hundreds of thousands of workers were idle, and production was shut down in

[29] Files on "O.P.A. and Price Controls, 1946," RFW Papers; 92 *Congressional Record*, 6466ff; Chester Bowles to RFW, March 13, 1946, RFW Papers.

[30] Files on "O.P.A. and Price Controls, 1946," RFW Papers; 92 *Congressional Record*, 7973ff, 8339ff; Lester V. Chandler, *Inflation in the United States: 1940–1948* (New York, 1951), pp. 216ff; Arthur S. Link and William B. Catton, *American Epoch: A History of the United States since the 1890s* (New York, 1963), pp. 674–675.

steel, automobiles, and other vital industries. In this atmosphere of turbulence the Administration and Congress embarked on reconsideration of the nation's basic labor legislation—the Wagner Act.

Truman himself started the ball rolling when, in a message to Congress on December 3, 1945, he proposed a "cooling-off period" and the establishment of presidential fact-finding boards in strikes that affected the national interest. The Chief Executive's recommendation was mild enough: the boards' findings would be made public, but they would not be binding on the parties to the strike. Yet it was significant in that it represented the first time since 1935 that the White House had endorsed a basic alteration in the nation's collective bargaining process.

As Bob Wagner anticipated, what started out as a relatively moderate measure soon paved the way for the conservative majority of Congress, who were determined to bring about a more thorough revision of the National Labor Relations Act. At the end of January, 1946, after the House Labor Committee reported Truman's bill favorably, the House Rules Committee substituted in its place, without any public hearings whatever, an entirely different and much more drastic measure, framed by Republican Congressman Francis P. Case of South Dakota. As passed by the House early in February, the Case bill embodied most of the restrictive provisions of the Smith bills of 1940 and 1941. In addition, it provided for sixty-day "cooling-off" periods and fact-finding commissions in strikes affecting the national welfare; it weakened the restrictions placed by the Norris-La Guardia Act on the use of injunctions in labor disputes; and it specified that in some instances workers might be deprived of their Wagner Act rights as the penalty for violating the bill's provisions.[31]

As in the past, the Senate's Education and Labor Committee did its best to preserve the Wagner Act intact. As reported to the floor by Chairman Murray in May of 1946, the House-approved bill was stripped of everything except provisions creating more effective federal mediation machinery along the lines that Wagner had been suggesting since 1940. The committee had rejected all proposals that would limit or abridge the right to strike, Murray explained, because inevitably they would lead to ever greater controls on both employees and employers and to a form of totalitarianism in labor relations. "I am in favor of the private enterprise system," the Montana liberal re-

[31] Files on "Labor Legislation, 1945–1946," RFW Papers; 91 *Congressional Record*, 11526ff; Thomas L. Stokes, "Case History," column clipped from an undated, unidentified newspaper (1946), RFW Papers; Harry A. Millis and Emily Clark Brown, *From the Wagner Act to Taft-Hartley* (Chicago, 1950), pp. 300ff.

minded his hearers.

Once the measure was on the floor, however, it was open to amendment, and Taft-led conservatives were ready to capitalize on the opportunity that a new rash of strikes in the nation's coal mines and on its railroads afforded them. During sessions that frequently ran beyond midnight, and while senators such as David I. Walsh of Massachusetts complained that "calm and wise judgment" had been swept aside by "the hysterical emotions of the hour," the Senate loaded Murray's bill with amendments that restored it to something like the Case bill passed by the House.

All the while Bob Wagner, under doctors' orders, remained silent. Younger men did his speaking for him, as when, on May 24, James E. Murray cited as the real cause of labor unrest Congress' failure to face up to the vital economic and social issues affecting the workers' interest that clamored for attention—inflation, the growth of business power and profits, housing, social security, and health legislation. The next day, when the final vote was to be taken, liberal Republican George Aiken of Vermont denounced "the million dollar campaign" waged by business on the Case bill's behalf; he would vote against it, Aiken announced, because his conservative colleagues openly described it as "just a beginning" of their antilabor crusade. During the hour before the roll call began, Claude Pepper of Florida berated that same crusade and the progress it seemed to be making. But "I anticipate the coming of the day when we will go back truly to the principles for which the Senator from New York has so long fought," the liberal Southerner declared. "He is sitting here now in the Senate chamber, I cannot but believe thinking sorrowfully of what he has seen done in the past few weeks."

The veteran New York lawmaker was sorrowful, indeed, but he knew that all the talking by his liberal colleagues would produce little effect. When the roll was called, the Senate approved Robert Taft's version of the Case bill by a convincing 49–29 vote.[32]

President Truman's subsequent veto of the Case bill was upheld by Congress. But in the meantime the President himself had added considerably to the antilabor sentiment brewing across the country. On the same day that the Senate passed the Case bill, and after two national railway brotherhoods had refused to accept a federal settlement of the wage dispute that had prompted the government to seize the railroads a week earlier, Truman asked Congress for legislation

---

[32] 92 *Congressional Record,* 4806ff, 4885ff, 5248ff, 5524ff, 5618ff, 5691ff, 5739, 5924ff, 5978ff, 6674ff; Millis and Brown, *From the Wagner Act to Taft-Hartley,* pp. 360ff.

that would empower him to draft into the Army any employee who refused to return to work voluntarily in government-sequestered industries.

The House of Representatives enacted the President's bill the same day he asked for it, but in the Senate, liberals and responsible conservatives alike demanded more sober deliberation. That Truman's proposal had been conceived in an atmosphere of White House hysteria or histrionics quickly became evident as, during the next few days, a rather disconcerted Alben Barkley did his best to carry out his job as majority leader in defending the Administration measure. Would workers be punished under martial law if they still refused to return to their jobs after the government inducted them, conservative Taft wanted to know. Would they still be eligible for benefits under state workmen's compensation laws if injured on the job, asked liberal George Aiken. Since the Administration's hastily constructed bill covered no such fine points as these, Barkley was hard pressed to provide any answers.

At that point, on May 29, Bob Wagner rose to deliver his first extended analysis of the labor legislation that had occupied so much of the attention of Congress during 1946. Addressing his remarks to fundamentals, the father of the National Labor Relations Act observed that "easy remedies are not to be found for industrial disagreements in a democracy." But as between reliance on the collective bargaining process, with all the inconvenience of strikes that it entailed, on the one hand, and the degrees of coercion and control envisaged in the Case bill and the Labor Draft bill on the other, Wagner continued to prefer the former, for the latter could only lead to the rise of a totalitarian state. And while he recognized the necessity for government seizure of strike-bound essential industries—the power to do so should be embodied in permanent legislation, he declared—seizure itself, combined with more adequate mediation machinery and the force of public opinion, should suffice to reduce public inconvenience to a minimum even in the most vital industries. The radical sanctions proposed in the President's Labor Draft bill, which had not been invoked even in wartime, were far too drastic to comport with American ideas of liberty.

At the conclusion of his speech Wagner formally moved to strike out the draft provision of the Administration measure; ironically, it bore the same designation, Section 7, as the article of the National Industrial Recovery Act that had inaugurated large-scale growth of the labor movement in early New Deal years. By a vote of 70–13 the Senate concurred in the New York member's motion, as only a sprinkling of rural Southern Democrats, and a somewhat embarrassed Alben Barkley, voted to carry out Truman's recommendation. "I was sorry that I had to disagree with Senator Barkley on the President's strike bill," Wagner wrote newspaper columnist Thomas L. Stokes a few days later. "We agree on so many things that I felt disturbed when I could not follow him on this bill. But my conscience and my philosophy just made it impossible." [33]

As a result of Truman's veto of the Case bill and the Senate's veto of Truman's bill, labor legislation remained essentially in *status quo* when the Seventy-ninth Congress came to an end early in August 1946. But the tinder against the Wagner Labor Relations Act had been piled up high, and it awaited just a spark of further encouragement to flare up.

Besides the labor and housing issues, still another question vexed Bob Wagner's relations with the Truman Administration during 1945 and 1946, and that was the matter of Palestine. Following unproductive talks with British Prime Minister Clement Attlee at Potsdam in the summer of 1945, late in August the President publicly called on Britain to allow the immediate entry of 100,000 Jewish immigrants into Palestine; on behalf of the American Palestine Committee, Senator Wagner applauded. But Attlee parried the President's demand for action by suggesting creation of a Joint Anglo-American Committee of Inquiry to study the problem and make recommendations for its solution. Truman acquiesced, to the vast disappointment of Zionists and their sympathizers. "We need no more facts! We need no more promises!" Wagner told delegates from thirty-one countries who attended an International Conference on Palestine in the fall. "Each day's delay means more Jewish dead. Another protracted inquiry may end the Jewish problem altogether by the total liquidation of the surviving Jews of Europe." [34]

In the meantime Wagner and Senator Taft pressed again for action on the resolution that would commit Congressional sentiment to the Zionist cause of creating an independent Jewish commonwealth in Palestine. On October 26, 1945, Secretary of State James F. Byrnes indicated that the Administration had no objection to their project. But during the next three weeks the executive department changed its position again; on November 18 Byrnes informed the House Com-

[33] 92 *Congressional Record*, 5709ff, 5752–5753, 5774ff, 5884ff, 5918ff; RFW to Thomas L. Stokes, June 3, 1946, RFW Papers.
[34] RFW Papers: files on "Palestine, 1945"; Wagner speech file, Nov. 1, 1945; also Richard P. Stevens, *American Zionism and U. S. Foreign Policy: 1942–1947* (New York, 1962), pp. 125ff.

mittee on Foreign Affairs that approval of the Palestine resolution at that particular time was inadvisable. At a press conference eleven days later, moreover, President Truman announced his personal opposition to the measure. In a letter to Wagner on December 10 Truman suggested that consideration of the Congressional resolution be postponed until after the inquiry committee had submitted its report.

By this time, however, Wagner and Taft were not to be deterred. Under their influence the Senate Foreign Relations Committee voted 17–1 to report the resolution to the floor (only Chairman Tom Connally abided by the President's advice), and on December 17 the Senate gave it overwhelming approval without even the formality of a roll call. Two days later the House concurred. The Congress of the United States, if not the Chief Executive, now stood firmly behind the creation of an independent Jewish state in Palestine, a project that Wagner described as "the touchstone of the postwar world's integrity." [35]

But Congress' expression of sentiment produced little immediate effect on those who formulated policy at the White House and in the State Department; it had even less impact on the formulators of British policy in Downing Street. In April 1946 the Anglo-American Inquiry Committee reported in favor of immediate admission to Palestine of 100,000 refugees, just as Truman had urged seven months earlier. But the committee's proposal for long-range development of an Arab-Jewish federation in Palestine, under continuing British suzerainty, left Zionist spokesmen crestfallen. Their disappointment was compounded further when in the months that followed it became evident that the British government intended to link the two parts of the committee's recommendations together by making stepped-up immigration contingent on acceptance of the political federation plan by both the Arabs and Jews. "It is perfectly clear that this means that the admission of the 100,000 is shelved indefinitely," Wagner told the Senate at the end of July, "for there is not the remotest chance of this scheme being accepted by all concerned." [36]

Most disturbing of all was the mounting evidence that an ele-

[35] RFW Papers: files on "Palestine, 1945"; RFW and Robert A. Taft to Carl A. Hatch and other senators, Nov. 16, 1945; undated memorandum of telephone call from Secretary of State James F. Byrnes to RFW, Oct. 1945; Abba Hillel Silver to RFW, Oct. 31, 1945; also transcript of press conference, Nov. 29, 1945, Harry S Truman Papers (Truman Library, Kansas City, Missouri); Harry S Truman to RFW, Dec. 10, 1945, RFW Papers; 91 *Congressional Record*, 10071, 11606, 11881–82, 12136ff, 12165ff, 12383ff; Wagner speech file, April 29, 1945, RFW Papers.

[36] Wagner speech file, April 30, 1946, RFW Papers; 92 *Congressional Record*, 10452.

ment in the American State Department was willing or even anxious to join the British in what Wagner called "a deceitful device to stifle the hopes of a long-suffering people." "My years of loyal friendship with both President Truman and Secretary Byrnes," Wagner told his colleagues, "gives me the right to call upon them to see to it that the policy announced by the President of the United States last August is not sidetracked or evaded by a group of subordinate officials in Washington or abroad who may be out of sympathy with that policy." On repeated occasions during the remainder of 1946 the New York Senator exercised that right, both in public pronouncements and in private conversations with the President that an eyewitness observer described as "very frank." [37]

Nevertheless, several members of a pro-Zionist Congressional delegation that called at the White House in midsummer of 1946 told newsmen afterward that Truman had seemed inattentive and brusque as they presented their case; the Chief Executive had intimated also that the reasons for their visit were "political." No doubt there was an element of truth in the President's assessment, for politically conscious Democrats were aware of growing signs that Jewish disenchantment with the Administration's temporizing policies might soon threaten their party's hold on the "Jewish vote." Late in September, for example, a group of prominent Jews published an open letter in *The New York Times* warning Democratic candidates that *"We will not be content with . . . speeches. We do not seek new promises or new planks. The old ones are good enough. What we ask is that our Administration fulfill those old promises now."*

Early in October, and perhaps partly in response to such promptings, the President issued another call for immediate admission of the 100,000 refugees seeking entry into Palestine. He also pronounced unacceptable any long-range plan that envisaged continuing British suzerainty over Palestine, and expressed the hope that a satisfactory compromise might be arranged on the basis of the Zionist leaders' recent proposal for partition of Palestine into viable Jewish and Arab states. Truman's position afforded Zionists a new basis for hope, but among some Jews a lingering doubt remained. Did this latest White House statement, together with those that ran back through the Roosevelt years, add up to "no more than mere vote-getting devices"? [38]

[37] 92 *Congressional Record*, 6378, 10452; files on "Palestine, 1946," and James G. McDonald to RFW, July 29, 1946, RFW Papers. See also Bartley C. Crum, "The State Department Sabotages," *Palestine* (Sept. 1946), pp. 92ff; Stevens, *American Zionism and U. S. Foreign Policy*, pp. 137ff.

[38] Files on "Palestine, 1946," RFW Papers; *New York Times*, July 31, Sept. 30, Oct. 5, 1946; clippings from the New York *Post*, Oct. 16, 17, 1946, RFW

By election time 1946, American Jews were not the only ethnic group disappointed with the postwar fate of their "homeland." Italian-Americans flooded Congress with protests against the tentative peace treaty drawn up for Italy; Greeks and Albanians contested over the disposition that should be made of the Dodecanese Islands; Polish-Americans were becoming convinced that at Yalta the Democratic Administration had "sold out" their old country. Meanwhile admirers of Franklin Roosevelt divided over whether President Truman's "get tough" policies toward Russia represented an abandonment of Rooseveltian ideals or a realistic facing-up to the harsh truths of the postwar power vacuum.[39]

Compounding the Democrats' dilemma were the divisive domestic issues that threatened to alter voting patterns that had ensured them control of Congress since 1932. President Truman's progressive utterances had already incurred for his Administration nearly the same revulsion that conservatives had lavished on the New Deal in earlier years. At the same time, however, the new Chief Executive had managed to alienate many among the liberal and labor elements that had formed the backbone of the Roosevelt coalition; as we have seen, even such a staunch party man as Bob Wagner had parted ways with Truman on several key issues. By the fall of 1946, moreover, inflation had put consumers in general in an angry mood; no one knew for sure just who was responsible for the shortages that existed and for the zooming cost of living, but the Republicans coined a catchy slogan, "Had Enough?," that proved capable of channeling public wrath against the "ins."

"Our party is in some difficulty just now," Senator Wagner confided as the election season approached, and in a public statement on Labor Day he readily conceded that "the last Congress failed to attain goals essential to the national welfare." Illness prevented him from participating actively in the campaign that ensued, but in a series of statements he did what he could to withstand the impending conservative resurgence. "This first postwar election . . . brings vividly to my mind the nationwide election in 1918," Wagner declared in one interview. "It was then that the American people made a tragic mistake. Apathy and impatience, after the strain of war, combined to produce in the nation a Republican swing" that, confirmed in the

---

Papers; *Palestine* (Oct. 1946), p. 105; "Statement by Dr. Stephen S. Wise . . . December 1, 1945" (mimeographed copy), RFW Papers.

[39] RFW Papers: files on "International Affairs, 1945–1946"; Anna Celletti to RFW, July 26, 1946; George E. Phillies to RFW, March 28, 1946; "Memorandum of the Polish American Congress to James F. Byrnes, Secretary of State . . . November 1946" (copy).

presidential election of 1920, led into a period of "false isolation and false prosperity." "Never again can we afford to repeat that tragic mistake," the Senator asserted as he summoned liberal Americans to elect a progressive Congress.

But the unity of the New Deal coalition had been decisively shattered, even if the courage of its remaining adherents was intact, and on election day 1946 the Republicans were assured control of both Senate and House in the Eightieth Congress. "The trend and tide were against us all over the country," Wagner conceded in a postelection letter to one liberal casualty, Senator Abe Murdock of Utah. "We will miss you terribly in the Senate, especially when the Republicans get going on the Labor Act and other measures. The prospect is not encouraging, but I do not intend to abandon my principles." [40]

Wagner was on hand in Washington when, during the first days of 1947, jubilant Republicans organized Congress for the first time in seventeen years. Before January was over, however, he retreated to Florida again in search of relief from another spell of influenza. During the next few weeks the corporal's guard of liberals left in Congress reintroduced the Wagner-Murray-Dingell bill and other measures that the New York Senator had sponsored in previous years; as anticipated, they received no consideration from the Republican-controlled committees to which they were referred.

Nor did Senator Taft's infinitely more moderate program of social advances fare any better. In 1947 he reintroduced what now became known as the Taft-Ellender-Wagner Housing Bill, his federal grant-in-aid bill to promote state health programs for the indigent, and a bill that would establish a program of grants-in-aid to the states for the improvement of education. But not even "Mr. Republican" himself could move his Congressional colleagues to act on these measures. Instead, many of them were intent on rolling back New Deal-type programs handed down from the pre-1939 reform era; functions ranging from the soil-conservation program to the United States Employment Service were starved for funds. [41]

In some instances Senator Taft's enlightened conservatism mod-

---

[40] RFW Papers: RFW to James B. McNally, June 14, 1946; Wagner speech file, Sept. 1, 4, 1946; RFW to Abe Murdock, Dec. 6, 1946. On the general political atmosphere leading up to the Republican victory in the 1946 elections see Eric F. Goldman, *The Crucial Decade—and After: America, 1945–1960* (New York, 1960), pp. 3–46.

[41] Files on "RFW Bills, 1947" and "RFW, Personal Correspondence, 1947," RFW Papers; Davies, " 'Mr. Republican' Turns 'Socialist,' " pp. 140ff; Goldman, *The Crucial Decade*, pp. 52ff.

erated the purposes of the reactionary crew in Congress; other intentions were negated by President Truman's frequent exercise of the veto. In the field of labor legislation Taft's views dulled somewhat the knife wielded by his party's business-oriented "vindictive" wing— the adjective was supplied by Republican liberal George Aiken of Vermont. But this time Truman's veto failed to prevent the Congress from enacting a far-reaching revision of the National Labor Relations Act in a form that the Ohio Republican approved. The Taft-Hartley Act of 1947 proved to be the only lasting contribution of the Eightieth Congress to the nation's code of domestic legislation, but it affected that area of the New Deal heritage that was closest of all to Bob Wagner's heart.

As passed by the house of Representatives in April 1947, Congressman Fred Hartley's bill embodied just about every labor-curbing device that antiunion employers had campaigned for since 1937. The Senate Committee on Labor and Public Welfare stripped away many of its more drastic provisions, and by a vote of 7-to-6 it even refused to approve several provisions that Senator Taft, who now presided over the committee as chairman, thought necessary or desirable. Liberal Republican Wayne Morse of Oregon called the committee version a "constructive contribution," and he ventured the opinion that the President would sign the bill if it remained unchanged. Even liberal Democrats like Claude Pepper of Florida and James E. Murray congratulated Taft on the fairness with which he had conducted the committee's deliberations.

But Taft himself remained dissatisfied with the group's handiwork, and during consideration of the labor bill by the full Senate in late April and early May he succeeded handily in having added to it those amendments that the labor committee had refused to sanction. When the final vote was taken on May 13, 1947, therefore, the Senate version of the measure revising the Wagner Act was entirely satisfactory to Senator Taft. It was weaker than the rabidly antilabor forces in the House desired, but as a result of the floor amendments, liberal Republicans like Wayne Morse had turned against it.[42]

There was no mystery, therefore, as to how Bob Wagner, who had returned to Washington late in April, regarded the Taft-Hartley bill. On May 12, the day before the final ballot, Wagner made his first and only contribution to the debate that had occupied the Senate during the previous three weeks. And his words that day constituted his last speech in the United States Senate.

[42] 93 *Congressional Record*, 3613–14, 3798ff, 5015, 5108ff; Millis and Brown, *From the Wagner Act to Taft-Hartley*, pp. 363ff.

In calm and deliberate tones, before a packed but subdued chamber, Wagner described the Taft-Hartley bill as a measure that was "untimely, trouble-making, reactionary, unfair, and unduly political." Untimely, because it would "disarrange the relationships between management and labor just as they are settling down" following a postwar period of reconversion in which, "compared with the period after the First World War, the results have been remarkable." [43] Trouble-making, because "it would generate friction over the interpretation . . . of new and untried definitions of rights and duties . . . in the courts and in the collective bargaining process . . . at the very time when we most need smoothness and stability." Reactionary, "because it seeks to strip workers of hard-earned rights which are at the core of industrial democracy" by means that were not novel but that in most cases had been advanced by labor's opponents "from the very beginning of the effort to afford legal protection to the industrial rights of workers." Unfair, because "it is based upon the idea that unions have acquired too much monopolistic power . . . at the very time when . . . business monopoly . . . is now even more than before the real evil. It is not labor, but the opponents of labor, who have too much power." Political, because it sought "to repress, to reprove, to demoralize, and to weaken the workers and organizations [who] have been the strongest and most consistent fighting force for economic progress and human betterment," while at the same time it would augment the strength of "those very employer organizations whose selfish policies are threatening our prosperity and blocking our progress."

Wagner's speech lasted only fifteen minutes, and it produced little effect on the conservative coalition that dominated the national legislature. Nor had the veteran liberal expected more than that. "Viewing the record"—a record on social legislation that was "as barren as the sands of the Sahara"—"it is too much to expect that a majority of the present Congress will bury this bill," he stated at the conclusion of his address. "But I earnestly hope that the President vetoes it. Such a veto would, I believe, be sustained here." [44]

Two of Wagner's predictions came true. The Senate passed the Taft-Hartley bill the next day by a vote of 68–24, and following conferences in which the House managed to restore some of the stricter provisions contained in its version, the measure went to the White

[43] In 1945, 12.2 percent of the work force engaged in strikes; for 1946 the figure was 14.5 percent. But this was far below the 1919 peak of 20.8 percent.

[44] 93 *Congressional Record*, 5010–11; Millis and Brown, *From the Wagner Act to Taft-Hartley*, p. 300; files on "Labor Legislation, 1947," RFW Papers.

House. Then, on June 20, President Truman returned it with his veto, together with a message that reiterated many of the points Wagner had stressed previously. But during the next few days—and here Wagner's forecast proved wrong—both the House and the Senate overrode the President, and the Taft-Hartley Act became law.[45]

Just moments before the Senate roll was called on the question of reapproving the conservatives' labor bill Senator Alben Barkley, who had come to the Senate along with Robert F. Wagner in 1926, secured unanimous consent for the reading of a message concerning his long-time friend. "Senator Wagner, the author of the act which the Taft-Hartley Bill will amend, is not able to be present to cast his vote in favor of sustaining the President's veto," the statement read.

> Because of his great devotion to the working men and women of this country, and because, in his estimation, this bill will destroy what he has so long labored to develop— industrial peace through democracy—every effort was made and every facility at the disposal of the great city of New York was made available to Senator Wagner in order to have him present here on the Senate floor today. It was Senator Wagner's most ardent hope that the doctors would see fit to let him come. But it was the unanimous and expert decision of his . . . physicians . . after thorough and final examination this morning, that "he not be permitted to make any trip whatsoever." It is their opinion that if he did so at this moment, it might well prove fatal. Senator Wagner has a heart ailment, and his blood pressure, most unfortunately, at the moment is at such a level that any strain or excitement would be sufficient to result in his death.

A few days later New York City's Commissioner of Housing, Robert F. Wagner, Jr., called on President Truman at the White House and delivered a message from his father. The passage of the Taft-Hartley Act over the Chief Executive's veto, the elder Wagner informed the President, was "one of the bitterest disappointments I have ever experienced. For I was forced to see the work of a lifetime destroyed, while I lay on my back in bed." [46]

[45] 93 *Congressional Record*, 5117, 6369ff, 6436ff, 7485ff, 7538.
[46] *Ibid.*, p. 7538; Wagner speech file, July 2, 1947, RFW Papers.

CHAPTER 18

The Next Move Is Ours

WAGNER'S MESSAGE to the President following the enactment of Taft-Hartley was uncharacteristically, and unduly, pessimistic. His more typical optimism soon reasserted itself. "I have no intention of resigning," the Senator announced in mid-July 1947. "I am rapidly regaining strength . . . and I want to serve notice now that I have only begun to fight."

The hope of recovering his health and returning to the "front line" helped account in part for the fact that Wagner retained his Senate seat for more than two years after his last physical appearance in Washington. Governor Thomas E. Dewey's action in having the Republican legislature change New York's election law in April 1947 in a way that was obviously designed to precipitate Wagner's early resignation also helped strengthen the Senator's determination not to have his hand forced. And, finally, there were the political and legislative considerations, urged by Democratic strategists in both New York and Washington, dictating that Wagner hold onto his seat and his vote as long as possible in the hope that the electorate might soon enter a more liberal mood.

Through statements issued from Wagner's New York office by Bob, Junior, then, the sentiments of the aging progressive continued to be heard on the issues that confronted the nation and Congress during 1948. In Washington Joseph P. McMurray and Minna L. Ruppert, who successively held the post of administrative assistant, arranged pairs on important Senate roll calls, so that Wagner's vote might at least offset that of a Republican counterpart while liberals tried to curb the designs of the conservative-dominated Eightieth Congress. During the first six months of 1949, too, Wagner's vote remained at the disposal of his party's Senate leadership as the newly restored Democratic majority tried, among other things, to repeal or fundamentally amend the Taft-Hartley Act.

But Wagner's health did not improve during his prolonged absence from Washington; instead it got worse. As the Eighty-first Congress unfolded, moreover, the conservative coalition in the national legislature remained strong enough to prevent the sort of vigorous resurgence of liberalism to which Wagner's vote might be vital.

On June 28, 1949, therefore, a few hours after conservative forces had carried an important vote in the Senate's deliberations on revising the Taft-Hartley Act, the last official statement of his public career emanated from Wagner's office. "My turn has come to step down," it read. "For some time past it has been my personal wish"; and although friends and party leaders still persisted in urging him to hold on, "in the last analysis I must square my conduct with my own conscience. That inner voice tells me that I should no longer rely on a hope so long deferred." [1]

Wagner lived four more years, but with his resignation from the Senate—and, indeed, with the end of his active participation in its affairs in May 1947—it may be said that the biography of this essentially public man came to a close. As senility progressively took its toll he lived out his span in virtual seclusion with his son and Susan and their children. During the summer, tourists who visited Islip, Long Island, occasionally glimpsed the retired statesman walking solitarily along the beach or contemplating the sea while his grandchildren scampered about him. When winter came Wagner returned to his son's apartment in Yorkville, where he had first learned to know America. And there, on May 4, 1953, he died.

The Senator was buried with the rites of the Catholic Church, which he entered as a convert in 1946. He had been "growing into Catholicism" gradually and seemingly inevitably, Wagner explained at the time, ever since his marriage to Margaret Marie McTague many years before. In death he was interred beside her, in ground that had been consecrated to her memory for over a third of a century.[2]

[1] Wagner speech file, undated statement (July 1947), and June 28, 1949, RFW Papers; *New York Times*, June 29, 1949; interviews with Robert F. Wagner, Jr., Joseph P. McMurray, Minna L. Ruppert, Marguerite Cummins Hayes, Harry S Truman, and Warren Moscow.
[2] *New York Times*, May 5, 6, 8, 1953; interviews with Robert F. Wagner, Jr., Simon H. Rifkind, Leon H. Keyserling, Joseph P. McMurray, Jeremiah T.

Wagner's departure from the national scene was thus undramatic and unobtrusive, befitting the manner in which he had gone about his work in the nation's capital during the previous two decades. He left behind few monuments of marble or stone; the "Legislative Pilot of the New Deal" is honored by no memorial such as the imposing carillon on the Capitol grounds that bears tribute to "Mr. Republican"—Senator Robert A. Taft.

Yet for Wagner in his twilight years there was the satisfying knowledge that he could count "more victories than defeats" in his "continuing battle for human rights," as he expressed it in his retirement statement. And there was the imposing testimony to the value of his legislative achievements offered across the years by a host of admirers, common men and exceptional men alike, culminating perhaps in the words that Franklin D. Roosevelt addressed to Wagner during the 1944 election campaign: "Your name is written indelibly across a second Bill of Rights for America." [3]

In contributing to the compilation of that bill of economic and social rights Wagner had been assisted by many individuals and groups, as this volume has indicated. Moreover, most important of all in accounting for his victories, in the broadest sense, was the impetus to reform provided by the vast social forces that remade the face of America during Wagner's lifetime: industrialization, urbanization, and immigration. For the nature and content of America's Second Bill of Rights were determined in large part by the needs and aspirations of the urban, immigrant-derived, industrial working class in which Wagner himself originated. His progression to political prominence, from obscurity as a Tammany ward heeler in the city of New York at the turn of the century, to state-wide reputation as Democratic leader of the Empire State's legislature during the Progressive Era, to national renown and responsibility during the New Deal—paralleled almost exactly the course that the growing political influence of his class followed. In an important sense Wagner did not make or originate or generate that influence; rather he reflected its unfolding, and he was its product. He was one of its instruments for gradually reshaping the nation's attitudes and institutions so that they might, under the changed conditions of modern life, continue to afford a degree of security and opportunity to even the less humble

---

Mahoney, Claire Dittrich Denzer; Robert F. Wagner, "Growing into Catholicism," in John A. O'Brien, ed., *The Road to Damascus* (Garden City, N. Y., 1951), *passim.*

[3] Wagner speech file, June 28, 1949, RFW Papers; FDR to RFW, Oct. 17, 1944, FDR Papers.

members of America's emerging industrial society.

That Wagner performed his role so effectively and honorably testifies, of course, to those inner individual qualities of mind and spirit
that made him perhaps the outstanding, and certainly one of the no-
blest, products of the broader social and political influences in which
he was rooted. And leadership of that high character was of no small
importance to the success of the movements he represented.

But because the kind of measures identified with the Second Bill
of Rights and with Bob Wagner were essentially the results of
broader societal forces, and not simply the aberrancies of a band of
stout-hearted individual New Dealers, events since Wagner's time
have tended to bear out the New York Senator's confident assertion
to fellow liberals in 1947 that "History is on our side." "We are fighting a holding action . . . ," he added then, "until we gain new recruits, young blood, and renewed vigor in the army of progress and
humanitarianism." Insofar as the Eightieth Congress did attempt to
turn back the clock, the voters who in 1948 returned Harry Truman
to the White House and a Democratic majority to Congress indicated
their concurrence in Wagner's observation two years earlier that
while "you can win elections with laissez-faire slogans . . . you can't
govern with them." [4] When the G.O.P. next assumed direction of
national affairs, under the Eisenhower Administration, it was with a
brand of "modern Republicanism" that acknowledged the need for
preserving, and at least moderately advancing, the kind of affirmative
government policies that were the legacy of the Progressive Era, of
the New Deal, and of men like Bob Wagner. And although the Taft-
Hartley Act remained in effect, it did not serve in practice the union-
busting purposes toward which, in 1947, Wagner feared it was directed, and toward which at the time many of its proponents aimed.

In short, Postwar II did not duplicate Postwar I. Instead, such
welfare-state concepts as the government's responsibility and role as a
"balance wheel" in the economy, institutionalized in the Wagner-
sponsored Employment Act of 1946, won increasing acceptance. In
1949 the Wagner-Ellender-Taft Housing bill finally secured Congressional approval. Under both Truman and Eisenhower old-age pensions, unemployment insurance, and other phases of the Social Security system established by the Wagner-sponsored, New Deal measure
of 1935 underwent considerable expansion and improvement. By the
latter part of the 1950s, moreover, the crusade for Negro rights, which
Wagner and a few others helped launch two decades earlier, had

[4] RFW Papers: RFW to David Dubinsky, June 26, 1947; Wagner speech
file, May 11, 1947, and undated statement of June, 1947.

grown to occupy the center of the nation's attention.[5]

Thus the liberals' "holding action" during the Truman and Eisenhower years not only proved successful, but in addition, as Wagner had predicted, "the frontiers of social responsibility" were enlarged. Yet even as the spirit of modern American liberalism seemed to quicken under the administration of John F. Kennedy, and for a while under Lyndon Johnson, the question persisted as to whether the historical forces pointing America in the direction of democratic welfare statism were being nourished sufficiently and quickly enough by "new recruits, young blood, and renewed vigor" to head off disaster. For while a growing proportion of Americans entered into the enjoyment of an affluent society guaranteed by the Second Bill of Rights, the plight of the remnant of society still denied those guarantees became ever more striking and more desperate, desperate to the point where some seemed ready to abandon the methods and goals of liberalism altogether. Would the affluent majority of Americans, distracted as they frequently were by the real and imagined responsibilities of international power, respond in time to the needs and aspirations of the still underprivileged minority? That is the question pressing for an answer as the second half of the twentieth century evolves.

The remnant of still underprivileged Americans was relatively small compared to the huge urban, immigrant-derived, industrial working class for whom Bob Wagner had emerged as a champion early in the century. Most of these workers or their progeny had graduated to middle-class affluence during the course of that century. Moreover, the programs whereby even the underprivileged remnant might also be afforded platforms of security and opportunity were ready at hand, most of them anticipated by measures for which the New York lawmaker had fought during his tenure in Washington. And America's resources for implementing those programs seemed unlimited. What was lacking, perhaps, was the kind of "strength and courage and public spirit in the Congress . . . no less than in the vicinity of the White House" that had been displayed so remarkably during Wagner's years in the nation's capital.[6]

For those who aspired to provide such leadership for the fulfillment of America's Second Bill of Rights the inspiration of Bob Wagner's words, as well as the precedents set by his programs, were

[5] See Eric F. Goldman, *The Crucial Decade—and After: America, 1945–1960* (New York, 1960), *passim.*
[6] Leon H. Keyserling, "The Wagner Act: Its Origin and Current Significance," *George Washington Law Review* (Dec. 1960), p. 227.

available. "Of what use are material resources and scientific resourcefulness, all our equipment, our enterprise, and our efficiency," he asked, "if the sum total of human happiness enjoyed by our people—*all* our people—be not increased thereby?" "I firmly believe that human welfare and social security will play a far greater role in the world of the future," he asserted, "than any mere political combination or military alignment." "A steadily increasing measure of security, a steadily rising standard of living, a steadily lengthening period of leisure well spent, a never ending increase in the value and nobility of life," he suggested, "—we can do no better than to devote ourselves without stint to make that the history of our country."

But "if we would conserve this civilization," he warned in another period of profound crisis, "we must take the initiative. We cannot wait until others who see in it nothing of value tear it up by its roots."

"The next move is ours."

Bibliography

Manuscript Collections

Senator Edward P. Costigan Papers. University of Colorado Library, Boulder, Colorado.
Leon H. Keyserling Papers. In Mr. Keyserling's possession, Washington, D.C.
Franklin D. Roosevelt Papers. Roosevelt Library, Hyde Park, New York.
Harry S Truman Papers. Truman Library, Independence, Missouri.
Senator Robert F. Wagner Papers. Georgetown University, Washington, D.C.

Interviews

Irene Osgood Andrews. April 29, 1962, New York City.
Henry Ashurst. January 25, 1962, Washington, D.C.
John A. Bell, Jr. June 13, 1960, New York City.
Hugo Black. January 23, 1962, Washington, D.C.
Mrs. Frederick W. Brooks, Jr. June 10, 1960, New York City.
Howard Cullman. June 14, 1960, New York City.
David Delman. June 15, 1960, New York City.
Claire Dittrich Denzer. April 27, 1962, New York City.
Paul H. Douglas. January 22, 1962, Washington, D.C.
Mary E. Dreier. June 15, 1960, New York City.
Morris Ernst. April 30, 1962, New York City.
Clarence Galston. April 26, 1962, New York City.
Theodore Granik. January 28, 1962, New York City.
Edythe Griffinger. April 26, 1962, New York City.
James Hagerty. June 16, 1960, New York City.
Milton Handler. May 1, 1962, New York City.
Carl Hayden. May 9, 1960, Washington, D.C.
Marguerite Cummins Hayes. April 10, 1958, New York City.
Dorothy Kenyon. June 13, 1960, New York City.
Leon H. Keyserling. January 23, February 19, 20, March 20, 1962, Washington, D.C.
Philip Levy. January 13, 1958, April 2, May 22, June 5, 1962, Washington, D.C.
John L. Lewis. May 22, 1962, Alexandria, Virginia.
Isador Lubin. June 8, 1960, New Brunswick, New Jersey.
Joseph P. McMurray. June 14, 1960, New York City.
Jeremiah T. Mahoney. April 8, 1958, June 9, 1960, April 24, 1962, New York City.

John P. Morrissey. June 15, 1960, New York City.
Warren Moscow. June 15, 1960, New York City.
Frances Perkins. April 10, 1958, Washington, D.C.
Francis J. Quillinan. April 9, 1958, New York City.
Victor F. Ridder. June 10, 1960, New York City.
Simon H. Rifkind. April 26, 1962, New York City.
Eleanor Roosevelt. June 10, 1960, New York City.
Anna M. Rosenberg. June 14, 1960, New York City.
Minna L. Ruppert. January 17, 1958, January 25, 1962, Washington, D.C.
Rose Schneiderman. April 26, 1962, New York City.
Boris Shishkin. January 29, 1962, Washington, D.C.
Kenneth Steinreich. June 13, 1960, New York City.
Nathan Straus. June 15, 1960, New York City.
Mrs. Myron Sulzberger. June 11, 1960, New York City.
Harry S Truman. January 22, 1960, Washington, D.C.
Robert F. Wagner, Jr. April 8, 1958, June 15, 1960, August 23, 1965,
    New York City.
Burton K. Wheeler. January 22, 1962, Washington, D.C.

REMINISCENCES, ORAL HISTORY RESEARCH OFFICE, COLUMBIA UNIVERSITY

Robert S. Binkerd. 1949.
Claude Bowers. 1954.
William H. Davis. 1958.
Thomas I. Emerson. 1953.
Charles Fahy. n. d.
Edward J. Flynn. 1950.
John P. Frey. 1955.
James W. Gerard. 1950.
John A. Heffernan. 1950.
Arthur Krock. 1950.
Jeremiah T. Mahoney. 1949.

Herbert Claiborne Pell. 1951.
Louis H. Pink. 1949.
William A. Prendergast. 1951.
Lawson Purdy. 1948.
Martin Saxe. 1949.
Boris Shishkin. 1957.
Lawrence A. Tanzer. 1949.
Rexford G. Tugwell. 1950.
Lawrence Veiller. 1949.
James W. Wadsworth. 1952.
Leonard Wallstein. 1949.

PERSONAL CORRESPONDENCE

Mary E. Dreier. May 21, 1962, to the author.
Elinore Morehouse Herrick. January 2, 20, 1962, to the author.
Constance J. Lawson. April 30, 1962, to the author.
Lawrence D. Weiner. May 16, 1962, to the author.

GOVERNMENT PUBLICATIONS

New York (State) Assembly. *Journal.* Albany, 1905–1918.
New York (State) Factory Investigating Commission. *Reports.* 13 vols.
    Albany, 1912–1915.
New York (State) Senate. *Journal.* Albany, 1905–1918.
U.S. *Congressional Record.* 1927–1949.
U.S. House of Representatives, 71st Cong., 2d Sess. *Message of the President of the United States.* House Document 176. 1929.
——, 71st Cong., 3d Sess. *Message of the President of the United States.*
    House Document 519. 1930.

U.S. Senate, 70th Cong., 2d Sess. Committee on Education and Labor, *Causes of Unemployment.* Senate Report 2072. 1929.
——, 71st Cong., 2d Sess. Committee on Commerce, *Unemployment in the United States: Hearings.* 1930.
——, 72nd Cong., 1st Sess. *Report of the Select Committee to Investigate Unemployment Insurance.* Senate Report 964. 1932.
——, 73rd Cong., 2d Sess. Committee on Education and Labor, *Hearings on S. 2926: To Create a National Labor Board.* 1934.
——, 74th Cong., 1st Sess. Committee on Education and Labor, *Hearings on S. 1958: National Labor Relations Board.* 1935.
——, 74th Cong., 1st Sess. Committee on Education and Labor, *National Labor Relations Board.* Senate Report 573. 1935.
——, 74th Cong., 1st Sess. Committee on Education and Labor, *Hearings on S. 2392: Slum and Low-Rent Public Housing,* 1935.
——, 75th Cong., 1st Sess. Committee on Education and Labor, *Creating a United States Housing Authority.* Senate Report 933. 1937
——, 79th Cong., 1st Sess. Committee on Banking and Currency, *Hearings . . . on S. 380: Full Employment.* 1945.

NEWSPAPERS

Albany *Evening Journal,* 1904–1918.
New York Times, 1904–1953.
New York *World,* 1904–1918.
Senator Robert F. Wagner Papers. Georgetown University, Washington, D.C. Scrapbooks and collections of newspaper clippings.

BOOKS

Allen, Frederick Lewis. *The Big Change: America Transforms Itself, 1900–1950.* New York, 1952.
Auerbach, Jerold S. *Labor and Liberty: The La Follette Committee and the New Deal.* Indianapolis and New York, 1966.
Bailey, Stephen Kemp. *Congress Makes a Law: The Story Behind the Employment Act of 1946.* New York, 1950.
Berle, Adolf A. *The Twentieth-Century Capitalist Revolution.* New York, 1954.
Bernstein, Irving. *The New Deal Collective Bargaining Policy.* Berkeley and Los Angeles, 1950.
Blum, John Morton. *From the Morgenthau Diaries: Years of Crisis, 1928–1938.* Boston, 1959.
——. *From the Morgenthau Diaries: Years of Urgency, 1938–1941.* Boston, 1965.
Buchanan, A. R. *The United States in World War II.* 2 vols. New York, 1964.
Burns, James MacGregor. *Roosevelt: The Lion and the Fox.* New York, 1956.
Burrow, James G. *AMA: The Voice of American Medicine.* Baltimore, 1963.
Catton, Bruce. *The War Lords of Washington.* New York, 1948.

Chamberlain, Rudolph W. *There Is No Truce: A Life of Thomas Mott Osborne.* New York, 1935.

Chandler, Lester V. *Inflation in the United States, 1940–1948.* New York, 1951.

Davenport, Russell W., *et al. USA: The Permanent Revolution.* New York, 1951.

Davies, Richard O. *Housing Reform during the Truman Administration.* Columbia, Missouri, 1966.

Davis, Kenneth S. *Experience of War.* Garden City, New York, 1965.

Derber, Milton, and Edwin Young, eds. *Labor and the New Deal.* Madison, Wisconsin, 1957.

Douglas, Paul H. *Social Security in the United States.* 2nd ed. New York, 1939.

Ellis, David M., James A. Frost, Harold C. Syrett, and Harry J. Carman. *A Short History of New York State.* Ithaca, New York, 1957.

Farley, James A. *Behind the Ballots.* New York, 1938.

Fine, Sidney. *The Automobile Under the Blue Eagle.* Ann Arbor, Michigan, 1963.

Fisher, Robert Moore. *20 Years of Public Housing.* New York, 1959.

Frankfurter, Felix, and Nathan Greene. *The Labor Injunction.* New York, 1930.

Freidel, Frank. *Franklin D. Roosevelt: The Apprenticeship.* Boston, 1952.

Friedman, Jacob A. *The Impeachment of Governor William Sulzer.* New York, 1939.

Galbraith, John Kenneth. *American Capitalism: The Concept of Countervailing Power.* Boston, 1952.

Gerard, James W. *My First Eighty-Three Years in America.* Garden City, New York, 1951.

Goldman, Eric F. *The Crucial Decade—and After: America, 1945–1960.* New York, 1960.

——. *Rendezvous with Destiny.* New York, 1952.

Goldmark, Josephine. *Impatient Crusader: Florence Kelly's Life Story.* Urbana, Illinois, 1954.

Halperin, Samuel. *The Political World of American Zionism.* Detroit, 1961.

Handlin, Oscar. *Al Smith and His America.* Boston, 1958.

——. *The American People in the Twentieth Century.* Cambridge, Massachusetts, 1954.

Hatch, Alden. *The Wadsworths of the Genesee.* New York, 1959.

Hays, Samuel. *The Response to Industrialism, 1885–1914.* Chicago, 1957.

Higham, John. *Strangers in the Land.* New Brunswick, New Jersey, 1955.

Hofstadter, Richard. *The Age of Reform.* New York, 1955.

Hoover, Herbert. *The Memoirs of Herbert Hoover: The Great Depression, 1929–1941.* New York, 1952.

Huthmacher, J. Joseph. *Massachusetts People and Political Politics, 1919–1933.* Cambridge, Massachusetts, 1959.

Ickes, Harold L. *The Secret Diary of Harold L. Ickes.* 3 vols. New York, 1953–1954.

Isakoff, Jack F. *The Public Works Administration.* Urbana, Illinois, 1938.

Janeway, Eliot. *The Struggle for Survival: A Chronicle of Economic Mobilization in World War II.* New Haven, 1951.

Kempton, Murray. *Part of Our Time.* New York, 1955.

Leuchtenburg, William E. *Franklin D. Roosevelt and the New Deal.* New York, 1963.

Link, Arthur S. *Woodrow Wilson and the Progressive Era, 1912–1917.* New York, 1954.

Lorwin, Lewis L., and Arthur Wubnig. *Labor Relations Boards.* Washington, D.C., 1935.

Lubove, Roy. *The Progressives and the Slums.* Pittsburgh, 1962.

Lyons, Eugene. *The Red Decade: The Stalinist Penetration of America.* New York, 1941.

Lyon, Leverett S., *et al. The National Recovery Administration.* Washington, D.C., 1935.

McDonnell, Timothy L., S.J. *The Wagner Housing Act.* Chicago, 1957.

Meriam, Lewis. *Relief and Social Security.* Washington, D.C., 1946.

Millis, Harry A., and Emily Clark Brown. *From the Wagner Act to Taft-Hartley.* Chicago, 1950.

Morgenthau, Henry. *All in a Lifetime.* Garden City, New York, 1922.

Moscow, Warren. *Politics in the Empire State.* New York, 1948.

Mowry, George. *The Era of Theodore Roosevelt, 1900–1912.* New York, 1958.

Munger, Frank J., and Ralph A. Straetz. *New York Politics.* New York, 1960.

Myers, William Starr, and Walter H. Newton. *The Hoover Administration: A Documented Narrative.* New York, 1936.

Nevins, Allan. *Herbert H. Lehman and His Era.* New York, 1963.

O'Brien, John A., ed. *The Road to Damascus.* Garden City, New York, 1951.

Perkins, Dexter. *The New Age of Franklin Roosevelt: 1932–1945.* Chicago, 1957.

Perkins, Frances. *The Roosevelt I Knew.* New York, 1946.

Pringle, Henry F. *Alfred E. Smith: A Critical Study.* New York, 1927.

Proskauer, Joseph M. *A Segment of My Times.* New York, 1950.

Riordon, William L., ed. *Plunkitt of Tammany Hall.* New York, 1905.

Rollins, Alfred B., Jr. *Roosevelt and Howe.* New York, 1962.

Romasco, Albert U. *The Poverty of Abundance: Hoover, the Nation, the Depression.* New York, 1965.

Roos, Charles Frederick. *NRA Economic Planning.* Bloomington, Indiana, 1937.

Ross, Malcolm. *Death of a Yale Man.* New York, 1939.

Salter, J. T., ed. *The American Politician.* New York, 1938.

Salvadori, Massimo. *The Economics of Freedom: American Capitalism Today.* Garden City, New York, 1959.

Schlesinger, Arthur M., Jr. *The Age of Roosevelt.* 3 vols. Boston, 1957–1960.

——. *The Vital Center: The Politics of Freedom.* Boston, 1949.

Seidenberg, Jacob. *The Labor Injunction in New York City, 1935–1950.* Ithaca, New York, 1953.

Sherwood, Robert E. *Roosevelt and Hopkins: An Intimate History*. New York, 1948.

Silverberg, Louis G., ed. *The Wagner Act: After Ten Years*. Washington, D.C., 1945.

Simkhovitch, Mary Kingsbury. *Here Is God's Plenty*. New York, 1949.

Smith, Alfred E. *Up to Now*. New York, 1929.

Smith, Mortimer. *William Jay Gaynor: Mayor of New York*. Chicago, 1951.

Spanier, John. *American Foreign Policy Since World War II*. New York, 1965.

Stein, Leon. *The Triangle Fire*. Philadelphia, 1962.

Sternsher, Bernard. *Rexford Tugwell and the New Deal*. New Brunswick, New Jersey, 1964.

Stevens, Richard P. *American Zionism and U.S. Foreign Policy: 1942– 1947*. New York, 1962.

Stokes, Thomas. *Chip off My Shoulder*. Princeton, New Jersey, 1940.

Strayer, Paul J. *Fiscal Policy and Politics*. New York, 1958.

Swanberg, W. A. *Citizen Hearst*. New York, 1961.

Truman, Harry S. *Memoirs*. 2 vols. Garden City, New York, 1955–1956.

Villard, Oswald Garrison. *Prophets True and False*. New York, 1928.

Warren, Harris Gaylord. *Herbert Hoover and the Great Depression*. New York, 1959.

Werner, M. R. *Tammany Hall*. Garden City, New York, 1928.

Wesser, Robert F. *Charles Evans Hughes: Politics and Reform in New York, 1905–1910*. Ithaca, New York, 1967.

White, Walter. *A Man Called White*. New York, 1948.

White, William S. *Citadel: The Story of the United States Senate*. New York, 1957.

———. *The Taft Story*. New York, 1954.

Wiebe, Robert H. *The Search for Order: 1877–1920*. New York, 1967.

Williams, Edward Ainsworth. *Federal Aid for Relief*. New York, 1939.

Yellowitz, Irwin. *Labor and the Progressive Movement in New York State, 1897–1916*. Ithaca, New York, 1965.

Articles

Auerbach, Jerod S. "The La Follette Committee: Labor and Civil Liberties in the New Deal." *Journal of American History*, December 1964, pp. 435–459.

Davies, Richard O. " 'Mr. Republican' Turns 'Socialist': Robert A. Taft and Public Housing." *Ohio History*, Summer 1964, pp. 135ff.

"The G— D—— Labor Board." *Fortune*, October 1938, pp. 52ff.

Huthmacher, J. Joseph. "Charles Evans Hughes and Charles Francis Murphy: The Metamorphosis of Progressivism." *New York History*, January, 1965, pp. 25–40.

———. "Urban Liberalism and the Age of Reform." *Mississippi Valley Historical Review*, September 1962, pp. 231–241.

Keyserling, Leon H. "The Wagner Act: Its Origin and Current Significance." *George Washington Law Review*, December 1960, pp. 119ff.

Pilat, Oliver. "A New Dealer—Sunday, Monday and Always." *New York Post Weekly Picture Magazine*, December 31, 1943, pp. 2ff.

Pollack, Jack H. "Bob Wagner, Liberal Lawmaker." *Coronet*, April 1946, pp. 36–39.

Pringle, Henry F. "Profiles: The Janitor's Boy." *The New Yorker*, March 5, 1927, pp. 24–26.

Rosenthal, Herbert H. "The Cruise of the Tarpon." *New York History*, October 1958, pp. 303–320.

Smith, Beverly. "Thanks to Brother Gus." *American Magazine*, December 1939, pp. 42ff.

Spivack, Robert G. "Valiant Crusader for Social Betterment." *New York Post Daily Magazine Section*, October, 1944, p. 1.

Stone, I. F. "Robert F. Wagner." *Nation*, October 28, 1944, p. 507.

Wagner, Robert F. "Company Unions: A Vast Industrial Issue." *New York Times Magazine*, March 11, 1934.

——. "Danger Ahead! A Frank Warning." *Liberty*, July 23, 1932, pp. 6–9.

——. "The Fight Has Only Begun." *American Magazine*, November 1933, pp. 14ff.

——. "The Ideal Industrial State." *New York Times Magazine*, May 9, 1937.

——. "The Meaning of 'The Right to Work.'" *New York Times Magazine*, September 23, 1945.

——. "Plan for Millions of Post-War Jobs Vital to Cushion End of Arms Boom." *American Laborite*, August 15, 1941, pp. 7ff.

——. "Planning in Place of Restraint." *Survey Graphic*, August 1933, pp. 395ff.

——. "Post-War Security for All the People." *The Progressive*, September 27, 1943, pp. 1ff.

——. "Problem of Problems: Work." *New York Times Magazine*, February 16, 1936.

——. "The Problem of 25,000,000." *New Outlook*, October 1932, pp. 35ff.

——. "Senator Wagner Tells How to Keep Tab on Unemployment." *Printers' Ink*, March 8, 1928, pp. 85–86.

——. "Sound Policy to Break the Bread Lines." *Independent*, April 14, 1928, pp. 353–354.

——. "Wagner Challenge Critics of His Act." *New York Times Magazine*, July 25, 1937.

Warner, A. L. "Legislative Prophet of the New Deal." *Literary Digest*, December 16, 1933, p. 6.

"Washington Correspondents Name Ablest Congressmen in *Life* Poll." *Life*, March 20, 1939, pp. 13ff.

Wesser, Robert F. "Charles Evans Hughes and the Urban Sources of Political Progressivism." *New-York Historical Society Quarterly*, October 1966, pp. 365–400.

White, Owen P. "When the Public Needs a Friend." *Collier's*, June 2, 1934, pp. 18ff.

Wood, Edith Elmer. "The Hands of Esau." *Survey Graphic*, October 1936, pp. 556ff.

Woolf, S. J. "Wagner Foresees a New Industrial Day." *New York Times Magazine*, November 12, 1933.

UNPUBLISHED STUDIES

Dubofsky, Melvyn. "New York City Labor in the Progressive Era, 1910–1918: A Study of Organized Labor in an Era of Reform." Ph.D. dissertation, University of Rochester, 1960.

Byrne, Thomas R., S.J. "The Social Thought of Robert F. Wagner." Ph.D. dissertation, Georgetown University, 1951.

Gillette, J. William. "Welfare State Trail Blazer: New York State Factory Investigating Commission, 1911–1915." Master's essay, Columbia University, 1956.

Lewinson, Edwin R. "John Purroy Mitchell, Symbol of Reform." Ph.D. dissertation, Columbia University, 1961.

Rollins, Alfred B., Jr. "The Political Education of Franklin Roosevelt." Ph.D. dissertation, Harvard University, 1953.

Wesser, Robert F. "Charles Evans Hughes and New York Politics, 1905–1910." Ph.D. dissertation, University of Rochester, 1961.

Zangrando, Robert L. "The Efforts of the National Association for the Advancement of Colored People to Secure Passage of a Federal Anti-Lynching Law, 1920–1940." Ph.D. dissertation, University of Pennsylvania, 1963.

Index

Index

355

Eightieth Congress, 312, 335, 336, 340, 342
Eighty-first Congress, 340
Eisenhower, Dwight D., 342, 343
Electric power generation and distribution legislation, 29–30
Ellenbogen, Henry, 207, 212, 215, 221
Ellender, Allen J., 240, 299, 300
Emergency Banking Act (1933), 138
Emergency Committee for Employment, 77, 84
Emergency Relief and Construction Act (1932), 98–102, 127–28, 139, 143
Emery, James, 165, 191, 195
Employment Act (1946), 342
Employment agencies, public, 30, 61–62, 84
Employment discrimination against Negroes, 275
Employment Service, U.S., 61, 75, 78, 84, 292, 293, 320
Epstein, Abraham, 176, 185, 186, 199
Epworth League, 14
Export-Import Bank, 272, 304

Fair competition codes, NRA, 154, 155, 157, 159
Fair Employment Practices Commission, 275, 325–26
Fair Labor Standards Act (1938), 203, 246–47, 249
Farley, James A., 102, 104, 181, 245
Farm Credit Administration, 141
Farm indebtedness, 141–42
Farm price legislation, 143
Farm relief legislation, 69
Featherstone, "Silent Maurice," 21–22
Federal Advisory Council, 152
Federal Communications Act (1934), 171
Federal Emergency Relief Act (1933), 140, 152
Federal Emergency Relief Administration, 139
Federal Employment Stabilization Act (1931), 78, 89, 297
Federal Employment Stabilization Board, 62, 244
Federal Home Loan Bank Act, 91
Federal Housing Administration, 171, 212, 237, 323
Federal Land Banks, 91, 141
Federal Power Commission, 102
Fess, Simeon D., 72, 128, 140–41
Filibuster of 1938, 239, 240
Finn, Dan, 123

Fishbein, Morris, 265
Five Cent Fare bill, 20–21, 28
Foley, James A., 36, 122, 310
Folsom, Marion B., 186
Foreign-aid bills, 313–14, 315
Fortune magazine, 57, 254
Foster, William Trufant, 67, 72, 73, 88, 110
Four Freedoms, 303
Frank, Jerome, 147
Frankfurter, Felix, 14, 65, 198, 200
Frawley, Jim, 25
Freidel, Frank, 35
Full Employment bill (1945), 296–99, 311–12, 317–19

G.I. Bill of Rights, 294–95
Gannett, Frank, 266
Garner, John Nance, 100, 181
Garrison, Lloyd K., 190, 191
Gavagan, Joseph A., 238
George, Walter F., 215, 291, 294, 295, 300, 319, 320
Gilbert, Clinton W., 86
Girdler, Tom, 188
Glass, Carter, 128, 197, 227
Glass-Steagall Act (1933), 138
Glenn, Otis, 83, 85, 87, 174
Goldwyn, Samuel, 230
Gompers, Samuel, 5, 30–31, 39
Good Neighbor League, 218
Goodyear Rubber Company, 165
Government spending programs, 89, 245–46, 257, 258; *see also* Public works programs; Relief programs
Grady, Thomas F., 23, 28
Graham, George S., 78, 79, 80
Grant-in-aid programs, 81, 94, 264
Gray, Howard, 228, 229
Green, William, 140, 144, 152, 160, 163, 191, 211, 260
Greenbaum, Fred, x
Grimm, Peter, 254
Gross, Bertram, 296, 297
Guffey-Snyder Act (1935), 200, 201, 203

Hamilton, Charles M., 5
Handler, Milton, 115, 145, 164
Handlin, Oscar, vii
Hard, William, 67, 112, 174
Harding, Warren G., 61, 62
Harriman, Henry I., 153, 191, 254
Harrison, Pat, 195
Hartford *Times*, 24
Hartley, Fred, 336

Wagner, Robert Ferdinand (*continued*)
176; World War I experiences, 39–42; World War II years, 281–310
Wagner, Robert Ferdinand, Jr., ix, x, 13 n., 22, 44, 51, 126, 230, 264, 283, 308, 309, 338, 339, 340
Wagner, Susan (Mrs. R. F. Wagner, Jr.), 283, 340
Wagner Act, *see* National Labor Relations Act
Wagner and Mahony, law firm, 15, 16, 22, 64–65, 147
Wagner Papers, Robert F., ix-x
Wagner-Ellender Housing bill (1945), 205–16, 301, 322–23
Wagner-Ellender-Taft Housing bill (1949), 324–25, 342
Wagner-Hatfield bill, 176–78
Wagner-Lewis unemployment insurance bill, 174–76, 185
Wagner-Lewis-Doughton social security bill, 199
Wagner-Murray-Dingell Health bill (1943), 292–94, 298, 320–22, 335
Wagner-Smith labor bills, 7–10
Wagner-Steagall bill, 224–30
Wagner-Van Buys-Gavagan antilynching bill, 238, 239–43
Wald, Lillian, 129
Walker, James J., 122
Wallace, Henry A., 282, 315–16
Walsh, David I., 94, 96, 133, 165, 167, 170, 192, 207, 215, 329
Walsh-Healey Act (1936), 203, 273, 274
War Department, U.S., 272
War Food Administration, 286
Warburg, James P., 138
Watson, James E., 72
Wealth of Nations, The (Smith), 149
Weir, Ernest, 170
Weirton Steel Company, 162
Welfare legislation, 30, 39, 40
Welfare state, emerging of, 292, 294, 295
Wheeler, Burton K., 63, 108, 134, 151, 223, 271, 313
Wherry, Kenneth, 327
Whiskeman, James, 5–6
White, Carl Robe, 74
White, Walter, 73, 98, 172, 173, 218, 242, 275, 308
White, William S., 113
Whitney, Richard, 138–39
Wilbur, Ray Lyman, 263
Wile, Frederic William, 113
Williams, George H., 81
Wilson, Woodrow, 26, 41, 200, 251
Winant, John G., 305
Wolman, Leo, 160
Women, employment of, regulation of, 7, 8
Women suffrage movement, 29
Women's Christian Temperance Union, 53
Women's Trade Union League, 4
Wood, Edith Elmer, 206, 211
Woodbury, Coleman, 211
Woods, Arthur, 77, 84
Woolf, S. J., 113
Working papers, issuance of, 8
Workmen's compensation act, 30–31
Works Progress Administration, 184, 206, 243, 245, 259
World Bank for Reconstruction and Development, 304–05
World Court, 58, 268
World Economic Conference, 132
World War I, 39–42, 61, 273
World War II, 256, 277, 281, 285–310, 311
Wyzanski, Charles E., 168, 169

Yale News, 126
Yalta Conference (1945), 307
"Yellow-dog" contracts, 65, 66
Yorkville, New York City, 14, 19, 21, 44, 124, 340
Young, Arthur, 77

J. Joseph Huthmacher is Richards Professor of History at the University of Delaware, Newark, Delaware. He is the author of *Massachusetts People and Politics, 1919-1933*.

Atheneum Paperbacks

Atheneum Paperbacks

STUDIES IN AMERICAN NEGRO LIFE